Negative Originals

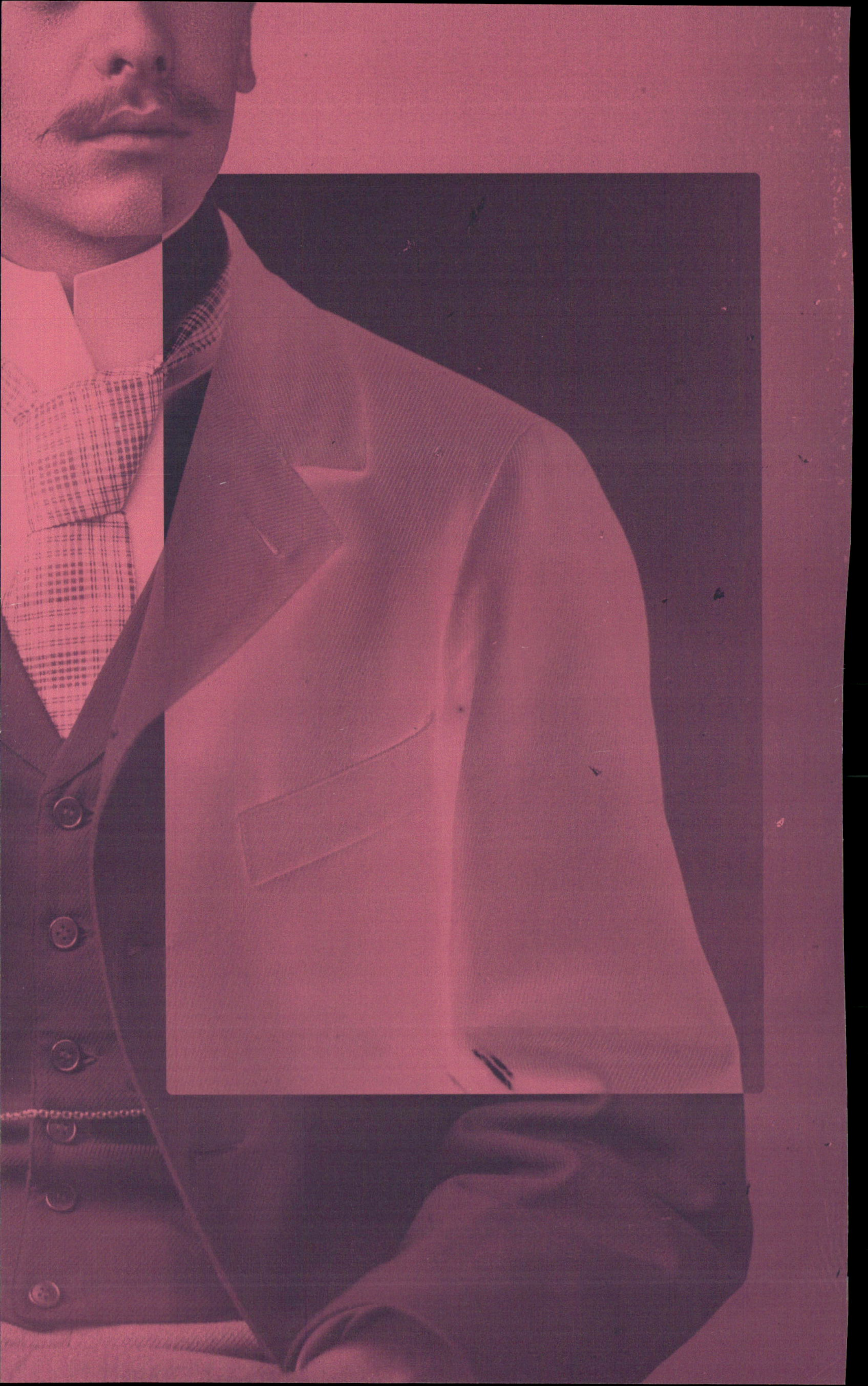

Negative Originals

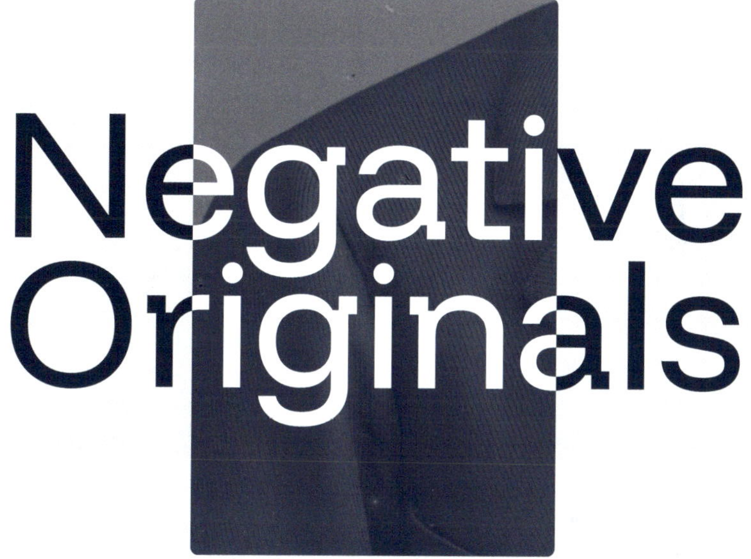

RACE AND EARLY PHOTOGRAPHY IN COLOMBIA

JUANITA SOLANO ROA

DUKE UNIVERSITY PRESS   DURHAM AND LONDON   2025

Printed in the United States of America on
acid-free paper ∞
Project Editor: Liz Smith
Designed by Matthew Tauch
Typeset in MeropeBasic, Funnel Display, and Recursive Sans
Linear Static by Westchester Publishing Services

Library of Congress Cataloging-in-Publication Data
Names: Solano Roa, Juanita, author
Title: Negative originals : race and early photography in Colombia /
Juanita Solano Roa.
Other titles: Race and early photography in Colombia
Description: Durham : Duke University Press, 2025. |
Includes bibliographical references and index.
Identifiers: LCCN 2024054109 (print)
LCCN 2024054110 (ebook)
ISBN 9781478031994 (paperback)
ISBN 9781478028758 (hardcover)
ISBN 9781478060963 (ebook)
Subjects: LCSH: Calle, Benjamín de la, 1869–1934 | Rodríguez Márquez,
Melitón, 1875–1942 | Rodríguez Márquez, Horacio Marino, 1866–1931 |
Photography—Colombia—Medellín—History—20th century | Photography
in ethnology—Colombia—Medellín—History—20th century | Photography—
Social aspects—Colombia—Medellín—History—20th century | Photographers—
Colombia—Medellín—History—20th century
Classification: LCC TR46.M43 S653 2025 (print) | LCC TR46.M43 (ebook) |
DDC 779.9861/26—dc23/eng/20250522
LC record available at https://lccn.loc.gov/2024054109
LC ebook record available at https://lccn.loc.gov/2024054110

Cover art: Fotografía Rodríguez, *Pedro P. Villa*, 1930. Detail of gelatin dry plate under raking light. Biblioteca Pública Piloto de Medellín / Archivo fotográfico. Photo: Esteban Duperly.

TO ALICIA

Contents

Acknowledgments

WHILE MY NAME stands alone as the author of this book, its creation is truly a collaborative effort. I firmly believe that the fields of photography and its history are woven through the fabric of collaboration. Therefore, I extend my heartfelt gratitude to the extraordinary network of friends and mentors who have been instrumental in bringing this project to fruition. My mentors and now colleagues Edward Sullivan, Shelley Rice, and Robert Slifkin have not only shaped my perspective on the history of art and photography but have also provided invaluable feedback, incisive criticism, and profound insights that have enriched my methodological approaches and expanded my knowledge of the field. I am equally indebted to my colleagues at the Universidad de los Andes, especially Verónica Uribe and Camilo Hernández, whose careful reading of sections of the manuscript and invaluable feedback contributed significantly to its refinement. I would also like to thank Esteban Duperly for his intellectual generosity on the history of Antioquia, his feedback, and his help in so many instances in the writing of this book.

The realization of this project has been facilitated by the support of two grants and institutions: the Fondo de Apoyo a Profesores Asistentes (FAPA) of the Universidad de los Andes and the Institute for Studies on Latin American Art (ISLAA), an institution founded in 2011 and dedicated to expanding and enriching the narratives of Latin American art. I am very grateful for this generous support. In particular, I would like to thank Ana Malaver, Alejandro Giraldo, Sair García, and Rondy Torres from the Centro de Investigación y Creación at the School of Arts and Humanities at the Universidad de los Andes, and Ariel Aisiks, Lucy Hunter, and Blanca Serrano from ISLAA for making this project possible. I am also indebted to the Biblioteca Pública Piloto (BPP) in Medellín, especially to Jackeline García, whose management of the photographic archive was invaluable in the publication of the accompanying photographs. Alejandra Builes's efficiency in navigating through thousands of photographs and securing the necessary permissions for publication was also indispensable.

The publication of this book owes much to the generosity and insight of three anonymous reviewers, whose careful reading of the manuscript and valuable feedback were instrumental in shaping the theoretical underpinnings of the book. I am grateful to the dedicated staff at Duke University Press, especially Ken Wissoker, who believed in and saw the potential of the manuscript from the beginning. I would also like to thank Ryan Kendall and James Moore for guiding me through the process of publishing my first book in the United States. The indispensable contributions of my student assistants, Juanita Bayona and Camila Panader, cannot be overstated; their patience, organizational skills, and diligence in securing permissions and revising the extensive bibliography were instrumental in bringing this book to completion.

I am deeply grateful to my close friends Rachel Kim and Blanca Serrano, whose unwavering support and wise counsel have been invaluable companions on this exhilarating journey. Without their boundless generosity, wisdom, and affection, this project would not have come to fruition.

However, the most special and profound thanks go to my mother, Marcela Roa, my father, Mario Solano, my sister, Natalia Solano, and my husband, Felipe Restrepo. Their truly unconditional encouragement, advice, patience, and love made this book possible. Thank you for believing in me.

Introduction

LET US BEGIN by comparing the negative and the positive versions of a photograph taken at the turn of the twentieth century by Colombian photographer Benjamín de la Calle (figs. I.1 and I.2). The positive depicts a standardized wedding portrait of a couple posing in a photographic studio before a painted backdrop. They pose, holding each other by their arms and looking directly at the camera. The woman wears a black dress that covers her feet and a long white organza wedding veil on her head, with small decorative flowers that cover the frontal part of her hairdo. The man wears a suit, a white shirt, and leather shoes. The lapel of his jacket has small flowers on the left side (fig. I.1). There is nothing particularly interesting about this photograph. Nothing differentiates it from the millions of similar images taken worldwide during this period. However, when one looks at the negative original, surprising elements emerge. We notice that the wedding veil was not part of the original shot. Instead, the photographer carefully hand-painted it with an intense red dye. He also applied the same color on the man's cheeks and painted a small curved line at the bottom of the woman's dress to hint at her feet (fig. I.2). However, why did the photographer intervene with so much detail in a generic portrait? What do these interventions mean and convey?

Through an analysis of both negative and positive prints, this book examines the contradictions at work in the construction of identity through the juxtaposition of traditional portraiture that reinforced racial ideologies and the subversive depictions of usually excluded individuals such as cross-dressers, black, and poor people portrayed in dignifying ways. This book delves into the study of race and photography in Colombia at the turn of the twentieth century through the study of negative

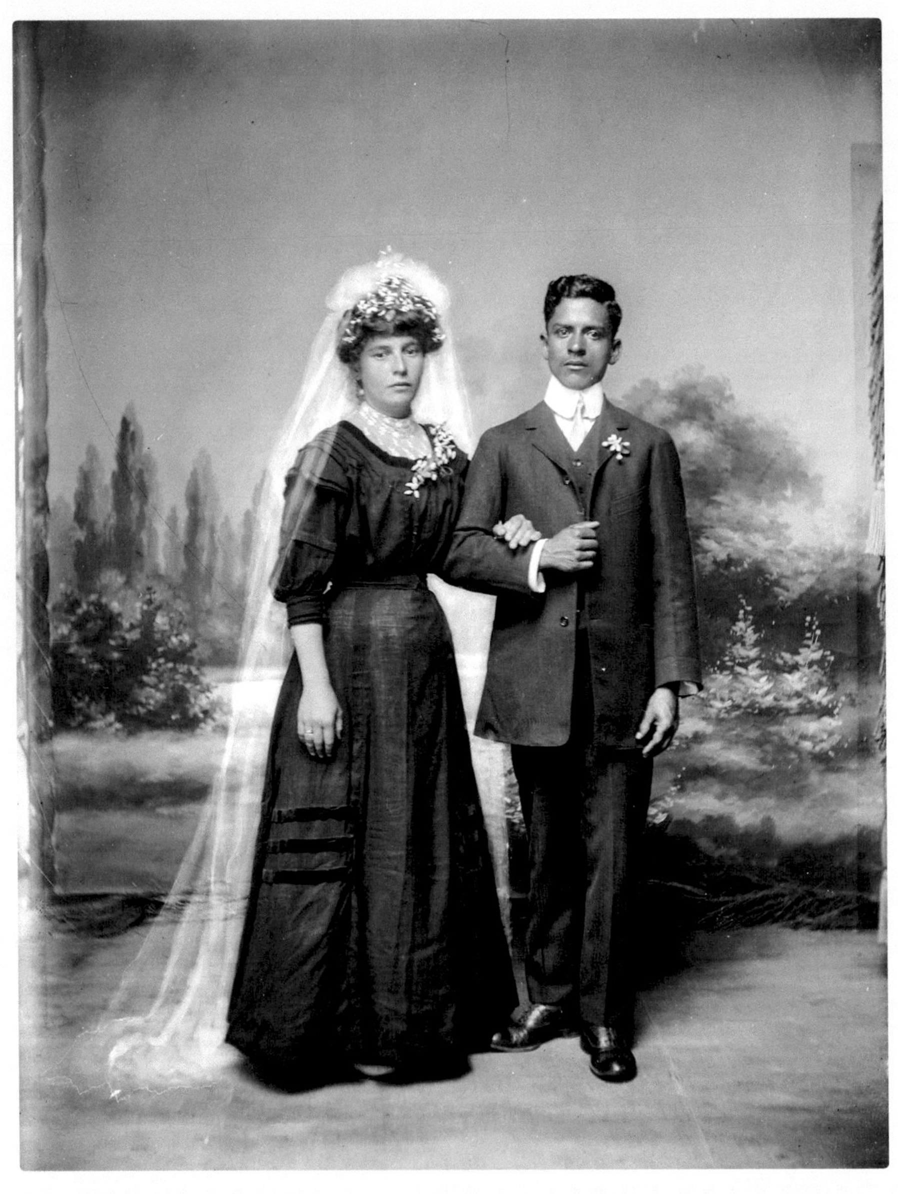

I.1. Benjamín de la Calle, *Tomás Morales B. y señora: San Cristóbal*, 1909. Digital positive from original gelatin dry plate, 16 × 12 cm. Biblioteca Pública Piloto de Medellín / Archivo fotográfico.

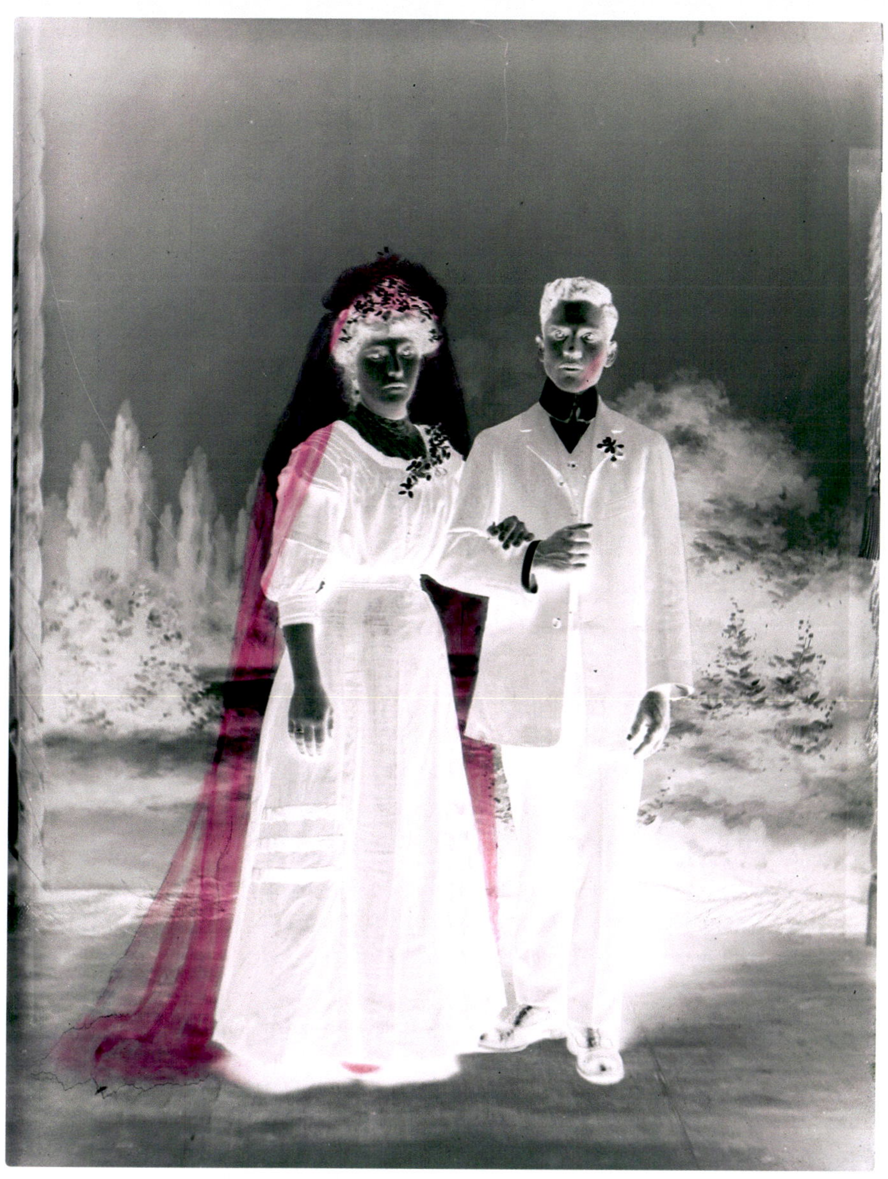

I.2. Benjamín de la Calle, *Tomás Morales B. y señora: San Cristóbal*, 1909. Gelatin dry plate, 16 × 12 cm. Biblioteca Pública Piloto de Medellín / Archivo fotográfico.

originals. It explores the construction of regional and national discourses that linked theories of race to those of progress and how such discourses were visualized or contested through photography. Through the examination of the work of Fotografía Rodríguez (Horacio Marino and Melitón Rodríguez) and Benjamín de la Calle, two photographic studios based in Medellín, Colombia, this book traces the construction, dissemination, and visual materialization of a racial discourse that emerged at the turn of the twentieth century in Colombia's Department of Antioquia.[1] It also looks at the resistance to such discourses through the same medium. Focusing on individual photographs, it addresses how these photographers challenged or circumscribed a discourse based on the invention of a new race. Working simultaneously in the same city, although surrounded by very different environments, de la Calle and the Rodríguez brothers addressed, sometimes resisting and other times supporting, distinctive ways of portraying a society that proclaimed itself more modern and progressive than the rest of Colombia and Latin America. By 1910, a group of intellectuals in the Department of Antioquia established a series of discourses surrounding identity in which the idea of a *raza antioqueña* (Antioquian race) emerged. They claimed that if "there is a place in Latin America where the ideal birthplace of a superior race exists, that place is Antioquia."[2]

This book focuses on the portraits produced by these two studios and the strategies employed in their artistic and commercial work through the ideas of regional progress, modernity, and the invention of a racial ideology. The Department of Antioquia cultivated a strong identity discourse around progress, with particular attention to the idea of the *raza antioqueña*. Since the early nineteenth century, and particularly after the devastating Guerra de los Mil Días (Thousand Days' War), the notion of progress became an agent that fostered and imposed material and ideological demands in the region.[3] These ideas reached their apogee when the two studios were active and, despite the critical development that such notions have received since then, such an ideology still underscores identity discourses in the region. The alleged *raza antioqueña* took advantage of the region's economic boom to proclaim a superior race that distinguished the antioqueños from the rest of the country.[4]

Both products of positivist thinking during the nineteenth century, race and photography have worked hand in hand since early on. However, racial photographic representation has usually been discussed through the analysis of typological or scientific photography that took advantage of the objectification and exoticization of Indigenous, mestizo, and black bodies. However, constructing these othered bodies would not have been possible without the simultaneous invention of a race that considered itself superior. Therefore, instead of expanding on the study of type and scientific photography in Latin America, my research analyzes the formation of racial discourses from the opposite perspective. I explore the construction of whiteness—and the discourses that challenged it—through the study of studio portraiture and its relation to the ideology encouraged by the intellectual elites in Colombia and promoted through publications, political policies, and social conventions. Taking as a point of departure the structuralist idea of binaries, I contend that the Latin American Other could not have been constructed without the invention of these whitening ideologies. My research explores this idea by analyzing the strategies used to promote this alleged racial superiority in materializing the discursive rhetorical practices into visual and physical forms. I explore the visual resistance that flourished in the work of lesser-known photographers who engaged with a more inclusive photographic approach.

Negatives and Race

From a theoretical point of view, the book addresses the duplicity of the photographic image. In opposition to traditional approaches, where the vintage positive copy of a photograph is the object analyzed, this study examines the implications of looking at the negative originals. The lack of institutional efforts in collecting and studying photography, the scarcity of funds, and the complicated sociopolitical situation of the country shaped the early history of Colombian (and Latin American) photography. These circumstances have led to collecting, conserving, and preserving the negatives rather than the positive prints. Previous analysis of most of the images included in this book, in particular those of de la Calle and Fotografía Rodríguez, has been achieved through modern digital copies (scans), overlooking other aspects of photography. If, as Ariella Azoulay suggests, we understand photography as an event, that is, as a series of actions, objects, relations, and encounters that are triggered by the (hypothetical) presence of the camera and the production of a photograph, then the negative is also a constituent part of the event of photography.[5] We can even think of something like a "negative event" as part of it. Most histories of photography in Latin America have focused solely on the exhibitional event of photography—that is, the exhibition and analysis of positive prints—overlooking this negative event. I argue that this negative event is not only closer to the photographed one, but it also constitutes a rawer and sometimes richer version of the final image. Negatives are imbued with manual interventions, retouching, and other types of image manipulation that have not played a role in the understanding of the photographs. Rather, they have been read only for what they visually represent and not for what they actively do. In this project, the material aspects of the photographic image play a central role because they speak about what lies behind the intended final visual result. Traditional analysis and display of photographic images only show positive prints or scans to the larger public in online or offline exhibitions. As stated by photo historian Olena Chervonik, "Its negative, its repressed Other, exists behind-the-scene, relegated to archival boxes and rarely seeing the light of day. . . . Even when collections choose to represent negatives alongside positives, often those negatives as tangible objects look different from their digitized forms."[6] I contend that looking at negatives expands our understanding of photography, giving us access to the process involved in creating an image and, thus, to the line of thought behind it. In this sense, photography is not a specific or decisive moment—that of capturing the event—but a longer and more complex composition of time that includes the process that led the photographer, the sitter, and all those involved to that event, and what lives and happens after it. Indeed, we can even think of a multiplicity of events and timelines that unfold at their own pace, triggered by the multiple copies that can come from a single negative. The negative is evidence of the fragmentation of the process and a step in the long temporality of photography.

But what exactly is a negative? Technically, negatives are fine silver particles suspended in a binder or emulsion of collodion, albumen, or gelatin, which is carried on a paper, glass, or film support.[7] From a purely visual perspective, negatives are objects that present inverted images.[8] In nineteenth-century monochrome photography, negatives reproduce the inversion of the shades of the photographed subject in its complete gradation of grayscale, modeling the subject and giving it a spectral quality. The values of the halftones play a pivotal role in the definition of the photographic negative, something that, as noted by Bertrand Lavédrine, most literature tends to oversimplify.[9] Definitions of the negative frequently describe the simple reversal of light areas of the picture into dark sections and vice versa, but negatives present a reversal of the complete tonal range. Moreover, the inversion of the negative is not only tonal but also spatial. Negatives show the images laterally reversed (from right to left), thus inverting the picture tonally and spatially.

In this book, I specifically engage with and study gelatin on glass negative plates, or dry plates as they are popularly known. Gelatin dry plates are glass negatives that use glass as support and gelatin as a binder. They represented a radical innovation in photography during the nineteenth century, in part due to their industrial production. In particular, dry plates shortened exposure times to less than a second compared to the longer time used in collodion or paper negatives. Besides, photographers could buy ready-to-use plates, meaning they did not have to prepare the emulsion in the studio.[10] The first records of this type of negative appeared in 1871 in a publication by Richard Leach Maddox. However, it was not until 1878, after several technical improvements, that these plates were commercially introduced.[11] In the archives of the Rodríguez brothers and Benjamín de la Calle's studio, there are original boxes containing dry plates from the Eastman Dry Plate Company and the Lumière Brothers, which speaks to both the wide circulation of these materials and the connections of these photographers with the international photographic industry.

The invention of the negative turned photography into a potent tool. Copies could indeed have been made through the reproduction of direct positives by contact or projection—as we know we can do today with slides—if the image produced by the camera obscura was a direct positive on translucent paper.[12] But this was not the case. Hippolyte Bayard's process, which produced direct positives on paper, was not fully developed when William Henry Fox Talbot used high-quality calotypes that created inverted images. Thus, the invention of the negative enabled photography's reproducibility, and the widespread dissemination of realistic images became possible thanks to Talbot's negative/positive process. He conceived this binary relationship of photography as early as 1835 and made it fundamental to the development of the calotype.[13]

Nevertheless, Talbot's version of photography was not immediately widely used because he held a patent that made it difficult to access. Many photo historians argue this was one reason the daguerreotype became so popular; it was available and free to practically the entire world. It was not, however, until 1851, when Frederick Scott Archer invented the glass negative wet-collodion process, that the negative/positive process commercially surpassed Daguerre's invention. From then on, photography entered a new phase in which its democratization was based on the negative's reproductive quality. This was noted in the press, instruction manuals, philosophical essays, and specialist articles.[14] The negative—not the positive—challenged what Walter Benjamin called "aura" and the notion of singular authenticity. To make an image no longer unique was essential for the peculiar qualities of the medium.

It can be argued that the lack of attention negatives have received in the history of photography is a result of the historiography of the medium during the twentieth century. During the nineteenth century, however, authors and photographers alike paid detailed attention to the photographic process and thus to the negative as a constituent part of the medium. In his experiments with photographic reproduction, British scientist John Hershel—the person who coined the words *positive* and *negative* when referencing photography—played in multiple ways with the negative to produce detailed positive prints. Similarly, in his well-known essay "Doings of the Sunbeam," American writer and physician Oliver Wendell Holmes noted how light became shadow in the making of a negative:

> Stop! What is that change of color beginning at this edge, and spreading as a blush spreads over a girl's cheek? It is a border, like that round the picture, and then dawns the outline of a head, and now the eyes come out from the blank as stars from the empty sky, and the lineaments define themselves, plainly enough, yet in a strange aspect,—for where there was light in the picture we have shadow, and where there was shadow we have light. . . . This is a *negative*—not a true picture—which puts darkness for light and light for darkness. From this we can take true pictures, or *positives*.[15]

For Holmes, the negative was a transient moment in which an image was inverted and thus "not a true picture." Photographic truth became available only when the positive was created. Indeed, the negative inverts the picture, but it is not a fleeting moment. Negatives are images that endure, were kept and sold by photographers, and represent a large part of nineteenth-century photographic archives today.

In Colombia, the negative also played a pivotal role in how photographers envisioned the medium. Indeed, the Rodríguez brothers, particularly Melitón, thought of photography in terms of the negative. Not only did he repaint and retouch many of the negative plates he created, but he also evaluated his work by analyzing the negatives. In his diary, he continuously refers to the number of negatives he created and their quality. For example, in a January 19, 1907, note, he stated, "The works are better in every way. Better negatives and more work."[16] In the following note from that same month, he wrote, "It [the day] ended with two negatives of children that should be very good, which I am going to develop on the spot."[17] This conception of photography as negative was crucial. The care and work in the studio were targeted toward creating excellent-quality negatives. The positive prints followed.

Since their invention, negatives were also racially coded. As noted by Darcy Grimaldo Grisby, in Holmes's description of the making of photography, the preservation of racial difference was a subtext of his description.[18] For him, a "true picture" was one of a white sitter who appears white and not "dusky," as in a negative. The term *dusky* referred to the diminution of light but was also used to describe African Americans.[19] Likewise, in 1839, John Herschel wrote in his diary that in a photographic negative, "fair women are transformed into negresses," emphasizing the inversion of the image from a racially coded perspective.[20] In 1854, Henry Morley and William Henry Wills also wrote in racial terms about the process of turning negatives into positive prints: "That negro stage was not, of course, the finished portrait, it was 'the negative'—or stereotype plate, as it were—from which, after it had been fixed with a solution of the sulfate of the peroxide of iron, any number of impressions could be taken. . . . The black face will obstruct the passage of the light and leave a white face underneath."[21] These analogies, commonly employed in the medium's early years, speak to loaded language and the racially inflected ways in which photography's negative/positive process was understood from the beginning.[22] They also signal the strong relationship between race and photography, two ideas that emerged in parallel during the nineteenth century and fed upon one another to install racial segregation through "scientific" perspectives. This issue has been widely studied, particularly the relationships between eugenics, anthropometry, and photography.

But rather than focusing on scientific photography, in this book, I examine the history of studio portraiture at the turn of the twentieth century to trace a parallel history of racial photography through which a construction of whiteness as an ideal standard in society was achieved. Considering the loaded racial history of the negative, I understand the negative not only in its material and physical form but also as a methodology that enables a different perspective. As noted by Tanya Sheehan, photography functions—beyond a technology of representation—as an instrument and metaphor for race relations.[23] Therefore, in this book, the negative is also understood as a metaphor for those categorized as the Other. Negatives are linguistically charged with a pejorative reading, just as poor, black, Indigenous, and nonnormative bodies have been relegated and associated with negative connotations. However, what happens when we think positively about those negative subjects? When we look at them from the reverse side of both photography and history? What happens when we understand the negative as a productive way of thinking through photography?

This methodology of the negative, as I shall call it, is an approach that invites the spectator to view the images studied here from the other side, that is, from the reverse. That other side is the reversal not only of the image but also of history. Thinking through the negative implies a trifold approach: material, symbolic, and spatial. Thus, in the following chapters, I return to the negative and use it as a concept to analyze the photographs through one or more of these approaches. For example, the negative is materially and symbolically understood in chapters 2, 3, and 4. In these chapters, I focus on the representation of subjects considered negative or positive by Antioquian society. I analyze how photography reinforced or challenged preconceived ideas of whiteness and alterity by appropriating local and international representational styles and themes, such as pictorialism, Orientalism, and *costumbrista* painting. In the last chapter, I focus on the negative space of the photographic image through an analysis of the backdrops used in studio photography. In other words, I study the negative from a spatial perspective. Just as negatives have played a minor role in photography's historiography, the negative space of the photographic image is rarely analyzed. Carefully chosen painted backdrops are the negative space of studio photographs. These backdrops, by themselves, already connote certain ideas. But when looked at and analyzed in juxtaposition to the sitters, their meaning expands, locating the portrayed persons in a very specific context that speaks of the racial morale of the *raza antioqueña*.

Moreover, when one looks at the photographic negative of these images—the object itself—hand-drawn additions appear on the surface of the glass plate, subtly altering the depicted background and thus its meaning. These additions respond to the photographer's effort to contain what Christopher Pinney has called a space of "unruly contingencies," that is, the photographic surface onto which everything that stood in front of the camera is imprinted with more information than the photographer can control.[24] The idea of photography as contingency was first enunciated by Walter Benjamin in his "Little History of Photography" and later developed by Roland Barthes in *Camera Lucida*. For Benjamin, contingency is the "here and now, with which reality has, so to speak, seared through the image-character of the photograph."[25] It is the unwanted element that, even in the most controlled of all the photographic practices, such as the mise-en-scène of studio photography, sneaks in. For Barthes, that contingent element is usually where he finds the punctum of the picture, the "shock," the "wound," which usually does not correspond to the photographer's intention. I argue that the intervention of negatives is a step in the process of controlling this "madness of photography," or its "exorbitance," as Barthes called it. Negatives reveal the diverse ways used to modify photography before the invention of Photoshop. With this in mind, we must ask ourselves why negatives have been secondary or supplementary to photography's history. One scope of this book is to question the hierarchies of the elements analyzed in photography and show that photographic history can be constructed by considering other aspects of the picture.

Examining the negatives has both advantages and disadvantages. The major inconvenience is not having access to the final printed image created by the photographer for the client. Indeed, this is a larger issue in the history of photography in Latin America. Perhaps the most well-known case is that of the Peruvian Martín Chambi, who toned his prints in shades of red, blue, or brown and sometimes even airbrushed them. The photographer and his contemporaries held these tinted images in high regard, and they became a commercial success. However, these pictures were not the ones that later became known to the larger international public. The images curators and critics picked and showed internationally were modern copies made from the original negatives after Chambi's death. These new copies aligned with modern photography's black-and-white aesthetic but did not reflect the photographer's original intentions. Indeed, when Edward Ranney curated the first exhibition of Chambi's work outside South America—at the University of New Mexico Art Museum in Albuquerque—Chambi's toned vintage prints were removed just days before the opening. Those photographs did not appeal to modern tastes.[26]

Likewise, printing digital scans created today from the negatives used by these photographers permits the enlargement of the photographs to enormous dimensions. Contemporary prints are thus manipulated to appeal to new tastes, distorting the original function of the photographs, which invited close inspection and physical intimacy. These photographers would have never considered printing their pictures life-size because their function and circulation spaces differed from today's art world. In Alois Riegl's terms, we are assigning them "present-day values." That is, we are not considering them in their original historical context, but putting them "on a par with a recently completed modern creation."[27]

Access to de la Calle's and Fotografía Rodríguez's photographs through digital scans has mainly enabled an understanding of their photographs as images, not as physical objects. The disembodied reading of the photographs has been further worsened by the lack of vintage copies and the relatively easy access to the scanned versions of the negatives. This use and reading of the photographs is a consequence of cultural shifts that tend to privilege content over the aesthetic, social, and sensory dimensions of the object of study.[28] This approach has obscured fundamental aspects of photography, such as its uses, functions, and other material dimensions of the photographic object that exceed visual representation.[29] "A photograph is a three-dimensional thing, not a two-dimensional image," noted Elizabeth Edwards.[30] This claim to think about photography—and art history more broadly—from a perspective that embraces both the visual and the material can be traced back to Alois Riegl's ideas when he separated the visual aspects of art from its haptic elements, establishing a framework that positioned artistic processes on a spectrum between the act of seeing and the act of touching.[31] I argue that one way of bringing this dual dimension back to the analysis of these photographs is through serious consideration of the negatives.

The analysis of negatives points to social, political, and economic circumstances that have not been fully considered in the histories told so far. For example, photographers carefully retouched many of the photographs of this period for different purposes, such as altering the color of skin, eliminating some elements from the pictures, or adding artifice and effects that were not part of the original shot. This manipulation of the photographs, usually visible only on the negative plate, completely changes the original understanding of the images and raises questions related to the transparency of the photographic object.[32] It also questions the indexical nature of the specific positive versions that result from a negative.

In *Camera Lucida*, Roland Barthes famously wrote that in a photograph the referent always adheres. I argue that it indeed adheres, but in positive/negative-based photography it adheres to the negative and not necessarily to the positive. He also noted that this "adherence makes it very difficult to focus on Photography" and not on what the photograph is depicting.[33] Here, I want to propose that engaging with negatives is a strategy to "focus on Photography." Through the inversion of tonal range and spatial direction, negatives make evident photography as mediation while maintaining its deictic language, contingency, and exorbitance. The negative reveals the photographic image as a photograph.

Another advantage of analyzing the negative plates is that it allows the possibility of looking beyond the final image. This *beyond* should be understood here in two senses: that of Roland Barthes and that of Ariella Azoulay. Barthes suggests that the "unruly punctum" of the photograph is in this "subtle beyond," in the potential that certain photographs have in launching "a desire beyond what it permits us to see."[34] To a certain degree, the negative points to this *beyond*—to an area of greater contingency that is noisier than its positive version. But this *beyond* is also that of the depicted scene itself. It is captured on the negative and usually cut out of the positive print. By looking at the negatives, we have access to uncropped versions of the photographs, revealing elements that lie beyond the backdrop of the settings, including other props, the arrangement of the studios, assistants, and other technical equipment, as seen, for example, in a photograph of Manuel J. Echavarría (fig. I.3). We also see the inscriptions and other interventions the photographers did on the negative plates. In other words, we have access to the unwanted aspects of the photographic images and, hence, to other central elements of the process of constructing the picture. This is the *beyond* proposed by Azoulay: a beyond that allows us to see the relationships established by the photographic event and, in the negative, become more evident.[35]

The reading and understanding of the final positive copies are often complicated when analyzing negative-based photography. The negative counterpart of the picture brings about other aspects of the photographic image that are usually not taken into consideration but—in

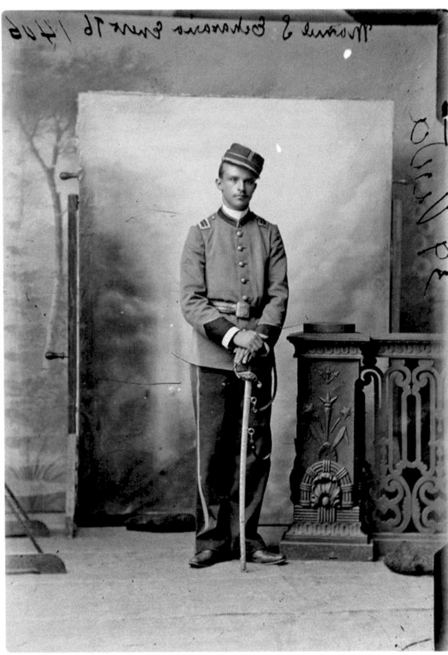

I.3. Fotografía Rodríguez, *Manuel J. Echavarría*, 1896. Digital positive from original gelatin dry plate, 13 × 9 cm. Biblioteca Pública Piloto de Medellín / Archivo fotográfico.

some instances, such as the ones analyzed in this book—affect the thorough understanding of the complete picture. I argue that examining photography should also engage these different instances of its production. Unfortunately, in most cases, re-creating the moment of the shot is impossible, leaving scholars with only the last two stages of the picture: the negative and the positive print. However, there is a certain bias toward privileging the latter because it is the last step of a chain process. However, what happens when the negative unveils aspects of the image that are not visible in the positive version?

The issue of the fragmentation of photography also plays in the opposite direction. What happens when the positive version distances greatly from its negative counterpart? Where lies the intention of the photographer? It is usually assumed that the positive copy is the one the photographer signed off as final and that the negatives were never intended to be looked at. This is an issue at stake in the analysis of the photographs in this project. A few versions of positive prints that have been found were, for example, hand-painted and cropped. This variation of the pictures opens another set of questions regarding the final version of the image. One might even wonder if there is something like a final version of a photograph. If one can produce several positive copies of a picture from a single negative and alter them, which is the original? These considerations inevitably take us back to the negative, as it seems to be a breaking point in the production of images, and nineteenth-century photographers were aware of this. Then why should we overlook histories of photography that do not engage with the final version of the images? Is it equally valid to create a history of photography through the negative version of the images?

If we agree that the photographic medium is fragmented—divided between the physical action of the camera, the selection of the image, the editing process, and the final positive print—then the negative as a point of reference might be just as important as, if not more important than, its positive version. Indeed, we can argue that the negative is closer to the photographic event, that it is the bearer of greater contingency, and that it embodies a noisier or rawer version of the photographic positive, which both photographers and sitters tried to tame, never really fully succeeding.[36] The negative can capture either too much or too little. Retouching the faces of sitters responded to a rejection of what photography captured: wrinkles, freckles, and pores that the sitters didn't want to see in their likenesses. On other occasions, it captured too little, and additions such as missing props and painterly effects were added.[37] It is precisely because it is an integral part of the photographic event that I consider the negative a critical aspect of understanding photography.

Although this method might be problematic precisely because we are not dealing with the final image, it sheds light on other issues that shaped and forged the construction of identities in modern Latin America. It also clarifies theoretical questions regarding photography's ontology and the construction of the photographic image. It forces us to question where exactly the image lies or if any state is more complete than another. As noted by Geoffrey Batchen, rethinking the history of photography through the negative points to troubling questions such as, "What exactly is a photograph? Is it just the negative, the original indexical trace of the world depicted? Or is it a single positive 'master' print generated from that negative? Or does a photograph necessarily comprise the two of them, symbolically joined in an eternal union?"[38]

These questions regarding the definition of photography from the point of view of the negative take me to questions regarding the definitions of race in light of whiteness. In Latin America, the latter concept involves an array of positive traits that generate profitable outcomes for people, communities, and social practices deemed white or aligned with whiteness in the eyes of society.[39] Attributes that deviate from this conception are undesirable. The concept of whiteness, like the concept of race, is an idea, not a fact. It has been appropriated and implemented in different contexts and societies to create relationships of power. As a concept, whiteness is also relative and subjective. For example, the notions of white and black in Latin America do not correspond to those of white and black in Europe or the United States. Whereas in the United States, a person with any visible signs of black ancestry is identified as black, in Latin America, only people who look identifiably African will be regarded as black. The opposite happens with the concept of white. While in the United States only people who appear to have a pure Caucasian lineage are considered white, in Latin America, the concept is broader and includes mixed-race people with a light(er) but not exclusively white skin color.

Indeed, the concept of whiteness is complex, frequently exceeding physical appearance, although not abandoning it altogether. During the nineteenth century in Colombia's Andean region, whiteness was also defined in terms of beauty, material consumption (mostly European material culture), and morality. In this sense, the concept of whiteness can be regulated, altered, and even lost. Yet, despite its flexibility, whiteness as a place of enunciation is validated as superior.[40] This is noticeable in the photographs analyzed in this book. In some cases, the concept of whiteness and white privilege is visible not in the color of the skin of the depicted subjects but in the morality traits that they express and in the social distinction of the sitters—usually seen in the material goods they wear and the behaviors and poses they perform for the camera. For example, in the negatives of pictures such as *Emilia Obregón* and *Carolina Carvallo,* the photographer decided not to retouch the sitter's skin color and instead focus on the theatricality of the scenes emphasizing the material and symbolic aspects that relate the sitters to a privileged upper and whiter class (figs. 2.2 and 2.5). I explore these ideas more deeply in chapter 2, where I analyze these particular photos.

Besides the racial concepts of black and white, a third one was introduced, usually used to refer to mixed-race people. The concept of mestizo, or mixed-race person, goes back to colonial times and has complex bifurcations, which I will not address here. There were dozens of categories used to refer to the different race-mixing processes among the three major groups of people during the Spanish colonial era: Indigenous,

African, and Spanish. During the sixteenth and seventeenth centuries, *mestizo* was a mutable concept which, as Joanne Rappaport has explained, included fleeting conditions that ranged from occupation to behavioral practices and more stable situations also subject to change, such as place of residence, gender, and religion.[41] Mestizo identity was not a stable marker during the colonial period and depended on the labeling person and the purpose of such labeling.[42] As opposed to the eighteenth-century *casta* painting system developed in New Spain (today Mexico), in New Granada (today Colombia) there were no such visual representations of race mixing, and there was no system for classifying *mestizaje* processes. *Casta* paintings depicted an idealized projection of racial combinations that appeared during the colonization process and usually emphasized Spanish supremacy.[43] They indicated, for example, how through the mixture of races over generations, an Indigenous person could become Spanish. *Casta* paintings have become the most significant and more salient visual examples of these complex processes of *mestizaje* in the Spanish Americas. Still, they do not represent the situation of all the Spanish colonies and, more importantly, they do not represent the realities of New Spain's society. They depict a projection for European consumption.[44] As noted by Rappaport, "'Casta,' the terminology used in colonial Mexico . . . to refer to a system of socio-racial categories including 'Indian,' 'mestizo,' 'mulatto,' and so on, does not appear in the archival record of the Nuevo Reino until the eighteenth century, and then only as an umbrella term used to refer to those who were not Spaniards, Indians, or black slaves; in the sixteenth-century Andes 'casta' referred to lineage in a more general sense."[45]

During the colonial period in Colombia, visual representations of race mixing—such as *casta* paintings—were not a popular genre. Explicit racial depictions of this type emerged only in the nineteenth century with the *costumbrista* painting—a genre intended to depict local customs and traditions. In this type of painting, people were not depicted as individual subjects but as types. The most prominent examples of this genre in Colombia are the plates produced as part of Agustín Codazzi's Chorographic Commission, the country's first and largest geographic exploration, which took place in the 1850s. The commission intended not only to survey the landscape of the newly formed nation but also to document the types and idiosyncrasies of its inhabitants.[46] To complete this task, Codazzi hired different draftsmen—Henry Price, Carmelo Fernández, and Manuel María Paz—the artists that did the well-known plates. When representing

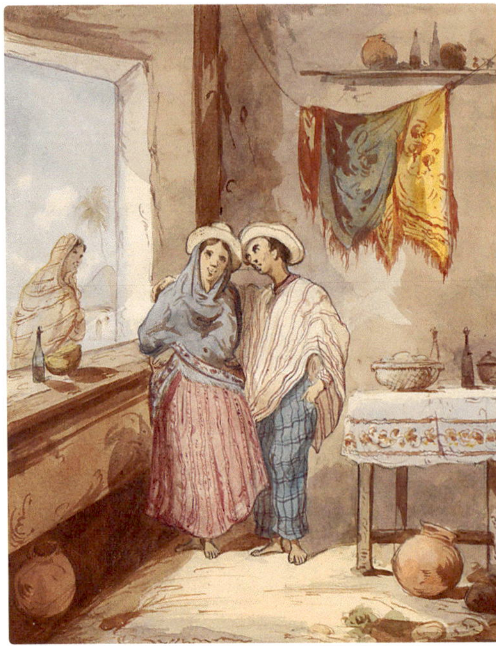

I.4. Manuel María Paz, *Mestizos de Cartago en una venta*, 1853. Watercolor on paper, 31 × 24 cm. Biblioteca Nacional de Colombia.

the diverse population of the country, the illustrations emphasized the different races as seen, for example, in *Mestizos de Cartago en una venta* (Mestizos from Cartago in a shop, fig. I.4). The surprising aspect of this plate is the fact that the sitters, which according to the caption are mixed-raced persons, are represented with fairly white skin. However, other aspects of the image point to their nonwhiteness and, therefore, to their negative identity: the bare feet of both sitters, the clothes they wear, and the ceramic vessels they possess.

Today, when we think about the concept of mestizo, what comes to mind is the idea of a mixed-race person, usually with Indigenous heritage. However, the notion of *mestizaje* was fluid and distinct from modern racial discourses. During the nineteenth century in Colombia, *mestizaje* described the process of becoming white rather than one of race mixture. The cultural imaginary in nineteenth-century Colombia saw race mixing as a path toward physical and cultural whiteness. In the official documentation and the fictional stories of the time studied, none of the subjects were classified or referred to as mestizos. This notion only appeared in the visual representations of types or public discourses encompassing larger population groups. Conversely, the process of *mestizaje* played a central role in national discourses, allowing the formation of the nation itself.[47]

I have not found nineteenth-century photographs of types that describe their subjects as mestizos. This intermediate racial category was not verbally announced in the pictures' accompanying texts, but it became visible in the "invisible" part of the photographic process: the negative. The retouching performed on many of the plates studied in this book speaks precisely to the process of *mestizaje*, leaving traces of a stigma that had to be improved or overcome on the surface of the negatives. But retouching was not the only way to visually announce the process of becoming white. In other instances, this process was not so literal, and it materialized in photography through the sitters' poses, clothing, props, backdrops, and the themes of the performed scenes.

The meaning of race shifts and changes according to the context and culture in which it develops. In Colombia, *race* was understood as *lineage* until the eighteenth century. Rather than focusing on a person's color, what marked the difference was status or religion.[48] People's social standing depended on purity of blood: a genealogy of descendants that traced its pure Christian past.[49] By the nineteenth century, race was considered a type. In other words, until the 1800s, race was a category that referred to a line of descendants from a single common ancestor, whereas by the nineteenth century, it had transformed into the concept that races could be divided into types: human beings with innate and permanent qualities passed from generation to generation could be classified based on this shared history of inheritance. In the twentieth century, conversely, race took on different connotations. The understanding of race as a permanent, unchangeable feature changed—partly because of Darwin's theories of evolution, which determined that breeding populations could adapt. This new scientific discovery paved the way for eugenics and the understanding of certain races as inferior. Scientific racism was later challenged through its own techniques, such as the anthropometric research of anthropologist Franz Boas and, more recently, Mendel's genetic discoveries, which finally forced the scientific community to determine that races do not exist and are indeed social constructions.[50]

Yet, knowing that race is a social construct does not mean it has no real, tangible consequences. Races are social categories of great tenacity and power, affecting large portions of the world population positively and negatively.[51] Although, relatively recently, some scientists have argued that races are social constructions built on phenotypical variations, that is, disparities in physical appearance, such a concept is also misguided. The features on which these variations are based are a small selection of recognizable physical characteristics that show continuity over generations, such as height, weight, and hair and skin color, but also, as stated by Peter Wade, those that "correspond to Europeans in their colonial histories."[52] In other words, the phenotypical variations selected to define racial types are also social constructs. Thus, the concept of race reflects a history of European thought about difference rather than one deploying objective scientific truth independent of its social context.[53]

The concept of race that emerged in Antioquia during the second half of the nineteenth century and peaked during the early twentieth is a mix of the notion of race as type and that of race as eugenics. It is interesting, however, to see how in Colombia, the concept of race is not addressed through the usual notions of black or white but is traversed by the symbolic process of the racialization of the regions.[54] In Colombia, race is not a national concept; the regions are allotted racial identities that determine the hierarchical organization of the departments. Territories in the Andean part of the country, including Antioquia, occupy the upper section of the pyramid and are considered of greater morality and progress (white) and thus positive. Whereas those in warmer climates, such as the Cauca region and the Caribbean coast, are relegated to the lower parts of the hierarchical structure. The regional identities of the warmer climate regions are usually associated with negative connotations: disorder, backwardness, and danger (mestizos or black). For this reason, the representation of races in Colombia is linked not to the concept of the nation but to that of the region, and Antioquia is the area with the best-defined racial identity.[55]

The Department of Antioquia is in the northwestern part of the country. It has an area of 63,612 square kilometers. A small section of its northern territory borders the Caribbean Sea, but most of it lies in the Andes Mountains (fig. I.5).[56] Medellín is the capital city and occupies a valley surrounded by rugged mountain ranges. Until 1914, it was incredibly isolated from the outside world and only accessible by mule. In 1812, Medellín had a population of 13,755. By the end of the nineteenth century, it had grown to 37,237; and by 1928, it had reached 120,000 inhabitants.[57] It went from the fourth most populated city in the country to the second one, with only Bogotá surpassing its numbers. The process of *mestizaje* was particularly

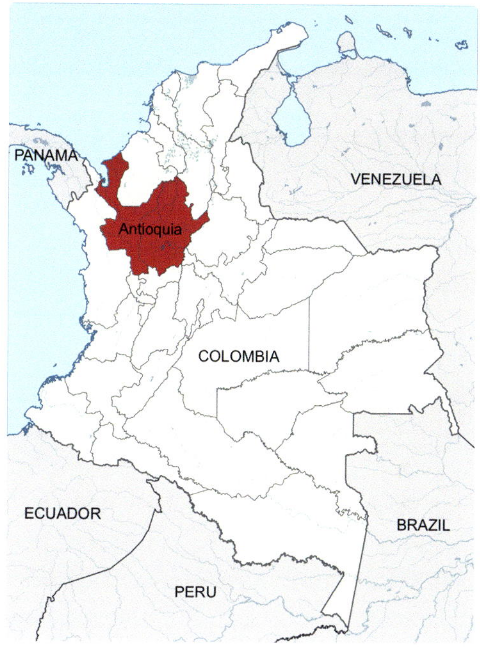

I.5. Map of Colombia, showing the location of the Department of Antioquia. Wikipedia.

strong in Antioquia. Although black enslaved populations were brought to the region to work in the gold mines, they made up less than 1 percent of the population by the mid-nineteenth century. This is surprising considering Antioquia borders the Department of Chocó, Colombia's region with the highest percentage of black people. The Indigenous population, on the other hand, was almost completely devastated, and the few survivors were confined to special reservations.

In Antioquia, as in many other Latin American regions, regional racial identities and nationalist discourses intertwined, turning racial discourses into political ones.[58] One of the major challenges posed by this situation was the risk of naturalizing these discourses and assuming them to be unchangeable truths. Yet, the notions of white, black, or mestizo are not fixed categories and, most times, gain meaning in relation to others, such as class and gender. Indeed, the idea of whiteness in the concept of the *raza antioqueña* emerged from the intersection with other discourses that privileged male subjectivity, Catholic religious beliefs, and class differentiation. The photographs analyzed in this book point precisely to these intertwined ideas and show the complex bifurcations that such a category entails. Although the rationale behind different notions of race may differ, the ideas are invalid because, as previously stated, every racial construction is fiction. These fixed definitions of race tell powerful narratives with actual consequences for the region and nation they represent but also for how individual subjects understand themselves and, thus, for the distribution of power. The first chapter of this book deals with this topic in more depth. However, the Antioquian race seen through the concept of the negative ultimately becomes the book's common thread.

This book, thus, embraces the negative as both an object that is closer to the photographic event and as a space where ideas can be inscribed after the photograph is taken and reproduced through the negative/positive process. One can draw an equation between the reproduction of an image through the negative/positive process (i.e., the material negative) and the reproduction of ideologies (i.e., the metaphorical negative) that are ultimately embedded in the negative plates. My argument is that these ideologies are later inscribed on the image. I assert that this is done through direct intervention on the negative plates (adding or removing information) or through the inscription of ideological ideas that come from the frameworks in which these images circulated, namely the racial morale of the *raza antioqueña*. These postevent ideas are not predetermined; they can change, and new ideas can be imprinted on these photographs, which is one of the aims of my project. Taking this into consideration, the negative can inhabit this apparent contradiction: being closer to the photographic event while simultaneously constituting a postevent writing space.

The Photo Studios: Benjamín de la Calle and Fotografía Rodríguez

In 1898, Benjamín de la Calle, a newcomer to the photographic world, wrote a letter—later published with its reply in the newspaper *El Espectador*—to Horacio Marino Rodríguez (1866–1931), an already recognized artist-photographer in Medellín, asking him to assess his work. De la Calle inquired if he could open a photographic studio in "any advanced society with the confidence of satisfying the most refined tastes."[59] Rodríguez replied with admiration, acknowledging de la Calle's photographs as some of "the best in the country in terms of good taste and exquisite execution" and confessing that some of them even "made [him] feel envy."[60] This conversation might seem paradigmatic as it evidences a connection between two of the three photographers involved in this history—Benjamín de la Calle, Horacio Marino Rodríguez, and his younger brother Melitón Rodríguez—whose production would later provide the foundation for two of the most significant turn-of-the-century photographic archives in Colombia, if not in Latin America. Despite their geographic isolation and the lack of museums, galleries, and institutions, these photographers created a compelling visual record focused on portraiture, one of the region's most diverse. For clarity throughout the book, I refer to the Rodríguez brothers by their first names, while I use the standardized reference by the last name when dealing with Benjamín de la Calle's work.

The photographers were the first to recognize the power of portraiture, as reflected in their self-portraits. As de la Calle stated in his letter of 1898, he aimed "to satisfy the most refined tastes" and simultaneously climb the social ladder.[61] This was not a neutral statement, as it came from an inexperienced and little-known photographer who had yet to realize such aspirations. For him, photography was the best way to achieve this goal, as seen, for example, in one of his most outstanding self-portraits (fig. I.6).[62] Standing in front of a poorly painted background, de la Calle wears an unusual outfit for an early twentieth-century, middle-class photographer. Sporting a bowler hat, a three-piece suit with a dotted vest, and a white bow tie, he holds a pair of gloves in his right hand while staring away from the camera. He stands in contrapposto, imitating a classic art historical pose, making a statement about his status in society. Through the pose, de la Calle claimed that even though he was a photographer who arrived in the city in the early 1890s from a small town high in the Antioquian mountains, he indeed had "refined taste" and was aware of the stylistic tropes and signifiers of the upper classes. This idea was ultimately a European appropriation that conveyed the beliefs of the white male elite. To fit in, de la Calle not only performed these ideas but also attempted to live his public life according to the assumptions of what refined taste was.

This image is a visual witness to his struggle for social acceptance and his radical approach to photography. De la Calle was born in 1869 in Yarumal, Antioquia. He studied photography with Emiliano Mejía (1864–1937), a carte de visite photographer who had studied in Paris and offered not only lessons in photography but also drawing, painting, and French language courses in his studio, located on Calle Pichincha in Medellín.[63]

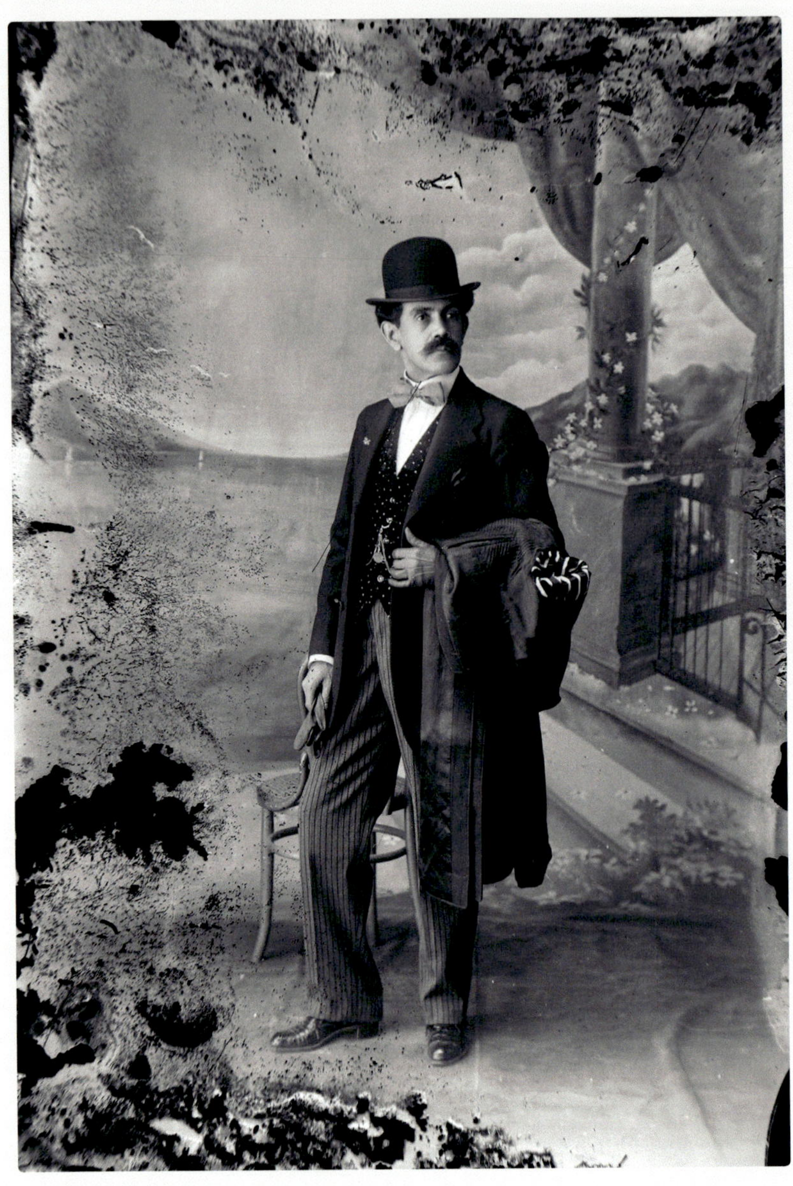

I.6. Benjamín de la Calle, *Self-Portrait*, ca. 1920. Digital positive from gelatin dry plate, 25 × 20 cm. Biblioteca Pública Piloto de Medellín / Archivo fotográfico.

After studying with Mejía, de la Calle returned to his hometown, where he established a photo studio with his brother Eduardo.[64] At the beginning of his career, he worked between Yarumal and Medellín until 1899, when he moved to the department's capital and opened a studio in the Guayaquil neighborhood. This part of Medellín developed parallel to, but separate from, the more cosmopolitan lifestyle of the historically more affluent downtown neighborhood. Guayaquil became a commercial neighborhood; within it, a distinct set of "values, beliefs, mythologies, and ways of thinking" emerged.[65] Although extremely productive and in many aspects successful, throughout his career, de la Calle struggled financially, as demonstrated both by the various letters he addressed to the city's council requesting tax reductions and by a classification in 1911 of the photographic establishments in Medellín in which his studio appeared as a "second class" establishment—in other words, a studio of lower prestige.[66]

In the same spirit manifested in his self-portrait, de la Calle's desire to belong to a higher social class was further evidenced by adding *de la* to his last name in 1909. The addition of a preposition to the surname underscored a heritage of illustrious ascendance, Spanish in most cases. By August of that year, he was signing his advertisements in the newspapers as "Benjamín de la Calle" instead of the simple "Benjamín Calle" that had preceded it.[67] This gesture could be seen as a further reflection of his desire to portray himself as a sophisticated gentleman of his time. Medellín's elite's urge to differentiate themselves from other social classes led them to develop a strict behavioral code embodied in the discourse of *urbanidad y etiqueta* (civility and etiquette).[68] The correct choice of clothing, for example, transmitted a message of good taste, education, and sophistication. No one who aspired to be part of the elite had the liberty to dress however they desired; they had to follow strict rules that reflected their educational background and social standing.[69] For de la Calle, a man sometimes described as "extravagant and complex," and who struggled to keep his homosexuality a secret in a highly conservative city controlled by the beliefs of the Catholic Church, following these codes was crucial.[70] The way he dressed and posed turned into a form of performing a constructed identity and presenting a latent self, which was enhanced and disseminated through photography, a medium that circulated and communicated a certain subjectivity as representation.

An example of the radicality of his images and specifically of this performativity, enhanced through the manipulation of photography, was the addition of a painted flower to the lapel of the suit in his self-portrait—a detail missing in the original shot but later added to the negative (fig. I.7). Although the addition of the flower seems initially a superficial detail, it was decisive. Carlos Coriolano Amador—the wealthiest man in the city, whose investments were considered outrageous at the time—was known for always wearing a red carnation on the lapel of his suit, as seen in a photograph taken by de la Calle himself in 1914 (fig. I.8). In this image, Amador poses wearing a three-piece suit with a white shirt and tie, a top hat, and a cane in his hands, in a posture very similar to the one de la Calle emulated in his self-portrait taken in 1920, after Amador's death in 1919. Some of his contemporaries noticed de la Calle's apparent intention to imitate Amador's manners, as stated by Roberto Álvarez, a merchant who declared that he saw de la Calle "several times on the street with a light-colored suit and a carnation on the lapel, in the manner of Coriolano Amador's style."[71]

But the painted flower on the lapel of de la Calle's suit may have referred not only to Amador but also to de la Calle's homosexuality. As is well known, the green carnation became a queer symbol worldwide after Oscar Wilde presented *Lady Windermere's Fan* in 1892.[72] Men who wore it identified with the dandy: a fashionable, flamboyant, and sexually ambiguous man. It can be said that in this self-portrait, de la Calle embodies the dandy through the pose, the outfit, and the carnation. The addition of the flower to the negative plate is a way of reaffirming his sexuality, albeit through a very subtle gesture. The visualization of such a symbol opened up a political field in which nonnormative gender identification began to take shape, to be represented, and to be visually inscribed. This is more evident in the photographs he took throughout his career of cross-dressed men and women, which are discussed in more detail in chapter 3. But the simple detail of adding a flower to the negative of his self-portrait is a good example to introduce both the radicality of his practice and the importance of looking at negatives.

The exemplary quality of de la Calle's photography permitted him to work with many of the elite, as seen in the pictures of Medellín's upper class and politicians of the time, which he photographed later in his career. He also worked for the police, creating interesting pictures of criminals, which is explored in chapter 3. However, he never abandoned his interest in portraying and giving voice to the urban Other, that is, the peasants who migrated to the city, the Afro-Colombian population from the Pacific

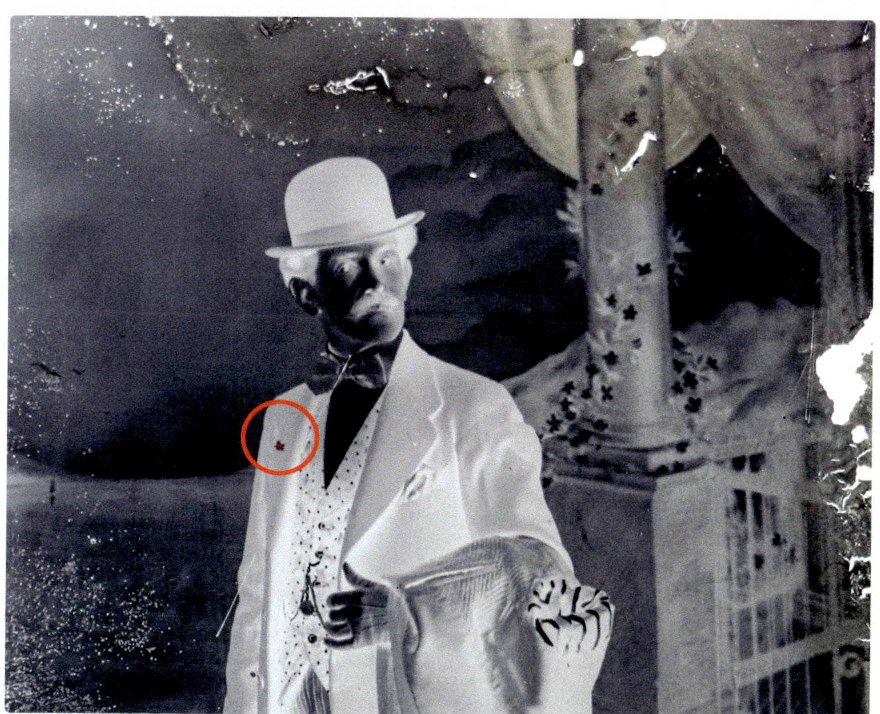

I.7. Benjamín de la Calle, *Self-Portrait*, ca. 1920. Detail from negative on gelatin dry plate. Biblioteca Pública Piloto de Medellín / Archivo fotográfico.

I.8. Benjamín de la Calle, *Carlos Coriolano Amador*, 1914. Digital positive from gelatin dry plate, 18 × 13 cm. Biblioteca Pública Piloto de Medellín / Archivo fotográfico.

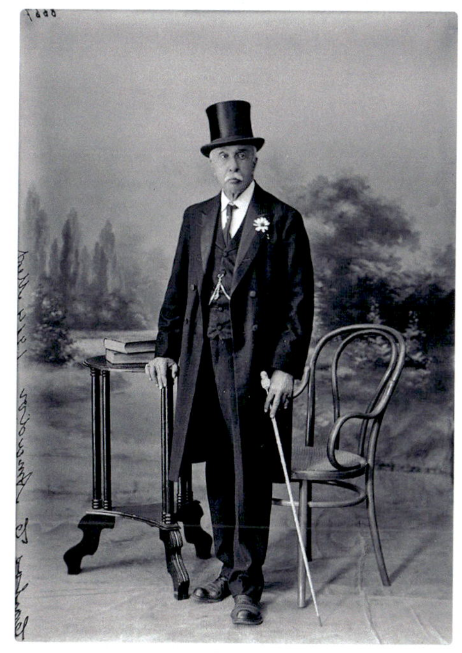

coast, and the prostitutes and cross-dressers that inhabited his neighborhood, among others. By openly assuming his sexual identity, de la Calle signaled his identification with a community that experienced political and intellectual forms of marginalization and segregation.[73] To counterbalance this position, he sought approval from the establishment as a professional photographer, a task he achieved relatively quickly after settling permanently in Medellín. Proof of his success as a photographer is found in the pictures he took for President Rafael Reyes (1849–1921), who visited Medellín in 1908. Reyes was one of Colombia's first presidents to leave his seat in Bogotá and travel around the country during his time in office. Part of his political program included documenting these journeys.[74] Photography played a fundamental role in this program, as Reyes understood the power of images as visual propaganda for his government. The photographs were later published in one of the first photo books in Colombia's history, *República de Colombia: Excursiones presidenciales* (Republic of Colombia: Presidential excursions), from 1909.[75] The official photographer of the president's journey around the country, and later editor of the book, was the chief of the national gendarmerie, Pedro A. Pedraza. His Kodak camera captured most of the photographs that accompany the publication.

It seems, however, that during his sojourn in Medellín, Reyes hired de la Calle to cover his visit. A letter written by the president—published in the newspaper *El Bateo* in 1908—states that "Colombia's incumbent president greets Mr. D. Benjamín de Calle [*sic*], thanks him profusely for the photographic works executed during his short stay in Medellín, and hereby recommends him as a skillful photographer and accomplished gentleman."[76] Although de la Calle received no credit in the final publication, the images seem to align with de la Calle's style when compared with the photographs he took of other significant events in the city, such as the arrival of President Pedro Nel Ospina in 1922 (fig. I.9). The bird's-eye view that allowed him to capture the multitudes that congregated in the main plazas of Medellín to witness the grandiloquence of the occasions characterized de la Calle's pictures of public events.[77]

By 1942, Lisandro Ochoa, a chronicler of the time, described de la Calle as a "practical and consecrated photographer," thus acknowledging the recognition the photographer had achieved throughout his career.[78] Yet de la Calle's best work is not what he created for Medellín's elite, presidents, or politicians but his portraits of anonymous people whose character, spirit, and aspirations were frozen in time through the photographer's

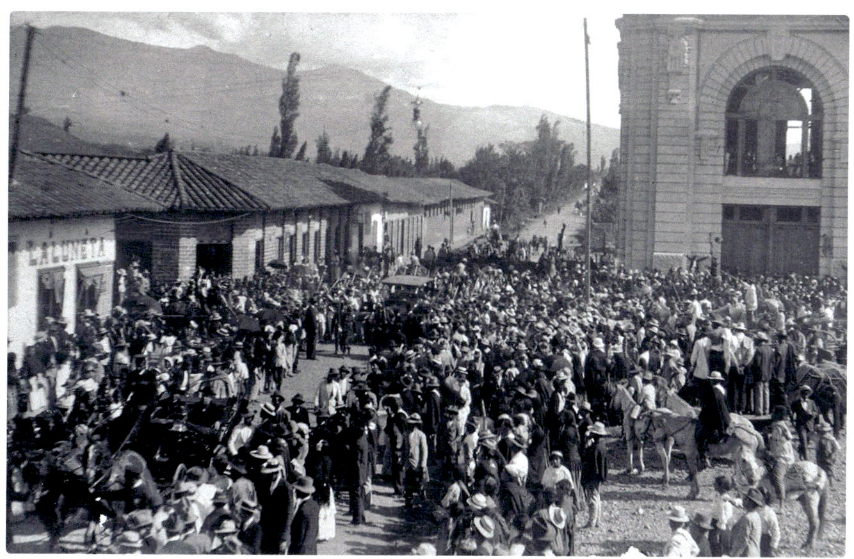

I.9. Benjamín de la Calle, *Untitled (Plaza de Cisneros Pedro Nel Ospina)*, 1922. Digital positive from gelatin dry plate, 9 × 12 cm. Biblioteca Pública Piloto de Medellín / Archivo fotográfico.

profound interest in documenting a different city. If representing likeness was, for some, photography's main achievement, de la Calle's work surpassed it. His portraits do not reveal likenesses but resemblances, that is, he documented the character and inner spirit of the people inhabiting a city seeking progress and civilization but also a sense of belonging.[79] This profound ambivalence is perhaps what best characterizes de la Calle's oeuvre.

Fotografía Rodríguez, the Rodríguez brothers' studio, gravitated instead toward establishing photography in the realm of the fine arts and their work as part of the hegemonic culture of the time. While de la Calle rarely pursued artistic aspirations, the Rodríguezes' studio was born with them. Horacio Marino Rodríguez and his cousin, the painter Francisco Antonio Cano (1865–1935), founded it around 1889 under the name Foto Cano y Rodríguez. Cano would become one of Colombia's most recognized nineteenth-century painters, an acknowledgment rooted in his close kinship to photography.[80] By 1891, Cano had left the photo business and Horacio Marino joined forces with his brother Melitón, opening Fotografía y Pintura Rodríguez y Jaramillo with an investor. This

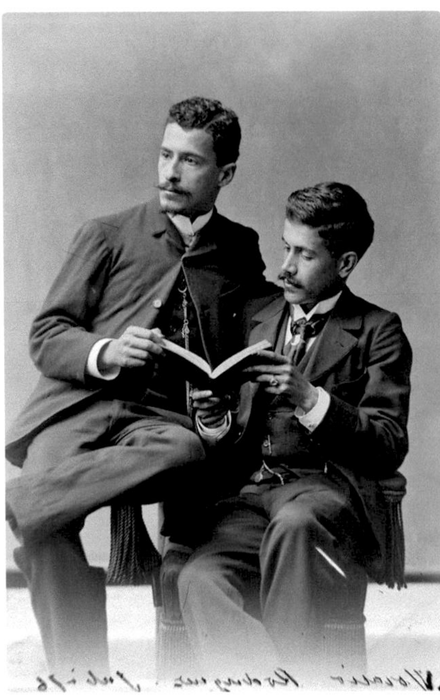

I.10. Fotografía Rodríguez, *Horacio Marino y Melitón Rodríguez*, 1896. Digital positive from gelatin dry plate, 18 × 13 cm. Biblioteca Pública Piloto de Medellín / Archivo fotográfico.

studio eventually became Fotografía Rodríguez, perhaps the most celebrated photographic atelier in the city. Around 1898, Horacio Marino left the photographic enterprise to immerse himself in other projects—such as the publication of the first photogravures in the region in the magazine *El Montañés*—and later became one of the city's most prominent architects.[81] Besides his intellectual curiosity, which permeated many spheres of the arts in the region, one of his most significant contributions was the publication of the first photography manual written in Spanish for the Colombian public. The book, *Diez y ocho lecciones de fotografía* (Eighteen photography lessons), was published in 1897, just before he left the photo business. His younger brother Melitón took over the studio, producing some of Antioquia's most celebrated images during his thirty-year career.

A dual self-portrait from 1896 of the Rodríguez brothers best exemplifies the characteristics of their work (fig. I.10). The two photographers pose against a plain backdrop while holding a book in their hands, marking their status as intellectuals in Medellín's elite society. Horacio Marino, the older brother, sits on the armrest, looking away, while Melitón stares attentively at the publication they are holding. They both wear modern dark suits, white shirts, and pocket watches, identifiable by the chains that contrast against their dark clothing. These elements were characteristic of the men of distinction and elegance they repeatedly photographed and whose interests they reflected.

If we understand the self-portrait as a mediation between the photographer's self and his audience, the Rodríguez brothers' image functioned as the materialization of this definition. The photographers present themselves not as artisans but as intellectuals, reflecting a concern with their professional identity and elevating their social standing. They portray themselves as educated, refined, and cultured men, relating their interests with those of an emerging group of thinkers, which differed from the purely artisanal work to which they were previously related. Their more sober style contrasts dramatically with de la Calle's elaborate, almost theatrical manner of portraying himself, which required numerous props and an exaggerated pose.

The Rodríguez brothers came from a tradition of marble gravestone carvers, a practice that their father pursued for many years and which Melitón continued during the early part of his photographic career. However, the family's open-mindedness and interest in spiritualism (a practice condemned by the Catholic Church) led to financial hardships and intense conflicts with the ecclesiastical authorities, who even prohibited their services to the public.[82] These circumstances drove them to turn to different practices and adopt photography as their chief source of income while distancing themselves from spiritualism. It is presumed that the Rodríguez brothers learned photography from their uncle, Dr. Ricardo Roldán, who trained as a medical doctor in Paris during the mid-nineteenth century and worked as a photography assistant in one of the countless ateliers of the city to support himself.[83] They also studied photographic publications, especially those produced in France, such as *La pratique en photographie* and *L'art en photographie*, both by Frédéric Dillaye, thus adopting the French tradition as their primary reference.[84]

They explicitly visualized their appropriation of a French style of artistic portraiture in their self-portrait. The sober background, as opposed to de la Calle's excessively theatrical backdrop, parallels their work with that of French masters such as Nadar or Étienne Carjat, who opted for a style in which the character of the sitter was the center of the composition, without an abundance of props. The personification of the Rodríguez brothers as members of the intellectual elite seems less artificial than de la Calle's effort to portray himself as a member of high society. Indeed, this constructed identity was concomitant with the Rodríguez brothers' new social stature. By the turn of the century, they were wholly absorbed within the circle of intellectuals who would develop a series of racial theories and identity discourses to explain the region's rapid economic growth and its impulse toward progress and to be civilized.

In their images, one sees an intense interest in producing photographs with artistic intent, especially through the appropriation of pictorialist strategies, such as the slightly blurred effect intended to imitate painting finishes or the creation of *tableaux vivants*. Their aesthetic project was utterly intertwined with the profound obsession with beauty that still characterizes the idiosyncrasy of the people in Colombia, particularly in Medellín.[85] Although beauty is a topic that has concerned different societies throughout history, the fixation on the topic in Colombia could be explained as a counterbalance to the beast, that is, violence, racism, and poverty.[86] Beauty, thus, emerged as another concept that, attempting to obscure the horrifying reality of the country with a positive image, promoted and encouraged patriarchal values and traditional gender roles. Moreover, beauty was codified in terms of whiteness. As noted by Mercedes López Rodríguez, beauty was part of the processes of racial differentiation: "The body and physical appearance . . . occupy the imagination of writers and artists, building an argumentative circle in which white people are more beautiful and, therefore, morally superior, so that whoever is beautiful and moral is considered white."[87] This phenomenon is clearly seen in the photographs studied in this book, particularly in the pictures of women taken by the Rodríguez brothers and discussed in chapter 2.

There was a profusion of articles and advertisements in newspapers and magazines promoting not only beauty products but also strategies to abolish the ugly, as illustrated, for example, in an article titled "No habrá feos en el Taller de la Belleza [*sic*]" (There won't be ugly people in the beauty workshop) from the newspaper *El Bateo* in 1907.[88] The brief article intended to promote new beauty products that could improve the skin, either by eliminating the holes left by smallpox or by "reforming the physiognomy" of the skin—a set of "corrections" also sought through the retouching of photographs.[89] It is no surprise then that photography played a critical role in perpetuating these values since the photographer could alter the images to satisfy the client's requests. In particular, there was a deep interest in changing the facial appearance and skin tone. As a chronicler of the time stated in the first short history of photography in Antioquia, the clientele had sundry demands: "ugly ladies who want to look pretty, one-eyed and cross-eyed people who want to appear with good eyes, whites who do not feel comfortable with the shadows, and blacks who must look white."[90] Fotografía Rodríguez deliberately took advantage of photography's alleged transparency—its most powerful rhetorical device—to convey the ideals of an identity's ideology.[91] Negative retouching, specifically the excessive amount used by this studio, played a critical role in this regard, as we will see in chapter 1.

In the work by the Rodríguez studio, the portraits of women are one example in which the aesthetic project was twofold: the concept of beauty served as a formal device but also embodied the function of the photographs. Among these images are portraits sent to the national beauty contests and photographs for magazines like *Sábado*, a weekly literary magazine that included coupons with pictures to vote for the beauty queen of the Fiesta de las Flores.[92] Other images appeared in government-sponsored publications dedicated to the international promotion of the country, such as *El libro azul de Colombia*, which, not surprisingly, devoted an entire section of the book to "Beautiful Colombian Women."[93] This type of portrait not only played with dramatic lighting effects and soft-focus techniques but also presented an image of the woman as a submissive, passive, moral, and extremely feminine character, sometimes reinforced by using flowers as props to signal purity, innocence, and humility. Another important aspect to note is that the vast majority of the women included in these publications were white members of the elite, who had to follow the intricate codes of etiquette and behavior dictated by the manuals of the time.[94] Perhaps without deliberate intention, promoting beauty became a way of reinforcing gender roles and underscoring a racial discourse hidden by the aesthetic project that ultimately perpetuated the power dynamics of the white male elite.[95] However, it is important to acknowledge that the Rodríguezes' studio also photographed the black population of Medellín in dignifying ways, particularly at the end of Melitón's career. Some of his photographs present blackness in honoring and powerful ways (figs. 1.10 and 1.13).

As seen in the two self-portraits previously analyzed, both the Rodríguez brothers and de la Calle had an increased concern with personal identity and exploited photography to mythologize their personality and business interests. Although the primary interest of both studios was commercial, they distinctly promoted different veiled agendas. On the one hand, the Rodríguez brothers were immersed in an artistic and intellectual project that produced some of the most compelling photographs of the period in Colombia. Specifically created with either artistic or commercial purposes, these images reflected an aesthetic interest that was ultimately permeated by a strong regionalist ideology that aimed to present Antioquians as more progressive and civilized than the rest of the country, or even Latin America, as I will further explain in this book.[96] Ideology emerged through these apparently innocent photographs: the elite class of Medellín wanted to look white, sophisticated, and European to parallel themselves with the Western modernist project and thus create distance from an uncivilized and underdeveloped environment.

Conversely, a sociopolitical project underscored de la Calle's work as a photographer. Employing photography as a tool of resistance against the embedded ideologies of race and progress, he gave voice to and documented a part of the Antioquian society that was otherwise overlooked. De la Calle broadened the idea of Antioquian identity by opening up the spectrum of documentation subjects. We see this, for example, in his photographs of peasants—where he covered their bare feet—or in those of cross-dressers, in which he profoundly questioned the ideas of gender identity. The Rodríguez brothers would not portray these types of sitters in their studio. These other identities are a part of our visual history only because de la Calle was willing to portray them. This is further discussed when analyzing these images in chapter 3.

Ultimately, what these images reflect—just as de la Calle's self-portrait does—is a plea for acceptance, a struggle to be acknowledged as equal and to be seen on their own terms. De la Calle's photographs work against the stereotype, bearing witness to a broader scope of Medellín's society and humanizing people who have not historically been treated as worthy of documentation. His photographs work as active witnesses, not in the legal sense of simple testimonies, but in a human sense. They activate a desire for knowledge and act as a form of witnessing, as humanizing devices, questioning and broadening the understanding of what photography can accomplish far beyond the medium's limits as a representation.[97]

Picturing Photography

In 1937, *El Bateo* published a caricature with the caption "Escena muda, pero . . . muy paisa" (Silent scene, but . . . very *paisa*) (fig. I.11).[98] It depicted a two-vignette scene of a portraiture shot. In the top vignette, a photographer—dressed in a Roman costume—instructs a man to sit calmly in front of the camera while he adjusts it to take the picture. The sitter sits silently and straight, waiting for him to take the photo. He wears what seems to be the typical garment of an antioqueño peasant with a striped scarf around his neck and a set of espadrilles covering his feet. In the lower vignette, the photographer hides beneath the cloth that covers the camera to take the photo while the sitter stands up to attack the photographer with a knife. The caricature directly addressed the presumed shrewdness of the antioqueños, an attitude promoted by the myth of the *raza antioqueña*. Allegorically, the caricature also commented on the opposition between refinement and culture and the uncivilized pueblo; it spoke about the power of photography as a tool of authority and control.

From another perspective, *El Bateo*'s caricature ironically presented the act of being photographed and its specific meanings at the time. Photography was an activity that was becoming accessible to a larger demographic population, and the caricature satirized, contested, and addressed the ritual of going to the photographer's studio to be captured in a static and never-changing picture. Despite important technological advances, the experience of posing for the camera changed very little over time. The caricature, published by the end of the period studied in this book, conveyed impressions similar to those described by Enrique Echavarría in a chronicle about the experience of visiting the photographer's studio at the time of collodion photography, that is, right before the Rodríguez brothers and de la Calle opened their studios in the 1890s. It is worth quoting the chronicle at length. Echavarría wrote:

> Humanity has three small martyrdoms in everyday life, and our benefactors caused them: the tailor, the barber, and the dentist. Formerly there were four because the photographer was included.
>
> When someone resolved to portray himself, back in the old days, he would be subject to the following: making an appointment and specifying if he wanted a group, a vignette, or a whole body shot; a complex operation. When the day arrived, it was necessary to adorn

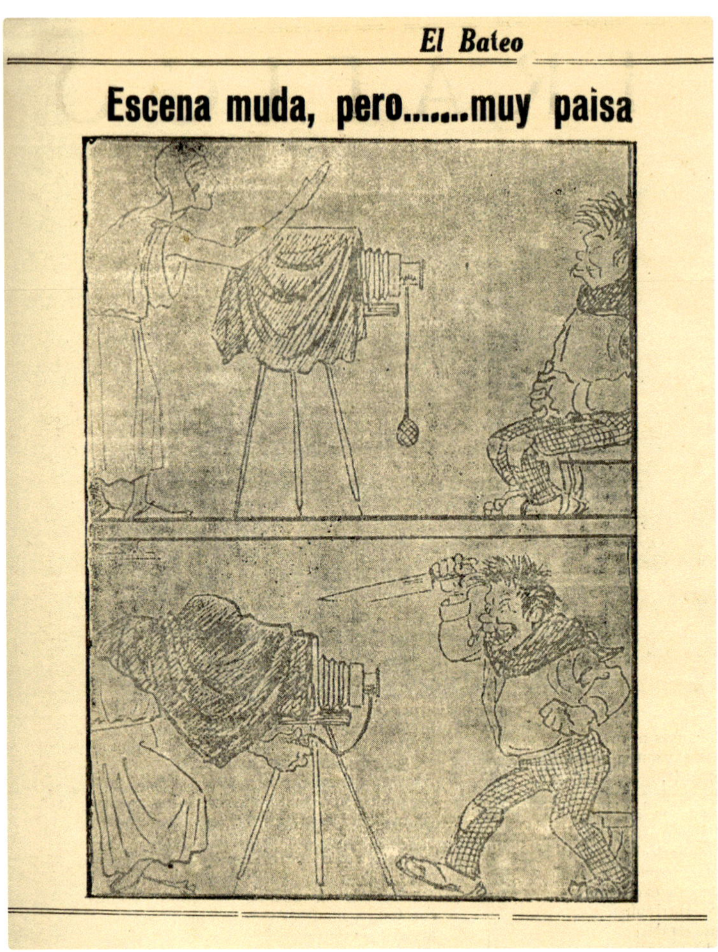

I.11. "Escena muda, pero . . . muy paisa," 1937. Page from *El Bateo*. EAFIT, Centro Cultural Biblioteca LEV, Sala de Patrimonio Documental, Medellín.

oneself and dress in Sunday clothes, especially if the sitter belonged to the fairer sex. Already in the gallery, and when the photographer was ready, it all began by positioning the patient; he was placed in a pose; usually lying on a table, where there were several scattered books, one or two open, as if he were a great thinker, then . . . even though he could not read. In such a position, a set of iron hooks, prepared in advance, were fastened behind him; these caught mainly the head and part of the body. They did all this to keep the sitter completely still.

One could not blink during the one minute that the shot lasted. In this situation, the photographer assumed a solemn attitude, as befitted such a delicate action; with one hand, he held the shutter and with the other the clock to measure time. He resembled a physician who took blood pressure from a patient. And counted very slowly . . . one, two, and three.

However, this was not enough; one had to wait a long time while the operator developed the plate to see if the print was good; most of the time, it was imperfect and bad, and it was necessary to repeat the portrait until success was complete.[99]

There seems to be little difference between the experience presented in the caricature and the one verbally described by the chronicler, even though the technological aspects of the medium had improved immensely: shooting times were faster, and thus the iron structure was no longer needed. New materials—such as gelatin dry plates—had been introduced to facilitate the photographer's task. There were a greater variety of cameras, and prices were more accessible. Yet the ritual itself had changed very little.

By the time the caricature from *El Bateo* appeared, parodies related to posing for a photograph were already a tradition. One of the best known was Honoré Daumier's *Croquis Parisiens* from 1853, a drawing that juxtaposed two photographic shots: one where the photographer took a frontal portrait of a man and one where the pose of the sitter is more artificial (fig. I.12). The captions read, "Pose de l'homme de la nature" (Natural human pose) and "Pose de l'homme civilise" (Civilized man pose), respectively. Here, Daumier satirized how the frontal shot had become a sign of "'naturalness,' of a culturally unsophisticated class," while the high class assumed more intricate and "cultivated" poses.[100] In the 1880s, under the influence of control and rehabilitation measures, the frontal photograph transitioned into a means of identifying and classifying individuals, particularly those seen as socially inferior such as criminals and Indigenous peoples.[101] In these photos, the subject faces the camera directly, and there is a confrontational aspect with both the photographer and the spectator. In contrast, in the more elaborate poses, the sitter rarely looks at the camera and instead presents herself as a subject for contemplation.

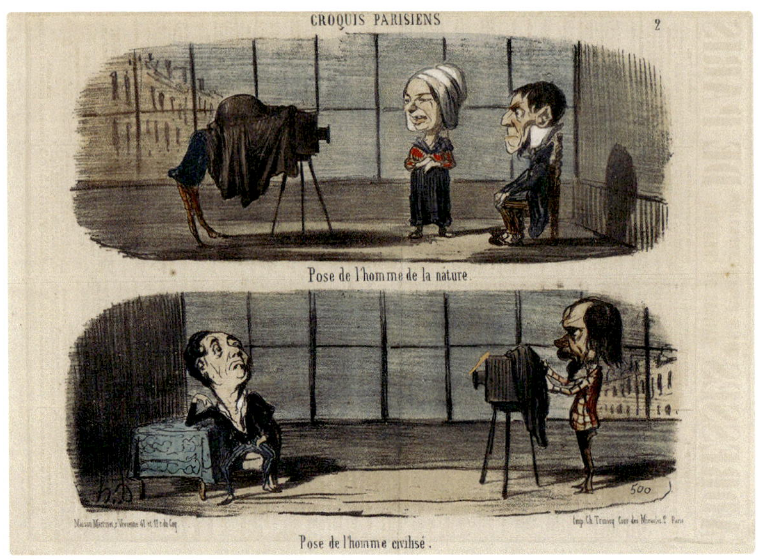

I.12. Honoré Daumier, *Croquis Parisiens*, 1853. Lithograph with watercolor, 22.86 × 33.02 cm (9 × 13 in.). Minneapolis Institute of Art, gift of Janet H. Spokes in memory of her parents, Angelica and Ignatius Houley, 2013.26.10. Photo: Minneapolis Institute of Art.

This phenomenon was not restricted to the Parisian environment. Indeed, it was an occurrence that extended across borders and was noticeable in Medellín during the nineteenth century. De la Calle and the Rodríguez brothers took pictures that aligned with the two poses identified by Daumier. Some photos speak to the frontal and natural poses, while others present more sophisticated and elaborate attitudes of the portrayed persons. Indeed, many of the sitters seen as negative subjects of Antioquian society appear to claim recognition, equality, and a sense of citizenship through photography. Some of de la Calle's sitters confront the camera so directly that they challenge the tendency to be stereotyped, giving the subjects agency through an act of self-representation.

Although in different ways, the Rodríguez studio and de la Calle, along with other photographers from the period, such as Rafael Mesa, were literally mapping the Antioquian society of the time.[102] Sitters and photographers alike were aware of the democratization of image culture that was transforming the way Medellín's citizens understood and disseminated their identity. Pedro Fernández distinctly addressed this in an article from 1889 where he noted:

> Any anonymous individual in this world is for their family a character to immortalize. Earlier, it was forbidden for most mortals to bequeath to their descendants the image of their ancestors. Photography has brought the entire world under identical conditions, painting with equal fidelity and economy an emperor with his shields and crests and an *arriero* with his wide-brimmed hat and *tunjana* shirt. The light of the sky is a great democrat: it paints with its camera obscura whatever stands in front of it. Today, the penniless boyfriend and the unhappiest father can, without going to Jamaica, give portraits to their girlfriends or own those of their children. And the light that leads home so many treasures of veneration and tenderness leads us from town to town and from nation to nation to the ends of the planet.[103]

By the end of the nineteenth century in Medellín, photography had become ubiquitous and changed how people related to and understood the world surrounding them. Although the city was geographically secluded, a medium that facilitated the recognition of their identity and allowed the appreciation of and engagement with other places far away and presumably unapproachable counterbalanced the presumed isolation. In particular, the elite class of the city was exceptionally well connected. Although it took enormous amounts of time and money to reach other places, such as Europe and the United States, they traveled back and forth, bringing ideas and objects that changed the way they perceived the world.[104] Antioquia also experienced a publishing boom between 1850 and 1920, much more than in other parts of the country, allowing its people to be informed and entertained. The city's archives house newspapers from Paris, cartes de visite by Nadar and Disdéri, and postcards from different European countries, as well as news about the latest advancements in technology and history—like the invention of the x-ray, the sinking of the *Titanic*, or the beginning of World War I.

Geographically, however, Medellín was secluded. In a map published in 1926 on the cover of a magazine called *Progreso*, the city was presented as both the center of the world and an isolated town. The map shows the time it took to travel by hydroplane from Medellín to other places in Colombia. Remarkably, a trip to the capital, Bogotá, took fifty hours—flying, with intermittent stops. Reaching one of the port cities on the Caribbean shore, such as Barranquilla, Colombia's principal point of departure, required the same time. This map merged and pictured the vanity of the antioqueños, a regionalist culture partly driven by the immense difficulty of communication in the preindustrial age and the "natural ties" with which the intellectual elite intensely tried to identify.[105]

Considering this, Medellín's development and rapid evolution from a small town into Colombia's second-largest city was a remarkable feat. The role played by the photographic negative was crucial for consolidating the ideological discourses that allowed for such a change. As photography became a more objective and portable medium, it also became a place to visualize and materialize ideology to share, support, or contest it, regardless of geographical isolation or historical distance.

The Chapters

This book is structured into five chapters. In chapter 1, "Envisioning a New Race: Photographic Manipulation and the Discourse of *la raza antioqueña*," I analyze a group of negative plates and the retouching performed on them to understand how the discourse of Antioquian race manifested visually or was challenged through photography. Although the visual alterations of the images remained invisible for most sitters, they transformed the photos in ways that had real and lived consequences. I argue that the implications of the Antioquian race and its counterdiscourse materialized on the negative plates literalizing each perspective's rhetoric. To achieve this, I explain in detail the invention and development of the Antioquian race discourse, which emerged in the second half of the nineteenth century in Medellín and which Libardo López epitomized in 1910 with the publication of the book *La raza antioqueña*. In this chapter, I trace the work of some authors who proclaimed the superiority of the Antioquian race to underscore the recurring dimension of this discourse. I look at some sources these authors drew from to understand what inspired their ideas and how eugenics was appropriated and adapted to fit the Colombian context. Then, through a careful analysis of negative glass plates, I introduce a comparative analysis of the different retouching techniques used by both Fotografía Rodríguez and de la Calle in their photographic practices. The context in which Fotografía Rodríguez worked and the elite status of their clients led them to produce highly manipulated images that aligned with the discourse of the *raza antioqueña*. Conversely, de la Calle's use of retouching aimed to elevate the social status of his clients and fulfill aspirational desires, thus challenging the discourses imposed by the elite. However, this straightforward narrative becomes complicated when analyzing the photographs of black sitters and how both Fotografía Rodríguez and de la Calle manipulated the negatives.

Chapter 2 focuses on the work of Fotografía Rodríguez. Here, I argue that the negative was central to the Rodríguezes' artistic practice and to reproducing the racial morality their photos promoted, a morality clearly based on the discourse of the Antioquian race. Through carefully analyzing some of their pictorial photographs, I examine how the Rodríguez brothers used pictorialism and the negative to reinforce the racial discourse of *la raza antioqueña*. Furthermore, in this chapter, I explore the multiple ways in which the Antioquian race reinforced whiteness as superior. Exploring a selection of their photographs—in both their negative and positive forms—I unravel the intricate layers through which this ideology conveyed notions of superiority that surpassed the understanding of race simply as skin color, complicating the conventional definitions of whiteness.

Within this context, my examination takes on a multifaceted approach to the concept of the negative. Not only do I study the physical objects themselves and the interventions performed on the negative plates to produce pictorial effects, but I also craft a theoretical approach to the negative from a symbolic perspective. Here, I introduce the notion of the negative Other: photographic images that purposefully accentuate distinctions and disparities rooted in race, gender, ethnicity, geography, or social class. This is seen particularly in pictures that tended to aestheticize subaltern subjects, whether through *costumbrista* scenes or depictions of women in theatrical scenarios.

Last, I explore the profound significance of negatives as the matrix for reproducing photographs—and thus the ideologies inscribed in them—hence facilitating their widespread circulation. These three ways of understanding the negative—materially, symbolically, and as reproduction's matrix—intertwine and collaborate, forming a comprehensive understanding of the manifold implications of this concept. Through this exploration, my aim in this chapter is to illuminate the intricate interplay between pictorialism, *costumbrismo*, the negative, and *la raza antioqueña*. By peering into the world of the Rodríguez brothers' photography, we can gain invaluable insights into the complexities of race, representation, and the formation of identities in the social tapestry of Medellín at the turn of the twentieth century.

Chapter 3 addresses the work of Benjamín de la Calle. In particular, I study a group of photographs in which he challenges the binary understanding of gender. Here, I examine the practice of cross-dressing in diverse contexts that range from allegorical representations to repressive practices by the police. I argue that, while de la Calle's work usually contests the elites' rhetoric, destabilizing the discourse surrounding the Antioquian race, in other instances, his photographs aligned with it. *La raza antioqueña* shaped the understanding of whiteness and enforced a rigid set of conservative norms and behaviors, including a strict gender dynamic. Through a meticulous analysis of de la Calle's photographs capturing the urban Other, I unveil inquiries about representation, visibility, and power dynamics. This chapter showcases how de la Calle's work demystifies and deconstructs the discourse surrounding the Antioquian race, shedding light on its complexities and unveiling alternative narratives. It also puts to the fore the ambivalences of his photographic practice, as he also worked for governmental institutions and their disciplinary apparatuses.

If, in chapter 2, race was understood beyond inherited physical traits, in this one, the negative is understood beyond its literal physical object. Here, I look at the negative from a symbolic perspective: the negative emerges as a metaphorical conduit to address subaltern subjectivities, often perceived as deviant, and thus negative subjects, within the late nineteenth-century Latin American context. These nonconforming subjectivities disrupt binary categorizations, such as negative/positive, compelling us to question the conventional understanding of the negative as a distinct and singular category. The pictures analyzed in this chapter present, in a positive light, subjects that have traditionally appeared as undesirable. Therefore, I argue that these images symbolically resist photography's binarism, so strongly embedded in the negative/positive process.

Chapter 4 delves into the analysis of Orientalist photography produced in Medellín, questioning the understanding of the concept as viewed uniquely from a Western perspective. These images broaden the conception of Orientalism, complicating its definition and the relation between Western and non-Western cultures. Analyzing a series of Orientalizing photographs produced by both Fotografía Rodríguez and de la Calle, I reassess the meaning of Orientalism, shifting the perspective usually given to this term and questioning the implications of Orientalist tropes outside the colonial and the colonist territories.

In this chapter, I build upon previous discussions of the negative—from material and metaphorical perspectives—and delve into the notion of alterity and the subaltern in photographic representations. I also emphasize the itinerant nature of photographs and their ability to circulate across geographical spaces, historical periods, and various mediums. The photographic negative played a crucial role in enabling massive-scale circulation, leading to questions of reproduction, originality, and the wide dissemination of images. In summary, I explore the appropriation and circulation of Orientalism, delving into its implications within the context of Medellín and its complex relationship with race and representation. I examine the role of the photographic negative in facilitating the dissemination of images, ultimately shedding light on the dynamic interplay between Orientalism, visual production, and notions of alterity and identity.

The book ends with a chapter that studies the backdrops employed by Fotografía Rodríguez and Benjamín de la Calle. Whereas in the previous sections the analysis of the photographs focused on the sitters, chapter 5 focuses on the other elements that compose studio portraiture. Here the negative is understood from a spatial perspective. Thus, I displace my analysis from the pictured sitters to the negative space of the images. In studio photography, the negative space of the pictures often displays painted backdrops. I argue that these background paintings, frequently disregarded in photographic analyses, contribute to the meaning of the pictures and prompt questions regarding the notion of the Antioquian race. Just as retouching served as a photographic supplement for both photographers, the negative space in the photographs also played a role in amplifying their meaning, sometimes in seemingly contradictory ways.

This project proposes a critical and detailed reading of the work of Fotografía Rodríguez and Benjamín de la Calle through the notion of the negative. It also serves as a model to analyze the materialization and reproduction of ideologies in studio photography, a poorly studied genre when it comes to national discourses and racial theories. The issues at stake here are by no means exclusive to the work of the Rodríguez brothers and de la Calle. This book is only a model to understand the copious instances in which racial discourses are materialized or challenged through photography. The intersections of race and photography are a worldwide phenomenon usually studied by other fields, such as sociology or anthropology, reflecting the hierarchies of the photographic medium and those of the disciplines through which these images are looked upon.

Before delving into the detailed study of the photographs, I want to clarify one last thing. Most of the positive versions of the photographs depicted in this book are the result of a scanning process done at the Biblioteca Pública Piloto in Medellín to make their collection available to a larger public. Conversely, the negative versions of the images are not public or digitally available. The photographs of the negatives included here were made exclusively for this publication.

The positive black-and-white digital versions of the photos in this book differ from the various forms these pictures could have taken in their positive versions during their production period. For instance, a few examples of positive copies were hand-colored. We can also sense how the pictures might have been cropped, eliminating the handwritten aspects visible on the negatives and other unwanted materials such as lighting devices. However, the archive does not hold a large volume of positive prints, making it hard to pinpoint exactly what the manipulations on these versions of the images could have been.

CHAPTER ONE

Envisioning a New Race

PHOTOGRAPHIC MANIPULATION AND THE DISCOURSE OF *LA RAZA ANTIOQUEÑA*

WHEN I FIRST held the negative plates studied in this book, I could not resist the temptation to examine them by looking at the different ways in which the reflected light affects the photographic image. How does the picture look when the light that hits the negative comes from a forty-five-degree angle instead of a perpendicular point of view? Does the image change if I turn the negative plate further and position the light source at ninety degrees? This might initially seem a strange way to look at photographs but, at the time, the fact that analog photographs—particularly those created during the earlier period—are not the transparent objects we are used to thrilled me. In 2015, when I began to study the archives of Benjamín de la Calle and Fotografía Rodríguez, I had recently taken a course on photography conservation that opened my eyes to other aspects of the photographic image. What particularly elated me was the different techniques used to manipulate photographic plates in their negative status. I was constantly looking for them, and changing the angle at which the light hits the negative was a productive way to discover these interventions.

The moment I slightly turned a negative plate created by Fotografía Rodríguez to see if the negative could unveil something new about the image, I was immediately shocked by how much retouching the photograph had gone through. Graphite strokes completely covered the sitter's face. Only his eyes and clothes were untouched. But why would the image of a young man need so much intervention? Wasn't retouching supposed to correct age defects such as wrinkles or minor skin imperfections? There seemed to be other reasons for these interventions that were external to the images and differed from those continuously referred to in photographic manuals. That was when I decided to study in depth the cultural context in which they produced these specific photographs.

Benjamín de la Calle's studio and Fotografía Rodríguez emerged as commercial enterprises precisely when Medellín became Colombia's second-largest city and the country's industrial center. The flourishing of new markets and rapid economic growth developed because of a series of circumstances that were unexplainable at the time. Considering the city's geographic isolation and, thus, the problematic access to not only goods but also information, intellectuals found it challenging to explain the transformation of Medellín from a small town into an industrial center in fewer than fifty years. The circumstances that allowed for such a rapid and radical change of the city were rooted in the early discovery and exploitation of alluvial gold mines, which attracted foreign engineers and new technology during the nineteenth century. The wealth associated with the extraction of gold brought an important accumulation of capital—as gold was the international currency used for economic transactions—and the development of an entrepreneurial attitude.[1] Although gold brought money to the region, the impetus for the city's growth came from the commercial mentality. Traders and dealers started commercial enterprises exchanging goods for the mines and later the coffee plantations, as Antioquia became the center of coffee production, Colombia's most important export crop. This commercial stimulus ultimately led to a robust industrial production of goods, mainly reflected in the textile business.[2]

In addition to this industrial shift, by the turn of the century, Colombia was immersed in the Thousand Days' War, a three-year violent confrontation that devastated the country and led to the loss of Panama.[3] In Antioquia, however, the war lasted only forty days: the first month and a half of 1900. This rare situation allowed Antioquia to develop while the rest of the country recovered from the war. When the war ended in 1903, the wealth in Antioquia was untouched. The miners from the region loaned their money to the Colombian government, most likely at high interest rates, to build infrastructure and repair the country.[4]

The new wealthy elite came mainly from a rural background, a fact that forced them to adapt to new bourgeois manners and to distance themselves from the other social classes as a form of legitimization, in this way creating cultural barriers.[5] One of the most striking strategies used by the elite to explain the rapid transformations that the region was undergoing was the invention of the idea of a new race, namely the *raza antioqueña*. This strategy developed further as time passed and became a kind of myth related to people from Antioquia. It can be argued that this myth, or imaginary, grew from the necessity to justify their new social standing and simultaneously understand the region's rapid economic growth.[6] In this chapter, I examine the development of the *raza antioqueña* discourse, its materialization in the negatives of Fotografía Rodríguez, and the partial disarticulation of this myth through the work of de la Calle. In particular, I study the use of negative retouching to support or challenge the myth of the *raza antioqueña*.

The Myth of *la raza antioqueña*

Historian Catalina Reyes argues that *mestizaje*, which was particularly strong in Antioquia, strengthened the myth of the *raza antioqueña*, a type characterized by hardworking standards, family-driven values, Catholic beliefs, honest principles, and business abilities.[7] In general terms and sometimes with slight differences, these were the hypothetical features of the antioqueño as described by many at the turn of the century. Yet the color of the skin and the Spanish origin of people from the region—who ultimately also claimed whiteness—were recurrent points in the various descriptions and notions of the *raza antioqueña* myth. Some native chroniclers, for example, stated that their race was of "Spanish origin, Castilian, with some Semitic blood in their veins" or that in the region "the white race dominates exclusively. The Indian race has left few records; the black race, by itself, has disappeared. . . . It has only left some strange *mulatos*."[8] These ideas, although dramatically exaggerated, were supported by historical facts that helped reinforce the legend of the antioqueños.

The Department of Antioquia experienced a dramatic loss of its Indigenous population with the arrival of the Spaniards. By the nineteenth century, the few survivors were confined to Indian reservations or *resguardos*. Although the hard labor of the mines was primarily undertaken by enslaved black people brought to the region from the sixteenth century onward, by the mid-nineteenth century, enslaved peoples had diminished to 0.7 percent of the population, and a broad mixture of races had occurred.[9] The claimed whiteness of the antioqueños was perhaps reinforced when compared with the rest of the country, a fact that positively surprised many foreigners who visited Antioquia. Although the number of white people was relatively high—31 percent by 1918—the mestizo and *mulato* population was the largest in the region, constituting around 52 percent.[10] Already in 1869, Charles Saffray, a French physician and botanist who visited the country, noted that in Medellín "everyone claims to descend in a straight line from blue-blooded gentry; but the truth is that brown [skin] colors, yellow and swarthy are common in almost every family."[11] This dichotomy between what was said and what was empirically documented can be traced back to Agustín Codazzi's Chorographic Commission (1850–59), Colombia's largest nineteenth-century state-sponsored enterprise intended to create a complete cartographic description of its territory and its inhabitants. Indeed, Codazzi described the people from Antioquia as a "white, vigorous, and healthy race."[12] However, as noted by Nancy Appelbaum, the commission's empirical observation did not necessarily coincide with the generalizations made in the written documents that accompanied the visual documentation they were creating.[13]

The *raza antioqueña* should be understood here as a myth in Barthian terms: it is a type of speech that took multiple forms and helped to naturalize a particular point of view of the world.[14] The discourse of the Antioquian race was so prominent that it deviated from reality, creating an ideology. It reached its apogee by the turn of the century when a series of intellectuals embarked on defining their own identity through the myth of this new race. Their ideas circulated textually and visually, imbuing the myth of a whiter, more progressive race deeply in the region's beliefs and extending the creed until today. Photography played a crucial role in establishing these ideas among the elite class of Medellín, as the medium visualized, in a supposedly unbiased manner, the whiteness, beauty, and sophistication of the people.

Additionally, the technological aspect of the medium aligned perfectly with the theories of progress that came along with those of the Antioquian race. Photography and its transparency acted as the visual evidence of the *raza antioqueña*, reflecting the racial discourse and partaking in its formation. If relatively few read the writings of the exponents of this new race, many saw the images that circulated.[15] They appeared in newspapers, magazines, cartes de visite, and family albums, among others. A large part of the population thus internalized and adopted these ideas, and they became part of the visual economy of modernity.

Visualizing the *raza antioqueña*

The Rodríguez brothers' studio was not only the place where Medellín's upper class was portrayed but also where the intellectuals gathered to discuss and share ideas. Two of the most recognized members of this small circle of thinkers were Horacio Marino Rodríguez and Francisco Antonio Cano, the founders of the photo studio. It is no surprise then to learn that their photographic practice and pictorial production reflected the beliefs that emerged from the meetings at the Rodríguez house. As with any ideology, their practice naturalized and became part of the normative vision, followed not only by themselves, the elite class, the government, and the church. Their production reflected a coherent system of ideas and beliefs that kept the status quo of a society divided by class that privileged the elite. It was not a one-way relationship but one in which both elements continually reinforced each other. Images such as the portrait of Henrique Uribe speak to these moments in which visual production and ideology intertwine (fig. 1.1). The negative depicts a half-body shot of the sitter: a man wearing an elegant suit, a collar shirt, and a big checkered tie, looking away from the camera as if mesmerized by something else. It is a sober picture, with minimal contrast but featuring all the ranges of gray and an ample gradation of light. The young man sits in front of a monochrome background, while the light that hits his face comes from the left side of the image, highlighting the shine of his dark hair and giving the portrait what Nadar would call "a moral grasp of the subject."[16]

When perpendicular light hits the negative of this image, it looks like any other portrait. However, when turned slightly to make the light hit the glass plate at an oblique forty-five-degree angle, the retouching process of the image becomes visible (fig. 1.2). The face of the sitter was manipulated to produce the effect of a whiter and smoother surface, somewhat imitating a porcelain effect. When analyzed with raking light, a series of graphite strokes covering the face's surface replace the smooth effect. This is especially striking in the portraits of young men and women, in which the

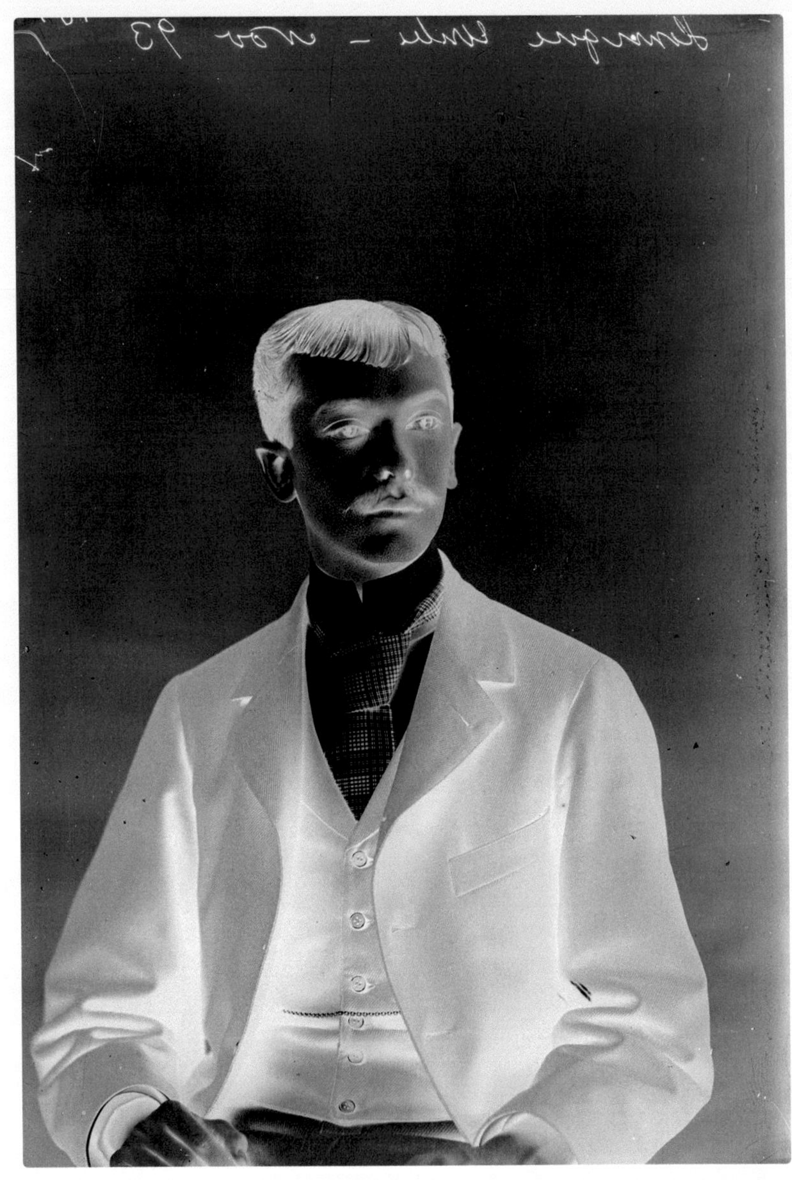

1.1. Fotografía Rodríguez, *Henrique Uribe*, 1893. Gelatin dry plate, 18 × 13 cm. Biblioteca Pública Piloto de Medellín / Archivo fotográfico. Photo: Esteban Duperly.

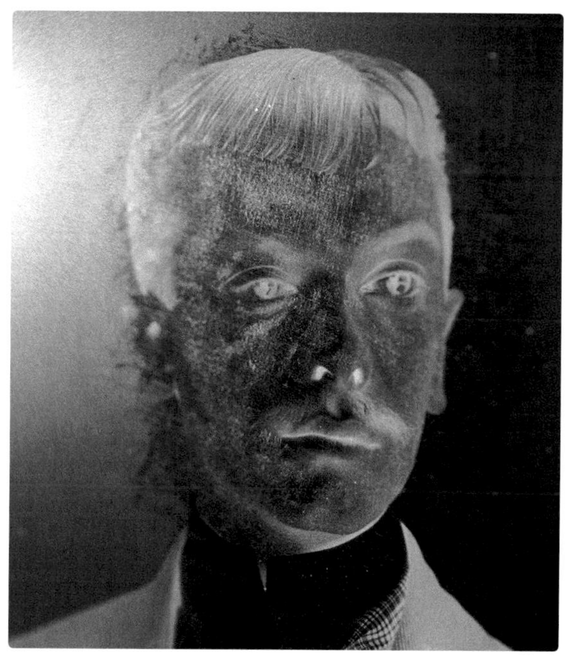

1.2. Fotografía Rodríguez, *Henrique Uribe*, 1893. Detail from negative under raking light. Biblioteca Pública Piloto de Medellín / Archivo fotográfico. Photo: Esteban Duperly.

intention was not only to correct wrinkles, freckles, or other skin defects or aging but also to whiten and smooth the faces of the sitters. Although negative retouching was a common practice globally, the amount performed on the negatives of the Rodríguez studio surpassed general practice. Barely any negatives in the archive have not undergone an extensive retouching process.[17]

In *Diez y ocho lecciones sobre fotografía*, the manual on producing photographs written by Horacio Marino Rodríguez in 1897, there is a section dedicated to the practice of retouching. He states, "The goal of retouching is only to fix imperfections such as the removal of stains, freckles, scars, and other accidental flaws of the human skin; to fix the strength of some shadows and to diminish the effect that strong lighting might have produced in the deepest wrinkles."[18] Most important, perhaps, was his concern with the effects of excessive retouching because it could "destroy individual character" and ultimately "reproduce a porcelain statue instead of a human being."[19] Nevertheless, these ideas seem to go against his practice when compared with the retouching performed on the images produced in his studio, which created precisely the porcelain effect that seemed to concern him so much. It is reasonable to think that the demands came from his clientele and not necessarily from his conviction. However, the images created an aesthetic associated with his practice, which defined his studio and differentiated it from his colleagues, creating a style that, perhaps unknowingly, perpetuated high-class values.

Another example among the vast array of retouched images is a portrait of Carlina Duque (of whom we know only her name) taken in 1894 (fig. 1.3). The sitter is a young woman who looks downward while her dark, curly hair falls behind her shoulders. Again, in this photograph, the skin of a young woman is overtly manipulated through the graphite strokes that cover the surface of her face. When viewed with raking light, the face reveals a somewhat disfigured appearance that materializes the racist discourse of the Antioquian race (fig. 1.4). Indeed, it was a discourse that played out on the bodies themselves, both representationally and physically, as reflected in the images when viewed in their full version, that is, with the physical intervention performed by the photographer. The final portrait naturally embodied the discourse as the graphite strokes literalized the rhetorical violence perpetuated by the theory of *la raza antioqueña*. Ultimately, what was seen as an imaginary—the invention of the idea of a new race—had real consequences.

The photographs from the Rodríguez studio exceeded common alterations such as the ones advised in other photographic manuals of the time and reflected on the images produced elsewhere. Take, for example, a wet plate collodion negative from an unknown American photographer from ca. 1851–85 (fig. 1.5). The faces of the sitters were retouched, and the intervention is visible to the naked eye. Since collodion was sensitive only to blue light, blemishes, rosy cheeks, and freckles appeared darker in the final prints; therefore, the sitters' skin had to be evened out. This process was primarily done using small lead pencil strokes—as seen in this negative—or watercolor techniques intended to smooth out the skin tone of the sitter. In this example, retouching is localized and applied only in particular areas of the face, as opposed to the more extensive, and even excessive, retouching done on the faces of Henrique Uribe or Carlina Duque at the Rodríguez studio.

Compared to the photographs by their colleague de la Calle, who, like any other photographer of the time, used retouching to reduce any imperfections on his sitters' faces, the excessive amount applied in the Rodríguez studio stands out. In the photograph *Margarita L.* (1928) by de

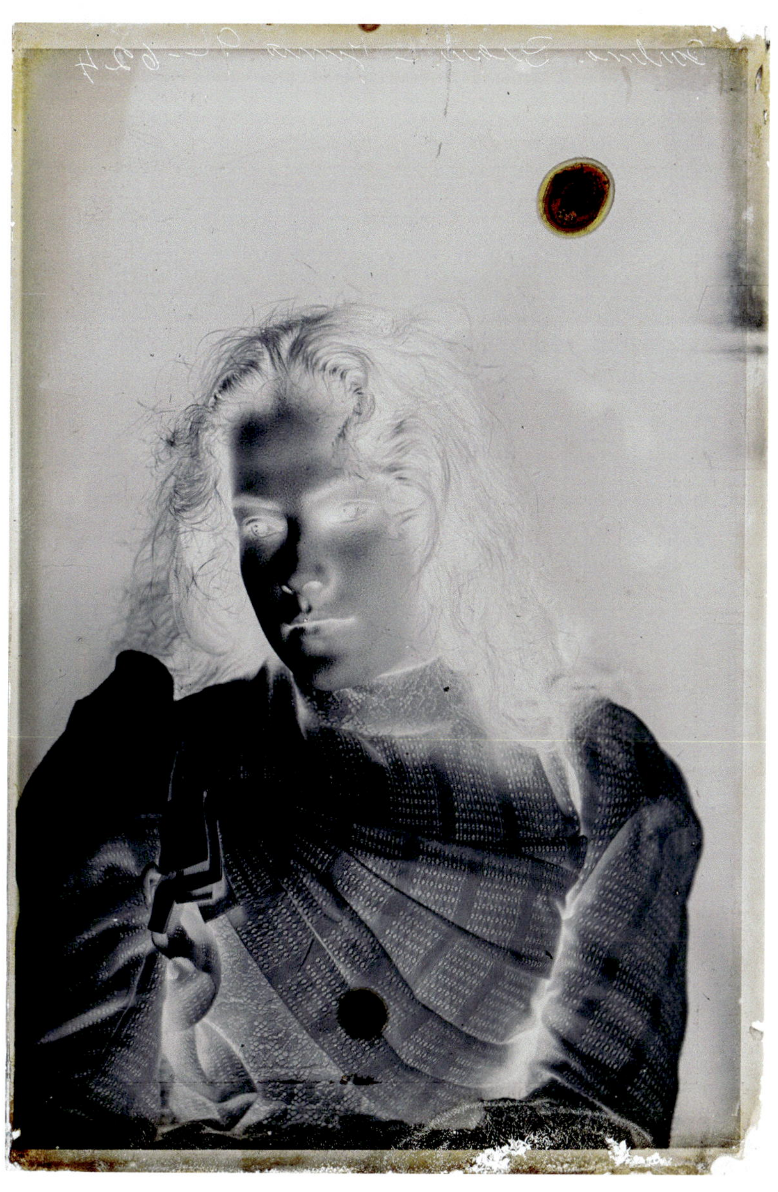

1.3. Fotografía Rodríguez, *Carlina Duque*, 1894. Gelatin dry plate, 18 × 13 cm. Biblioteca Pública Piloto de Medellín / Archivo fotográfico.

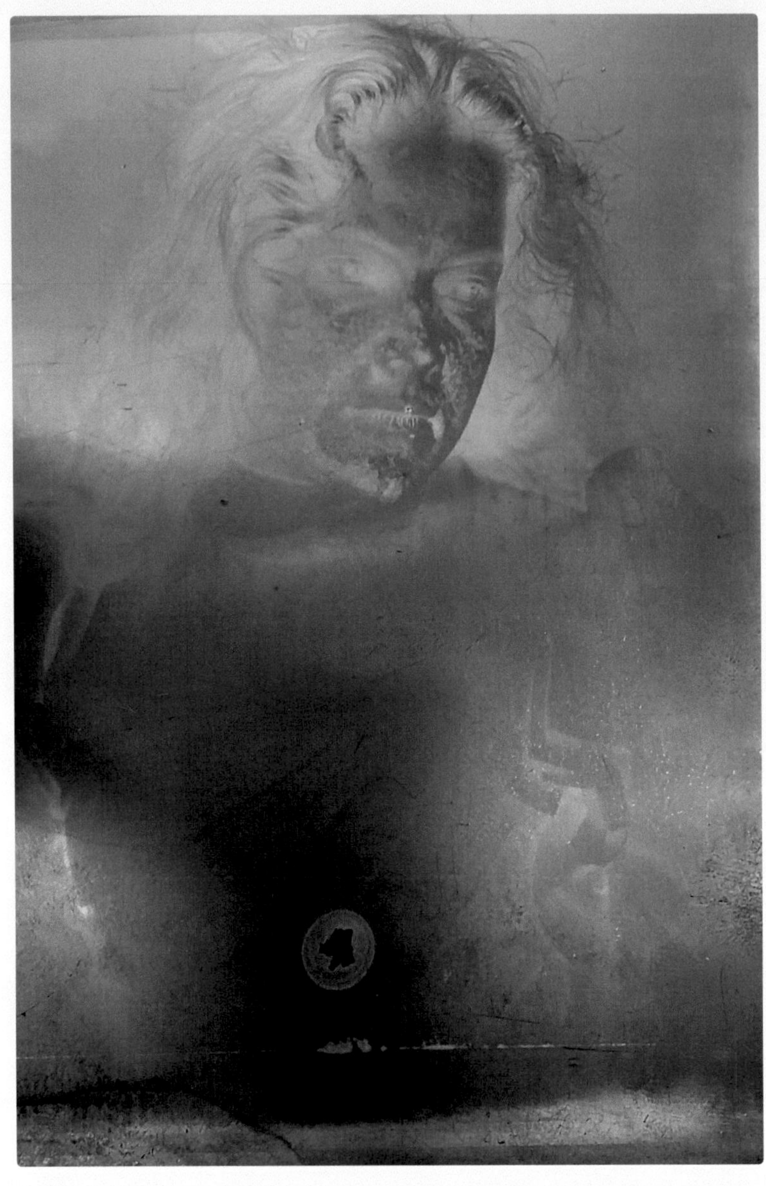

1.4. Fotografía Rodríguez, *Carlina Duque*, 1894. Gelatin dry plate, 18 × 13 cm. Detail from negative under raking light. Biblioteca Pública Piloto de Medellín / Archivo fotográfico. Photo: Juanita Solano Roa.

la Calle, for example, only some areas of her face—not coincidentally, those precisely advised to be manipulated in most of the manuals, that is, the nose, the labial furrow, and the section right below the eyes, among others—have been altered through the use of subtle graphite strokes (fig. 1.6). The manuals circulating in the world during the second half of the nineteenth century recommended that "the retoucher has to accustom himself . . . to be able to tell, upon seeing unusually deep lines or peculiar marks, whether they are photographic exaggerations or really characteristic points of the subject, and if exaggerations, to decide to what extent and amount of modification they will bear without destroying the character of the face upon which he is at work."[20] It was undoubtedly a matter of personal taste, but in the case of the Rodríguezes, taste aligned with the interests of the elite class, thus producing images that reflected their ideals, aspirations, and unquestionably, ideology. I do not pretend to say that the Rodríguezes were intentionally and deliberately creating these images to promote the ideals of the *raza antioqueña*, but to suggest that such values were so embedded in the beliefs of the antioqueños that they were naturally reflected in the visual representations of themselves.

The excessive retouching was certainly noticed more than once, and the debate reached the pages of the newspapers in Medellín. In an extensive article in *Las Novedades* in 1896, P. N. G. (presumably Pedro Nel Gregory, the same author who wrote the first comprehensive history of photography in Antioquia) argued that "retouching [was] one of the first and most important advances reached by the art of Daguerri [*sic*]" and that it was necessary to correct the distortions that the lenses produced, for example, the enhancement of defects in the skin.[21] According to the author, the camera took away something from reality that was given back to the image through the art of retouching, advocating in this way for a balance between reality and the photographic image.[22] He thought that, on the one hand, the supporters of excessive retouching adhered to a "system of ideals that distort[ed] the reality of things . . . and ma[d]e retouching an antithesis of *truth*," and on the other, that those who were against it were "too passionate about realism" because for them a portrait should be "as natural as possible," something that he did not seem to agree with.[23]

It is important to note that the understanding of realism during this period and its relationship to photography differed from what we discern

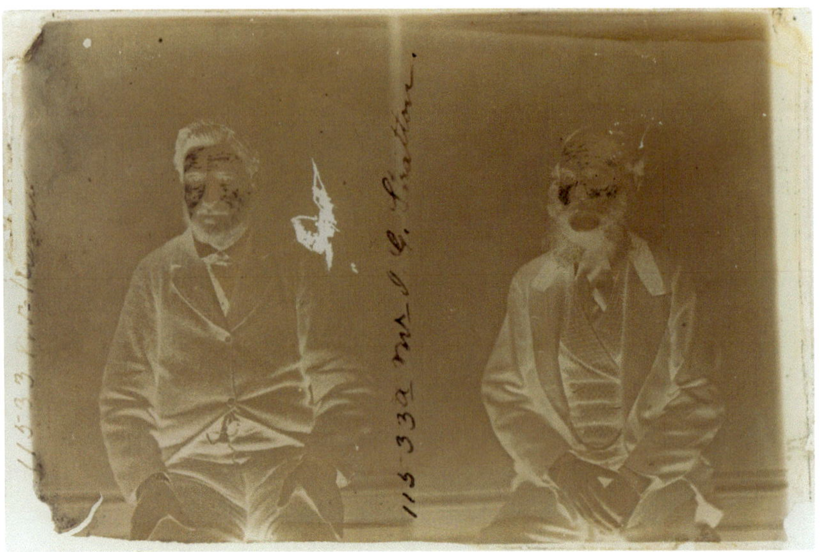

1.5. Unknown American photographer, *Untitled*, 1851. Wet plate collodion negative. Graphics Atlas from Rochester Institute of Technology (RIT).

today. Notions of indexicality, objectivity, and transparency in photography were not so firmly embedded in the medium's understanding. For the nineteenth-century practitioner, photography should represent what was true (as understood in their context) and not what was necessarily real. Thus, manipulating the photographic medium to convey a determined message was completely valid. For example, Pedro Nel Gregory explained in his article that photographic lenses "can prodigiously augment small things; the result [from this effect] is that in a portrait, which is 30 or 40 times smaller than the original, we see the wrinkles, freckles, pores, stains, and other skin flaws relatively bigger than the natural [ones]."[24] He saw this as a mistake, something that the camera distorted. In this understanding of the medium, fidelity was not equal to reality; therefore, photography's shortcomings could be fixed through different techniques.

This notion of realism and resemblance went back to the Victorian understanding of photography. It was akin to that of the photographers in Medellín who, knowingly or not, adopted a similar impression of the medium. In Victorian England, Henry Peach Robinson and Peter Henry Emerson, two of the foremost advocates of pictorial photography, set forth a debate between the use of combination printing methods and

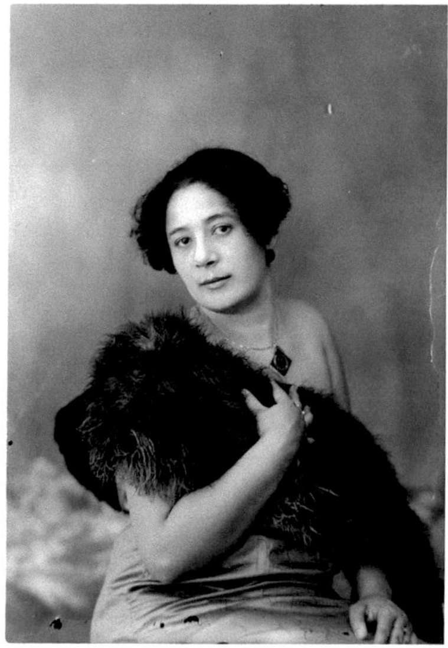
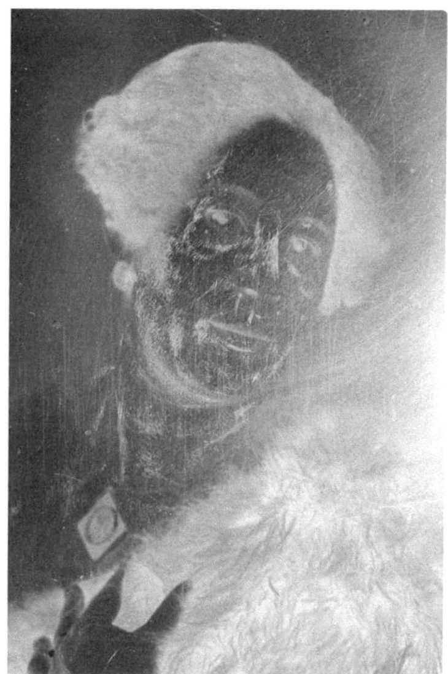

1.6. Benjamín de la Calle, *Margarita L.*, 1926. Left: Digital positive from original gelatin dry plate. Right: Detail from gelatin dry plate under raking light. 18 × 13 cm. Biblioteca Pública Piloto de Medellín / Archivo fotográfico. Photo: Esteban Duperly.

pure or straight photographic printing. This debate, which was not a new one and indeed was somewhat absurd since combination printing was and would continue to be used widely, regarded the conflict between scientific and artistic truth.[25] As photo-historian Shelley Rice put it, "the constant referral to 'truth' in these debates . . . tends to mask, for the modern twentieth-century viewer, the often-fluid definition of veracity that existed in the eyes of the 19th-century audience."[26]

The notion of resemblance was at the core of nineteenth-century debates. As Jan von Brevern demonstrated, portrait photography posed interesting and sometimes contradictory arguments about this notion.[27] During this period, a good portrait was not the realist depiction of someone's likeness but one that showed the painter or photographer's capacity to render the full character and inner spirit of the sitter, not just their external appearance. Indeed, it was not uncommon—as it still is today—to find oneself unrecognizable in a photographic image, sparking the debates regarding photography's capacity to render a real likeness. Resemblance was thus an idea that surpassed the notion of mimetic representation and was sometimes even in direct opposition to it. How could photography, a medium characterized by its intrinsically mimetic character, produce images that did not resemble its sitters? To counter this apparent contradiction, art photographers looked for strategies to capture true portraits. For an image to resemble the entire person (the inner and outer character)—and not only a fleeting, superficial moment—time was required. Resemblance was a "synthetic category" and it "could only be achieved by *transformation* of the real."[28] For these photographers in Medellín, this "transformation of the real" was achieved mostly through retouching. The negative was the matrix that permitted the incorporation of that which surpassed simple replication, and thus retouching became a critical tool for achieving resemblance.

Although neither Horacio Marino, Melitón, nor de la Calle left Colombia during their lives, their photography knowledge was quite extensive. Through the few magazines they had access to, and the books, prints, and postcards that circulated, ideas regarding the art of photography—such as the ones proposed by Robinson and Emerson—were adopted, processed, transformed, and finally incorporated by the Colombian photographers in their work. Again, this is not to suggest that they were directly looking at and/or reading the texts by the English photographers but that the ideas developed in Victorian England had striking resonances with those proposed in Medellín. Using retouching, at least in theoretical terms, was for the antioqueños a way to counter the challenges of inaccurate likenesses of oneself (as in photography) and trivial resemblance (as in painting), putting photography, even with its flaws, at the forefront of naturalistic representations and good portraiture. The episode that probably describes this best is the story of a painter in Medellín, surnamed Palomino, who charged for his portraits depending on how mimetically accurate they were: "Without resemblance for $5.00, with family resemblance for $8.00, and an exact likeness for $10.00."[29] The painter's varying prices, based on the accuracy of his work, not only signaled the difficulty of representing someone as true to reality as possible but, most importantly, it evidenced that the interest when representing people at the time was more related to an ideal—accurate or not—than to an exact copy of reality. Furthermore, it quantified and valued an ideal of truth and resemblance, making this point even more apparent.

In this context, the images that visualize the myth of the *raza antioqueña* emerged. The part of Antioquian society that aspired to look white, sophisticated, and civilized found in photography a medium that not only portrayed them with an unbelievable likeness but also gave them an allegedly real resemblance of how they saw themselves. For the public at the turn of the century, the primary goal was not mimetic accuracy but the representation of their ideal selves.

Eugenic Discourses

The ideals of representation and identity I outlined in the previous section were closely intertwined with the discourses of race that emerged at this time in Colombia and Latin America.[30] Unlike the beliefs that developed in other countries of the region and promoted national identity through the recovery and exaltation of their native roots—such as *indigenismo* in Peru or the ideas of a *raza cósmica* (cosmic race) as elaborated by José Vasconcelos in Mexico—in Colombia these discussions gravitated toward the other side of the spectrum through the definition of a national identity that looked to become whiter and imitated European culture, thus improving the country's race.[31] It was not until the late 1920s, with the emergence of a small group of artists identified as the Grupo Bachué, that the local became synonymous with pride, and a slow recovery of Indigenous and pre-Colombian cultures emerged, at least in the art world.[32] Constitutionally, however, Colombia only defined itself as a multicultural and multiethnic country in 1991, leaving the efforts of the art world as isolated and insignificant chapters in terms of real political and social repercussions.[33]

Some of the most complex and striking debates regarding race in Colombia took place during the late 1910s and early 1920s, when a group of intellectuals gathered and publicly presented their thoughts at the Congresos Médicos Colombianos (Colombian Medical Congresses) and later at the Teatro Municipal de Bogotá (Municipal Theater of Bogotá).[34] Doctor Luis López de Mesa, born in 1884 in Donmatías, Antioquia, adapted the hygienist and eugenic theories of a degenerated race in Colombia, as first proposed by Miguel Jiménez López. The latter, a highly recognized psychiatrist, politician, and scholar, argued that the Colombian population suffered from "unmistakable signs of a collective degeneration; physical, intellectual, and moral degeneration. . . . Many facts of functional nature demonstrate the biological inferiority of our race when compared with the average of the human species."[35] Appropriating degenerist ideas from the French psychiatrist Bénédict Morel, Jimenez López understood degeneration as a "regression in the vital and productive capacity of the race."[36] He also linked hygienist proposals with eugenics, a science that aimed at improving the human species through selective breeding and which, not surprisingly, exploited photography as one of its primary tools to prove its theories.

These degenerist and ultimately racist philosophies emerged from the ambivalence between the transition to modernity in an industrialized, progressive, and civilized world and Colombia's persistent social, economic, and political problems, which in turn manifested in a society considered wild, uneducated, and sick. Underpinning these ideas was the conviction that the nation's capacity for progress depended on its racial characteristics. Considering this, López de Mesa went so far as to propose that the solution to the Colombian problem was improving the race by introducing white immigrants, mainly Italian and Spanish, in certain zones of the country to "reinforce our future economy and our blood."[37] The areas selected for the insertion of immigrants were carefully chosen, taking into account the region's original race, since the latter would have to interbreed with the newly imported one.[38] Antioquia was, of course, one of the regions selected by López de Mesa for the insertion of white immigrants; according to him, since "this department [is] the geographical center of the republic and also the vigor of our race, everything that implies strengthening and purifying it is useful."[39]

It is unknown if López de Mesa and Jiménez López took advantage of photography to favor their theories, but the strong connection between photography and eugenics can be traced back to the invention of the latter and Francis Galton's experiments in England. During the second half of the twentieth century, Britain went through great social and economic flux, with increasing numbers of immigrants arriving in the country and thus contaminating the predominant Protestant Anglo-Saxon culture. Besides portraying the inhabitants of the colonies as uncivilized and technologically underdeveloped, the diaspora and Celtic populations—mainly composed of Jews and Irish people—became the focus of debates around race contamination. Galton was conducting his experiments with photography precisely at this moment, using reliable means to investigate both racial contamination and racial uplift through the identification of specific types.[40] This led him to the invention of "composite photography," a series of photomontages in which the faces of several persons were superimposed one over the other to identify physiognomic traits, creating a type from the repeating features of the different layers. Galton described his process as follows: "Composite portraits are made by successfully throwing the images of many different portraits for a short time, on the same portion of the same photographic plate. Features common to all appear in full strength; individual peculiarities leave too faint an impression to be seen, thus a typical or averaged figure is the result."[41] Photography served Galton as a scientific tool that made visible his theories and measured them. As a scientist, he believed racial characteristics were reflected in the mind and body of each person, determining an individual's race and social worth from their physical appearance.[42]

Deborah Poole has traced the genealogy of racial photography to the cartes de visite of types taken in places like Bolivia and Peru. She argues that these images, with their repetitiveness and apparent neutrality, became the perfect device for the exploration of racial hierarchies and categorization. Scientists such as Louis Agassiz, Alfred Haddon, and Arthur Chervin collected cartes de visite depicting Indigenous people from South America and used them as evidence in their new racial studies.[43] Poole argues that the Andean cartes laid the groundwork for further uses of photography as a tool for control, categorization, and comparison of Othered subjects, such as Bertillon's "signaletic system" and Chervin's system for measuring racialized populations.[44] In this sense, the history of disciplinary and ideological systems that emerged during the nineteenth century is highly intertwined with colonial photography, and specifically with the Andean carte de visite.[45]

Although the notion of the *raza antioqueña* never went as far as the eugenic and racial theories proposed by national and international scientists, doctors, and politicians, it served as a basis for the racial discourses further developed during the twentieth century in Colombia and, perhaps most importantly, evidenced the underlying ideology that characterized the elite classes of the time. One of the most prominent exponents of the *raza antioqueña* was the liberal attorney Libardo López, who published his essay, *La raza antioqueña*, in installments in a local newspaper in 1908 and later as a book in 1910. Revisiting French anthropologist Gustave Le Bon's ideas published in *Lois psychologiques de l'évolution des peuples* (*The Psychology of Peoples*, 1894), in which he argued that the Latin American countries reflected the "decadence of the Latin race in general," López appropriated the concept of a "superior race" to contradict this generalization and assured his readers that "if there is a place in Latin America where the ideal of a superior race exists, that place is Antioquia."[46] López saw in the antioqueños the same characteristics Le Bon found in the "Anglo-American race," namely initiative, high moral standards, religiousness, control of the self, and a clear idea of duty.[47] His observations led him to reaffirm once more what some of his colleagues had repeatedly stated: that the antioqueños were of Spanish descent and thus of "noble caste," and that they were a hardworking *pueblo* with strong Christian values.

Some intellectuals who contributed to the myth of the *raza antioqueña* were the doctor Andrés Posada Arango, engineer Tulio Ospina, and genealogist Gabriel Arango Mejía. In 1870, Posada Arango presented his *Ensayo etnográfico sobre los aborígenes del Estado de Antioquia en Colombia* (Ethnographic essay about the aboriginal people of the Antioquian state in Colombia) to the Anthropologist Society in Paris, a work where he first noted ideas regarding the study of the Antioquian type. The ideas presented here were later developed in his *Estudios científicos* (Scientific studies) from 1909, which allowed him to propose some of the first studies relating notions of race, inheritance, and climate to analyze the Antioquian people.[48] Tulio Ospina defended the Basque origin of the antioqueños as a way of explaining the spirit and independence of its people.[49] By attributing a Spanish origin and race, he also acknowledged white supremacy over the local mixed-race population. Finally, one of the most significant studies about the Antioquian race was *Las genealogías de Antioquia y Caldas*, published in 1911 by Gabriel Mejía Arango. His work emphasized the purity of the race by tracing a genealogy of the Antioquian population back to its Spanish origins. He stated that his work "aimed to prove that the *raza antioqueña* is of pure Spanish *casta*."[50]

All the authors mentioned above shared an evident emphasis and interest in defining the Antioquian people as white, moral, of Spanish descent, and thus a superior race. These ideas materialized in the photographs through the retouching techniques described above and, in some instances, became even more explicit, as in the case of a nun's portrait (1894). Her face was whitened by applying red ink on her skin to attain a paler tone in the positive copy (fig. 1.7).[51] The portrait depicts a young girl posing in an interior setting. She holds a Bible in her right hand and looks at the camera, proud of the prize she had recently won—symbolized by the large medal hanging on her chest. Under raking light, it is possible to detect additional retouching made with a pencil to remove specific

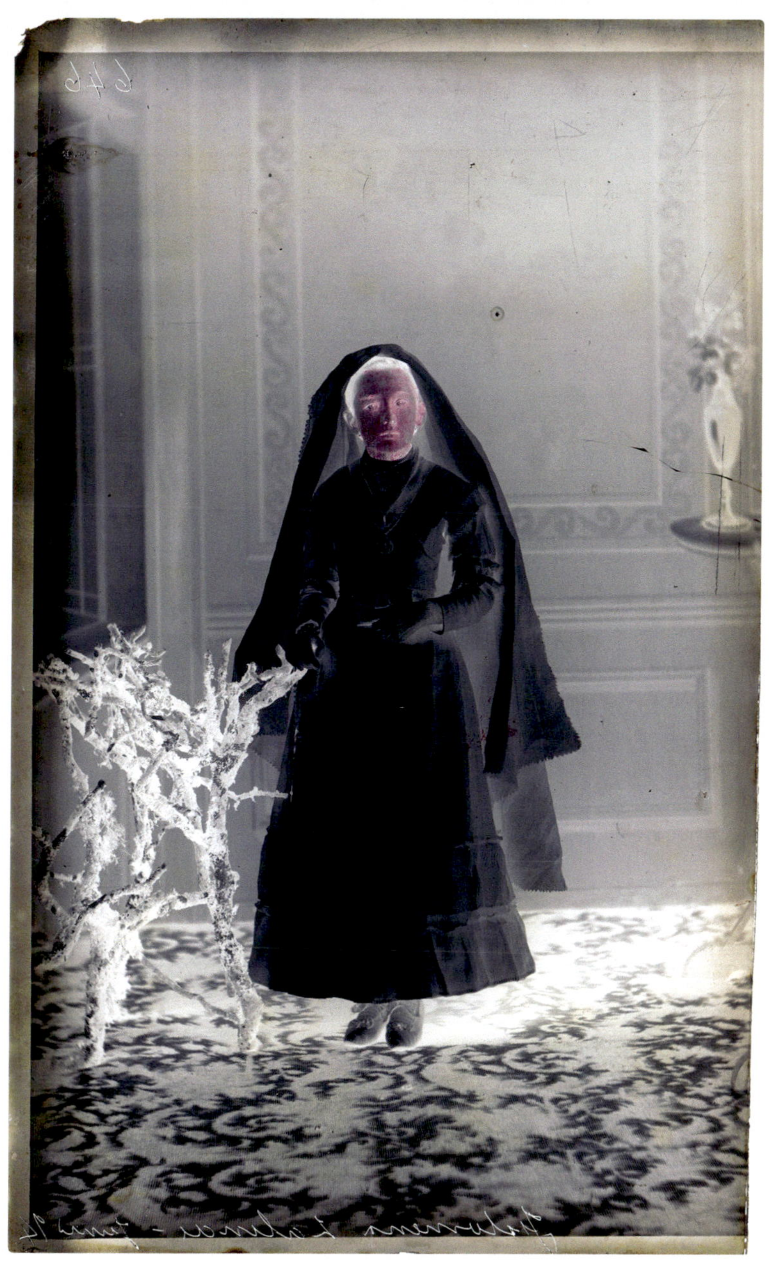

1.7. Fotografía Rodríguez, *Filomena Lalinde*, 1894. Gelatin dry plate, 18 × 13 cm. Biblioteca Pública Piloto de Medellín / Archivo fotográfico.

details of her facial features. In this image, not only is the discoloration of the skin very evident, more so than in the other photographs of the Rodríguez archive, but also the subject of the portrait, namely a young nun, represents the moral standards and Christian beliefs that the intellectuals of Antioquia were proposing in their writings.

The thin red fluid applied to the nun's face in the Rodríguez photograph was a technique widely used by photographers during the nineteenth century. This red layer helped lighten up the sitters' skin, particularly those whose skin color veered toward yellow, brown, and red tones. The application of red ink was used mainly in small negatives where the pencil was harder to apply. It blocked some of the light used in the positive print, "resulting in lighter skin according to the aesthetic appeal of the time."[52] The interesting aspect of this particular retouching process in the photographs of the Rodríguez brothers is that it enhanced the rhetoric around the Antioquian race. However, the practice of whitening the skin of sitters was not exclusive to Antioquian photographers. We see it in the work of other Latin American practitioners, such as the Peruvian Baldomero Alejos, who "retouched his images by reworking minute and prominent details in negatives, often to whiten and make younger the sitters in his photographs."[53]

Retouching was a practice undertaken mainly by women in the studios of male photographers. As very few females could practice photography themselves, they disrupted the medium through their work as active, although unseen, subjects.[54] It was a strongly feminized practice and considered apt for women as it embodied the delicate work associated with female labor. Retouching was, in a way, domestic. It was invisible and not publicly appreciated, but it was fully present. In this way, gendered characteristics moved from bodies to practices. The female intervention was usually "cast as irrational, less reliant on facts, and with an inherent propensity for manipulation"—yet their work was a highly detailed job.[55] Therefore, their effort was relegated to the sphere of the unseen even when their work was overtly visible on the negative plates and, more importantly, instrumental to the discourse of the Antioquian race. Retouching was a laborious task. Most photographic manuals remarked on the difficulty of this practice and the need for practical experience.[56] However, even though retouching was done by women, in photographers' international trade journals, "the retoucher was almost exclusively constructed as male."[57] As stated by Harriet Riches,

> With journals substituting male for female workers and thus defining their readership as men, the widespread practice of retouching was inserted into a masculine discourse of science, aligned with objectivity and truth, while anxieties about the retoucher's so-called deceptive arts in the remaking of the print were allayed. Just as the trace of the artist's hand was hidden in the doctoring of photographs at this time, so the bodily presence of the retoucher herself was concealed; real busy hands that carried out the detailed, reproductive, and painstaking work were suppressed beneath the masculinized veneer of photography as a professional pursuit.[58]

Interestingly, before becoming the official photographer of the Rodríguez studio, Melitón worked as a retoucher (together with his sister Rafaela) of the photographic plates taken by his brother Horacio Marino. The latter taught Melitón how to do the retouching while he slowly learned all the necessary abilities to run the photographic studio himself, which he did from 1904 until his death in 1942.[59]

As seen in this section, photography, retouching, and hygienist politics worked hand in hand. The myth of the Antioquian race was the base for racial politics and debates later developed during the twentieth century in Colombia. Theories of eugenics in the country lasted until 1941—just one year before the death of Melitón Rodríguez—with the professionalization of studies on racial alterity, the foundation of the Instituto Etnológico Nacional (National Ethnologic Institute), and the poorly received association of eugenics with National Socialism in Germany. Photography, but particularly the negative as an unseen constituent of the medium, played a considerable role not only as a tool that helped scientifically prove these theories but also to subtly but effectively make visible the ideologies that circulated among the Antioquian elite class.

Resisting *la raza antioqueña*

In Medellín, a city where most of the population was illiterate and did not belong to the small elite class who had access to the fine arts, photography—and with it, the democratization of image culture—became an opportunity to truly give representation to a broader part of the population. The photograph served as a commemorative, social, and political device; it became an active object capable of triggering affective engagements through images often considered objective and transparent. Just as photography could materialize ideologies, it could also resist them by working as a tool that visualized other realities, which would be forgotten unless photographed or articulated through visual media.

A photograph by de la Calle materializes this idea, a wedding portrait of Tomás Morales B. and his wife, a couple who most likely had a low socioeconomic status. They pose in front of a landscape backdrop—the same painting found in many of de la Calle's photographs with cypresses on the left side of the picture. He wears a black suit, and she a somewhat simple dress for a bridal costume, including some orange blossoms on her coiffure and left shoulder (fig. I.1). Her dress is not a proper wedding dress but, most likely, the best dress in her wardrobe, which she, like many other women across the globe, wore only to commemorate special occasions. What stands out in this negative is the woman's veil, which is not real but an addition made by the photographer's hand. The bride did not wear a veil for the picture, but the photo includes one to commemorate this moment. The photographer incorporated it through retouching. With the same red ink that the Rodríguez brothers used for whitening the skin of their sitters, de la Calle subtly hand-painted the veil, which the bride presumably could not afford (fig. I.2). The photographer's intervention is barely visible in the positive copy of the photograph, but it is evident in the negative. De la Calle probably used another picture as a model, such as one of Gregorio Montoya and his wife (fig. 1.8)—a couple from Medellín with more means—who had visited his studio for their wedding portrait. The style of the veil is almost the same in both photographs. However, one was indexically printed, and the other hand-painted. This intervention acknowledged that what really mattered was the visual representation of something, and thus its affective transcendence, rather than the enactment of that moment.

However, what is the real meaning of the photographer's intervention? De la Calle deliberately took advantage of photography's presumed objectivity to convey his desired message. By incorporating the hand-painted veil, de la Calle was simultaneously elevating the couple's social standing and fulfilling an aspirational desire that could only become real through photographic representation. As Christopher Pinney stated about postcolonial Indian and African photography—and whose words can apply to the present case—"there is an articulated recognition by photographers

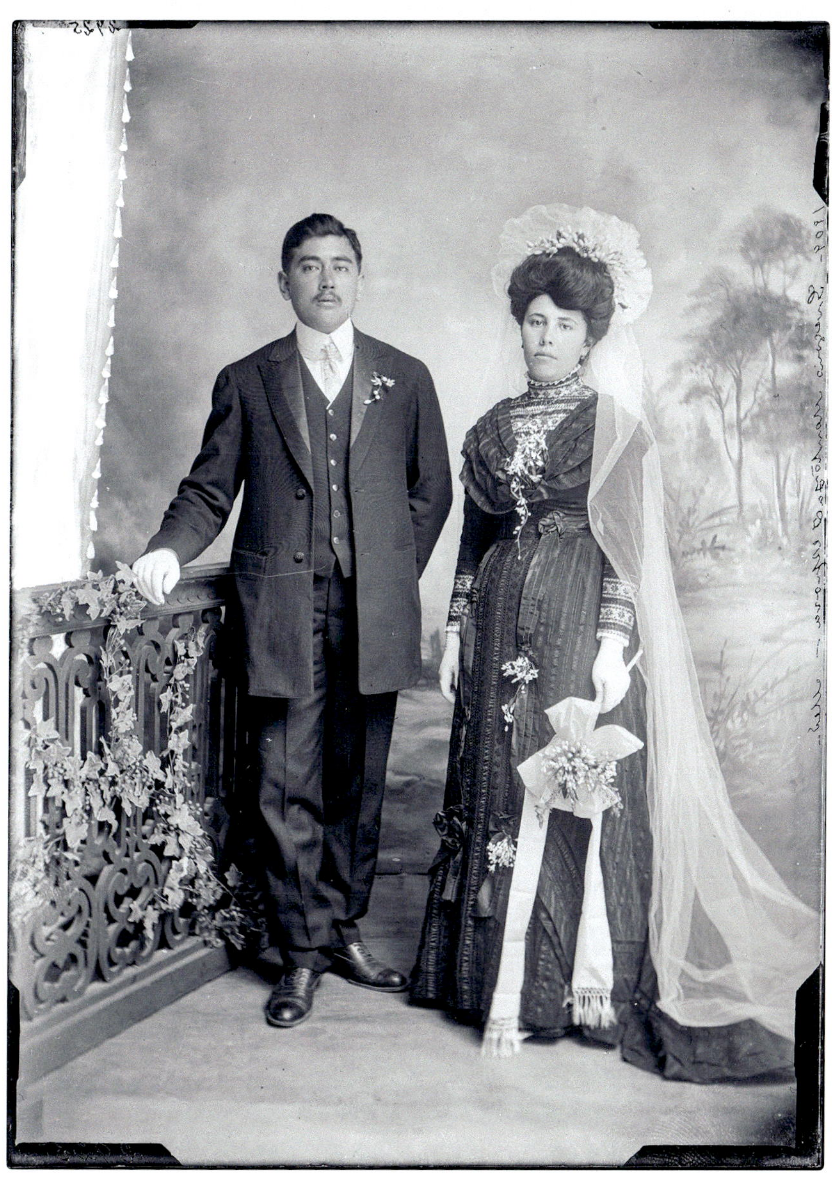

1.8. Benjamín de la Calle, *Gregorio Montoya, y señora: Medellín*, 1909. Digital positive from gelatin dry plate, 18 × 13 cm. Biblioteca Pública Piloto de Medellín / Archivo fotográfico.

that their task is to produce not an imprisoning trace of their sitters but to act as impresarios, bringing forth an ideal and aspirational vision of the bodies that sitters wish themselves to be."[60]

The wedding photograph represents one of the most important events in a woman's life. Thus the correct and complete representation of the event, with all its paraphernalia, was a determinant of social standing. Without the veil and a white wedding dress, the couple's portrait would have been just another photograph, not the wedding picture they hoped to acquire. The veil is a placeholder for the sacrament of matrimony and its importance. On many occasions, getting married represented a transition into adulthood and an ascent in social standing, depending on whom the person was marrying. For the middle class, photography became a way of displaying their resources and, by incorporating the veil, a reality that did not exist became truth. Marriage was, besides the first communion, a sacrament that antioqueños celebrated to a greater extent than elsewhere in the country; therefore, the wedding portrait held particular significance.[61] This photograph embodies Allan Sekula's concept of "sentimental realism." According to him, this type of photography captures the intimate and personal longing for authentic photographic representation, in direct contrast to photographic endeavors focused on social control and diagnosis, which Sekula termed "instrumental realism."[62]

This domestic and vernacular type of photography had particular uses. The images were displayed and circulated, found in frames and albums, or served as decoration in people's houses. In other words, they were objects to be exchanged and manipulated. In Deborah Poole's terms, they were part of a "visual economy" in which not only the image's content was important, but also its production, consumption, material form, ownership, institutionalization, exchange, possession, and social accumulation.[63] The use of photography in daily life enhanced the emotional experience of these objects. Therefore, the images became of primary importance for the people—not only the elite but also the middle and lower social classes. Lisandro Ochoa, a chronicler from Medellín, made clear this aspect of photography, highlighting the affective qualities of the pictures. In 1942, he remembered how, during the nineteenth century, people did not photograph themselves as often as in later years: "they did it only in special circumstances, such as on the eve of a trip to leave a picture of remembrance for the family" or "after formalizing the wedding, the bride and the groom used to give each other a portrait."[64]

The addition of hand-painted elements in negatives, such as the one discussed here by de la Calle, speaks to the importance given to the affective quality of portraits as opposed to the indexical trace usually attributed to photography. Elizabeth Edwards has noted, for instance, how in some popular practices in India and West Africa—and I would extend it to Latin America—the reality effect of the photograph is "imagined" or "constructed through additive techniques of overpainting and collaging. . . . Such work points to the provincial nature of Eurocentric notions of photography and demonstrates the inseparability of social practices, material practices, and imaging practices, as material forms are used to expand, enhance, and cohere the image content itself."[65] In the case of the wedding portrait of Tomás Morales B. and his wife, the intervention also shows how photography can work as a counternarrative to the hegemonic discourses circulated in Medellín at the turn of the nineteenth century.

Black Antioquia

Let us compare two photographs. The first was taken in 1912 (fig. 1.9) by Benjamín de la Calle. It depicts a dark-skinned boy who confronts the camera provocatively while resting his chin on his right hand. He poses in front of a landscape backdrop and sits on artificial stone props. He appears wearing a modern outfit: striped pants, a white shirt and black suit, a bow tie, and a boater hat. The second photograph is by Melitón Rodríguez and was taken almost twenty years later (fig. 1.10). It shows four elegant middle-class black women wearing long dresses, jewelry, stockings, and high-heeled shoes. It seems to be a commemorative portrait, perhaps taken after losing a loved one.

These two photographs are remarkable documents of the Afro-Colombian population in Antioquia, taken during a time when the myth of the *raza antioqueña* was so strong that blackness, both physically and rhetorically, was practically erased from the region. However, the portraits of de la Calle and Melitón Rodríguez are proof of the opposite. Although both photographers took pictures of black Colombians, they presented their subjects in differing and sometimes conflicting ways. The time difference between these two photographs, one taken in 1912 and the other in 1930, speaks precisely to these divergent perspectives, which ultimately reflected the beliefs and contexts surrounding the photographers.

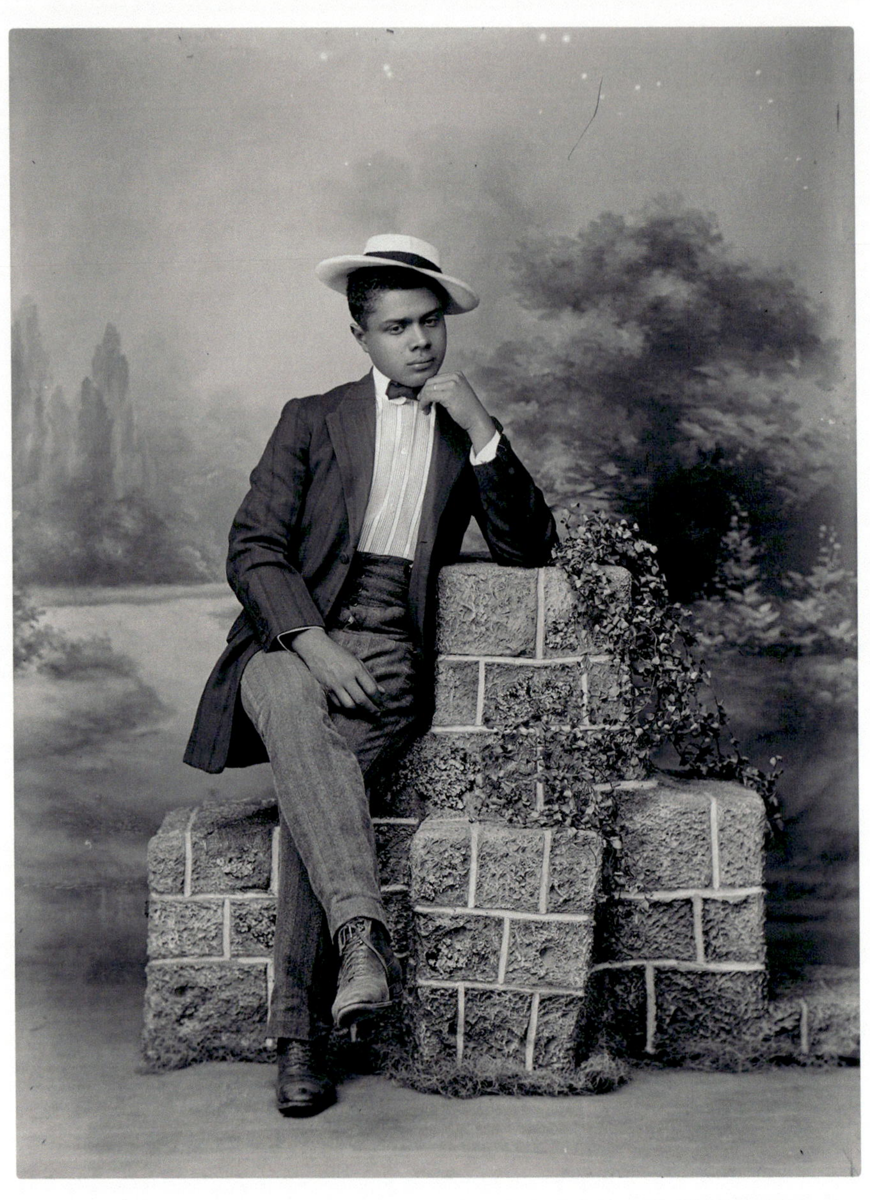

1.9. Benjamín de la Calle, *Martín E. Castaño M.*, 1912. Digital positive from gelatin dry plate, 16 × 12 cm. Biblioteca Pública Piloto de Medellín / Archivo fotográfico.

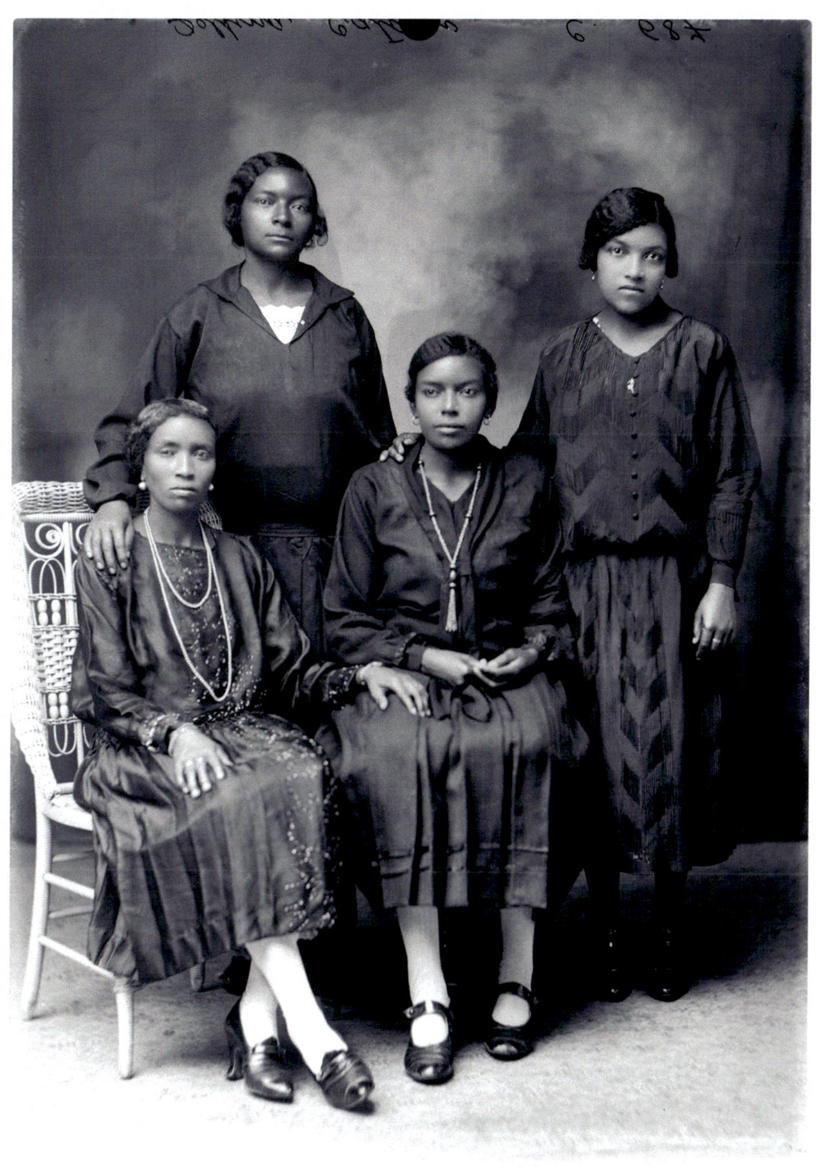

1.10. Fotografía Rodríguez, *Delfina Castaño*, 1930. Digital positive from gelatin dry plate, 18 × 13 cm. Biblioteca Pública Piloto de Medellín / Archivo fotográfico.

Indeed, Melitón took pictures like the one of this women's group, not at the peak of his career but only in the last stages of his work as a photographer.

Some of his few early portraits of black people ascribe to type photography rather than to what I call "dignifying portraiture" (i.e., pictures with first and last names that enhance the positive characteristics of the individualized sitter), as seen in an untitled photo of an older couple from 1900 (fig. 1.11). In this photograph, the confronting gaze of the woman takes prominence. Her bare feet and the couple's torn clothes emphasize their poor living conditions. When one compares this picture with the more common type of portraits he was taking, Melitón did not provide the usual nineteenth-century setting with the European-like backdrop and decorative props. Instead, he used a stark, plain backdrop and left the scene empty, including only the sitters' personal accessories. This empty scenario positioned the sitters in an undetermined space, further fostering the scrutiny of their bodies.

Other photographs present blackness solely as a backdrop. In these images, black bodies are present only because they perform an auxiliary role in the picture and not because they were thought to deserve visual representation. Such is the case of the photograph of three "white" upper-class children in which a black woman, presumably their nanny, appears in the middle of the picture holding the youngest child by her shoulders (fig. 1.12). Considering the girl's age, the photographer included the nanny just to keep the girl still while he took the picture. But the photograph's subject was not the nanny but the children. Moreover, the white color of the girls' clothing not only highlighted the subjects against the black backdrop but also reinforced their presumed whiteness, while the dark color of the nanny's dress camouflaged her body, further absorbing her into the backdrop and thus literalizing her presence as a simple prop and not as a subject worthy of being photographed.

The photograph recalls the so-called hidden mother portraits taken in England during the Victorian era. This tradition extended to Latin America, and Beatriz González-Stephan studied it in the context of Venezuela.[66] In these portraits, children appear in carte de visite photographs sitting on top of subjects covered by curtains and blankets. These erased subjectivities, which echo the hidden presence of negatives in photography, are presumably domestic workers, whose bodies, although visibly present, are absent. They appear as props and not as subjects, even in photographs where their presence is uncovered, such as the one by

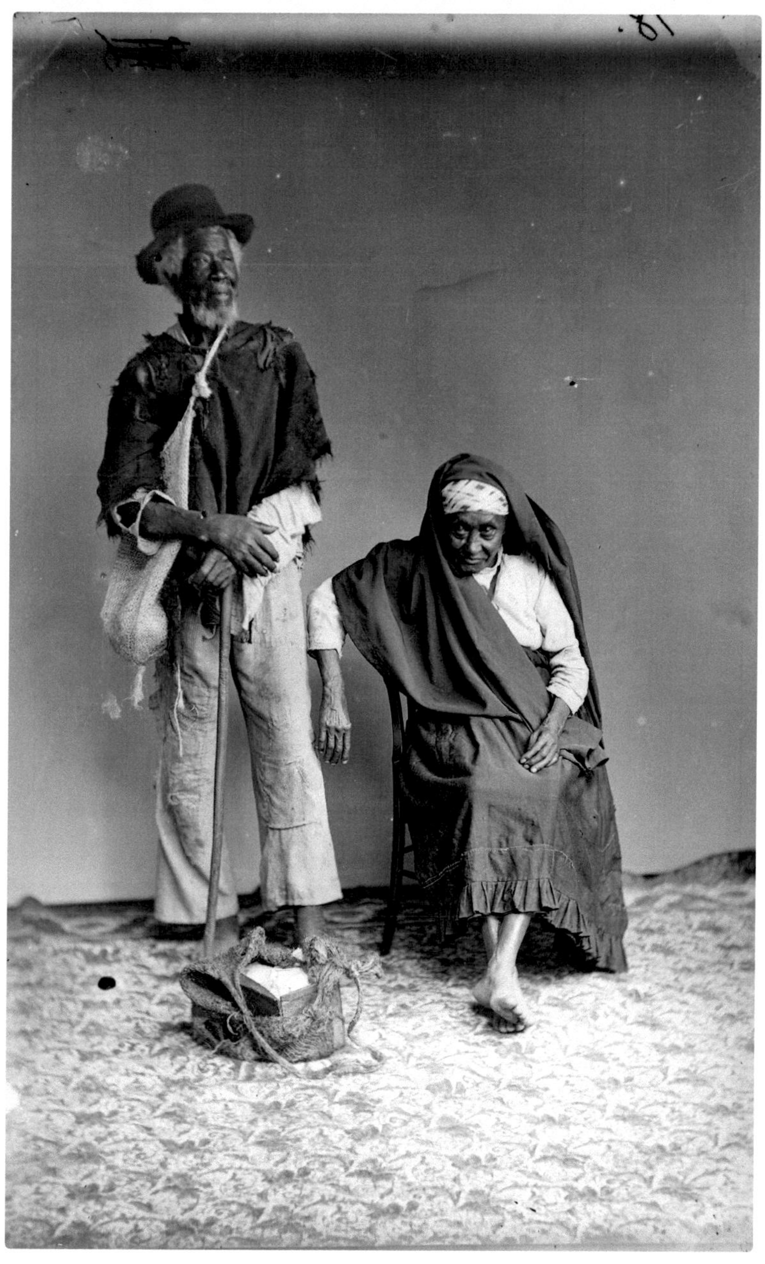

1.11. Fotografía Rodríguez, *Untitled (Ancianos)*, 1900. Digital positive from gelatin dry plate, 18 × 13 cm. Biblioteca Pública Piloto de Medellín / Archivo fotográfico.

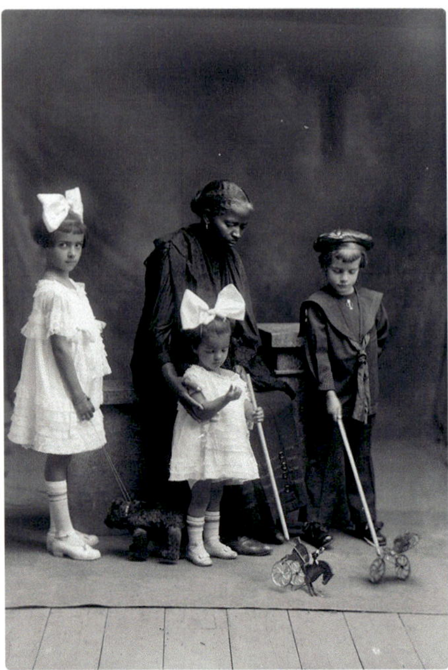

1.12. Fotografía Rodríguez, *Eva Jaramillo*, 1919. Digital positive from gelatin dry plate, 20 × 15 cm. Biblioteca Pública Piloto de Medellín / Archivo fotográfico.

Melitón Rodríguez previously discussed (fig. 1.12). In this picture, the black woman is absent, while the three children in the foreground play a role of power over her body. He does not portray her as an individual but as a blurred presence. As noted by González-Stephan, the inherent contradiction of these portraits reveals a society that sought to be modern while preserving the colonial order. She states, "Taking the colored domestic workers out of the visible field . . . could create the effect of a modern, homogenous and even de-racialized social group, and even play at racial democracy."[67]

This picture articulates the quotidian life of some black people in Antioquia. Following Tina Campt's proposals, I understand the "quotidian" here as "a practice rather than action. It is a practice honed by the dispossessed in the struggle to create possibility within the constraints of everyday life."[68] This photo shows a woman working rather than posing for her picture. She is a caregiver whose daily life is constrained by the necessities and whims of an upper-class and presumably white family, or even by the requirements and stipulations of the kids themselves. She looks, however, dedicated to her work. Her gaze focuses on holding

1.13. Fotografía Rodríguez, *Julia Castrillón*, 1898. Digital positive from gelatin dry plate, 12 × 9 cm. Biblioteca Pública Piloto de Medellín / Archivo fotográfico.

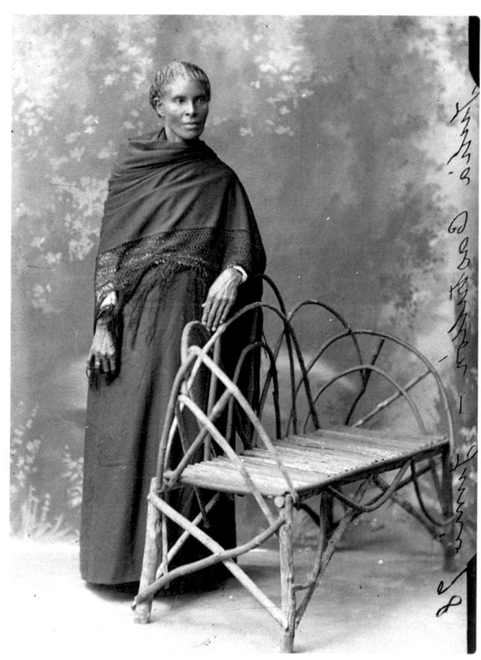

the little girl by her shoulders while simultaneously transmitting a sense of dispossession.

And yet, people of color also appear in Melitón's more dignifying portraits, hindering straightforward categorizations of his work. An early picture of Julia Castrillón, from 1898, portrays a middle-aged woman standing behind a bench in a typical studio scenario (fig. 1.13). She wears a long skirt and covers her torso with a black scarf. These clothes do not differ from the outfits worn by the proclaimed white elite, thus presenting the black body as equal. In opposition to exploitative portraits such as the one of the couple in rags (fig. 1.11), this image represents a black woman embodying a reality that was rarely acknowledged. In this picture, Melitón presents the sitter as an alternative record that worked against the standard iconography of racism.

De la Calle's work, on the other hand, is more consistent in presenting a wider share of Antioquia's society. Unlike his colleague Melitón, de la Calle photographed black people throughout his career. Perhaps his decision was an act of resistance to the discourses implanted by the elite. His photographs showed compassion, care, and sympathy for the people he was picturing, regardless of where they came from, the color of their skin, or their social and economic standing. De la Calle related to his sitters from within, and it became an act of affirmation. If the myth of the *raza antioqueña* had enhanced the belief that black people did not exist in Antioquia, then de la Calle's work actively challenged this idea. Early portraits such as the small but powerful photograph of María Loaiza (fig. 1.14) not only contested the discourses that presented the black population as subjugated or scrutinized but also presented the sitters in dignifying ways that visualized other aspects of their lives. The woman in this picture wears a white embroidered dress, a black lace pectoral, a three-strand pearl necklace, earrings, and a headband. Her jewelry—a standardized symbol of wealth—and her position contrast strongly with some photographs taken by Melitón. Her pose is defiant; her torso is straight, and her gaze is extremely penetrating. Composing a three-quarter view of a challenging figure, María Loaiza presents herself on her terms and not through those imposed by others.

However, examination of the negative complicates the narrative. When one looks at the glass plate with raking light, the skin of María Loaiza's face appears distinctly retouched (fig. 1.15). Slight strokes or "touches"—as they were called—appear throughout the surface of her skin, creating a ghostly figure. De la Calle employed a graphite pencil to smooth the look of her skin. Technically, these marks brightened the face in the positive image by blocking the light during the printing process. These marks were not visible in the positive versions of the image, and they were perhaps unknown to the sitters, who did not have access to the negatives.

Melitón also retouched his portraits of dark-skinned persons. The photograph of Pedro P. Villa and his family exemplifies Melitón's manual interventions on the negatives (figs. 1.16 and 1.17). His touches on the sitters' faces are longer and more consistent than those in de la Calle's example. Here, the graphite strokes follow one direction, the line moving up and down and covering larger areas of the skin's surface. The touches were done with meticulous technique. Conversely, de la Calle's touches are shorter and more scattered, have diverse forms, and follow different directions. They are more spontaneous and less deliberate.

As discussed earlier in this chapter, making modifications to correct errors or defects in the photographs was a common practice during this period. Nonetheless, the excessive retouching used by both photographers

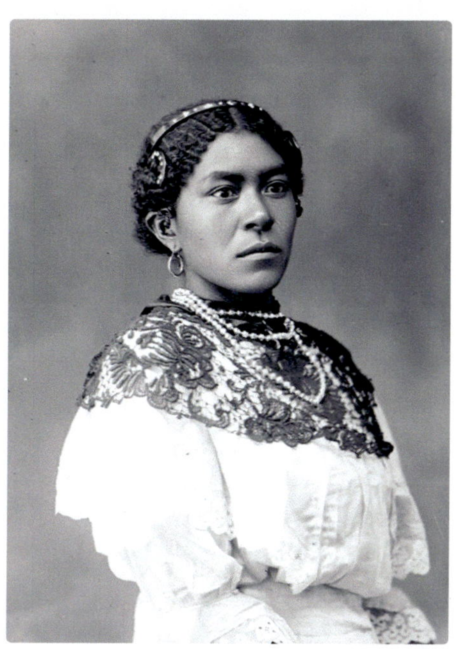

1.14. Benjamín de la Calle, *María Loaiza*, 1918. Digital positive from gelatin dry plate, 9 × 6 cm. Biblioteca Pública Piloto de Medellín / Archivo fotográfico.

1.15. Benjamín de la Calle, *María Loaiza*, 1918. Detail from gelatin dry plate under raking light. Biblioteca Pública Piloto de Medellín / Archivo fotográfico. Photo: Esteban Duperly.

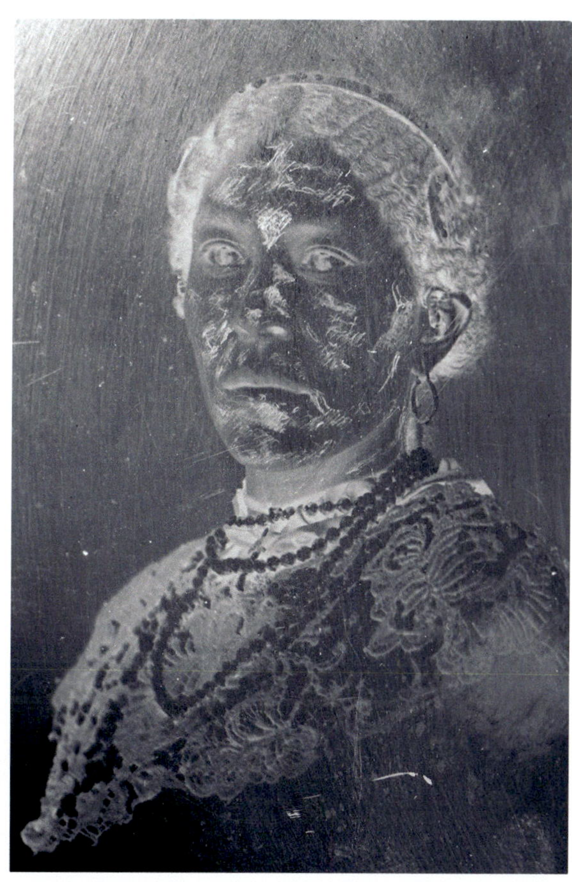

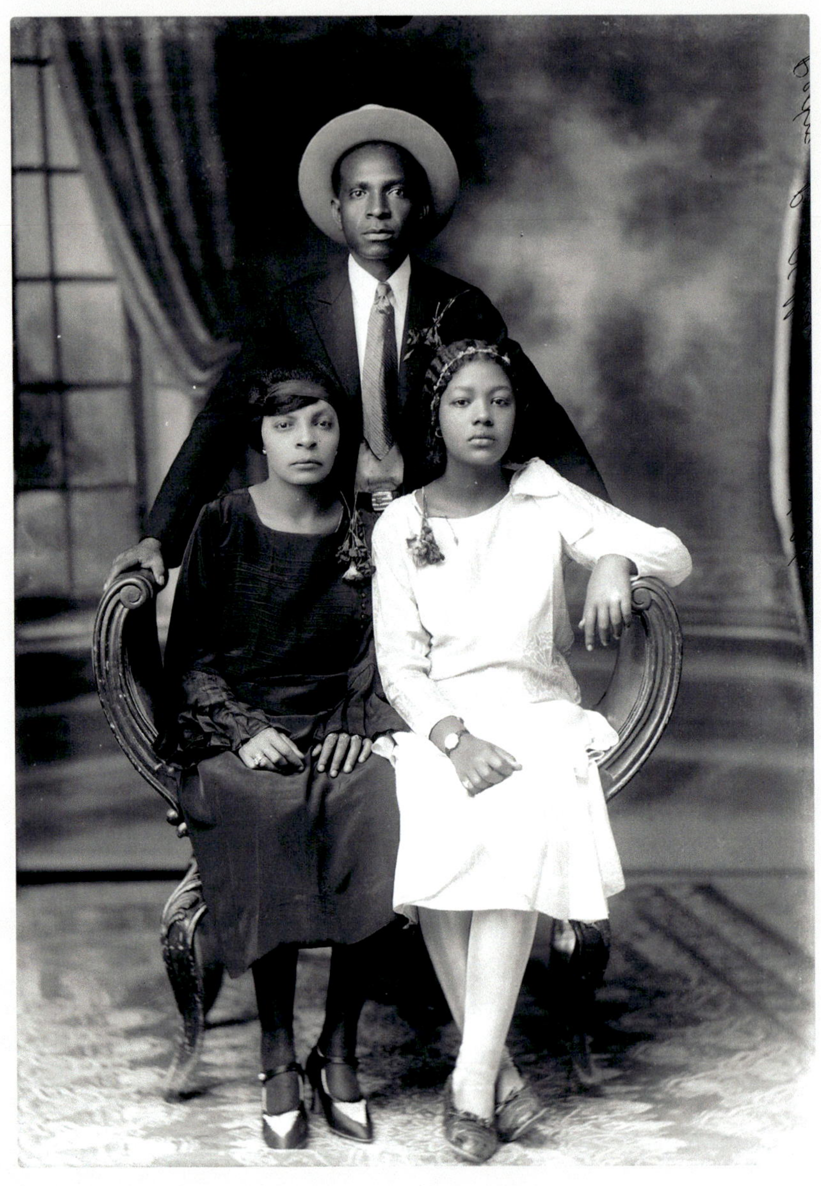

1.16. Fotografía Rodríguez, *Pedro P. Villa*, 1931. Digital positive from original gelatin dry plate, 18 × 13 cm. Biblioteca Pública Piloto de Medellín / Archivo fotográfico.

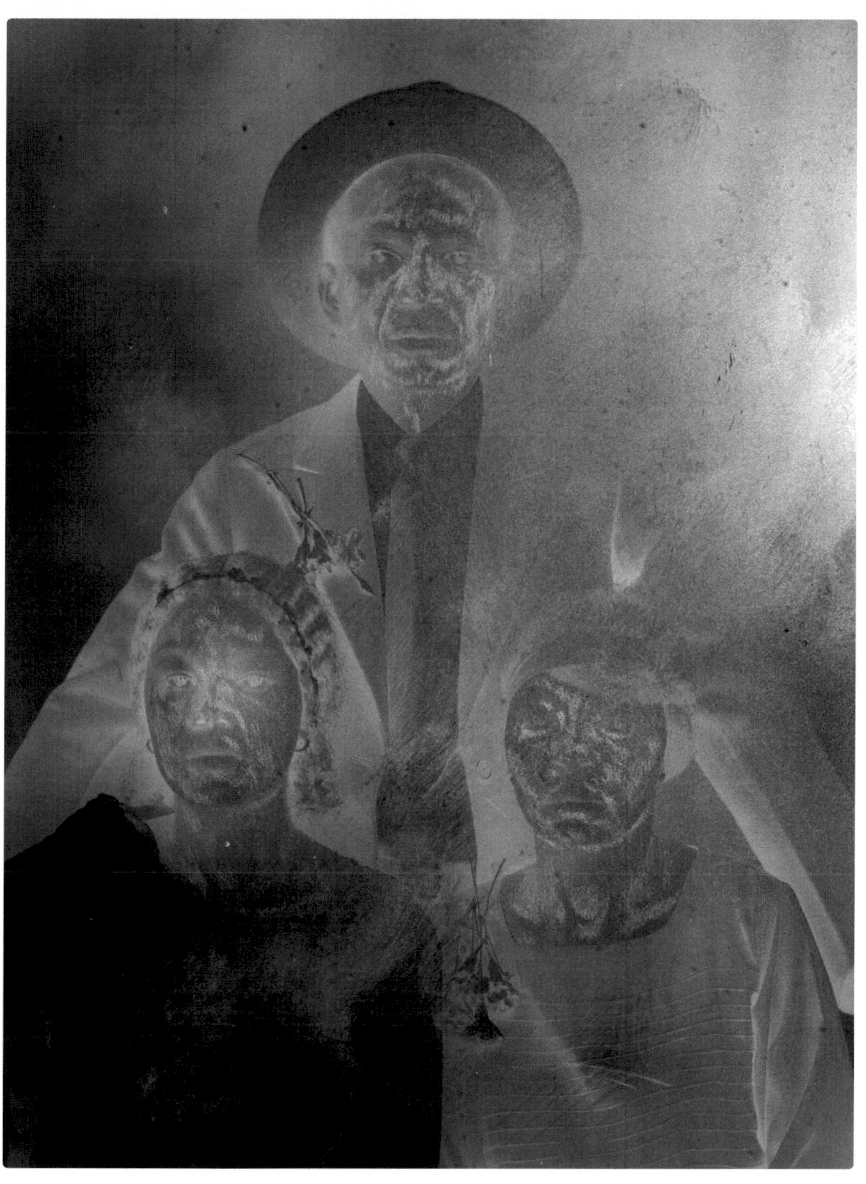

1.17. Fotografía Rodríguez, *Pedro P. Villa,* 1930. Detail of gelatin dry plate under raking light. Biblioteca Pública Piloto de Medellín / Archivo fotográfico. Photo: Esteban Duperly.

in these cases complicates straightforward narratives. Why were both studios performing this kind of manipulation on the negatives of their black sitters? Who encouraged disproportionate retouching, and for what purposes? Although it is clear that Fotografía Rodríguez's practice adhered more cohesively to the discourse implanted by the Antioquian race, do these images question de la Calle's work concerning this discourse? Perhaps this manipulation aimed to enhance the beauty of the sitters in the same way that Melitón would do with the portraits of white people. One could also argue that retouching the image on the negative plate was the most effective way these photographers had to achieve resemblance, that is, reflecting through the flawed medium of photography the inner or full character of a sitter. As stated by von Brevern, "Long before theories of indexicality were formulated, it was resemblance that positioned photography against notions of identity, and therefore against ideas of simple mimetic reference between image and object."[69] Ultimately, the purpose of portrait photography was to reflect the intricate equilibrium between a person's individuality and its resemblance.

The modifications made in the photograph of a group of four black women (fig. 1.10)—taken by Melitón Rodríguez and first described at the beginning of this section—are also remarkable because of the yellow color of the material used (fig. 1.18) and visible in the white stockings and the hands of the sitters, which are illuminated by rays of light coming from the left side of the portrait. The use of colored dyes, as opposed to pencil, raises the question of the effects the employment of a specific color had on the positive versions of the photographs. Color dyes were applied for different purposes when retouching negatives. The most common were red, yellow, and green. Photographers used a yellow dye in portraits when the aim was to highlight specific areas by occluding light waves in the purple range. Using colored pigments followed the same principles of contemporary photography: different filters are used in the lens of the camera to produce diverse effects. In the case of the negative analyzed here, the yellow pigment aimed to block the passage of violet light rays to differentiate the white stockings and the white light that hit the women's hands from the darker background.

It is also important to highlight that photographic emulsions, cameras, and other technical tools were rarely produced to photograph black skin adequately. Usually, the sensitivity of the emulsions was calibrated for white skin and not tailored for darker, brown, or yellow tones. Other

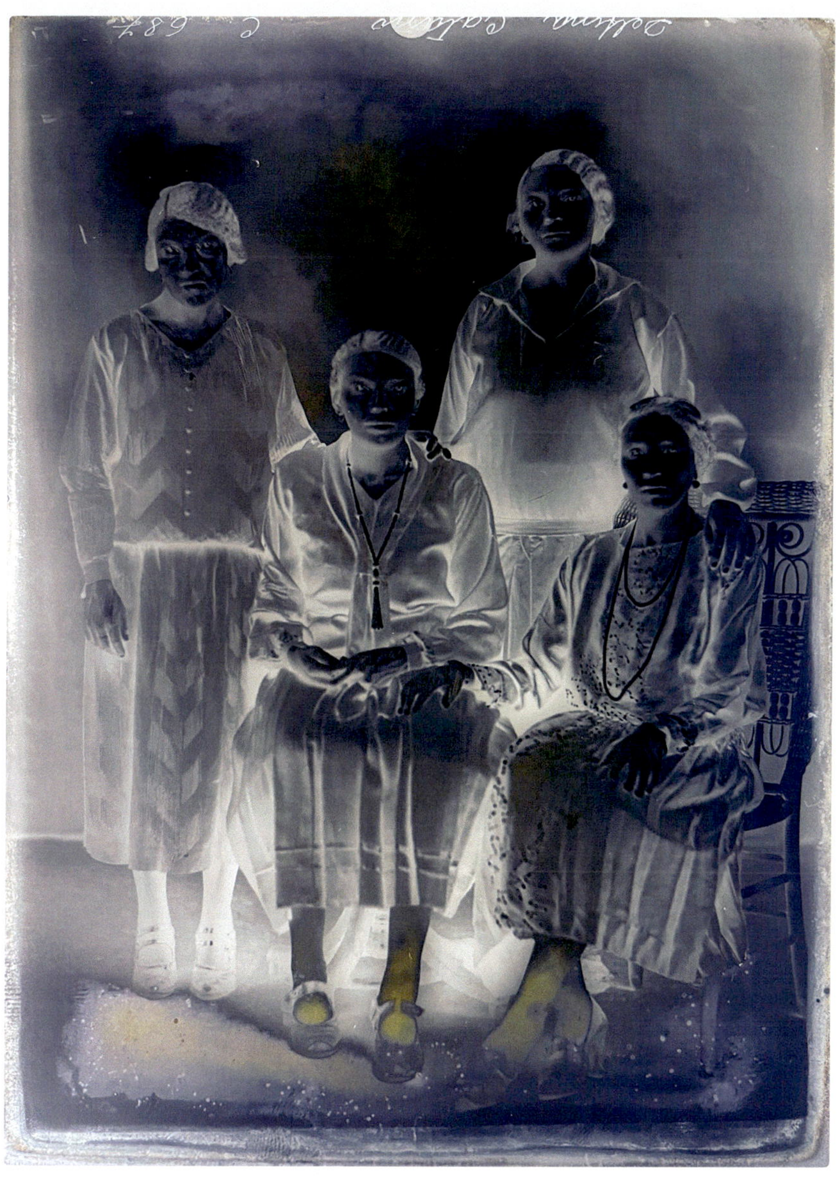

1.18. Fotografía Rodríguez, *Delfina Castaño*, 1930. Gelatin dry plate, 18 × 13 cm. Biblioteca Pública Piloto de Medellín / Archivo fotográfico.

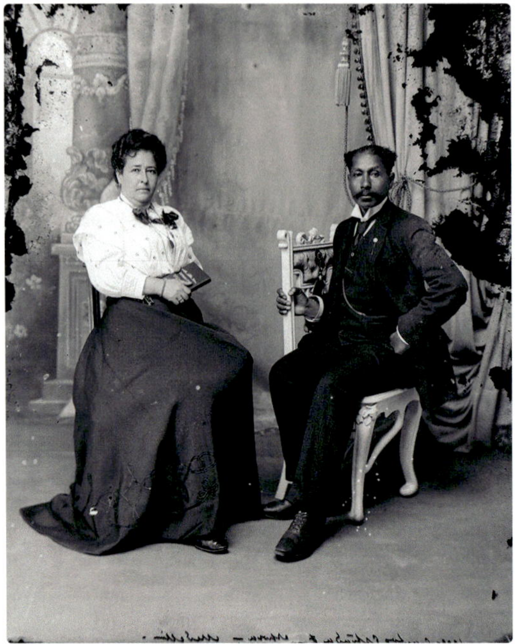

1.19. Benjamín de la Calle, *Carlos Estrada y señora,* 1906. Digital positive from original gelatin dry plate, 25 × 20 cm. Biblioteca Pública Piloto de Medellín / Archivo fotográfico.

tools, such as light meters, had similar restrictions. Therefore, photographers used retouching to alter the color of the skin, but this time, to improve the flaws of standardized photographic products. This was not only the case of Fotografía Rodríguez and Benjamín de la Calle but also of other practitioners who photographed black individuals—such as James Van Der Zee, to cite one example of the same period.[70]

Other portraits by de la Calle questioned even further the erasure of blackness in the imaginaries of the Antioquian population. Pictures such as the portrait of Carlos Estrada and his wife (fig. 1.19), representing an interracial couple using all the resources necessary to convey wealth and high social status through photography, are a good example. They appear against a highly ornate backdrop, wearing elegant clothes and jewelry. Incorporating these items was important because clothing was a key signifier. Interracial portraits are a significant visual testimony of the process of *mestizaje* in Colombia. Although such unions were known since the nineteenth century, images such as this one were uncommon. Nancy Appelbaum notes that the Chorographic Commission created no pictures of interracial couples, although those relationships were often insinuated.[71] Therefore, photographs such as this become fundamental witnesses to a process that had been erased until then. For de la Calle, these photos worked as visual claims to a different reality because they revealed a distinctive world. He presents the sitters as subjects, with first and last names, their personalities reflected through the photographic shot, and poses dictated by negotiation between the sitter and the photographer, not by a hegemonic, colonizing gaze.

Indeed, this was arguably the first historical moment in Antioquia in which the African population of the region represented itself through photography as subjects and not as types. The visualization of black people had been constantly neglected. When discussed at all, it had been through the lens of a hegemonic discourse that perpetuated the role assigned to them since the colonial period: slaves, servants, maids, and so on. For example, there are a few cartes de visite from the nineteenth century in which blacks perform these assigned roles, such as *Trabajador negro de Antioquia* (Black worker from Antioquia, ca. 1870) or *Chapolera recogedora de café* (Peasant coffee picker, ca. 1870), both taken by the Wills i Restrepo studio in Medellín—a pioneering photo studio in the region (fig. 1.20).[72] Both photographs are half-body shots taken inside a studio. The subjects pose wearing the clothes and props associated with their jobs: the worker holds a stick from which a crawling snake hangs, and the woman carries a basket on her head, presumably in which she collected coffee beans. These props enhance the exoticism with which the black population was portrayed and imagined. In particular, the photograph of the black man reinforces this idea by including the snake hanging from the stick he is holding. The snake is an animal associated with the concept of sin and with the idea of the wilderness and the noncivilized. Thus, blackness conveyed ideas of backwardness and depravity. These images were most likely intended for albums, which the local and foreign elite collected. Contrary to the photographs by de la Calle and the Rodríguez brothers, here the subjects have no names, and the images are identified solely by the role that the man and the woman perform: worker and peasant. The elimination of subjectivity perpetuated segregation and disseminated hegemonic values that had not changed since colonial times.

The cartes de visite described above strikingly parallel the photographs of Brazilian slaves taken by José Christiano de Freitas Júnior, a Portuguese photographer who settled in Rio de Janeiro during the 1860s. His pictures, portraying subjects picked off the streets and brought into the studio to be photographed, show black slaves as types, just as Wills

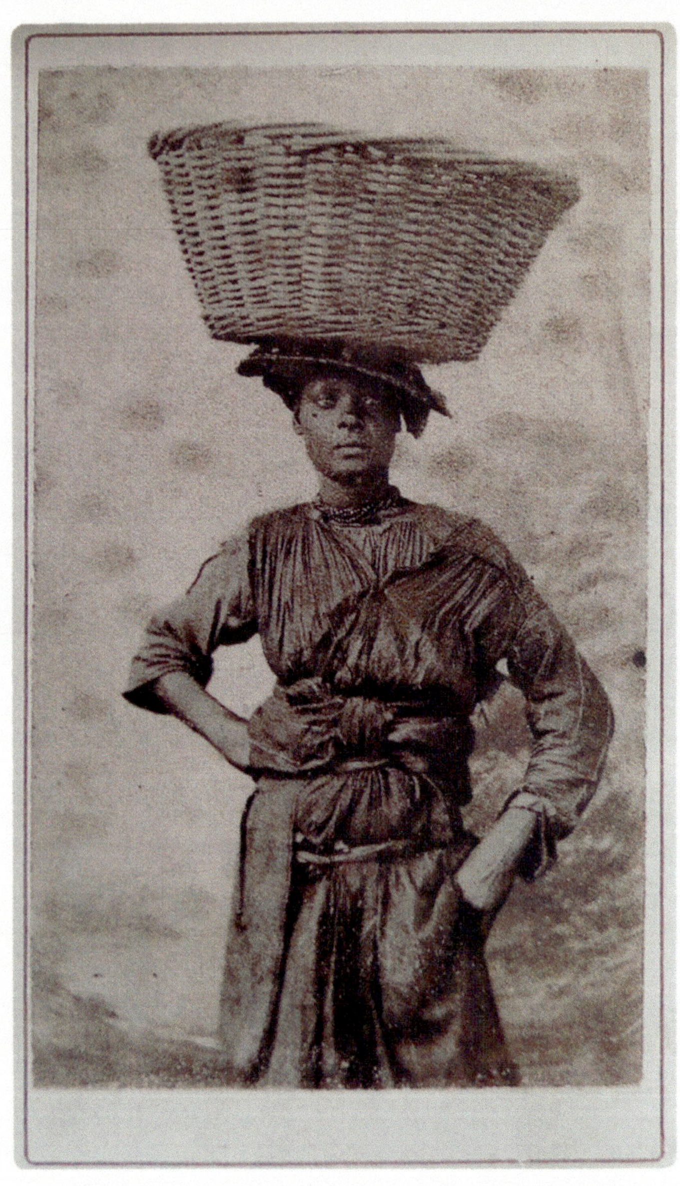

1.20. Wills i Restrepo, *Chapolera recogedora de café*, ca. 1870. Albumen print on carte de visite. Photo: Sonia Rojas.

i Restrepo did in Medellín some years later. Take, for example, the photograph of a *timbre,* which depicts a black man carrying a wooden barrel on his head—probably used to collect excrement and other garbage from the houses of Rio late at night (fig. 1.21, ca. 1860s).[73] Here again, the man appears performing his work and annulling his identity as an individual. What stands out in this type of photography, as observed by Poole, is "the repetition of form and gesture, rather than the singularity of the individuals": the coffee picker holds a coffee basket, the *timbre* carries a disposal barrel, the water carrier poses with a water jar, and so on.[74] This repetitiveness reveals the uses of the images, created to classify and compare, turning individuals into facts and categories to be scientifically studied. Poole noted that, in opposition to the cartes de visite created for the bourgeois population, the photographs of Othered individuals were not objects exchanged by the portrayed person but rather silent and unidentified depictions of distinct types.[75] This ultimately led to the development of photographic practices specifically used for racial categorization and control.[76] Ultimately, what differentiates Christiano Júnior's photographs from those of Wills i Restrepo is not visible in the images themselves; it is a historical fact: Júnior's subjects were slaves, whereas Wills i Restrepo's were not. During colonial times, blacks arrived in Antioquia from thirty-two different African nations, mainly from the Bakongo.[77] They were subjected to slavery until 1851, when President José Hilario López abolished the practice. Conversely, slavery lasted in Brazil until 1888.

Fotografía Rodríguez and Benjamín de la Calle's images work as models of a new visualization of black people in Antioquia. They bear witness to the fact that the African population was not absent in the Department of Antioquia and that the racial discourses promoted by the white elite were not sustainable.[78] In other words, these photographs show that segregation and exclusion through ideological discourses could not persist in a diverse society.

• • • • •

The myth of the *raza antioqueña* was a strong and tenacious discourse that embodied different forms. The historical circumstances that affected the Department of Antioquia from colonial times until the late 1800s fostered the construction of an ideology that took the form of a new race. By the turn of the nineteenth century, the emergence of eugenics in the European scientific world encouraged the responses of their

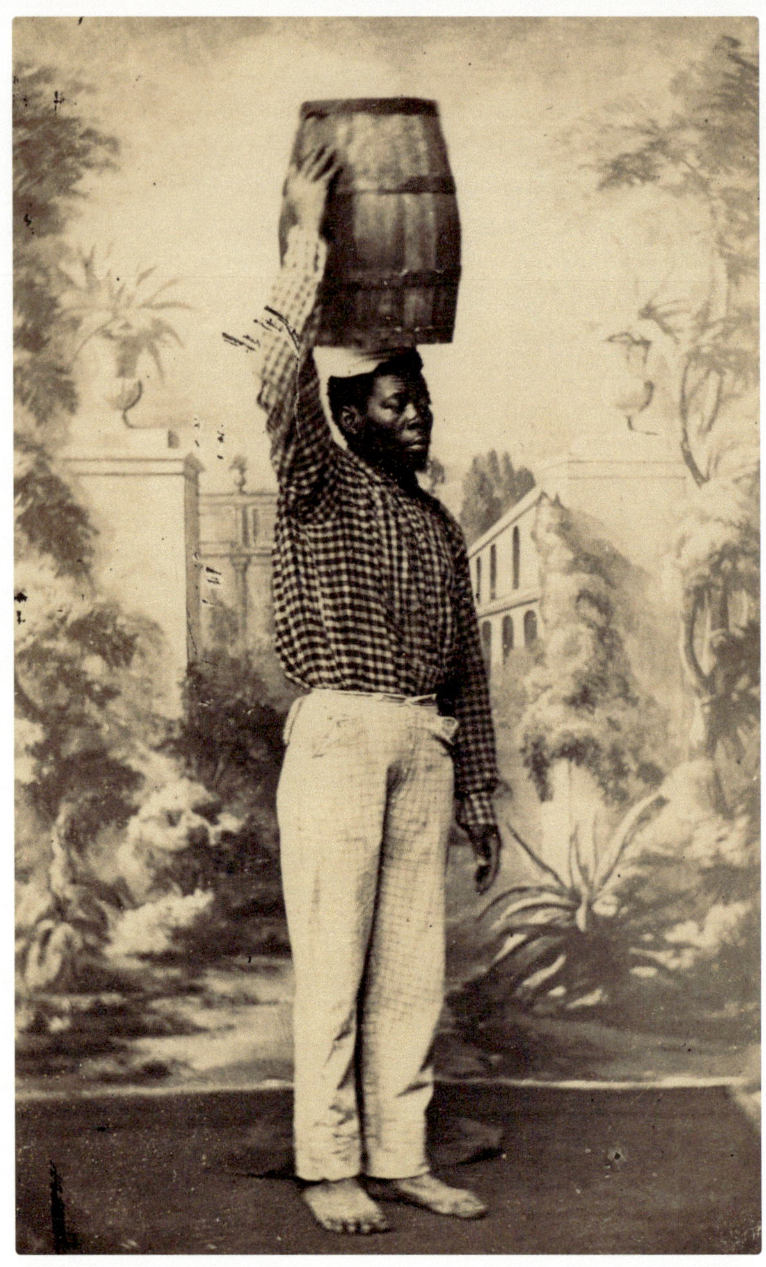

1.21. José Christiano de Freitas Júnior, *Male Street Vendor with Barrel on Head, Brazil,* ca. 1860s. Albumen print on carte de visite, 9 × 5.5 cm. Metropolitan Museum of Art, purchase from The Horace W. Goldsmith Foundation Fund, 2017.

Latin American counterparts. Attempting to redeem their own race, the Latin Americans replicated similar discriminatory ideals in their native countries. In Colombia, this was particularly reflected in Antioquia with the invention of the *raza antioqueña*. Here, the racial discourse not only took the form of a traditional speech but also materialized in persuasive visual forms. In particular, photography played an important role, as it visualized—in an apparently transparent and objective manner—the bodies of those immersed in this ideological discourse.

A careful examination of some negatives by Fotografía Rodríguez revealed how the alleged transparency of the medium was, in fact, manipulated to convey a standardized idea of a white elite. The negatives show evidence of excessive retouching in most of the portraits to smooth and whiten the sitters' skin. It is particularly revealing in the faces of young people who presumably did not need the improvements performed by the photographers. More importantly, the revealing graphite strokes literalized the rhetorical violence imposed by the *raza antioqueña*.

If the Rodríguez brothers employed the medium to spread the belief of a white Antioquian population, Benjamín de la Calle contested this idea. De la Calle also used retouching to alter certain aspects of his sitters' skin, but his manual interventions followed standard procedures. The retouching performed by de la Calle was usually not excessive. When he overtly manipulated the images, it was to elevate the social status of his sitters and fulfill aspirational desires, as seen in the photograph of the hand-painted veil (fig. I.1). De la Calle also resisted the *raza antioqueña* discourse by portraying other aspects of Antioquian society, including its black population, one of the most powerful acts of resistance. In a context where people of African descent were never acknowledged, neither physically nor rhetorically, photographs of black people performed an active role of resistance by asserting their presence. The study of photography is necessary to visualize the counterdiscursive practices of silenced bodies.

The relationship between race and photography has been poorly explored in Colombia, but as I have shown in this chapter, it is strong. The discourses that fostered this relationship were completely naturalized, but they become apparent when one studies the photographs in detail. None of the images by de la Calle and the Rodríguez brothers analyzed in this chapter correspond to the anthropological uses of photography promoted by the European tendency to categorize, study, and ultimately dominate the Other. On the contrary, these images were created from within for local commercial and artistic purposes. It is precisely in this context where an analysis of the issues of race is more pressing because these ideas, and their visual materialization, appear to be natural and, therefore, less evident. By appearing less scientific and thus lacking a strict method, they hide a reality that has to be challenged. Underscoring these images is the use of photography as a medium that developed in tandem with the construction of national and regional identities and served as a tool to promote or resist various discourses.

CHAPTER TWO

The Pictorial Negative

THE WORK OF HORACIO MARINO AND MELITÓN RODRÍGUEZ

IN A 1913 PHOTOGRAPH TITLED with the name of one of the sitters, *Emilia Obregón*, Melitón Rodríguez created an allegorical scene depicting a woman standing on a boat with a long rope tied around her waist and a tiara adorning her head. She holds a large flag in her right hand (fig. 2.1). In the foreground, a young girl sits on the edge of the boat wearing a winged hat, presumably representing Hermes, the god of progress and commerce, and holding a large paddle with both hands. The photograph is heavily retouched, with the bright red pigment used by the photographer particularly noticeable in the negative version of the picture (fig. 2.2). The negative was modified with visible brushstrokes to create a painterly effect on the image's background, giving the impression of a cloudy sky and a surging sea. Through retouching, Melitón created the illusion of the paddle immersed in the sea. During the nineteenth century, allegories were a popular topic not only in Colombia but in pictorial photography worldwide.[1] They often appeared during periods of rising nationalist sentiments and were used to reinforce these ideas through visual representations. In *Emilia Obregón*, the photograph uses a classic mythological scene, that of Hermes and Athena, to represent Colombia or Antioquia under the symbols of commerce and civilization, two central ideals of the Antioquian race discourse.

This photograph thematizes many of the issues I discuss in this chapter. It shows how pictorial photography reflected the civilizing discourse of the Antioquian race and highlights how the negative was central

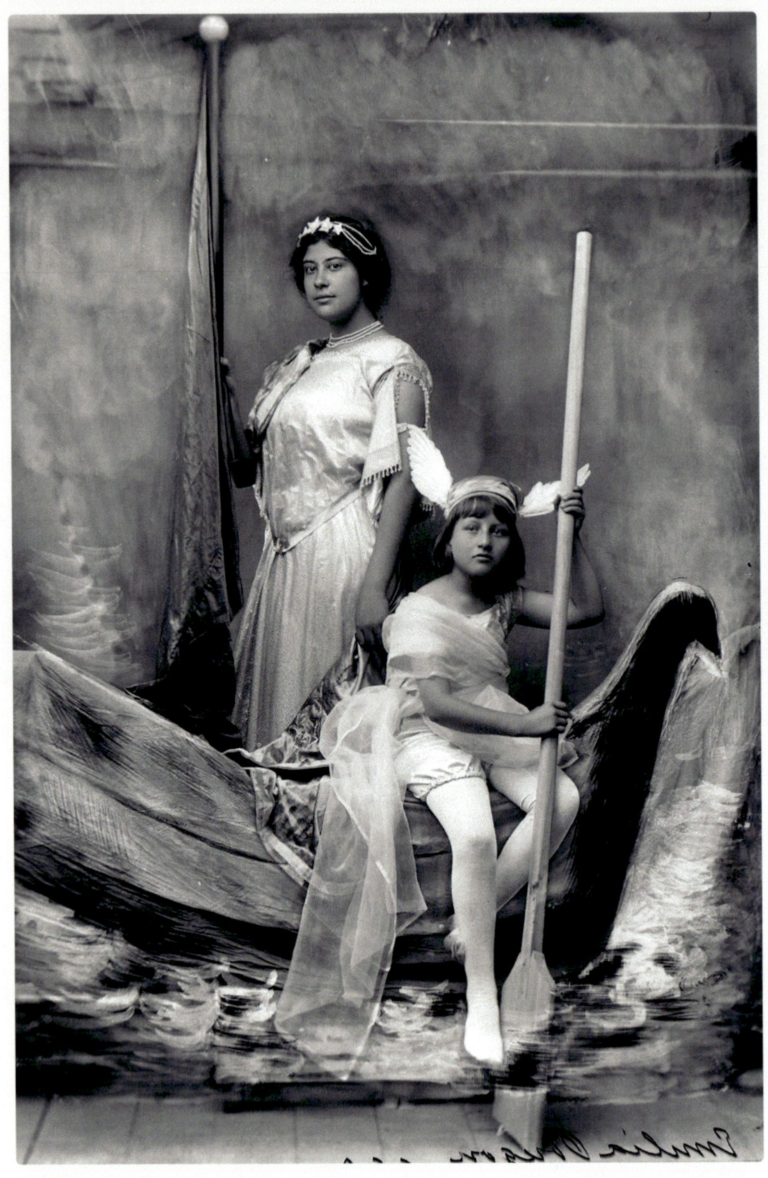

2.1. (*above*) Fotografía Rodríguez, *Emilia Obregón*, 1913. Digital positive from gelatin dry plate, 20 × 15 cm. Biblioteca Pública Piloto de Medellín / Archivo fotográfico. Photo: Esteban Duperly.

2.2. (*opposite*) Fotografía Rodríguez, *Emilia Obregón*, 1913. Glass plate negative, 20 × 15 cm. Biblioteca Pública Piloto de Medellín / Archivo fotográfico. Photo: Esteban Duperly.

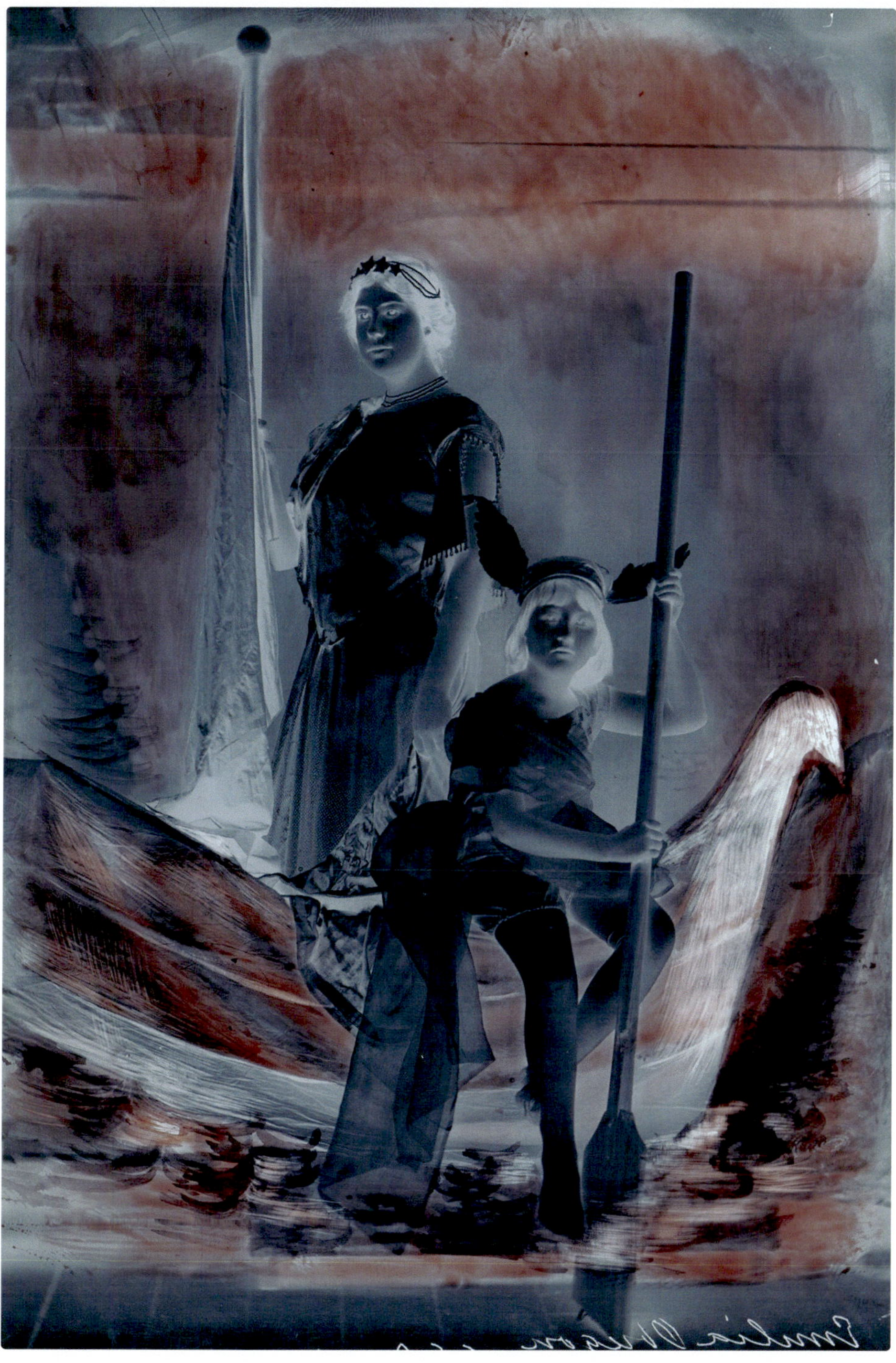

to both this artistic practice and racial morale. In this chapter, I examine how the Rodríguez brothers used both pictorialism and the negative to reinforce the racial discourse of *la raza antioqueña*, carefully analyzing some of their pictorial photographs. I also show how this racial discourse displayed racial superiority in nuanced ways that sometimes went beyond the color of the sitters' skin, thus complicating straightforward definitions of whiteness. Here, I will examine the concept of the negative from multiple perspectives: first, by looking at the objects themselves, given that negatives became central to the production of the photograph's pictorial effects, eventually leading to the creation of images that reflected the tastes and consumption patterns of Medellín's higher social class. This was an integral part of the creation of whiteness. Second, I will introduce the "negative Other" concept, that is, photographic images that deliberately highlight distinctions and differences related to race, ethnicity, geography, or social class. And last, I will discuss the importance of negatives as the matrix for reproducing photographs and thus responsible for their wide circulation and multiple connotations. These three ways of understanding the negative will appear in no particular order, sometimes working together one with another.

The Pictorial Negative and Ordinary Whiteness

Let's begin by explaining what pictorial photography is. First developed in Britain during the last decade of the nineteenth century and then appropriated and promoted by Alfred Stieglitz (1864–1946) and his circle in the United States, pictorialism—as the pictorial photographic movement was eventually called—aimed at elevating the status of photography to the realm of the fine arts by distancing itself from the connection to the machine-like aesthetic associated with the medium. Instead, it proposed a style that emphasized the allegorical, poetic, and expressive qualities of the photographic image and its formal characteristics.[2]

British pictorialism swung mainly between two ideas: the use of combination printing techniques to stage compositions as advocated by Henry Peach Robinson, or a type of photography that followed with fidelity the perceptual experience of life as proposed by Peter Henry Emerson in his book *Naturalistic Photography* (1889). In the United States, Alfred

Stieglitz became the driving force of the American version of this transnational movement. Stieglitz promoted photography as a legitimate art form and gathered a group of artist photographers experimenting with the pictorial tradition. Photographers such as Gertrude Käsebier, Clarence H. White, and Edward Steichen, among others, joined Stieglitz in an unprecedented exhibition titled *The Photo-Secession* held at the National Arts Club in 1902. The exhibition's title informed the approach to photography promoted by the artists. They believed that photography had a unique aesthetic worth recognizing. However, this was contradictory, considering that pictorial photography intentionally appropriated a painterly look. The impact of Stieglitz's pursuit is reflected in the profuse diffusion of the pictorial style not only in the United States but across the globe. Pictorial photography was eventually practiced in places as diverse as Japan, Singapore, Spain, Australia, and Peru.[3] Colombia was no exception. The impact of pictorialism and its profuse dissemination might be due to the ubiquitous emergence of amateur photographic clubs, the proliferation of exhibitions, and, most importantly, the abundance of magazines and journals promoting this type of photography.

In pictorial photography, the negative played material and symbolically significant roles. Many photographers manipulated their negative plates to produce the desired pictorial effects. Others saw the negative as the genesis of photographic art. For example, in a photograph from 1857 titled *The First Negative*, British photographer Oscar Gustav Rejlander depicted a scene in which a woman draws the shadow of a man on the backdrop of the picture (fig. 2.3). The scene is based on a classical account that comes from Pliny the Elder's story of the invention of art. In it, the daughter of the Corinthian potter Butades draws the silhouette of her beloved's face before he travels to a foreign land. With this photograph, Rejlander intended to evoke the invention of photography. Through the association with the classical story, he presented the new medium as an established artistic discipline. The scene not only recalls the use of the physionotrace to produce silhouettes—an important precedent in the history of photography—but, perhaps more importantly, it emphasizes the negative as photography's ground zero.[4] Rejlander interpreted the shadow and its subsequent inscription on a surface as "the first negative." He understood the double function of the shadow evoked by Pliny in his account and translated it to the context of photography. On the one hand, the inscription of the projection (shadow) created by Butades's daughter

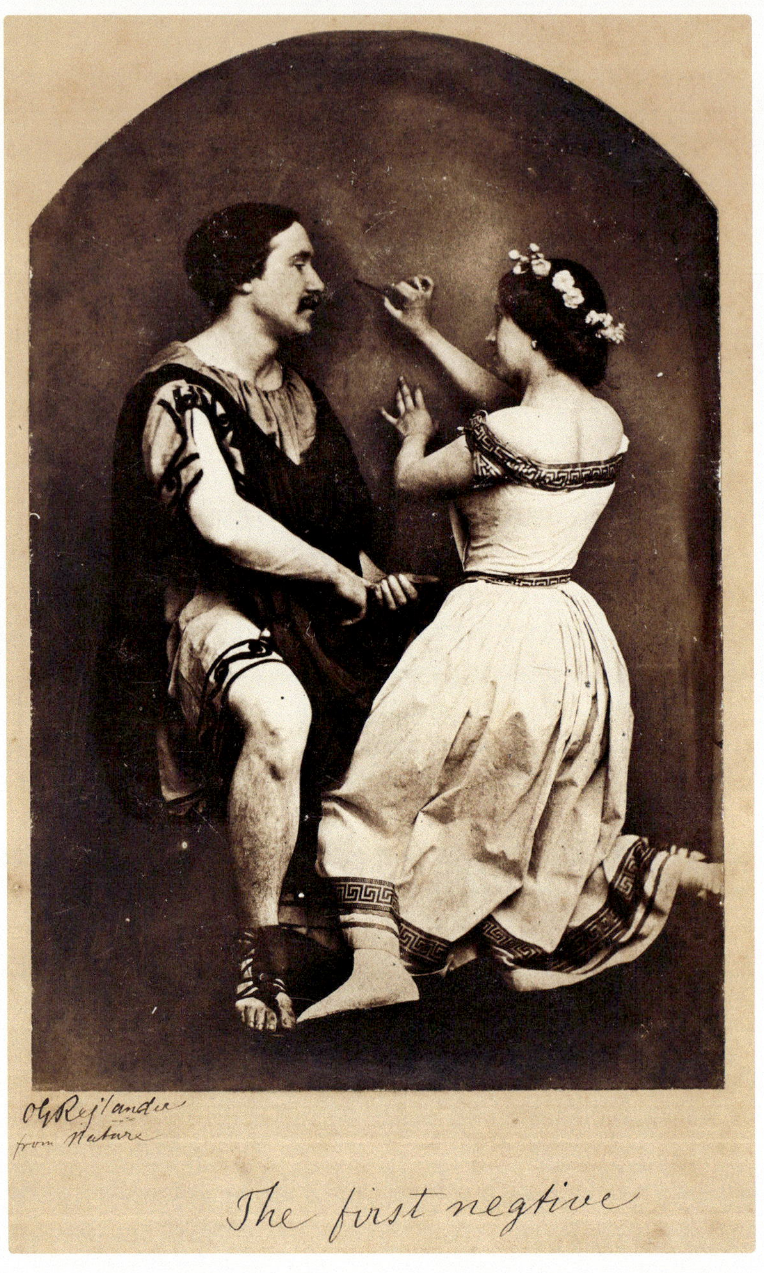

2.3. Oscar Rejlander, *The First Negative*, 1857. Albumenized salted paper print from a wet collodion glass negative, 29 × 15 cm. Musee d'Orsay, Dist. RMN-Grand Palais, purchased 2011. Photo: Patrice Schmidt.

made the absent subject present. Just as in photography, resemblance played an important role here. On the other hand, the inscribed image bears not only this relationship of resemblance to the referent but also one of direct contact, that is, an indexical relationship.[5]

As in *Emilia Obregón*, the scene departs from a classical account, a common practice in British allegorical representations.[6] In Colombia, photographic allegories were also common during the nineteenth century. They began to appear from the 1860s onward as a response to the nationalistic spirit exacerbated by the many nineteenth-century wars. Patriotism and a general interest in *costumbrista* painting fostered nationalist photographs representing the country's national heritage and cultural identity. As in nineteenth-century Britain, tracing the origins of the antioqueños to ancient Greece and Rome, a moral guidepost based on heroic legends, justified the idea of Antioquia as a civilized and racially superior enterprise. As noted by Jeff Rosen, images that depicted allegories were naturally emotional, frequently dramatic, and consistently contained a storytelling aspect. Such visuals showcased ordinary situations with individuals or small groups alongside picturesque themes from famous historical, mythological, religious, and literary narratives.[7]

But in opposition to the pictorial photographs created by British photographers such as Rejlander's *The First Negative* or Julia Margaret Cameron's "fancy subjects"—as she called her allegorical pictures—the Colombian photographers avoided the use of titles that referenced the specific iconographies they were departing from. As in most allegorical images, the idea of the nation or state and the claimed truth of a past related to Western classical values were represented indirectly in these photographs. Consequently, identifying the sources is more complex, and the meanings of the photographs are harder to decipher. Rather than giving a title to these photographs, the Rodríguez brothers continued their tradition of writing the sitters' names on the negative plates. One possible explanation for this decision might be that they didn't produce many allegorical photographs, and practically all had the patriotic intention of representing Antioquia or the nation. However, as I will further examine in this chapter, some of the strategies used in allegorical photographs, such as *Emilia Obregón*, were also used in other pictorial photographs that do not necessarily function as allegories.

Although the identification with a Greek and Roman past was a way to establish a direct relationship with the Western tradition and thus with the white race, photographs such as *Emilia Obregón* complicate this otherwise direct relationship. Indeed, the picture evokes Hermes and Athena and the association of these figures with the notions of progress and civilization, but the model is a woman of color whose features were not manipulated to make her look white. This suggests that the photographer might be familiar with more traditional allegories of America, such as Cesare Ripa's, in which America is described as a woman of color.[8] Alternatively, it could be that in *Emilia Obregón*, the costumes, the mise-en-scène, and the manual interventions on the negative were enough to convey the association between the classical past and the Antioquian race, making the model's skin color less critical. This picture demonstrates how in Antioquia the concept of race was a slippery term and, in the case of this photograph, was understood more as a moral than in terms of skin color.

The painterly intervention on the negative of this photograph also speaks to local Latin American practices of photography. In particular, it recalls the oil painting interventions that photographers such as the Peruvian Juan Manuel Figueroa Aznar made on the surfaces of his images. According to Deborah Poole, Figueroa Aznar traveled through Ecuador and Colombia before returning to Peru and embracing photography. She suggests that Figueroa Aznar may have learned art photography from the Rodríguez brothers and Benjamín de la Calle, who were already practicing this type of photography when he visited Colombia.[9] But instead of manipulating the negatives to create painterly photographic effects, as in *Emilia Obregón*, Figueroa Aznar developed a technique he called *foto-óleo*. It consisted of painting with oil over the positive versions of photographs to create idealized subjects, add color, and produce other special effects. In this way, he maintained the aura of the original work of art while preserving the allure of modernity attributed to photography.[10] This technique was also practiced by Colombian photographers and artists such as Duperly and Son and Epifanio Garay.[11] They may have learned the technique from Luis García Hevia, a Colombian pioneer photographer who promoted it under the name of *oleotipos* in the 1860s.[12] In all of these case studies, however, the most relevant aspect of the interventions had to do with strategies to open up a commercial avenue in this highly competitive business. But the oil interventions on the positive copies distanced photography from its democratic intentions, making the images unique again and available only to the higher social sphere. On the contrary, the intervention on the negative plate of *Emilia Obregón* allowed the image to be widely disseminated while maintaining its association with the Antioquian race.

Emilia Obregón is not the only picture in which whiteness was conveyed through strategies beyond the sitter's skin color. In 1897, the Rodríguez brothers photographed four women posing with hunting rifles in front of a seascape backdrop (fig. 2.4). They used a remarkably complex technique to create this photo. The backdrop was crafted using separate sections, which are barely visible on the positive copy of the picture but become apparent when looking at the negatives (figs. 2.5 and 2.6). Moreover, the photographer captured the image twice. In the first version of the photograph, the backdrop montage and scenery are visible within the image frame. This picture iteration was retouched, enhancing the effect of the waves and hand-painting the flying birds in the background. Then the doctored image was photographed a second time using a bigger plate and retouched again, adding the bird on the hand of the woman that appears in the foreground. The photographer also emphasized the waves and finally cropped the scene to make it seamless. Moreover, the large size of the negative and the elaborated mise-en-scène suggest that the photograph could have been quite expensive to produce.

The picture deploys a romantic landscape juxtaposed with the incongruous scene of presumably high-class women from Medellín posing armed for the photographer's camera. The empowered poses assumed by the women, particularly the woman standing in the boat holding a gun with her right hand and the left hand resting on her hip, defy the conventional female roles of the time. Hunting was a practice reserved for the elite in Medellín, but it's unclear if women participated. Although women in Victorian England increasingly engaged in hunting from the 1860s onward, this was likely not the case in Medellín, where hunting was considered a male activity that reinforced masculinity through the use of guns and the implicit violence of the sport.[13] Nevertheless, the Rodríguez brothers and the sitters might have been inspired by images of women in hunting attire produced in print and photography, mainly in England and the United States. These images could have reached Antioquia and inspired the duck-hunting scene captured in the photograph.

Indeed, the picture shows the sitters' theatricality and lack of hunting knowledge. The woman standing on the boat places her hand over the muzzle of the gun, a position that no trained shooter would have ever taken. In the photograph, the guns function as empowering and

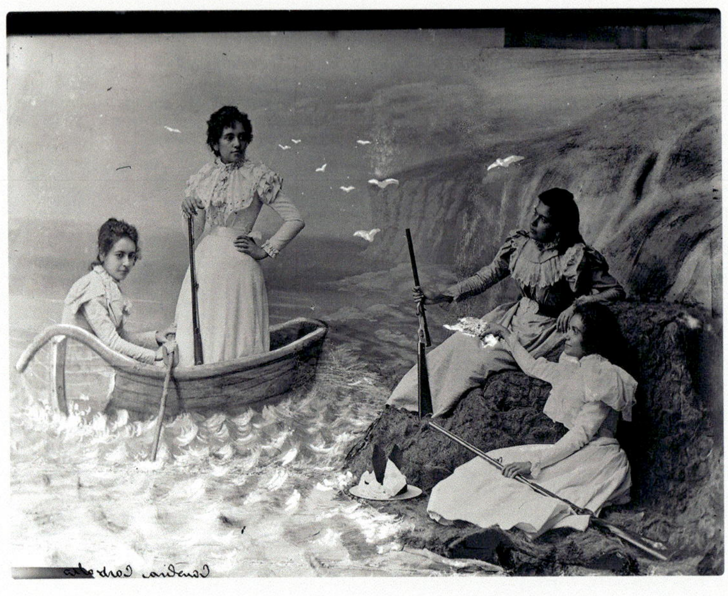

2.4. Fotografía Rodríguez, *Carolina Carvallo*, 1897. Digital positive from gelatin dry plate, 20 × 25 cm. Biblioteca Pública Piloto de Medellín / Archivo fotográfico.

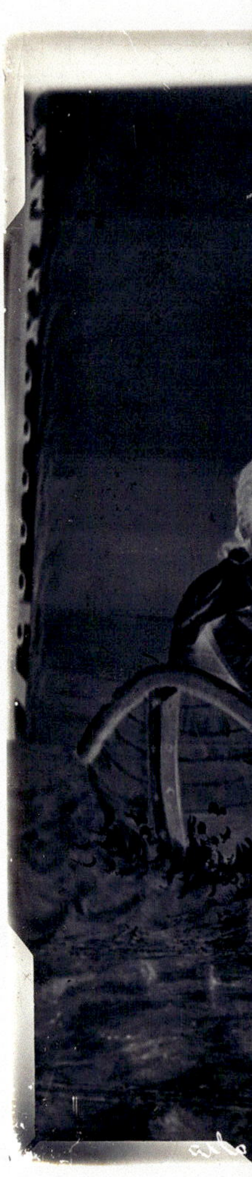

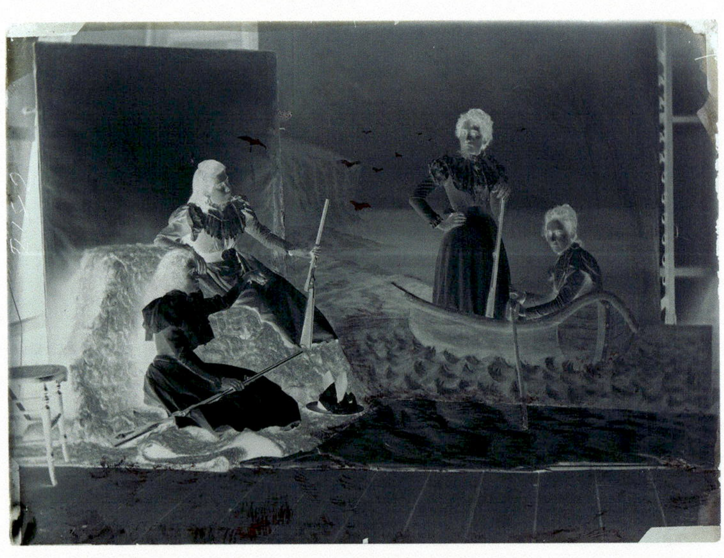

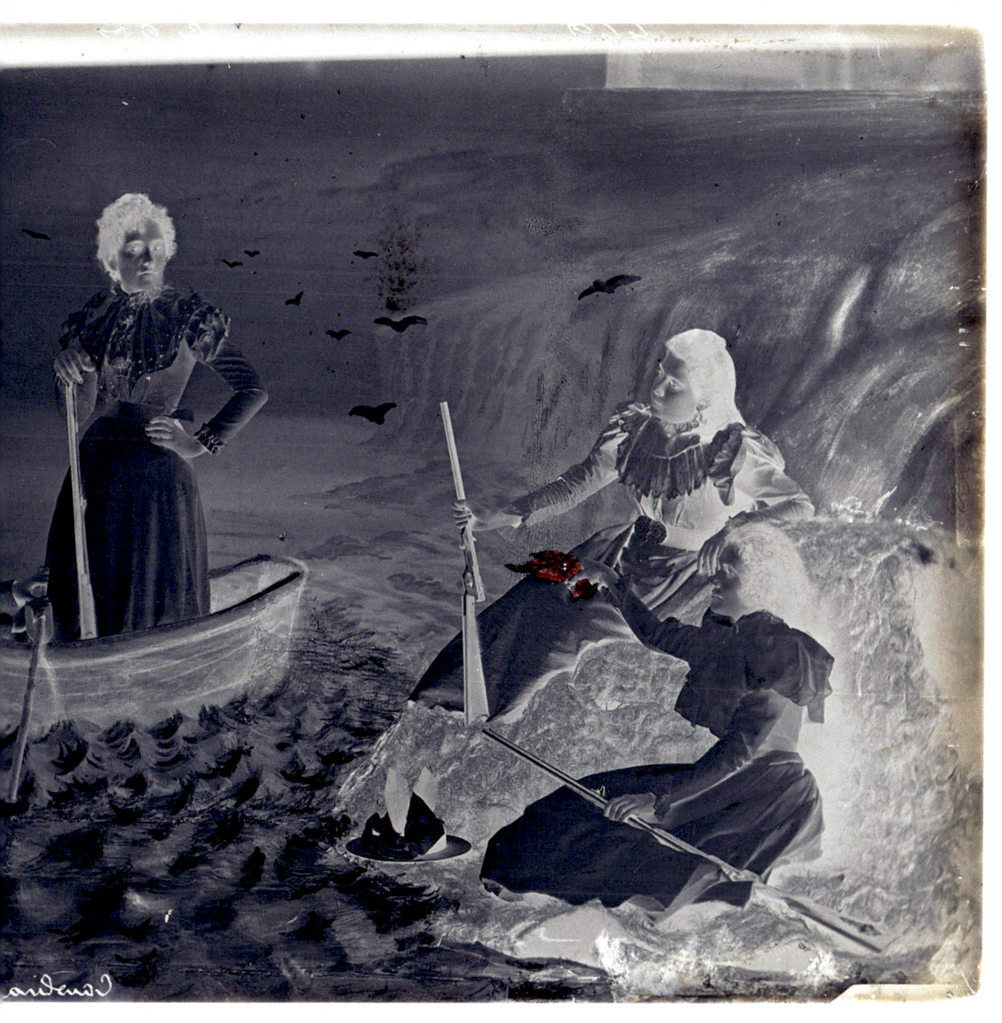

2.5. (*opposite*) Fotografía Rodríguez, *Carolina Carvallo*, 1897. Gelatin dry plate, 20 × 25 cm. Biblioteca Pública Piloto de Medellín / Archivo fotográfico. Photo: Esteban Duperly.

2.6. (*above*) Fotografía Rodríguez, *Carolina Carvallo*, 1897. Gelatin dry plate, 20 × 25 cm. Biblioteca Pública Piloto de Medellín / Archivo fotográfico.

emancipatory tools for women in the studio but also as signifiers of high class—as hunting was certainly a leisure activity related to the upper social sphere—and thus of whiteness. In pictures such as this one, race and class work hand in hand, evidencing how whiteness could be expressed through the sitter's skin color but also through material culture and activities that evidenced leisure time. This latter point is what recent scholarship has called "ordinary whiteness," that is, racial privilege performed in everyday activities and thus less explicitly visible.[14] The women depicted use the combination of racial and class dynamics in this photo to express their sense of belonging to an upper white social sphere. The women are not only engaging in leisure activities related to men; they also present themselves performing it while wearing long white dresses, a wardrobe unsuitable for this activity and rather indicative of material privilege. Therefore, this photo reinforces the white claim of the sitters through the props and staging of the picture, not through their skin color. If on the more standardized portraits the power of the Antioquian race discourse was made apparent through the retouching techniques applied to the sitters' skin on the negatives, in these more theatrical and artistic pictures, the manipulations modified other sections of the image, such as the background. As noted in the introduction, whiteness in Antioquia exceeded physical appearance, and it was also conveyed through notions of beauty, class-based behavior, and consumption patterns, as seen in the photographs analyzed in this section.

Costumbrismo as Pictorialism

In 1895, the Rodríguez brothers took one of their most famous pictorial photographs: *Los zapateros* (The shoemakers, fig. 2.7).[15] The image depicts a bucolic scene of a group of shoemakers (three men and three children) working on the production of handmade shoes. The picture is set in the veranda of a middle-class house, where the men sit surrounding a table while stitching and needling leather pieces. Material leftovers, old shoes, wooden lasts, and garbage lie around on the dirty floor and function visually as an index of the men's hard work. In the middle ground, a sewing machine and a boot hanging from the wall remind the viewer of both the process and the product of the men's labor. The Rodríguez brothers used a shallow depth of field to focus on the working scene and direct the gaze

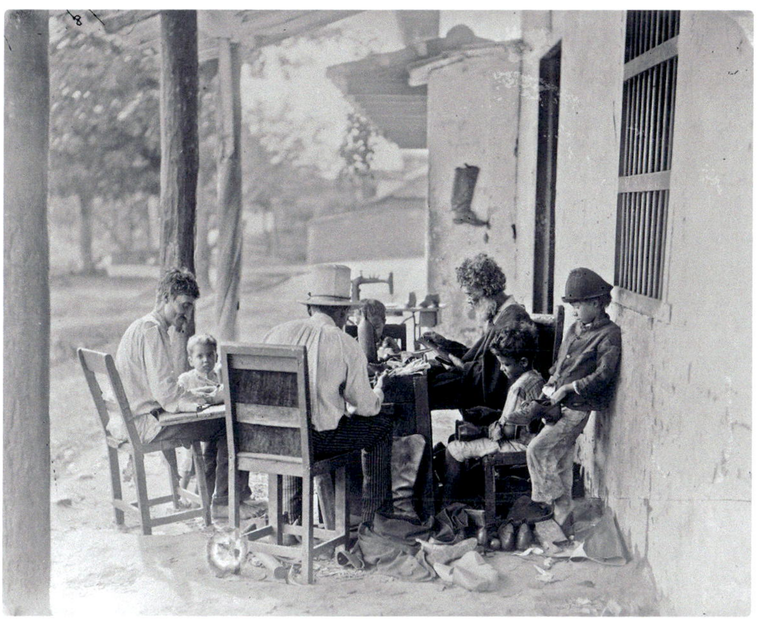

2.7. Fotografía Rodríguez, *Los zapateros*, 1895. Digital positive from gelatin dry plate, 20 × 25 cm. Biblioteca Pública Piloto de Medellín / Archivo fotográfico.

toward the people rather than the landscape, thus creating an image that evokes a romanticized idea of Medellín's lower middle class.

At first glance, the subject of *Los zapateros* seems to go against the Rodríguez brothers' practice, characterized by photographing the elite and promoting a sophisticated, Europeanized vision of Antioquian society. Although the photograph thematizes a different model of the ideal antioqueño, it still underscores the values of the hardworking, family-driven, and business-oriented man promoted by the myth of the Antioquian race. *Los zapateros* was not conceived as a candid documentary photograph. Instead, it was an artwork right from its conception and, within this context, romanticized topics from the working class and peasant culture aligned with the underlying racial ideology. Following the tradition of *costumbrista* painting and literature on the one hand and photographic pictorialism on the other, the Rodríguez brothers created a scene that described a local type, its customs, and environment while employing the visual language of an international photographic movement characterized by its use of soft focus and painterly subjects.

Although paradoxical, cosmopolitanism—presented through the idea of progress and civilization—and *costumbrismo* were two sides of the same ideology. In the same manner that photography needed the negative to produce a positive print, the *raza antioqueña* required *costumbrismo* to define itself. They did not radically oppose each other but worked hand in hand. The *costumbrista* tradition, which was appropriated by photography, particularly in the creation of types, shaped what I call the negative Other: a photographic image that intentionally emphasizes difference and alterity, whether in terms of race, ethnicity, territory, or class. By consciously creating art through photography and aligning their subjects with international trends, the Rodríguez brothers were positioning themselves at the forefront of the ruling classes' tastes, values, beliefs, and, ultimately, the dominant racial ideology that shaped and justified the political, social, and economic status quo of Antioquian society.

Costumbrismo was an important painterly tradition in Spain and Latin America during the nineteenth century. Broadly defined, it aimed to represent the types and customs of society. In Colombia, in particular, painters such as Auguste Le Moyne (1800–1880), José Manuel Groot (1800–1878), and Ramón Torres Méndez (1809–85), among others, created a substantial body of *costumbrista* images that circulated throughout the country during the nineteenth and early twentieth centuries.[16] Although formally diverse, what characterized the pictures were the scenes depicting types, costumes, and the social behavior of the people, often satirically. These paintings represent a radical transformation in Latin American visual arts because they moved away from the fictional space of colonial depictions toward a realm closer to an objective description.[17] They offer a more truthful depiction, closer to a documentary. Although the genre emerged before the invention of photography, it developed parallel to it. Indeed, the understanding of *costumbrismo* was very akin to the seemingly objective features of photography. The Spanish writer Miguel de Unamuno even described it as "the invasion of the photographic minutiae."[18] The idea of copying, rather than inventing, formed part of the subtext of *costumbrista* painterly and literary production. Therefore, the appropriation of the genre in photographs such as *Los zapateros* was accepted without dispute.[19]

As seen in the drawing *Vendedor de tejidos en el mercado de Bogotá* (Textile vendor in Bogotá's market, ca. 1835) by José Manuel Groot and Auguste Le Moyne, one subgenre of *costumbrista* painting was the creation of types that showed the jobs of the depicted subject within their working context (fig. 2.8). As opposed to the decontextualized characters that appeared in other images, the *Vendedor de tejidos* appears on the street, with visible colonial architecture in the background, and the picture includes the props used to construct his selling stand. Including the setting was a particularity of Colombian *costumbrismo,* especially when compared with Ecuadorian or Peruvian genre variants, which tended to present types in a vacuum.[20] Although images depicted some professional activities and crafts, the topic of the shoemaker—that is, the theme of *Los zapateros*—was not central in the painterly tradition of *costumbrismo* in Colombia, perhaps because the use of shoes was not a common practice.[21] This is evident not only in *costumbrista* watercolors but also in the photographs of Benjamín de la Calle, who tried to conceal the bare feet of his sitters by placing props—such as plants and fur—in the foreground of the pictures (fig. 2.9).[22] In this sense, the Rodríguez brothers' photograph was a modern one, signaling the change of a tradition and romantically exalting the work of a little-appreciated craft.

As in *Vendedor de tejidos,* in *Los zapateros,* the space where the men are plays an important role in the image: it describes their profession and environment. The surrounding space was an essential signifier of class and a geographical reference. In 1935, Enrique Echavarría, a chronicler, identified not only the location of the picture but also the figures that appear in it, relating them to Christian iconographies. According to Echavarría, the scene takes place in a shoe workshop sited in a small alley close to La Playa, one of Medellín's most important streets at the time; the Mejía Bridge is identifiable in the background. The main characters in the photograph are Ño Miguel Dulce, on the right, a man whom Echavarría describes as "a sort of Saint Peter, devoted to his work," and the maestro Villamil on the left.[23] In the same text, Echavarría compared and read the photograph as a *cuadro* (picture or painting) more than once, calling it the "famous picture" with which the Rodríguez brothers had "resounding success."[24]

Echavarría's insistence in calling the photograph a *cuadro* points to the will to insert the image into the realm of art, closer to painting or literary tales, than to a personal memento or document. In other words, there was a determination to push the boundaries of the photograph from its previous understanding and elevate its status to that of art. Although a *cuadro de costumbres* or genre scene did not precisely occupy the highest

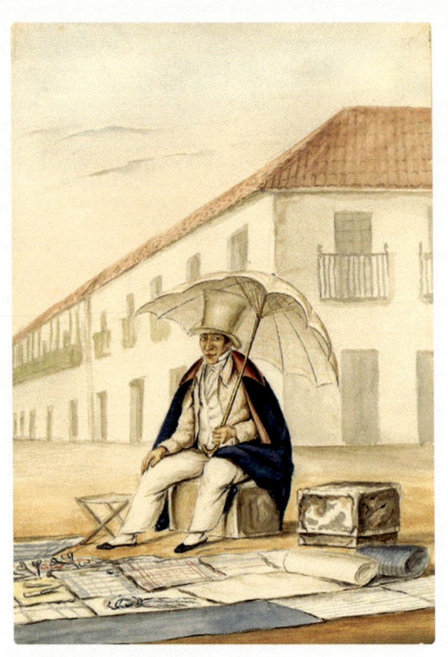

2.8. José Manuel Groot and Auguste Le Moyne (attributed), *Debitant d'étoffes au marché de Bogota / Vendedor de tejidos en el mercado de Bogotá*, ca. 1835. Watercolor on paper, 27.5 × 18.4 cm. Museo Nacional de Colombia, reg. 5502. Photo: Museo Nacional de Colombia / Samuel Monsalve Parra.

2.9. Benjamín de la Calle, *Mariano Hernández and Wife*, 1909. Digital positive from gelatin dry plate, 18 × 13 cm. Biblioteca Pública Piloto de Medellín / Archivo fotográfico.

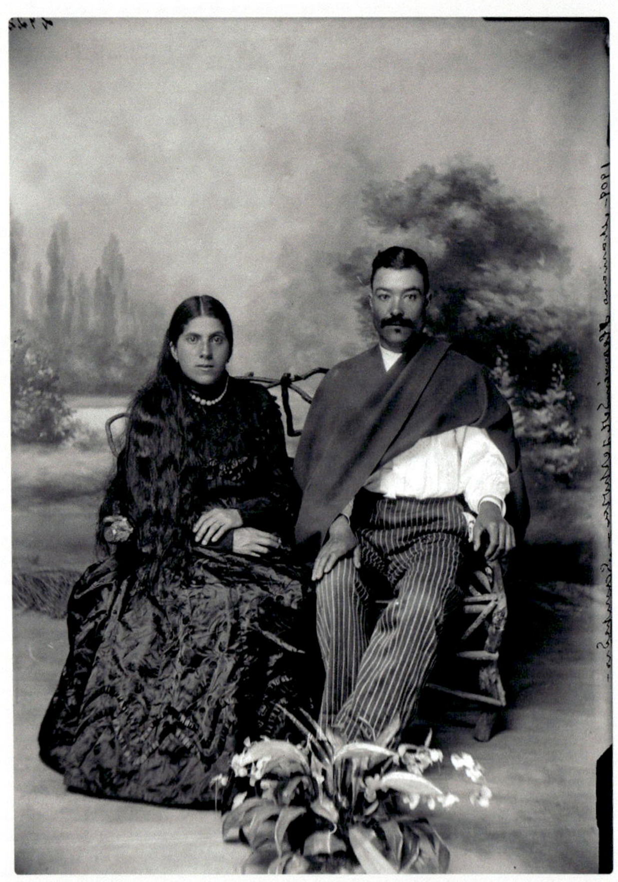

rank in the artistic hierarchy, it still pertained to the traditional pictorial genres.[25] Rather than alluding to the eighteenth-century pictorial tradition that preceded the British allegories discussed above, the Rodríguez brothers looked at *costumbrismo* for inspiration. The romantic, sentimental, and nostalgic scenes depicted in *costumbrista* paintings inspired *Los zapateros*. The photo represents a longing for a simpler, bygone era and an uncomplicated way of life while portraying a scene of working-class labor that aligns with the values of the *raza antioqueña*. Moreover, it fixes the lower-class Other, the negative subject, as a static image to be scrutinized.

Indeed, this classification of the negative Other through the lens of *costumbrismo* circulated widely in photography. However, rather than resorting to pictorial photographic tropes as in *Los zapateros*, most of these photos drew inspiration from *costumbrismo* painting to produce types circulated in the carte de visite form. In these images, the subjects are usually presented with neutral backgrounds, looking directly at the camera and dressed in costumes that relate them to either a racial type or a specific job. This is evident in Wills i Restrepo's cartes de visite of racialized black workers analyzed in chapter 1 (fig. 1.20). While people who identified themselves as white appeared in cartes de visite performing the role of a developing bourgeoise subject, the negative Others were presented as stereotypes emphasizing alterity. Rather than providing identities of particular individuals, type photographs made the subjects recognizable as part of an organized sequence of categories.

In contrast to Europe, where established art academies existed before the invention of photography, in some Latin American countries such as Colombia, the medium developed concurrently with nation-building processes. The Fine Arts Academy was only founded in Colombia in 1886, decades after the arrival of photography in its territories. Photography, invented in 1839, was introduced to Colombia shortly after that when Baron Jean Baptiste Louis Gros (1793–1870) took the first daguerreotypes of Bogotá in the 1840s.[26] Thus, photography became an essential tool in consolidating national identity, democratizing access to images. Despite this, in a highly stratified society, the elite created a set of cultural rules to differentiate themselves from *el pueblo*, the negative Other.

The relationship between painting and photography was even stronger in Medellín, where the first local academy of fine arts opened in 1910. These two mediums were conceived as part of a more extensive understanding of visual production. Although following the French tradition, the limits and boundaries between one medium and the other seemed more flexible. Indeed, several photographers opened their studios with painters as business partners, working together collaboratively. Among them were the Rodríguez brothers, who started their business in collaboration with their cousin, the painter Francisco Antonio Cano, and Ecuadorian photographer Carlos Endara, who worked in Panama with the Colombian painter Epifanio Garay.[27]

Costumbrismo played a significant role in Colombia's painting and literary tradition. The country had a prolific production of *cuadros de costumbres* (sketches of manners), which had artistic and literary connotations. One of the most famous examples is the novel *María* (1867) by Jorge Isaacs, which became a "foundational fiction" and one of the most important literary works of the nineteenth century in Latin America.[28] This book became so popular that people in Medellín reportedly passed a single copy from house to house, soaked in tears from the entire neighborhood.[29] The impact of literary *costumbrismo* in Medellín was enormous, and one of its most prolific writers was Tomás Carrasquilla (1858–1940). Carrasquilla's stories depicted characters that typified the realities of Antioquia, often from the lower and middle classes, and he emphasized his characters' use of local language, customs, and traditions. His most celebrated novel, *Frutos de mi tierra* (Fruits of my land), published in 1896, is considered today one of the best examples of Latin American literary *costumbrismo*.[30] This tendency continued with many authors adopting the realist *costumbrista* style. Their work, including Carrasquilla's, was published in several literary magazines that proliferated in Medellín during the second half of the nineteenth and early twentieth centuries.[31]

Among these magazines was *El Repertorio* (1896–97), an illustrated cultural journal published by the photographer Horacio Marino Rodríguez and the writer Luis de Greiff.[32] One of its aims was the promotion of photogravures, a technique introduced and developed for the first time in Medellín by Horacio Marino and the photographer Rafael Mesa.[33] Including images in a magazine based on the *costumbrista* tradition was an intelligent decision since some literary *cuadros* were more visual than textual. *Cuadros costumbristas* relied on ekphrasis, a verbal description of an image or scene meant to suggest mental visualization and evoke an emotional response.[34] Therefore, inserting images in the magazine reinforced and materialized this practice. Ekphrasis placed language at the service of vision, and the photographs sparked mental visualizations that granted the literary tales an even greater realist effect. In this sense, the magazine was innovative: until then, most artistic and cultural publications in the region had focused solely on literature. Photogravure technology enabled *El Repertorio* to reproduce images like artworks, photographs, and prints, and cover various topics like music, anthropology, engineering, and cartography.[35] Consequently, it is unsurprising to find in *El Repertorio* no. 6 a reproduction of *Los zapateros*, a photograph that aligned with the *costumbrista* literature pieces in the magazine and, by then, had international recognition. *Los zapateros*, like most of the images in *El Repertorio*, did not illustrate an accompanying text. Instead, it was published as an independent piece.

Although charged with artistic aspirations, *Los zapateros* also circulated as a postcard until the second decade of the twentieth century.[36] In the postcard version, the image's title changed to *Zapateros remendones*, emphasizing the act of repairing shoes, and was more a snapshot of rural life than an artwork. The artifice once given to the aesthetic decisions of the photographers was replaced by a sense of repetition and ordinariness, most certainly because of the new form the image acquired. Postcards were the place where photography became mundane and repetitive.[37] Circulating by the thousands worldwide, postcards became a communication medium and a form of visual interchange. However, those images responded to the demands of the masses, who consumed images that followed standardized tropes. The *costumbrista* aspects of the image, the labor scene of a group of poor shoemakers, were regulated through its circulation as a typical genre scene of the third world.

The publication of the same image in different contexts speaks to the clear interest these photographers had in photography's reproductive qualities, and the negative was the technique that allowed for the proliferation of multiple copies. *Los zapateros* first appeared in 1895 in the magazine *Luz y Sombra* (Light and shade)—a periodical published in New York beginning in April 1894 by Maurice G. Gennert and edited by Santiago M. Moreno—and won a silver medal in an international photographic contest promoted by the magazine.[38] *Luz y Sombra* was perhaps one of the first Hispano-American photographic publications directed to a Spanish-speaking public. It was conceived as a photo-scientific magazine but sometimes included art photography from Latin America and elsewhere. The articles focused mainly on improving photographic processes through discoveries in the study of light, optics, reproduction techniques, and chemical procedures.

In the few volumes that have survived, the magazine included two articles written by Horacio Marino in 1897 (the same year he published his book on photography): "Fotomicrografía" (Microphotography) and "Fotozincografía" (Zinc photography). In his article on *fotozincografía*, Rodríguez explained the technique he had developed to reproduce drawings and illustrations for newspapers or books through a photographic process that did not require a camera or any complicated procedure. Both articles sought to explain—to a larger photographic community—the techniques to amplify and reproduce photography using less equipment and expensive materials. They also draw attention to the lack of supplies available in Latin America and the photographic creativity that, despite difficulties, allowed for artistic invention.[39] Once again, this is evidence of the importance these photographers placed on the negative, photography's reproductive technique par excellence. The Colombian photographer was more interested in finding means to reproduce and disseminate the images—one of photography's most important features—than in creating unique positive copies. Indeed, many of the pictorial effects created by the Rodríguez brothers were performed on the negatives, thus permitting the reproduction of the artistic interventions.

Luz y Sombra was extensively distributed. Gennert had agents in Spain, Cuba, Puerto Rico, Santo Domingo, Curaçao, Mexico, El Salvador, Nicaragua, Venezuela, Chile, Peru, Ecuador, Bolivia, Uruguay, Argentina, and Colombia. With over fifteen agents in Mexico, eight in Cuba, and ten in Colombia, these countries made up the centers of a photographic network. The agents in Colombia, among them Aristides Ariza and Quintilio Gavassa, were recognized photographers.[40] The ubiquity of the magazine evidenced the connections between practitioners around the Western Hemisphere and the transnational character of the photographic practice. It also showed how Hispano-American photographers were active proponents of new theories and inventions and not only recipients of Eurocentric ideas and techniques.

Los zapateros won the second prize in the contest promoted by *Luz y Sombra* in July 1895.[41] The first prize went to the Valleto brothers, two Mexican photographers active in Mexico City, who also dedicated their work to documenting the elite class in their country and practiced *costumbrismo* through photography. Indeed, the winning picture was also described as a "*cuadro de costumbres*," pointing again to the ubiquity of this imagery within the Latin American photographic world.[42] While the repercussion of the award was relatively small for the Mexicans, the Colombians turned the prize into one of their most significant achievements.[43] *Los zapateros* became an emblematic image that intended to place the medium in the realm of art and thus within the hegemonic cultural sphere.[44]

Los zapateros was a photograph that held great artistic value due to its appropriation of the *costumbrista* tradition of painting and its reference to the international movement of pictorial photography, although it never fully aligned with it. In contrast to other Latin American photographers, like the Peruvian Juan Manuel Figueroa Aznar, who did not create photographs with artistic intention, the Rodríguez brothers embraced this aspect of the photographic practice.[45] In this sense, their work is more similar to that of Martín Chambi, an exception among Cusqueño photographers of the time, but it is unclear if the Rodríguez brothers were familiar with his work. However, the formal elements of the Rodríguez brothers' practice are more reminiscent of European pictorialism, specifically the work of Peter Henry Emerson, who utilized selective focus to imitate natural vision—a technique also used in *Los zapateros*. The photograph's relatively early date reaffirms this connection with European photography, which served as a reference for cultural production in Latin America.[46]

In terms of content, *Los zapateros* resonates with the pastoral scenes staged by Emerson, who, preoccupied with the rise of industrialization and tourism, documented Britain's people and landscape in his East Anglian series. But it also invites a parallel with the photographs of the *indigenistas* in Peru, even if their conceptual intentions were far removed. Figueroa Aznar took staged photos of idealized Indigenous types, theatrical groups, and self-portraits where he represented himself as part of the Cusco bohemian scene. He documented a constructed artifice of identity, regardless of who he was photographing. For him, as for other *indigenistas*, photography was a means to imagine new identities and not a medium used to represent or express them.[47] In a way similar to that of *costumbrismo* in Colombia, the *indigenistas* were taking elements from foreign styles to construct a new local avant-garde language that responded specifically to their context. Although there is no evidence that the Rodríguez brothers knew of Emerson's or the *indigenistas*' work, the images speak to an international interest in representing traditional rural occupations and local types through pictorial photography. Another case worth mentioning is the Spanish photographer José Ortiz Echague (1886–1980), who created a vast body of photographic work from traditional Spanish types and costumes utilizing the pictorial style.[48] Therefore, it begs the question: Why was there a need to document traditional types and costumes in a relatively conservative way precisely at the moment of industrial and economic development? Why was there an impulse to preserve a subject of the past by the turn of the century?

The Rodríguez brothers produced other less famous but equally provocative compositions in which the dichotomy between traditional pictorial photography and *costumbrismo* emerges. Photographs such as *Arrieros en Palacé* (Muleteers on Palacé, ca. 1905, fig. 2.10) deploy the scene of three muleteers posing with a group of oxen in the middle of Palacé Street, a road that led to the central market of the city. Although the formal qualities of the picture—such as the sharp focus and frontal composition—differ from those of *Los zapateros,* the image still refers to the tension between the progressive desire fostered by the discourse of the Antioquian race and the *costumbrista,* more nostalgic, environment. Although seemingly contradictory, *costumbrismo* and cosmopolitanism were two sides of a larger project that aimed to discipline and define the nation while maintaining a local spirit. Through the documentation and categorization of the negative Other, the subjects in power could define themselves against these constructed identities traversed by racial and class characterizations. By making these subjects art—through a nostalgic and stylized presentation—they were patronized and thus disciplined, allowing the new liberal and presumably more progressive subjects, which in many cases were the photographers themselves, to reign and impose a gaze that supported the whitening discourse promoted by the elite. The *cuadro de costumbres* was ultimately a child of the Enlightenment in Europe and the incipient development of the scientific discourse in Latin America; it was the precursor of the ethnographic project, which led to the eugenic practices discussed in chapter 1.

Pictorial photography stresses the formal qualities of the pictures. Exploiting the material aspects of the image as part of the rhetoric to frame photography as an art form, pictorialists argued that photography's creative process was analogous to those of any other medium. The pre-

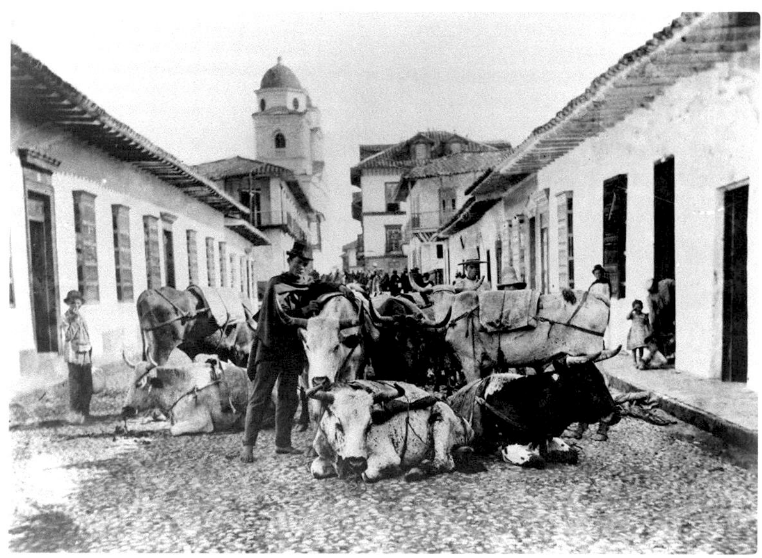

2.10. Fotografía Rodríguez, *Arrieros en Palacé*, 1905. Digital positive from gelatin dry plate, 13 × 18 cm. Biblioteca Pública Piloto de Medellín / Archivo fotográfico.

occupation with the material characteristics of the negatives was key in the technical research pursued by Horacio Marino, who sought to achieve images of the highest standards and new ways to reproduce them. This is clear in the articles he published in *Luz y Sombra*. However, Horacio Marino's intentions differ drastically from one of the main characteristics of hegemonic pictorialism: the use of intricate and elaborate photographic processes, such as gum bichromate or gum bromoil, which favored the creation of unique copies. Rodríguez's interests pointed precisely in the opposite direction.

Establishing a distance from local roots was common in Latin America's nineteenth-century cultural sphere. It intended to raise the worth of local cultural production to equal that of the dominant one. However, this line of thought was a "misplaced idea," to quote Roberto Schwarz's analysis of the phenomenon.[49] The Rodríguez brothers deliberately hoped to emulate European models, but they were creating their own in their attempts to imitate a different culture. As seen here, some of their photographs not only drew upon the hegemonic conception of art photography but also appropriated the local tradition of *costumbrista* painting, thus creating a new local style that ultimately established itself as the new role model for the region. This also happened in other Latin American regions. In Peru, for example, *indigenismo* as a vanguard movement embraced such contradictions: on the one hand, they subscribed to the ideal of an avant-garde while simultaneously rejecting the languages of abstraction and modernity that constituted its European version. As stated by Poole, "Far from being a carbon copy (much less, an imperialist imposition) of European modernism, indigenismo was deliberately an iconoclastic pastiche of philosophical, aesthetic, and discursive borrowings."[50] Although pictures such as *Los zapateros* incorporated *costumbrista* and pictorial photography characteristics, they proposed a new subject that was purposefully local and spoke to the specific realities that the antioqueños experienced at the turn of the century. The romanticized scene of the shoemakers visualized, idyllically, the nostalgia for the handmade object in a moment of industrial transformation (especially in the textile industry) and exalted the artisanal labor force to which the photographers also belonged.

The negative in photography enabled its reproducibility and portability, facilitating the widespread circulation of images and the convergence of various visual languages. The negative allowed for the creation of the most popular forms of photography by the end of the nineteenth century, including cartes de visite, stereographs, and postcards, which were widespread across the globe. The exchange, circulation, and consumption of these images allowed, for example, a person from Medellín to understand how the French or Egyptians would represent themselves or their imaginaries. They could also absorb the geographical description of places that, thus far, were only available through drawings, prints, or literary tales. Most importantly, it permitted the now more knowledgeable spectator to decide which aspects, forms, and symbols of a given cultural identity to highlight or resist, when, and why.[51] *Los zapateros*, as well as the other images analyzed in this chapter, materialize precisely this phenomenon: the emergence of a new visual language that borrowed something from the dominant European cultural sphere, as well as something from the local, historically rooted milieu, to construct the visual representation of themselves. These photographs became the bearers of the solid ideological discourse reflected in the myth of *la raza antioqueña*. Just as a photographic print required a negative, *costumbrismo* was necessary to create a positive image of the *raza antioqueña*.

From Hope to Work

One of the most emblematic pictures by the Rodríguez workshop is *El ángel de la esperanza* (The angel of hope), taken in 1909 (fig. 2.11). The picture depicts a lumberjack sitting in the middle of a theatrically staged forest. The man holds an ax in his right hand and leans his head on his left one. Behind him appears the ghostly figure of an angel. The winged character lays a hand on the man's head, looks up, and points the other hand at the heavens. Intense rays of light coming from the upper left section of the picture hit the angel's face directly. With blocks of chopped wood scattered on the right side, the spectator witnesses a private moment of spiritual force, changing the destiny of a harried soul.

El ángel de la esperanza was first intended as an artistic photograph. It depicts a tableau that conveys an allegorical Christian message—namely that of the guardian angel—and testifies to the photographer's mastery of the medium. *El ángel de la esperanza* is a double exposure, a process in which two photographs are taken, one after the other, on the same negative plate. The picture of the angel was taken with a shorter exposure time to create the ghostly figure, while for the sitter the photographer used the regular time length necessary to capture a clear image. In Medellín, such photographic tricks were a complete innovation. If photography had hitherto been conceived as a machine-made product, images such as *El ángel de la esperanza* challenged that understanding of the medium. On the one hand, this picture alluded to the iconography of painting; on the other, it could not be the work of an amateur photographer.

In a society ruled by Catholic beliefs, the representation of such an iconic figure through photography must have enhanced the spiritual convictions of its spectators. However, this photograph was the creation of photographers whose family had been firmly aligned with spiritualist practices.[52] Indeed, the Rodríguez family had previously gone through a difficult moment when the ecclesiastical authorities excommunicated them for practicing spiritualism. In the Medellín of the time, excommunication also meant a lack of work because the clergy advised potential clients not to support the services provided by anyone not a member of the Catholic Church. Melitón's mother, Mercedes Márquez, was the most famous medium in the city, and his father, Melitón Rodríguez Roldán, had direct links with spiritualism, a common practice among the radical liberals.[53] Texts such as Allan Kardec's *The Spirits' Book* were translated

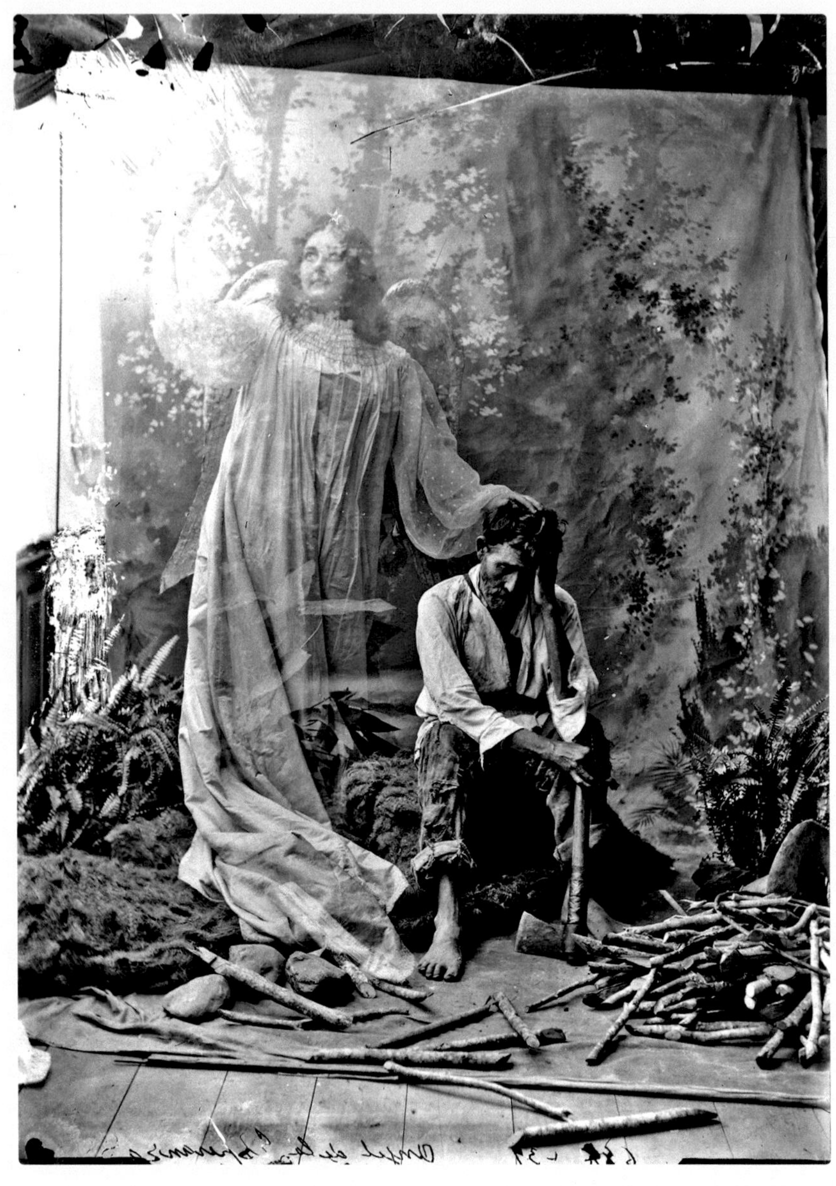

2.11. Fotografía Rodríguez, *El ángel de la esperanza*, 1909. Digital positive from gelatin dry plate, 25 × 20 cm. Biblioteca Pública Piloto de Medellín / Archivo fotográfico.

into Spanish and published in Medellín by Velásquez y Compañía in the 1870s, evidencing the growing interest in the field. It is unclear if all members of the Rodríguez family were practicing spiritualists, a practice in which photography played a significant role. When *El ángel de la esperanza* was taken, Melitón and his brother had distanced themselves from spiritualism. And yet the photo linked them back to the practice.

Indeed, when this picture was conceived, spirit photography had become a commercial success in Europe and the United States. In 1861, American engraver and photographer William H. Mumler discovered a way to include in the portraits of his sitters the ghostly appearance of another person.[54] The growing interest in spiritualism in the United States contributed to the photographer's success in the business and increased the proliferation of photographer-mediums across the globe. Frederick Hudson in England and Édouard Isidore Buguet in France emerged as spirit photographers during the 1870s.[55] The practice flourished, especially during or following periods of war, in which families and victims would accept anything to establish a connection with their loved ones. The discourse surrounding spirit photography was close to scientific photography, in which the medium's ability to capture the invisible was used to convey truths that were not visible to the naked eye.

Unlike the spirit photographs created abroad, Melitón's picture did not attempt to prove the existence of recently departed loved ones, nor did it intend to deceive the spectator. Rather, by creating a metaphorical relationship between religion and photography, it aimed to underscore both Catholic beliefs and aesthetic experience without abandoning the reference to his family's spiritualist ties. By doing so, he changed the then-negative connotations of spiritualism to the positive ones promoted by the Catholic Church. Just as in photography, the negative could be easily turned into positive. *El ángel de la esperanza* appropriated the standard representation of sacred subjects such as the guardian angel, an iconic figure profusely depicted in baroque and Renaissance paintings and common in printed media.[56] Melitón sought, like many other photographers of his time, to emphasize the material manifestations of the unseen, exploiting a shared visual vocabulary of mass-produced religious imagery. In Colombia, the guardian angel was a popular figure, especially among children, who prayed to him every night before going to bed. In *El ángel de la esperanza,* the photographer opted for a popular subject well known by his viewers and thus engaged an immediacy of spiritual commitment.

In opposition to other pictorialists who created similar effects by juxtaposing two or more scenes onto the positive print, Melitón chose a picture in which the whole scene was fixed on a single negative plate. When one inspects the image closely, it is possible to tell that the rays of light coming from the top left were created through manual intervention, such as scratching the plate or painting over it using a technique similar to the one employed in the background of *Emilia Obregón*. However, none of these interventions are visible on the final negative kept in the archives, leading me to speculate that the photograph was created from two different negatives and then rephotographed onto a single negative plate, which is the one he ultimately kept. This final negative plate served to reproduce the image in other contexts.

In 1912, the same photograph was published in a journal called *Avanti*—"to move forward" in Italian—a title that referred to the idea of progress. In this version, *El ángel de la esperanza* had transformed into *El ángel del trabajo* (The angel of work), a description that better suited its new printed context. Although it was the same photograph, this time, its reading was linked to one of the *raza antioqueña*'s most central ideological features: the hardworking man protected by his faithful devotion to God. If there were an iconic image of the Antioquian race, it would be a combination of a white working man, Catholic beliefs, and the antioqueños' progressive attitude. In *El ángel del trabajo*, the attention given to the angel in the previous version of the photograph shifts to the man. Here, the inferior quality of the reproduction de-emphasized the artifice created by the photographer, directing the attention to the subject itself. The new title also signaled a shift from a purely religious to a more functionalist image. Taking advantage of photography's polysemic characteristics, the magazine editors changed its title. They noted that "considering the absence of a more appropriate name, we have given it [the title of] *El Angel del Trabajo* [*sic*], which is, in our opinion, the one that most closely approaches the beautiful ideal it represents."[57] The morality of the *raza antioqueña* was so firmly embedded in the mentality of the intellectual elite that the title chosen to describe Melitón's photograph reflected this already naturalized mentality.

Avanti was a magazine that captured the Antioquian ideological race discourse in different ways. First, the design of the magazine, particularly the modern font used in its title, spoke to the progressive discourse embedded in the title itself. Second, the use of an Italian word—beyond its meaning—capitalized on the idea that Europe was an essential reference point. Third, the magazine contents grouped articles on culture and industry, which were ultimately signs of progress and civilization. The magazine included, for example, two texts written by Horacio Marino Rodríguez on the characteristics of cement and its industry; interviews with famous actresses of the time accompanied by pictures; notes related to women's fashion and behaviors; and photographs to be collected by the enthusiast readers, among others. Tellingly, the first photograph of the *Avanti* collection was a photograph of the Amagá railway station in Medellín, a symbol of progress. The caption next to the picture read, "The Amagá Railway is, despite its defects and the ill-will that many bear towards it, a work of high civilization, demonstrating that alcohol and other ills have not yet succeeded in completely destroying the energies of the Antioquian race."[58] Ironically, the photographer was Benjamín de la Calle, precisely the man whose work challenged these readings. In the course of three years, from 1909 to 1912, the meaning of *El ángel de la esperanza* shifted from a religious and aesthetically challenging reading to one that represented the ideology of a discourse based on race, progress, and civilization. The imprint of this image on a negative plate permitted precisely this divergence.

Embodying Faith

In the vast number of photographs constituting the Rodríguez archive, the subject of women posing as virginal Madonnas appears repeatedly. The most striking of them is a half-body shot of a woman whose hair is covered with a drape while she holds a flower bouquet in her hands (fig. 2.12). She looks like—or indeed, she embodies—the figure of the Virgin Mary. The photograph is as solemn as it can be. Besides the symbolic function of the flowers—lilies are associated with the Virgin in Christian iconography—and the drape, the traditional clothing of the Madonna, there are no other props in this picture. The woman is in a completely abstract and neutral space, making the image ahistorical. The theatricality that distinguishes all the other photographs analyzed hitherto is emphasized in this picture solely through the pose and the gaze, not through a plethora of objects or a particular backdrop. The simple frontal shot, the positioning of her hands in front of her chest, and—above all—the

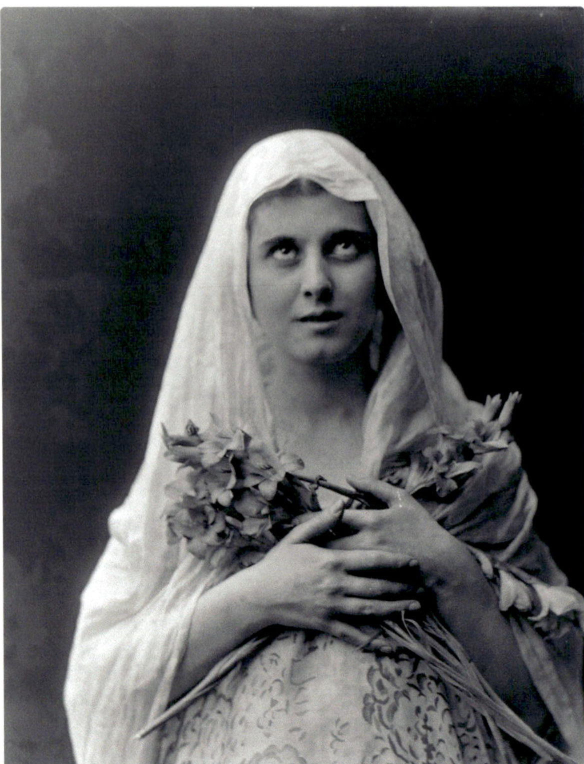

2.12. Fotografía Rodríguez, *Untitled*, n.d. Digital positive from gelatin dry plate, 25 × 20 cm. Biblioteca Pública Piloto de Medellín / Archivo fotográfico.

penetrating gaze directed skyward convey devotion. It recalls the familiar iconography of the Virgin Mary in common depictions of Renaissance and baroque art.

The picture is larger than most of Melitón's portraits and has no title. This was not a common practice for the photographer because, even in his untitled pictures, he usually wrote the sitter's name on the negative. It seems that Melitón intended to establish this photograph as a religious icon, so there was no need to identify the sitter. Indeed, it can be argued that by not linking it to a particular person, the photographer intentionally drew attention to the Virgin. Therefore, the photograph was not conceived as a representation of the Virgin Mary (i.e., someone posing as the Virgin Mary) but as the image of the Virgin Mary herself. The photograph was meant to work in the same way as pictorial religious imagery: it was an image whose potential function was to be worshiped, and thus, the real-life referent had to be removed. During the nineteenth century, religious faith was a significant motivation for photographers, as the medium rendered visually and thus made real that which the eye could not see. In a world increasingly dominated by science, religion was scrutinized and its doctrines questioned by a growing community who saw in material and scientific evidence a verifiable, accountable, and objective explanation of the world.

This positivist perspective was supported and further enhanced by the publication of Darwin's *On the Origin of Species* in 1859. The very existence of God was questioned when scientist Thomas Henry Huxley coined the term *agnosticism* in 1869. However, religious beliefs did not seem to have decreased in an era of growing secularism. Instead, science was increasingly used to prove the existence of that which the eye could not see.[59] Religion and science were, in some aspects, completely intertwined, and photography played a crucial role in promoting Christian beliefs (which needed a boost in an increasingly secularized period) and supporting scientific discourse.

In Colombia, the debates around faith and religion between 1850 and 1930 went back and forth. They moved between the most liberal lines of thought, from the constitution of 1863 (considered "the most anticlerical" in the country's history) to a highly conservative one of Catholic orientation, instituted in 1886 with the Regeneración project.[60] The first marked the birth of a federal state led by radical liberals, which considerably reduced the authority of the Church: they secularized education and separated the power of the state and the Church.[61] However, radical liberalism lost control in 1880, and in 1886 a new constitution, which was in force until 1991, was instituted. This new Magna Carta centralized the state and returned power to the clergy, and Colombia was officially declared a Catholic country. The Church recovered control over the educational system and had a special fiscal regime.

Catholicism was more deeply rooted in Antioquia than in the rest of the country. It flourished even during periods of radical liberalism. The limited economic impact of the Church on the department and the active involvement of many families in religious life (many members of traditional families were nuns and priests) might partially explain such a situation.[62] In 1864, during the very period when Colombia experienced its most radical liberal moment, the conservative Pedro Justo Berrío was appointed governor of Antioquia. He adjusted the anticlerical reforms to preserve the education system imparted by the Church in Antioquia—an action that seemed to reinforce Catholicism in the region.[63] Tellingly, by 1928, in a census performed by the government, 99 percent of the population declared themselves Catholic.[64]

The Virgin Mary was a role model for women. After the dogma of the Immaculate Conception proclaimed in 1854, the idea of being chaste and maternal determined how women should behave. They were supposed to follow an angelic path, a life of hidden desires and innumerable prohibitions.[65] The role played by women was fundamental in the moral and religious discourse of churchmen. They became their best allies because women, through their motherhood role, introduced the Christian discourse into family values. In other words, the Church not only exploited formal institutions, such as schools and universities, to propagate pious beliefs but also saw to the internalization of a moralizing discourse. As a result, religion was a domestic activity. In exchange for their evangelizing role, women gained the status of "queens of the house," again, an idea related to the symbol of the Virgin Mary, since she was the "queen of heaven."[66] The identification of women with the Virgin was ubiquitous; it was imposed not only by the Church and the educational system but also by the deeply embedded cultural values circulated in the etiquette manuals of the time and other publications. Anything that deviated from this was considered negative behavior.

Familia cristiana (Christian family), a journal published from 1906 to 1932, was one of the leading media to disseminate these ideas. It was a magazine created by the Jesuit order, a community that played a determining role in the educational system and in forming the larger Catholic cultural sphere. Its target audience was middle- and upper-class women who were expected to be mothers and housewives. The magazine's discourse centered on the creation of "a woman archetype," a woman subdued to a man but redeemed through her role as a "good mother" and her imitation of the Virgin Mary.[67] Considering this, it is no surprise to find so many photographs of women performing the role of the Virgin or other saints with which they felt identified to reinforce an identity considered positive. In pictures such as *Carlina Duque* and *María Olorsaga* (figs. 2.13 and 2.14), the women do not embody the Virgin Mary as in the first photograph examined in this section, but they do align with the standard representation of a white, pure, innocent, and chaste woman, which ultimately was what the Virgin represented and what they were conditioned to imitate.

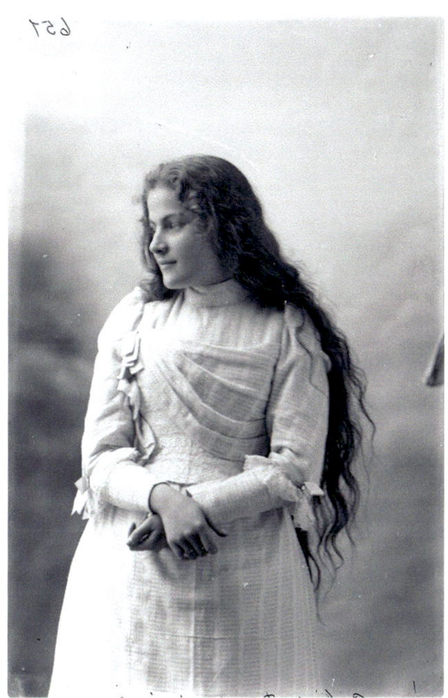

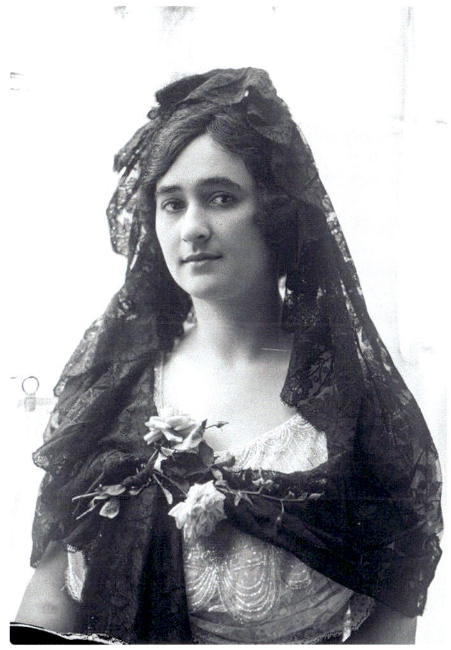

2.13. Fotografía Rodríguez, *Carlina Duque*, ca. 1890s. Digital positive from gelatin dry plate, 18 × 13 cm. Biblioteca Pública Piloto de Medellín / Archivo fotográfico.

2.14. Fotografía Rodríguez, *María Olorsaga*, n.d. Digital positive from gelatin dry plate, 18 × 13 cm. Biblioteca Pública Piloto de Medellín / Archivo fotográfico.

Other images, such as *Elena Uribe* (fig. 2.15), were more theatrical. Elena posed as the Virgin Mary at the foot of the cross or as Mary Magdalene, a figure usually portrayed as a penitent beside the cross. In this photograph—unlike the one of the Virgin or even those of *Carlina Duque* and *María Olorsaga*—the artifice was more obvious. The lack of a convincing background, the cross standing on a covered pedestal, and the exaggerated pose presented the image as a deliberate simulacrum, an artificial reality to which the turn-of-the-century viewer was accustomed.[68]

While photography opened a space for women to challenge moral impositions—as seen, for example, in the photograph of a self-confident female sitting in a stage-prop crescent moon (fig. 2.16)—the picture of *Elena Uribe* functioned more as an icon: it remained in the sphere of devotional representation. This picture did not confront the moralizing racial discourse; on the contrary, it supported and enhanced it through a

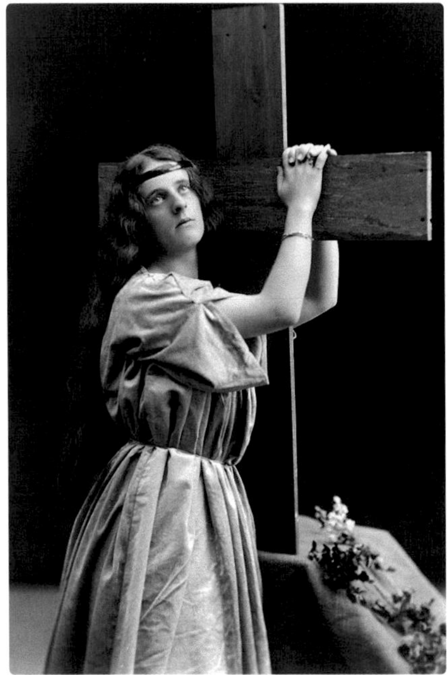

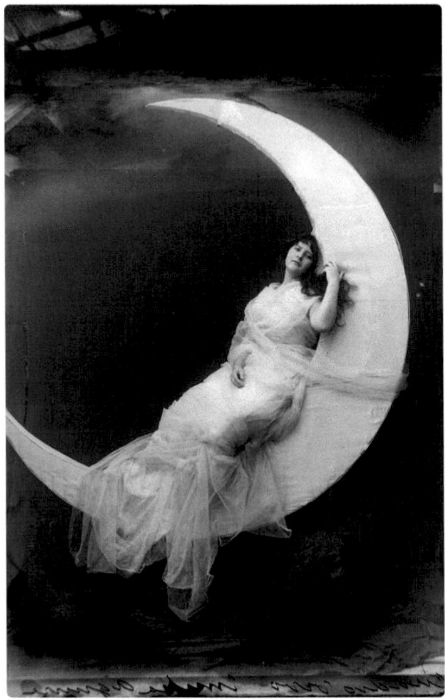

2.15. Fotografía Rodríguez, *Elena Uribe*, 1910. Digital positive from gelatin dry plate, 18 × 13 cm. Biblioteca Pública Piloto de Medellín / Archivo fotográfico.

2.16. Fotografía Rodríguez, *Emilia Aguirre*, 1915. Digital positive from gelatin dry plate, 20 × 15 cm. Biblioteca Pública Piloto de Medellín / Archivo fotográfico.

medium that supposedly reinforced objectivity and truthfulness—even in its extreme artificiality.

Catholic values were part of, and to some degree essential to, the modernization process in Medellín. As opposed to secularization in other parts of the country and Latin America, in Medellín, religion opened a space that, although extreme in its conservatism, permitted the integration of social classes in spaces such as the Church, religious associations, and charities.[69] Religion was so embedded in the cultural behavior of the Antioquian society that it created a social order that shared similar consumption patterns and, more importantly, the same ideology around the Antioquian race. As a result, the region grew economically and technically but not socially, culturally, or politically, a process that some historians have called "traditional modernization."[70] Photographs such as that of the Virgin enact this apparent contradiction: they depict and support traditional Christian values using modern technology that permits the wide-scale dissemination of such images.

The new medium had understandable advantages over the painting tradition, which was still embedded in academic rules. Photography provided a space to escape, at least to some degree, the stiffness of the academic style. Indeed, Melitón's decision to embrace religious imagery through photography did not distance him from his attempts to communicate the same through painting. Still, his photographs conveyed more strongly the professed faith. In an untitled picture, he painted the head of a Virgin covered with a white cloth and holding her hands together in prayer. The palette's colors appear dirty, lacking brightness, and the image seems to be painted with thick impasto. He depicted the creases of the Virgin's girdle and cloth, and the borders defining the figure, very sharply, delineating the figures with a thick line. The painting struggled between the academic tradition and a more modern style, strongly rejected at the time in Colombia.[71] It failed to convey the sweetness and tenderness usually associated with the Virgin Mary. Instead, the photographic version of the same topic was compelling. The Virgin appeared in a state of grace, easily transmitted to the pious spectator.

If, in scientific terms, photography was "the pencil of nature," here it enacted "the pencil of God."[72] The photograph appeared with no title or author; the light acted by itself to create an extremely devotional image. In its negative version, the light had further consequences: the Virgin appears when one places the glass plate against it (fig. 2.17). It is a ghostly, spiritual image that evokes a mystical and transcendent experience that could only be conveyed through light. Not coincidentally, God was represented as light and, in this case, light created the image. In this sense, photography was the perfect medium to invest the image with a spiritual aura that the photographer could not convey through painting.

As opposed to other pictorial photographers, such as Julia Margaret Cameron and F. Holland Day, who also engaged with religious imagery during the nineteenth century, Melitón's depictions affirm his daily life. He did not generate nostalgic images, nor did they emerge as part of a religious revival. Rather, his photographs were a response to his context and a reflection of a society immersed in a robust ideological discourse, which showed in speech, in text, and visually. This image became a privileged site for materializing proof of Christianity's truthfulness, ultimately one of the bases of the *raza antioqueña* myth. Melitón's religious

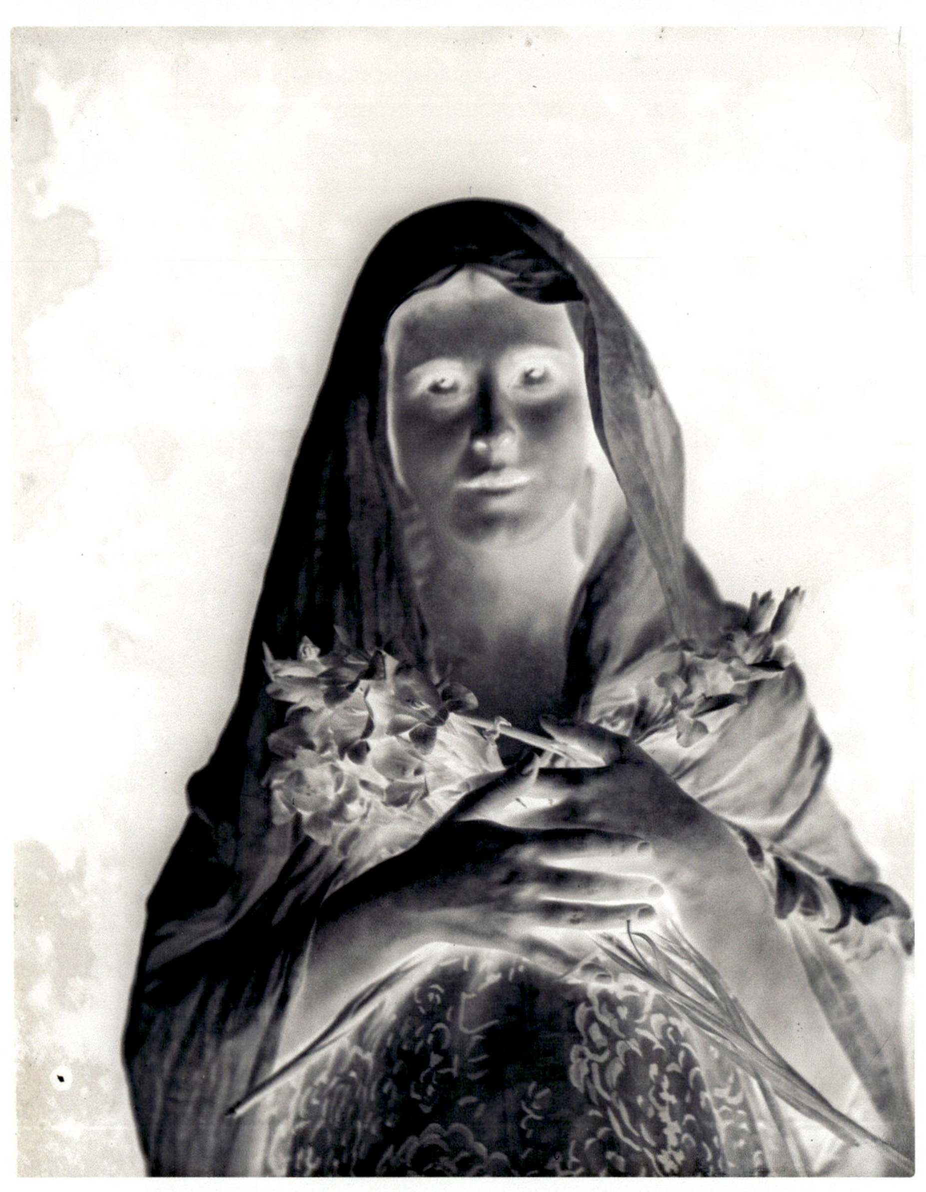

2.17. Fotografía Rodríguez, *Untitled*, n.d. Gelatin dry plate, 25 × 20 cm. Biblioteca Pública Piloto de Medellín / Archivo fotográfico.

photographs reflect his controlled production of the image to explain morality and its fictive grasp of the body, particularly the female one.

Liberating Spaces: Photography's Theatricality

Women who performed roles that transgressed the norms of behavior assigned to them in Marian terms were seen as negative subjects. The theatrical space of photography allowed women to challenge the extreme constraints of their daily life. Even if only for the time of the shot, posing allowed women to perform uncharacteristically. Using excessive makeup, flamboyant dresses, and costumes and adopting explicitly seductive attitudes were only possible in the space of theatricality. Posing became an opportunity to exaggerate the performative dimension of the self, which derived precisely from the censorship women suffered. If chastity, submission, and compliance were the female ideals of their real world, they were, to a certain extent, challenged in the photographic space. As in the photographic negative, reproduction—at the time considered the female's primary function—was taken to a secondary level, opening a space to explore other aspects of female identity that tried to relate their personas with different aspirations.

During the nineteenth and early twentieth centuries in Medellín, upper- and middle-class women were expected to speak little and be modest, educated, and discreet. They had to hide the fact that they were driven and determined.[73] Although by the 1910s the codes were somewhat more flexible than those of the previous century, women were still disciplined if their behavior in public deviated from the norm. In 1912, *Avanti* magazine published an article titled "La señorita de la calle" (The woman of the street). The anonymous author described some behavioral directives that single women had to follow in public. For example, the author stated, "the single lady has to avoid being noticed, both on the street and in the different places where she passes by" or "she must proscribe any untimely manifestation of exuberance," meaning that women should not speak out loud, cry, or even laugh freely.[74] Although the author pointed out that during that historical moment women had more liberties than in previous times, he explicitly stated that "a serious man would never accept as a wife a lady who, without being completely committed, had allowed criticism to take advantage of her."[75] Marriage was the ultimate goal of young women because it opened a different reality that, although still restrictive, gave them a slightly more liberal space. If deviations from the strict rules prevented women from marrying, those rules would be followed as rigorously as possible. Ultimately, the patriarchal values were as strong as they had been in the past century, and the conservative, Catholic, and male-driven morale of the Antioquian race still dictated women's bodies, spaces, and behaviors. Women were viewed as primarily responsible for reproduction, just as the photographic negative is responsible for producing an image.

On the photographic stage, women could be spontaneous and transgressive, attributes seen as negative traits by conservative groups if shown in public.[76] This might partly explain the proliferation of photographs like *Emilia Aguirre*, where women posed and assumed different characters, which they would not perform in actual life situations (fig. 2.16). The evident lack of this type of portrait with men as sitters speaks to the imbalances of a society in which women had to behave in one specific way, with any deviation from the rule publicly punished through social embarrassment and moral sanction. Thus, photography became a fruitful space for exploring a different world, where the female body could assume other roles, including a more open exploration of their sexuality.

Emilia Aguirre is a clear indication of the new space photography was opening up for women. In the picture, she lies wrapped in a tulle fabric in the curve of a monumental crescent moon, posing seductively. Although most of her body is fully covered, her pose—particularly the gesture she performs with her left hand holding her dark, loose hair—invests the image with a seductive character, a prohibited behavior outside photography's theatrical space. The explicit artificiality of these images allowed the sitters to explore other aspects of their bodies and a multiplicity of identities, which became real in the photographic studio. Barthes noted this transformation of the body when he stated, "I constitute myself in the process of 'posing,' I instantaneously make another body of myself, I transform myself in advance into an image."[77] In this phrase, Barthes points to three key results of the confrontation with the camera: the consciousness of the self, the transformation of identity, and the process of becoming an image. This is precisely what is happening in the photograph of Emilia Aguirre. But the exaggerated pose is also an indication of a desire to be seen, to force the gaze of the other, to force a discourse.[78]

As Sylvia Molloy argues about the homosexual pose, which applies to this case study as well, "the fin-de-siècle pose problematizes gender, its formulation and its boundaries, subverting classifications, questioning reproductive models, proposing new modes of identification based on the recognition of a desire rather than on cultural pacts, inviting to (playing at) new identities."[79]

These photographs created in the studio deploy the tensions between the concepts of the *corps* and the corpus, as identified by Christopher Pinney.[80] In *Camera Lucida*, Barthes stated that "in the Photograph, the event is never transcended for the sake of something else: the Photograph always leads the corpus I need back to the body I see; it is the absolute Particular, the sovereign Contingency, matte and somehow stupid, the This (this photograph, and not Photography)."[81] In other words, the photograph always takes us back to what was standing in front of it, the "this was there," the sovereign contingency of the *corps*. In the case of *Emilia Aguirre*, the photograph only points to the event: she posed in front of the camera, wrapped in tulle fabric, on a monumental moon. This is what is indexed on the negative plate. However, the broader narrative of the photographic corpus (the thing that the sitter or the beholder imagines the photograph to do, and adheres to it using strategies that escape the image) operates here in a creative way. By playing a different role, the sitter was not imitating someone else's character but building her own and rendering it present.[82] In this sense, the pose and the performativity in photography's theatricality became empowering tools for women.

The relationship between the performance for the camera and the theatrical one was very close. Before the proliferation of a society of the spectacle, where the many forms of entertainment accessible to the modern public emerged, people in Medellín complained of boredom.[83] In this still relatively small and reclusive city in the middle of the Andes, there was no entertainment—no World Fairs, museums, panoramas, or other spectacles often linked to technological advancements. However, there were other forms of amusement grounded in popular local expressions—such as cockfights and boxing, horse rides, dancing balls, and musical presentations. In this context, the emergence of theater as a leading form of entertainment was a crucial aspect in forming dramatic narrative art and creating more complex characters personified by actors and actresses. Although for most of the nineteenth century women could not perform on the theatrical stage, and men had to play both male and female roles, by the end of the century that changed.[84] These were, however, scarce roles and, in many cases, female actors were associated with liberal lifestyles that went against the conservative values of the Antioquian elite, thus making such roles inappropriate for most women.[85] In other words, women who performed them were seen as negative subjects. Therefore, most actresses who became celebrities in Medellín at the time were foreign women who did not follow the expectations of the Antioquian racial discourse. These more liberal women performed unreservedly, freely showing their characters and bodies to a primarily male public.[86]

The admiration of the local male counterparts toward the foreign actresses might have fostered the desire of local women to identify with the foreign divas. Thus, photography became a safe space to perform and relate to these unorthodox role models. In a two-dimensional mimetic representation, further distanced by the translation of the performance into a static picture and thus not seen live, women could enact other aspects of their personalities and live fantastical roles, often forbidden to them in real life. There was also a paradoxical turn regarding identification: if, in real life, women were expected to identify with the role of the Virgin, in the photographic theatrical space, the role of the diva or any other liberating subjectivity could easily replace that identification. Photography permitted the displacement of an imposed identity toward one created under their own terms, thus constructing a new subjectivity invested in the visual.[87] In other words, they could perform the role of the negative Other without any social sanctions.

But like the negative/positive principle in photography, this had two intimately connected perspectives. On the one side, the liberating space of photography permitted the emancipation of female identities; on the other, these images fostered an increased objectification of those bodies, thus standardizing the notions of beauty to which women had to subscribe. Hence, there is collusion between the subject and her objectification. The photographic negative, the matrix of a reproducible commodity easy to circulate, contributed not only to the fetishism of the female body but also to patriarchy and the fetishism of the photographic object itself. As Abigail Solomon-Godeau stated, women's "self-worth and social value [were] contingent on [their] status as object of desire" to the point that the male gaze was so internalized "as to produce a near total identification with it."[88] That is to say that, although photography opened a liberating space, women were, in many cases, the ones that voluntarily subscribed to the traditional roles assigned to them. Moreover, even when a liberating window opened, their roles contributed to objectifying their bodies to please the male spectator.

But the theatrical aspect of photography was not limited to the exploration of female identities. It was indeed a space that opened the possibilities of experimentation within the medium. The aim of the pictures was not to deceive; instead, from the outset, they were theatrical fictions where illusions and visual tricks made photographic realism even more appealing. Commercial photographers highly valued these images, because amateur photographers could not take them with the already popular Kodak cameras.[89] To complete the depicted illusion, photographers sometimes had to perform complex tricks to create the desired image. The simplest technique was cutting and pasting parts of different negatives to produce a new image to be rephotographed. Other strategies were more complex and implied using multiple exposures, masking devices, and precise aligning techniques to reproduce the same person several times in a single image or to include different scenes in the same print.[90]

Scenes such as the one depicted in a photograph of Pablo Echavarría Echavarría taken in 1906 were extremely popular in photographic practice across the globe (fig. 2.18). In this crime scene picture, the shooter and the victim are the same person. In other words, the sitter is his doppelgänger. Echavarría appears simultaneously as the assassin holding a gun and the dead body lying on the floor. This type of trick photograph was called a duplex or polypose picture. Melitón used the double exposure technique to create the illusory scene, dividing the composition horizontally in two. Although the result is quite convincing, the photographer had to manipulate the negative by hand-painting part of the dead body's left knee, which appeared initially fragmented, to create the seamless illusion of the finished picture. He also added the blood by retouching the negative.

Echavarría was an influential member of the Antioquian elite. He, along with other colleagues and family members, founded two of the country's most successful textile manufacturing companies: Fabricato in 1903 and Coltejer in 1907. He was also a founding member of the Sociedad de Mejoras Públicas (Urban Improvement Society) in Medellín and a board member of the Ferrocarril de Antioquia (Antioquian Railway)—a major enterprise for the region, founded in 1914.[91] Considering his privileged status, it is no surprise that Echavarría's portrait aligns with

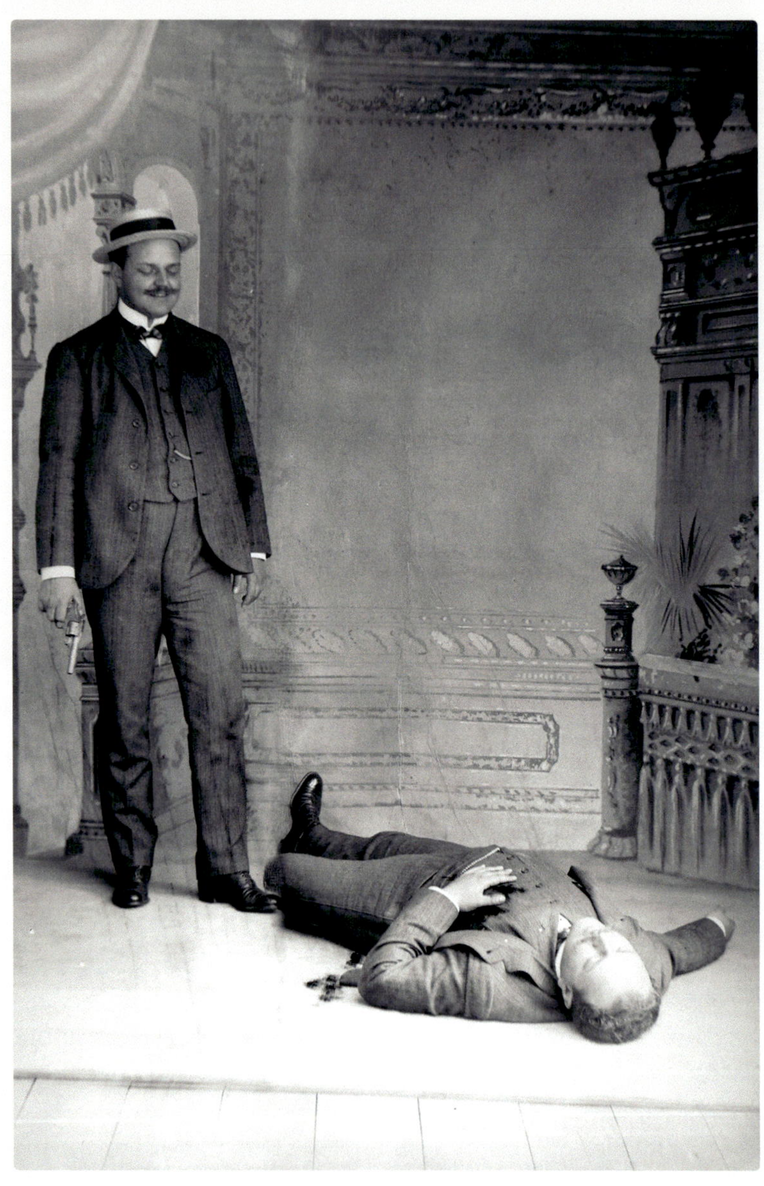

2.18. Fotografía Rodríguez, *Pablo Echavarría Echavarría*, 1906. Digital positive from gelatin dry plate, 18 × 13 cm. Biblioteca Pública Piloto de Medellín / Archivo fotográfico.

a type of picture popular in European and North American photography. Representing Echavarría using the latest trends was a strategy to position himself within the realm of hegemonic culture. It was an approach that played favorably on both sides: the Rodríguez brothers' studio aligned itself with international photographic trends, while Echavarría adopted a unique image that proclaimed his authority in a symbolic, even cynical, way. If Echavarría was to lose his position of power, only himself—his doppelgänger—the empowered subject could do it. The control remained in the hands of the same subject.

In Melitón's photograph, Echavarría is simultaneously dead and alive, a trick that speaks to the medium's understanding as a binary mediation between past and present, life and death, negative and positive. The imminent condition of photography is that of becoming history, of being always part of the past and therefore always acknowledging its subjects' future death. In photographing something, there is an embedded claim to immortality, a fact that Echavarría seemed to understand early on. Seen through photographs, people become icons of themselves, and their portraits are reflections on their mortality. As Barthes continuously reminds us in his book *Camera Lucida*, death is the eidos of photography. Barthes wrote about the sense of death when being photographed since, for an instant, the subject becomes an object.[92] However, there is also the imminent realization that any photographed subject will eventually die and thus become part of history. There is a paradoxical aspect in portrait photography: on the one hand, it makes someone's absence visible by transforming it into an iconic presence, and on the other, when the portrayed person dies, its meaning changes to represent absence.[93] In Melitón's photograph of Echavarría's murder scene, the spectator is confronted with both scenarios simultaneously, thus making that symbolic exchange, in a single image, a continuous one.

Trick photography appealed to famous personalities across the globe because it was an original way to present themselves. The Latin American elite quickly adopted these strategies, as seen, for example, in the portrait of writer Lucio V. Mansilla by the Argentinian photographer Alejandro Witcomb.[94] In one of his most celebrated images, the photographer presents Mansilla reproduced several times, forming a circle with the repetition of the sitter's body. Utilizing mirrors and other technical strategies, Witcomb created a unique portrait that aligned the Argentinian writer with the latest technological amusements. Another example of distinctive polypose pictures made in Latin America is *Los 30 Valerios* (The 30 Valerios). Brazilian photographer Valerio Vieira constructed a concert scene where he appears thirty times, each as a different character: waiter, pianist, audience member, and even painted subject. In 1904 this image won Vieira a silver medal at the St. Louis Purchase Exposition, signaling once more not only the connections between photographers and audiences across the Americas but also the dominant models of visualization emerging beyond the cultural centers. Photographers and sitters alike were part of a global network of valuation and desire that developed on a broader scale and was not constrained to the hegemonic centers.

The theatrical space of photography introduced new forms of visualization and opened up a space for exploring alternate identities and subjectivities. The bodies of both sitters and observers transformed, becoming components of a new regime of visuality. In other words, the elite found an explicitly differentiated way of picturing itself. The manipulation of the negative was fundamental in creating these complex photographs. Working within the naturalized discourse of the Antioquian race, these pictures became novel forms of knowledge and power operating directly on the bodies of the individuals. The photographic stage became a space where behaviors considered negative elsewhere could be performed.

Cupid's Arrow

The work of the Rodríguez brothers, chiefly of the younger Melitón, is a paradigm of how photography was instrumental in constructing a hegemonic cultural discourse in the context of Medellín. This construction is exploited as forms of differentiation: racial identity, religion, gender issues, public performance, the exoticization of the Other, and the appropriation of international artistic trends. Although the Rodríguezes were not from an elite family, their efforts to provide the upper class with an image of themselves gained them access to it. Even if sometimes one finds images and attitudes intended to challenge the *raza antioqueña* discourse, the truth is these photographs were an integral part of it. The aesthetic agenda manifested through their high-quality photographic production—which could easily compete with the most recognized international photographers in the dominant cultural centers—became a reflection of the tastes, values, and beliefs of the *raza antioqueña*. The negative played a fundamental role here. It was the material and symbolic source for constructing the Antioquian race discourse. Creating a negative Other was as important as the negative plates used to create differences through pictorial photography.

The role photography played in visualizing this racial discourse was determinant as it developed parallel to painting. In some instances, there seemed to be no distinction between the two media, as exemplified in a review from 1892 in the newspaper *El Espectador*. In an article supposedly dedicated to a painting exhibition, the anonymous author highlights the photographs of the Rodríguez studio and omits painting. He wrote, "With close attention, we dedicate ourselves to the study of the works exhibited, and we are pleased to say that in the middle of so much artistic beauty, the photographs sent by our friends Rodríguez y Jaramillo, owners of the best photographic establishment in the country, stood out."[95] The fact that they were first trained as painters and not photographers might have also played an important role in understanding their production within the realm of art. They were described as "not only skilled in the art of photography but accomplished artists, with the exquisite taste exhibited in their commissioned work."[96]

Sara Mejía's portrait (fig. 2.19) encapsulates many of the issues discussed thus far. The photograph portrays a young white woman pierced by an arrow that Cupid places in her heart. A naked, genderless child standing on her lap represents the god of love, and his arrow, according to the Greek myth, should fill her with uncontrollable desire. Cupid's attributes were delicately hand-painted on the negative plate: the wings, the arrows, and the bow on the left side of the picture. Not only is the photograph an exquisite example of pictorial photography created in the middle of the Andes early in the twentieth century, but it also places at the forefront the photographers' awareness of international trends, in particular the work of Julia Margaret Cameron and painters such as William-Adolphe Bouguereau, whose pictures might have served as inspiration to the photographer.

This photograph uses aesthetic elements to map whiteness onto antioqueños' daily life by appropriating popular European imagery. Sara Mejía's photo particularly recalls the work of William-Adolphe Bouguereau, a well-recognized painter in Parisian academic circles whose work has been deemed an example of extreme conservatism.[97] His pictures were also desirable among the higher social classes of the United

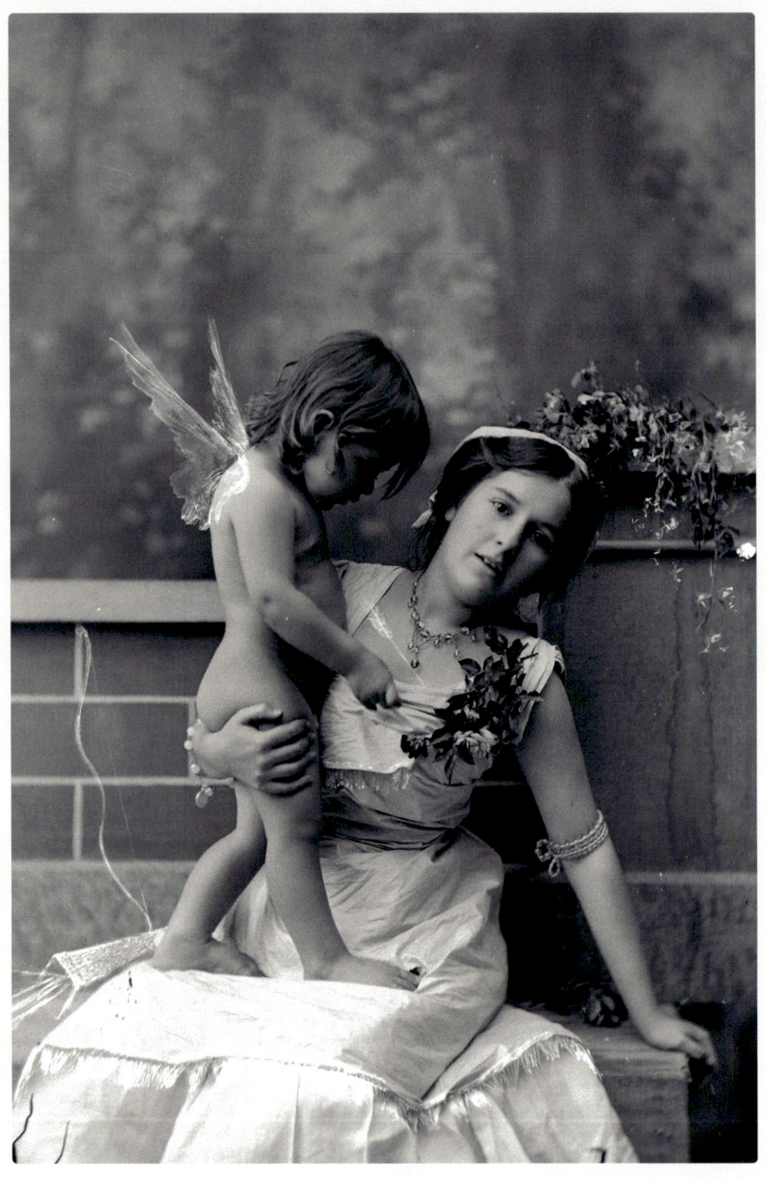

2.19. Fotografía Rodríguez, *Sara Mejía*, 1910. Digital positive from gelatin dry plate, 20 × 15 cm. Biblioteca Pública Piloto de Medellín / Archivo fotográfico.

States' Gilded Age and other European countries and massively reproduced through print media, which allowed for their international recognition.[98] Considering the conservative values of Antioquian society and its interest in relating itself to a wider cosmopolitan society, it is no surprise that the Rodríguez brothers were using Bouguereau's art for inspiration. These pictures introduced them and their clients to an international circle of image production that connected them to whiteness via European mythological themes and a shared visual aesthetic.

Moreover, as previously discussed, Sara Mejía's portrait is also an allegory, a common practice at the turn of the century. In this portrait, however, the allegorical aspect of the picture did not refer to the nation or a historical moment. Instead, it emphasized identification with a classical past and, thus, with a Western and white cultural tradition. The photograph also stressed gender roles and the *raza antioqueña*'s morality. It makes evident the passive attitude that women were required to maintain, even when filled with uncontrollable feelings. Sexual desire, however, is placed not on the adult woman but on the genderless child who opens the upper part of her dress and directs the gaze toward her breasts, thus emphasizing the patriarchal values so vigorously promoted by the myth of the *raza antioqueña*.

In this chapter, through a detailed analysis of their pictorial photographs, I have demonstrated how the Rodríguez brothers employed both pictorialism and negative techniques to bolster the racial ideology of *la raza antioqueña*. The objects themselves reveal the centrality of negatives for producing the photographs' pictorial effects, ultimately leading to the creation of images that reflected the tastes and consumption patterns of Medellín's higher social class. But the negative did not only play a central role as the material basis of pictorialism. It was also understood symbolically. Some of the Rodríguez brothers' photographs tended to aestheticize subaltern subjects, whether through *costumbrista* scenes or depictions of women in theatrical scenarios. These othered subjects were seen and understood as negative subjects—people considered less civilized and less cultured—and therefore subject to appropriation to strengthen, through difference, the construction of an ideal Antioquian type. In this chapter, I have revealed how this racial ideology conveyed notions of superiority in complex ways that transcended the mere skin color of the subjects, thereby adding layers of complexity to conventional understandings of whiteness.

CHAPTER THREE

The Negative in Suspense

DEVIANT SUBJECTS AND BODIES IN THE WORK OF BENJAMÍN DE LA CALLE

IN PREVIOUS CHAPTERS, I addressed the notion of the negative from a material and symbolic perspective. In this one, the notion of the negative will take a different form. As explained in the introduction, the negative is also a way of metaphorically speaking about subaltern subjectivities, traditionally regarded as deviant bodies, particularly in Latin America's late nineteenth century. These nonconforming subjectivities challenge binary categorizations, such as negative/positive. Therefore, in this chapter, the notion of the negative as a singular and discrete category is suspended.

The negative is understood here as an ambivalent entity, such as the image produced by a daguerreotype, which is simultaneously positive and negative.[1] Although I am not dealing with nonbinary images, since the photos analyzed here were made using the glass plate negative/positive process, ambivalences of gender are visualized through different strategies that aim at representing, positively, bodies that have traditionally appeared as negative subjects. If we understand the negative as a transparent object subject to reversal, then the images analyzed here materialize that idea. With this in mind, in this chapter, I analyze a group of photographs created by Benjamín de la Calle in which such ambivalences become apparent.

One of de la Calle's earliest photographs in which such a reversal occurs is a picture taken in 1897, in which a black woman appears confronting the spectator. Her name was María Anselma Restrepo (fig. 3.1).

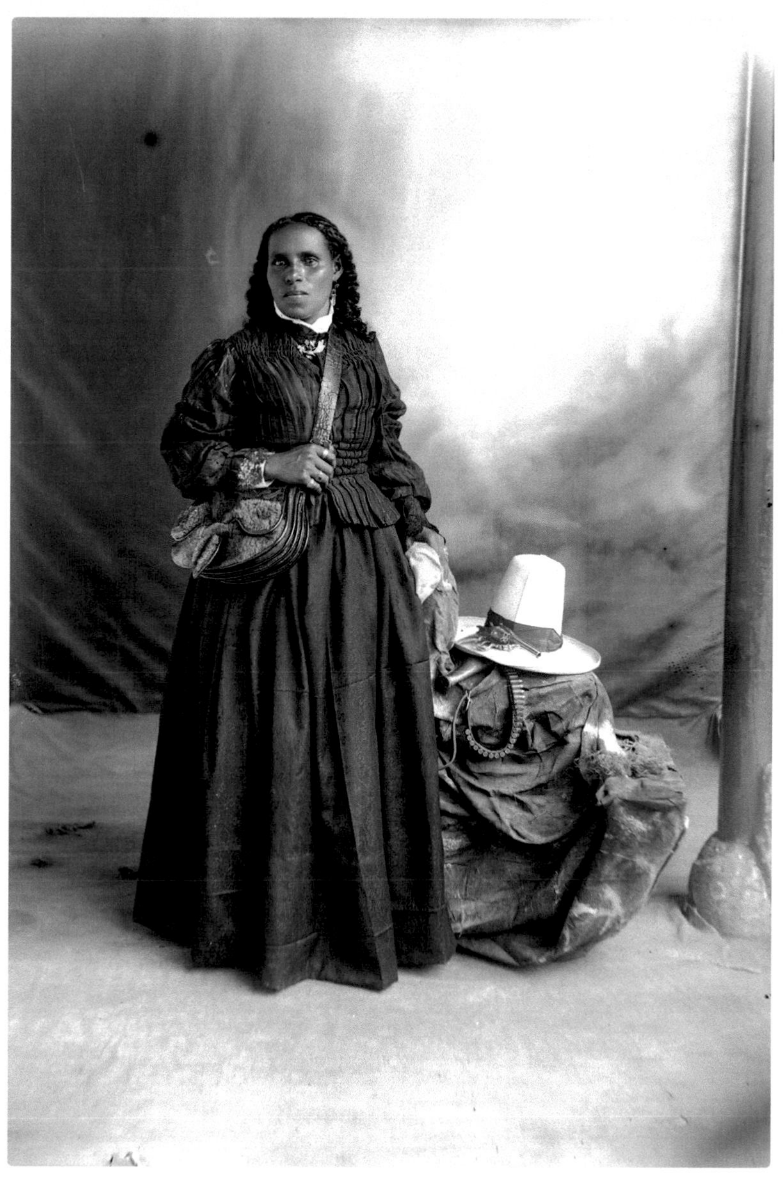

3.1. Benjamín de la Calle, *María Anselma Restrepo*, 1897. Digital positive from gelatin dry plate, 18 × 13 cm. Biblioteca Pública Piloto de Medellín / Archivo fotográfico.

In the picture, she stands next to a covered studio prop upon which lies a hat, a revolver, and an ammunition strap. Her clothes suggest contradictory gender conventions: while the long black dress expresses femininity, the *carriel* purse is an accessory typically used by male peasants in the Antioquia region.[2] These peculiar characteristics, paired with the photograph's early date, draw immediate attention, particularly when considering the deeply conservative and patriarchal context in which the portrait was taken. Compared with the stereotypical representations of women that followed normative gender roles, as seen in most of the images by the Rodríguez brothers, this photograph brings to the fore the rather rare but equally valid positions that women had assumed by the end of the nineteenth century.

Similarly, during the first decades of the twentieth century, de la Calle took pictures of men wearing women's clothing. In a picture dated 1927, a man named Emilio Sierra wears a lace dress partly covered by a silk vest, a belt with a big, elaborate metal buckle, stockings, and a feathered headpiece (fig. 3.2). He sits on a wooden chair, touching his chin delicately with his right hand while holding a fan with the left one. The elaborate outfit seems more like a costume than the quotidian clothes a woman in Medellín would wear during that period. He does not gaze directedly toward the camera but to the left, outside the picture frame. These photographs, like the others that are analyzed in this chapter, pose several questions regarding the meaning of cross-dressing and the different readings and implications fostered by such a decision. In this chapter, I mainly explore how the photographs of cross-dressed people operate in late nineteenth- and early twentieth-century Colombia. The readings that emerge are based not only on the context in which the cross-dressing act takes place but also on the sitter's gender, class, and race.

Although many of de la Calle's pictures challenged racist discourses, especially the rhetoric of the *raza antioqueña*, other photographs aligned with it. As a photographer who did not belong to a privileged family and identified with the disenfranchised, de la Calle in his images portrayed a vision of commonality that embraced difference and equality, and sometimes suggested self-identification with his sitters. As in the images of María Anselma Restrepo and Emilio Sierra, his photographs claimed an identity that differed radically from stereotypes. His deliberate decision to represent alternative and marginal identities in a positive light is fundamental to his role as a photographer. However, he simultaneously

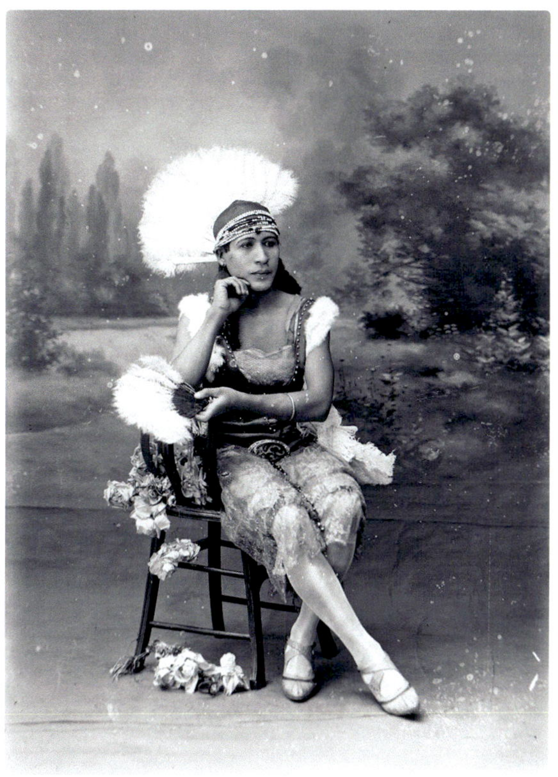

3.2. Benjamín de la Calle, *Emilio Sierra S.*, 1927. Digital positive from gelatin dry plate, 18 × 13 cm. Biblioteca Pública Piloto de Medellín / Archivo fotográfico.

worked for the police and other governmental institutions, documented executions, and took pictures of ostracized subjects used for repressive purposes. These images speak about the photographer's ambivalence, his role as a respected picture maker in a very conservative society, and the negotiations he had to make to survive in his profession.

The question of representation is critical, driving the means for creating meaning and culture in a specific society.[3] This motivation also translates into a question of power: Who should be represented and how? Who has access to the images and the tools required to produce them to give sense to the world one inhabits? De la Calle's photography works as a counterstrategy in the politics of representation established by the elites and solidified by the hegemonic cultural sphere in Colombia. The idea of representing difference is at the core of his photographic practice and is frequently elicited by the ambiguous nature of the images, their inherently queer nature, and their lack of documentation.

This chapter examines a selection of de la Calle's photographs in which questions about gender, representation, visibility, and power dynamics are at the forefront. Unlike the exoticization and typification of people who defy stereotypes, some sitters in de la Calle's photographs are independent subjects who look back at their beholders and challenge preconceived definitions of reality. Other photographs of his operate within the conventional repressive systems that were in place during that time. This chapter analyzes de la Calle's photography with particular attention to gender issues and how they can be understood through the ambivalence of a nonbinary image, that is, through images that escape the negative/positive opposition, not because they are not based on the binary photographic process but due to how the subjects are represented. De la Calle's photographs and the multiple identities he represented complicate the construction of the *raza antioqueña*; in some instances, they reveal his disagreement with this idea in favor of a more affective expression of regional identity, and in others, they align with it. His photographs also complicate the notion of the negative as a repressed Other since, as mentioned before, they present negative subjects in positive ways.

Militant Antioquia: María Anselma Restrepo, the Black *guerrillera*

Popularly known as the "*guerrillera* from Santa Rosa de Osos," María Anselma Restrepo's photograph has become an icon within de la Calle's production.[4] The photograph not only predates by at least a decade the famous photographs of *soldaderas* and female captains taken during the Mexican Revolution but also challenges stereotypical representations of female roles and black identities during the nineteenth century in Latin America.[5] The dark tone of Restrepo's skin and the ambiguity of her gender identity provoke questions not only regarding race and gender stereotypes but also about class distinctions. The discrimination against people of color, the marginalization of women, and the strict categorization of social classes were not discrete components of the Antioquian race discourse. On the contrary, they went hand in hand. The myth of the *raza antioqueña* was defined by its hypermasculinity, the representation of women in Mariological terms, and an emphasis on its white European past. De la Calle's photograph presents an individual that destabilizes the discourse in many of its foundational pillars, thus becoming an icon of the counterstrategies of visualization. In this sense, the image of María Anselma Restrepo embodies the notion of the positive Other, as opposed to the negative subaltern identity linked to black people.

The photograph is an aspirational portrait. In other words, it is an image intended to fulfill the sitter's desire to assume a role that she could hardly embody in real life. Thus far, there is no documentation of the sitter besides the picture itself. Restrepo's portrait relies on the symbolic connotations of the props included in the photograph—the hat, ammunition, revolver, and the *carriel*—to convey the idea that she was an active participant in one of the many wars fought in Colombia during the nineteenth century.[6] The deliberate inclusion of these elements in the picture presents a woman defying gender conventions. The props are signifiers not only of her aspirational role as a soldier but also of masculinity. However, why would a female sitter want to portray herself as a self-possessed and confident combatant?

One first possible answer to this question relates to both the photographer's and María Anselma's desire to challenge society's imposed gender roles. As stated in chapter 2, during this period, women were expected to assume private and domestic roles, take care of children, and abstain from participating in the public and political sphere. Just as photography was characterized by an opposition of binaries (negative/positive process), femininity was defined in opposition to something else, that is, masculinity. While men inhabited the public space, women were relegated to the domestic one. Men were supposed to go to war when called to do so, and women were supposed to stay at home and take care of the family that longed for and awaited the return of the male fighters. War was indeed a common situation during this period; it almost became an everyday activity. Since the nation's independence in 1810, Colombia's history can be summarized as a continuous war for power between the conservative and the liberal parties. Although we believe that the role of women during the nineteenth-century wars was relatively restricted, some documentation indicates that some actively participated in the war effort. These numbers increased as the nineteenth century progressed. By the time of the Guerra de los Mil Días (Thousand Days' War, 1899–1902)—the most deadly conflict since the birth of the nation and the one that led to the loss of Panama—the participation of women had increased dramatically, even if they mainly performed supporting roles of a medical and administrative nature.[7] Some of these women, however, became members of the revolutionary forces: they went to the battlefield and even ascended the military ranks to become captains.[8] Women who became part of the fighting troops have historically been called Juanas, a name most likely inspired by the figure of Joan of Arc.

Among the most renowned of those female figures was María Martínez de Nisser, a woman from Sonsón, Antioquia, who fought in the Guerra de los Supremos in 1841.[9] She convinced her family that actively fighting in the war was a political commitment and enlisted as a soldier, cutting her hair and changing her clothes for a man's uniform.[10] It is reasonable to think that the role of Martínez de Nisser might have motivated other women from Antioquia to join the troops or at least triggered a desire to do so. Her legacy was widely disseminated through public recognition and her writings. During her involvement in the war, she wrote a diary titled *Diario de los sucesos de la revolución en la provincia de Antioquia en los años de 1840 i 41* (Diary of the events of the revolution in the Province of Antioquia in 1840 and '41), printed in book format in 1843.[11]

Her participation in the war was publicly condemned, and she was called a prostitute for exposing her body in the public sphere.[12] During the patriarchal nineteenth century, when a man volunteered to serve the nation, he was a leader who offered his intellectual capacities to the public realm, but when a woman volunteered to do the same, she was simply offering her body for public display.[13] In other cases, women who participated heroically in the war were presented as selfless individuals who sacrificed themselves in the name of love for their husbands, fathers, or even the nation. In these narratives, beyond affective motivations, women seemed to have no serious political or social interests, much less personal commitment. Martínez de Nisser's book, one of the first written by a woman in Colombia, became not only a tool to fight the misogynist condemnations of women but also a document that could inspire other women to do the same. With the public documentation of a strong example of a woman from Antioquia who actively participated in the war, it is feasible to believe that such a model existed in the imaginary of women in the region and may have thus inspired portraits such as Restrepo's.

There is little visual documentation describing the role of women during the turn-of-the-century wars. One of the few identified representations is a painting titled *Soldados marchando* (Soldiers marching) by the little-known artist Eladio Rubio (fig. 3.3). The picture, dated 1902,

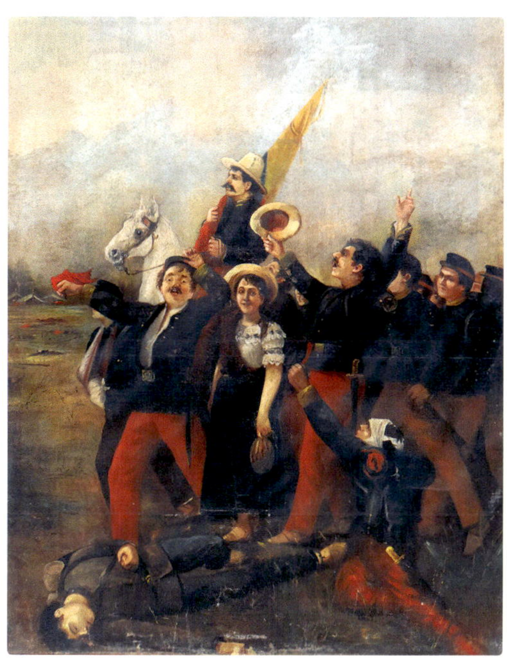

3.3. Eladio Rubio, *Soldados marchando*, 1902. Oil on canvas. Museo histórico Casa de la Cultura, Marinilla, Antioquia.

presumably depicts a scene from the Guerra de los Mil Días. It represents not war itself but a group of conservative soldiers simultaneously celebrating the victory and drama of the armed conflict. At the center of the composition appear three men: one on a white horse proudly carrying the national flag, and two standing in the foreground raising their hands in triumph. In the bottom section, there is an injured man requesting help and a dead soldier. Between the standing men is the figure of a woman who, although at the center of the composition, does not draw the beholder's attention immediately. She wears a typical *campesina* costume: a black skirt, white blouse, and espadrilles. Her hair is braided, and she carries a canteen in her left hand.

The inclusion of a female figure in one of the few existing paintings of the Guerra de los Mil Días suggests the active presence of women during the war.[14] Although the role they played was usually of a supporting kind, working as spies or messengers, or carrying water or ammunition, women had an unacknowledged presence during the revolution. The nature of their jobs was critical, even if their labor was covert or invisible, just as the woman in Rubio's painting is hidden in the composition (and title), yet actually in plain view. Other historical documents, such as the sketchbook by soldier-artist Peregrino Rivera Arce during the Guerra de los Mil Días, depict women accompanying the liberal campaign (fig. 3.4). Rivera Arce, however, limits his role to portraying the *cholas*—another name given to the women who had active roles during the war—rather than depicting them engaged in the revolution.[15] Perhaps the best-known representations of women during the nineteenth-century wars are the battle paintings by José María Espinosa, known as the *pintor abanderado* (soldier-painter) for his role as both painter and active soldier during the Campaña del Sur (1813–16), a series of military actions led by Antonio Nariño to stop the royalist troops in the country's south.[16] Espinosa did not paint on the battlefield but later during his life, beginning in 1845, although the exact dates are uncertain.[17] He created eight paintings depicting the confrontations between the patriots and the Spanish troops. Interestingly, the paintings do not portray just the war but also the landscape, the locations, and the many individuals that played a role during bellicose confrontations, including women. Indeed, female figures appear in three of the paintings: *Batalla de Calibío*, *Batalla de Tacines*, and *Batalla de los ejidos de Pasto* (fig. 3.5). In all three, women appear playing an auxiliary role: helping injured men or carrying water and munitions.[18]

De la Calle's photograph does not align with these visual representations. He presents an armed, empowered woman, suggesting an active role and not a supportive one such as those depicted in the paintings and drawings mentioned above. In that sense, de la Calle's portrait is closer to early twentieth-century depictions of female soldiers, such as the photographs of *soldaderas* and captains of the Zapatista Revolution in Mexico or the pictures of armed women in Brazil, such as Maria Bonita.[19] The close relationship between these later depictions and de la Calle's photograph can be read as a fulfillment of the sitter's desires. Although there is a geotemporal distance between the Mexican and Brazilian pictures and de la Calle's photograph of Restrepo, the comparison acknowledges the soldier embodiment that the Colombians were trying to convey with the picture. For example, in a studio photograph of Coronel Amparo Salgado taken by Mexican photographer Sara Castrejón in 1911, we see the revolutionary woman soldier posing with a carbine, a pistol, and cartridge belts while wearing a delicate flower dress (fig. 3.6).[20] As opposed to other women who posed with carbines as a simple trope, we know Salgado led men and women of the revolutionary troops. She was undoubtedly an

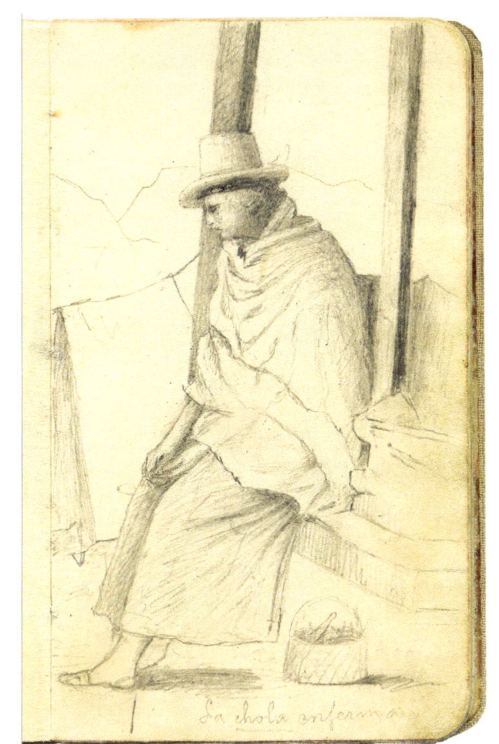

3.4. Peregrino Rivera Arce, *La chola enferma*. In *Recuerdos de campaña*, 1900. Pencil on paper, 16.5 × 10.5 × 1.3 cm. Museo Nacional de Colombia, reg. 3355, p. 37. Photo: Museo Nacional de Colombia / Samuel Monsalve Parra.

3.5. José María Espinosa, *Batalla de los ejidos de Pasto*, ca. 1850. Oil on canvas, 80 × 120 cm. Museo Nacional de Colombia, reg. 2515. Photo: Museo Nacional de Colombia / Ernesto Monsalve.

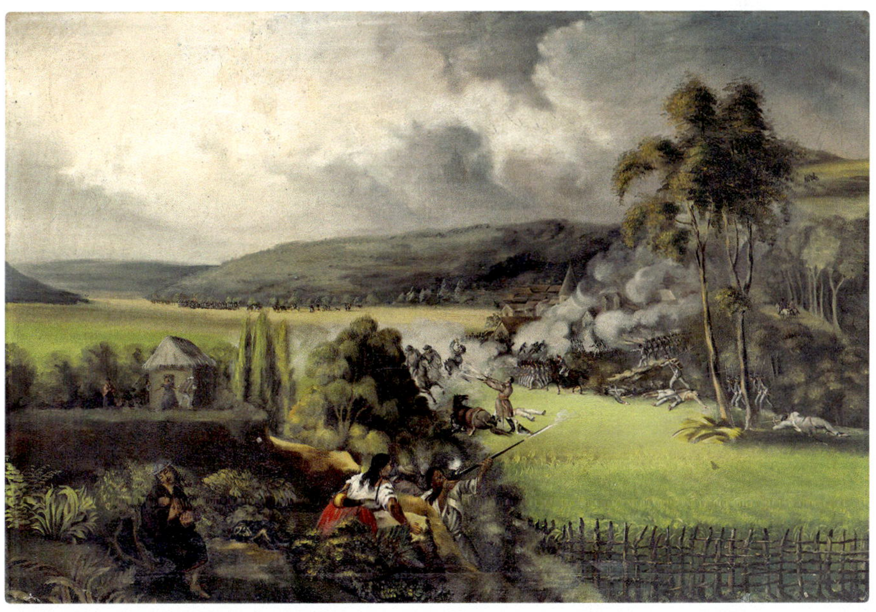

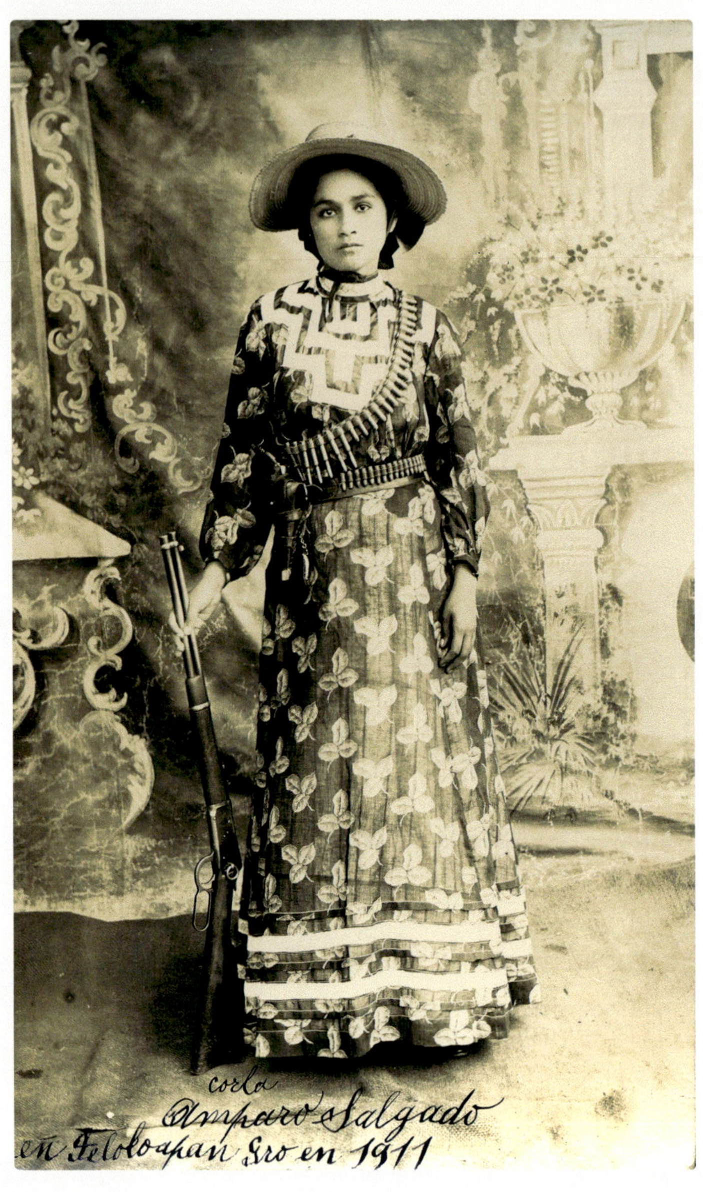

3.6. Sara Castrejón, *Coronel Amparo Salgado*, 1911. Courtesy of Consuelo del Rayo Castrejón. Digital restoration: Karina Herazo.

active participant in the Mexican Revolution.[21] The similarity between the two pictures is striking. Both photos respond to the codes of studio portraiture: they use painted backgrounds, present their sitters in the foreground looking frontally, and use similar props to convey the intended message. In the two images, the women wear long, delicate dresses that contrast strongly with the arms and ammunition that accompany them: a pistol or revolver, a carbine, and ammunition. Even the hat appears in both photographs.

However, de la Calle's photo of Restrepo differs from Castrejón's picture in some significant ways. The first one concerns the inclusion of the *carriel*, an essentially masculine accessory typical of the Antioquia region, usually used by muleteers. It is a leather purse with a fur front usually made of otter or jaguar skin. It is worn as seen in the picture, with a wide leather strap crossing the chest from the opposite shoulder.[22] The inclusion of this wardrobe piece is important because, like the gun, it destabilizes her gender identity. I have not seen other pictures from this period in Colombia of women wearing this typical peasant and male accessory, nor other images of women who purposefully represent themselves with men's garments. What makes this picture even more fascinating is that Restrepo wears a long black dress, thus simultaneously signaling femininity. The tensions between these male and female signifiers put her gender identity in suspense, as a photograph without a negative would bring the positive/negative binary into question. In this sense, we could consider representational images, such as María Anselma's photograph, and some photographic objects, such as daguerreotypes and ambrotypes, as nonbinary images.[23]

De la Calle's negotiation with the sitter and their mutual agreement to create such a photograph reveal historical erasures. Conceiving women as historical actors in their own right, whether real or aspirational, opens up a place for inclusion. Would we question the sitter's role if she were a white man from the city instead of a black woman from a small town? The performative nature of gender de-linked it from biology in intricate and significant ways. In Restrepo's photograph, this performative aspect was doubled. In the picture, she showcases manhood through the position of her body, the *carriel* she is wearing, and the man's hat that sits next to her. Nevertheless, these male signifiers do not undercut her femininity, performed in this case by donning a classic nineteenth-century long black dress.

This slippery model of womanhood opposed the premises of the civilizing discourse of the Antioquian race. This was associated with a negative construction of identity. The dark color of her skin already distanced her from the imported ideal of white femininity, grounded on notions of decency, chastity, and domesticity. White womanhood was not only respected and admired; it was necessary for the grounding and dissemination of the Antioquian race discourse. On the other hand, blackness was associated with lower social standing, lack of education, and the distress of hard physical labor. Blackness equaled backwardness, and thus the negative, a concept that directly opposed the discourse of progress. However, de la Calle's photograph of Restrepo did not convey these notions. She was presented in a nonsexualized way, empowered, and ready to go to war to fight with her male counterparts. It is known that Santa Rosa de Osos, the town where Restrepo came from, was part of a series of small enclaves in Antioquia where the black population had a strong presence since colonial times. Runaway slaves and other blacks formed *palenques* (places populated by maroons or enslaved Africans who escaped the colonial slave regime) and practiced gold mining in the alluvial mines of this area of the department. This group of people was able to rise socially and economically through this economic practice.[24] However, as Virginia Gutiérrez de Pineda notes, in Antioquia, in order for a black person to rise in the social hierarchy, the person had to adopt the emblems of whites.[25]

One possible iconographic model for de la Calle's photograph could have come from the allegories that circulated widely and were popularized in the photographic medium during the second half of the nineteenth century. One such example is an anonymous photograph of a young girl wearing a tall helmet that recalls a Phrygian cap and a feather plume (fig. 3.7). She holds a large flag in her left hand and a laurel crown in her right. These *tableaux vivants* evoked patriotism and were popular around national holidays such as Independence Day.[26] In allegorical representations of America, the iconography of the armed woman with a plume, bow, and arrows was appropriated and adapted to symbolize the nascent republic. Throughout the nineteenth century, it evolved from depicting a partially naked Indigenous woman to representing a woman wearing classical Greek or Roman costumes, anchors, laurel crowns, and flags. These latter representations related directly to depictions of liberty, nation, and the republic, most famously presented by Marianne's figure in Delacroix's *Liberty Leading the People*.

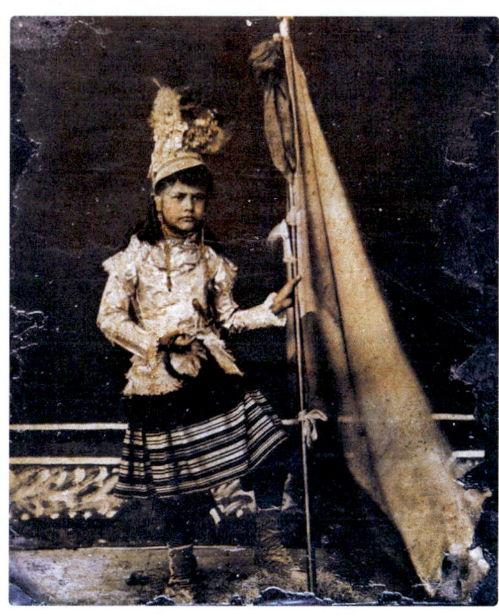

3.7. Anonymous, *Allegory*, ca. 1870. Tintype, 8.3 × 7 cm. Private collection.

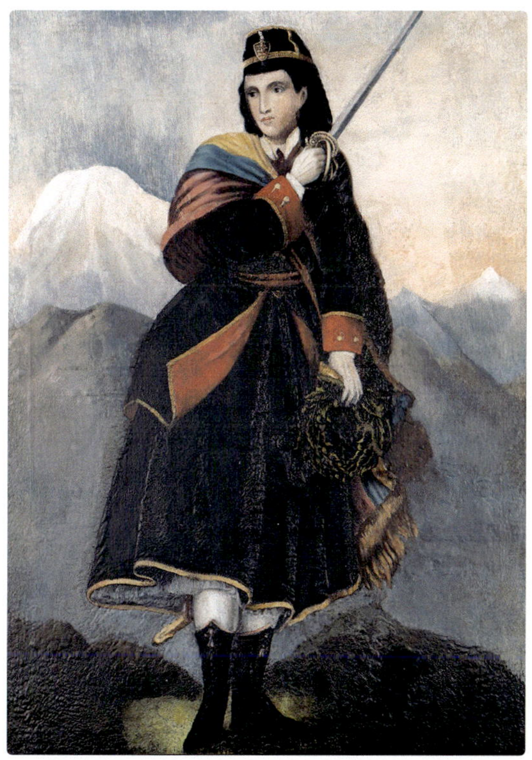

3.8. Leopoldo Carrasquilla, *Antioquia militante*, ca. 1880s. Oil on canvas on hardboard, 102 × 73.5 cm. Museo de Antioquia. Photo: Carlos Tobón.

This type of representation could also symbolize the local territories of specific departments, as exemplified in the painting *Antioquia militante* (Militant Antioquia) by Leopoldo Carrasquilla (fig. 3.8). The painting depicts a woman wearing a female adaptation of the military uniform, with the Colombian flag as a sash, raising a sword with her right hand and holding a laurel crown in the other. Some scholars have argued that the painting also represents Martínez de Nisser, thus uniting allegory and history in a single image.[27] The striking similarity between Restrepo's pose and Carrasquilla's characterization of Antioquia resides in the angle of their heads, the position of the right arm, the black dress, and the direct references to the Department of Antioquia, insinuating a connection that we should not ignore. Considering this, Restrepo's photo could also be understood as an allegory of militant Antioquia. Her depiction, however, challenges generic representations. It is an Antioquia that goes against the premises of the *raza antioqueña*. In de la Calle's representation, Antioquia is not white but black, and she does not conform to gender stereotypes but questions them.

Another detail worth mentioning in Restrepo's photograph is the rings that so prominently stand out on her right hand. The intentional inclusion of jewelry in her outfit can be read as a fundamental element in constructing a positive and individualized black identity. Like the negative in photography, black people have been invisibilized, racialized, and relegated to second-class subjects. Although slavery was officially abolished in Colombia in 1851, black subjects only began to appear as individuals and not as types, enslaved or caricatured subjects, or simply as backdrops in visual representations other than photographs well into the twentieth century. Photography thus became a tool for black empowerment. When comparing this picture with a watercolor created in 1850 as part of Colombia's Chorographic Commission, we can see the striking differences (fig. 3.9). In this image, Carmelo Fernández depicts three women from the region of Ocaña, a town located in the eastern part of the country. They stand forming a triangle. Two of the women, who are distinctively white, look to the left of the image, while the black woman faces the right side. It is a collective typological portrait like many created during this nine-year expedition that, among its various goals, aimed at portraying the country's population in catalog fashion.[28] What is startling about this particular image is its title, *Mujeres blancas, Ocaña* (White women, Ocaña), which blatantly erases the presence of the black woman. As noted

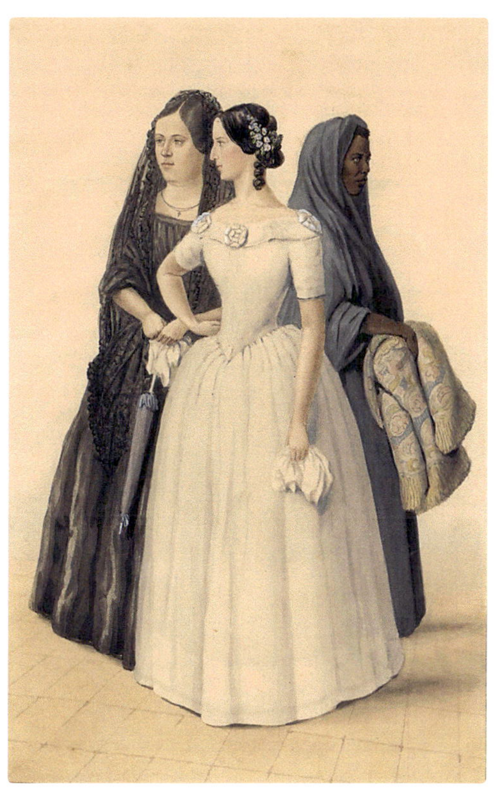

3.9. Carmelo Fernández, *Mujeres blancas, Ocaña*, 1853. Watercolor on paper, 31 × 22 cm. Biblioteca Nacional de Colombia.

by Sol Astrid Giraldo, although she is a structural element of the composition, the artist obliterates her presence in the title because black females were seen as shadows, as negative bodies.[29] The black enslaved woman is just a backdrop in the image. She is a prop and not a subject.

Conversely, in de la Calle's photograph, not only does María Anselma wear a dress similar to that of the white women in Fernández's watercolor, but she and the photographer also decided to include other material signifiers that separate her from previous negative connotations. The rings are significant in this sense, as well as the white cloth she holds in her left hand, which is very similar to the ones the white women hold in the watercolor. These elements connote wealth and place the sitter in a horizontal relationship with her white counterparts. According to Santiago Castro Gómez, during the colonial period, "the symbolic capital of whiteness was made evident through the ostentation of exterior signs that had to be publicly exhibited and demonstrated."[30] However, by the mid-nineteenth century, such imaginaries of race and class were still prevalent, as the watercolor shows. Going back to the question I posed at the beginning of this section, I argue that de la Calle's photograph of Restrepo is not only an aspirational portrait but also an active way of resisting the stereotype and opposing the negative. If blackness connoted everything that whiteness was not, then de la Calle's photo reverses this idea. It works as a reversed negative/positive process. As noted by Tanya Sheehan, one of the negative's features that made nineteenth-century photographic thinkers characterize it in pejorative ways was precisely its radical reordering of the black-and-white binary.[31] This is exactly what de la Calle's picture does: it reorganizes symbolic capital in order to resist negative portrayals.

Cross-Dressing

Wearing a flapper dress, dark stockings, high heels, gloves, earrings, and a feather headpiece, Alfonso Echavarría appears in perhaps one of Benjamín de la Calle's most fascinating photographs (fig. 3.10). Posing for the photographer in 1927, Echavarría sits on a studio chair, crosses his ankles, leans his head on his left hand, and directs his gaze to de la Calle's camera.[32] He appears in this image not exoticized as an extravagant Other but as just another sitter who went to de la Calle's studio for a portrait. More than once, de la Calle photographed cross-dressed subjects, especially men who felt comfortable posing for his lens wearing feminine clothing. Echavarría's picture is not an exception to the rule.

De la Calle's photographs of cross-dressed men are some of the earliest known examples of explicit photographic gender subversion found in Colombia. In a country ruled by a Christian perception of the world, any transgression of Catholicism's "natural" rule was a sin. Nonnormative gender identities and transgressive sexual orientations had to be camouflaged, coded, and hidden because they were seen as adverse to society's development. They undermined the dualism on which Christianity rests: good and evil, pagan and holy, hell and heaven. In this sense, as proposed by Sheehan, the metaphor of the negative and positive process in photography can be apt to analyze how these unstable identities operated.[33] Although the law did not penalize queer behaviors or alternative identities by the time this picture was taken, whoever deviated from the socially

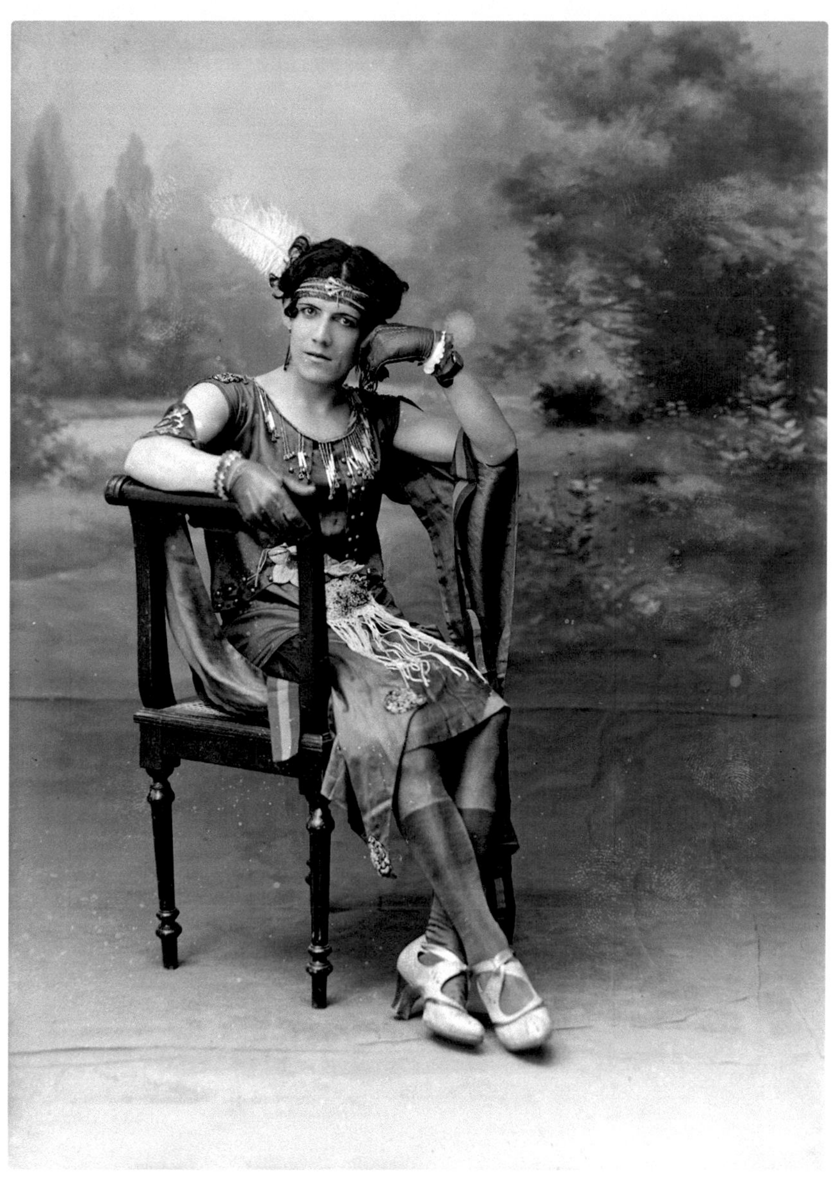

3.10. Benjamín de la Calle, *Alfonso Echavarría,* 1927. Digital positive from gelatin dry plate, 18 × 13 cm. Biblioteca Pública Piloto de Medellín / Archivo fotográfico.

acceptable was morally sanctioned.[34] Gossip and word of mouth made everyone aware of any transgression of the rules dictated by the Catholic discourses and imparted at home and in school. Thus, it was society itself and not the law that exerted control over alternative subjectivities. Ironically, although forced to alienate and become invisible, these marginalized subjects looked precisely to photography, the most powerful tool to document reality, to be immortalized. This paradox between visualization and erasure materializes in de la Calle's photographs, evidencing the dichotomy of the medium itself. On the one hand, photography served as a tool of institutional power and control and, on the other, it worked as a mnemonic device and an empowering medium. Photography created a reality that few visual media achieved with such intensity. For these men, who felt comfortable performing an alternate identity in front of the camera but perhaps not in their daily lives, having their portraits taken solidified a continuously alienated reality. In other words, if something can be photographed, it exists in the real world. As Karen Strassler rightfully proposed concerning studio portraiture in Java, and whose ideas we can extrapolate to this case study, rather than duplicating the world, these photographs create new ones.[35] In her words, "studio portraits exploit the illusionistic potential of photography to bring into material, tangible proximity a fantasy portrayed 'as if' it were real."[36] As pointed out by Christopher Pinney, these portraits of the "as if" are not only in the domain of the subjunctive or proleptic but are also medium-specific to photography.[37]

There are no portraits of cross-dressed persons in other photographers' archives in the city, neither in the Rodríguez brothers' nor in any other of their contemporaries. This raises the question of why these sitters went specifically to de la Calle's studio. It is presumed today that de la Calle was a gay man and that his sexual orientation made him, perhaps, more attuned to photographing the urban Other.[38] Indeed, recent sources reveal he led a cooperative of gay men in the city to take care of its members' health and financial issues. To raise funds, de la Calle asked men who seduced any of the cooperative members for cash as a way of supporting the cause.[39]

As a victim of the same social control as his sitters and part of the same patriarchal society, de la Calle identified with those who posed for his camera and vice versa. Precisely because his sexual identity had to be camouflaged, there is no material documentation to prove this orally transmitted myth. Some stories told by people who met him or heard about de la Calle while he was alive give some sense of how he was perceived during the early twentieth century. For example, Roberto Álvarez Jaramillo, a merchant from the Guayaquil neighborhood in Medellín where de la Calle had his studio, denied talking to the photographer "because he was seen as homosexual."[40] Other people described him as "effeminate," "*florindo*," or "*cacorro*" (gay).[41] It is clear from interviews that the pressure and social condemnation for being gay in this context were assumed not only by the person (in this case de la Calle) but also by any other social actors who associated with him, regardless of their gender. Dora Soto, a woman who worked as de la Calle's assistant writing down the names of his sitters and classifying the negatives, felt ashamed of her job, not because it was a dishonorable occupation but because de la Calle's name was associated with homosexuality.[42] In other words, de la Calle was associated with the idea of the sinner, the Other, and the negative.

Ultimately, these comments reflect a society that was (and still is) extremely homophobic: homophobia explicitly promoted by moral and religious discourses. As Eve Sedgwick explained, referring to Western society's homophobia, it "is not arbitrary or gratuitous, but tightly knit into the texture of family, gender, age, class, and race relations."[43] Being gay or openly assuming any identity that differed from the patriarchal discourse embedded in the notion of the *raza antioqueña* meant challenging one of the fundamental pillars of the rhetoric of this regional identity. It meant opposing the idea of the nuclear heterosexual family and male and female power relations. Gayness was synonymous with being deviant and criminal and thus a symbol of underdevelopment. In the same way blackness conveyed backwardness, queer identities were considered detrimental and thus harmful to society. These ideas explicitly opposed the discourses of civilization and progress so strongly promoted by the ideology of the *raza antioqueña*.

It is important to remember that the notion of sexual identity as we know it today did not circulate during the early twentieth century. Indeed, the concept of homosexuality only appeared in the Antioquian context in the second half of the twentieth century.[44] It was used to designate a sexual identity and also a sensibility, a behavior, and anything else that could translate into gender subversion. During this early period, there was no perceived difference between gender and sexual orientation, and any deviation from standard heterosexual behavior fell under the category of *marica* or *cacorro*, both words charged with negative connotations and used to designate male homosexuality.[45] These issues are only now being reconsidered in academic studies that deal with notions of sex and gender in the history of Antioquia. This very recent shift might also explain why authors who have dealt with de la Calle's photographs of cross-dressed men have immediately assumed that the sitters were gay. However, it is not possible to make such a statement just by looking at the photographs. Cross-dressing does not imply homosexuality, just as homosexuality does not imply cross-dressing. The questions posed by these photographs are more complex and subtle. It does not mean that people did not identify with, dress, and perform other genders, only that these ideas cannot be assumed just by looking at the pictures. They need to be researched in the specific contexts of photographic production, which in most cases do not exist precisely because of the presumed clandestine circulation. Last, before delving into a more in-depth analysis of the pictures, it is also important to point out that the concept of homosexuality referred to male homosexuality and not female, which was barely discussed.[46]

Alfonso Echavarría is not the only photograph of a cross-dressed man taken by de la Calle. He also photographed others, such as Emilio Sierra and José Celada, in 1927 and 1928, respectively. Both men wear distinctive feather headpieces, high heels, stockings, dresses, and jewelry (figs. 3.2 and 3.11). The exaggeration in the costumes speaks to the performative aspect of the photographs, a twofold performance: first, in posing for the camera, and second by the act of *trans-vestirse*—the literal act of cross-dressing—a performance of gender itself. As Judith Butler argued, "gender is not a performance that a prior subject elects to do, but gender is *performative* in the sense that it constitutes as an effect the very subject it appears to express."[47] The act of being photographed wearing the opposite gender's normative clothing emulates here a coming out, not of gender identity, but of a Self that was kept out of sight and suddenly gained a form of (re)presentation. Likewise, this coming out parallels the photographic process of transforming a negative into a positive copy: the image kept out of sight, existing behind the scenes, sees the light through its transformation from a transparent material into an opaque print. If transvestism represents for the outside viewer the Other and thereby becomes a tool that helps to position oneself in the place of the

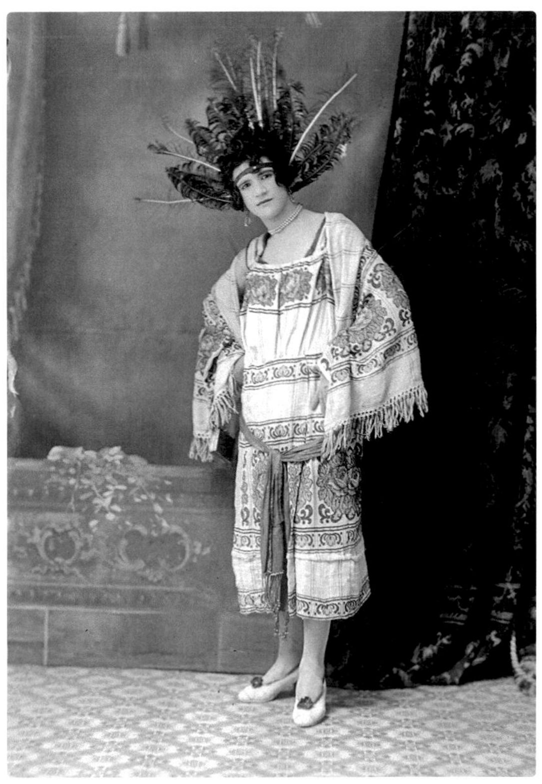

3.11. Benjamín de la Calle, *José Celada P.*, 1928. Digital positive from gelatin dry plate, 18 × 13 cm. Biblioteca Pública Piloto de Medellín / Archivo fotográfico.

Other, for the transvestite subject, cross-dressing is about representing the Self, becoming the Self, and (re)creating the Self.[48] It is not necessarily about becoming someone else but about personal realization. In this sense, transvestism can be an operating strategy that questions, deconstructs, and paradoxically emphasizes gender binaries and hierarchies. Butler wondered, "is drag [in this case transvestism] the imitation of gender, or does it dramatize the signifying gestures through which gender itself is established?"[49]

Today, it seems that many forms of alternative gender identity are unequivocally derived from or imitative of the normative, whether male or female, as if there was an original that the others copied, transformed, or appropriated, as in the negative/positive photographic process. Butler argues that drag, or in this case transvestism, "is not an imitation or a copy of some prior and true gender" but rather, it

> enacts the very structure of impersonation by which any gender is assumed. Drag is not the putting on of a gender that belongs properly to some other group, i.e., an act of *ex*propriation or *ap*propriation that assumes that gender is the rightful property of sex, that "masculine" belongs to "male" and "feminine" belongs to "female." There is no "proper" gender, a gender proper to one sex rather than another, which is in some sense that sex is cultural property. Where that notion of the "proper" operates, is always and only improperly installed as the effect of a compulsory system. Drag constitutes the mundane way in which genders are appropriated, theatricalized, worn, and done; it implies that all gendering is a kind of impersonation and approximation.[50]

The parallel with the photographic medium cannot be more astonishing: behind every photograph—a copy by definition—is an original negative. However, which one is the original: the positive, the negative, or reality itself? Neither in drag nor in photography is there an original or primary source to imitate. Instead, they are both an imitation for which there is no original: "In fact, it is a kind of imitation that produces the very notion of the original as an effect and consequence of the imitation itself."[51]

There is also an issue of self-presentation at stake here. In de la Calle's photographs of cross-dressed men, the gender performance enacted by his sitters is not based on just any kind of woman but specifically on the New Woman of the 1920s. Although the outfits were clearly exaggerated costumes, the decision to wear flapper dresses—shapeless and shorter than the previous styles—feather headpieces, and stockings showed an interest in the new type of woman that emerged after World War I. Internationally, the New Woman was interested in consuming modern goods, leisure activities, and media culture. She took part in politics, fought for women's rights, worked to penetrate men's middle-class professions, and was outspoken about intellectual and sexual issues. All this was reflected in the fashion, which did not emphasize the curvilinear body shape but showed more skin and encouraged the use of makeup and flirty accessories. Wearing trousers and other items traditionally considered male garments was revolutionary.[52]

In Colombia, World War I and the consequent sudden rupture of commercial ties created a lack of imported supplies and the necessity to produce locally. In this context, women became an important part of the workforce during the 1910s. Manufacturing industries were growing exponentially, and there were few inexpensive and efficient workers to take over these jobs. Therefore, women were employed mainly in textile and cigarette factories. Although the paid female employee index was still low—between 10 and 15 percent of the economically active population—the number was significant because it was part of the most dynamic branch of the national economy.[53] These working women usually came from low- and lower-middle-class backgrounds. In the textile industry in Medellín, one of the most important in the city, the workforce was approximately 73 percent female by 1923.[54]

Medellín's Catholic and conservative environment did not welcome the worldwide change in attitude toward women. The impression that women were inferior to men and should stay home was widely accepted until the 1950s. Vanity, flirtation, and interest in things such as fashion were strongly criticized because they directly conflicted with the idea of the chaste and pure woman destined to take care of her family.[55] The Church's opposition to this new attitude was among the strongest. In 1927, the same year that de la Calle took the pictures of Echavarría and Sierra, a priest from Santa Rosas de Osos, a city approximately seventy kilometers north of Medellín, condemned any woman who dared dress provocatively or showed more skin than necessary.[56] That same year, a group of women was shocked when a local business owner placed a reproduction of the *Venus de Milo* in his storefront window. They persuaded the mayor to have the "nude" taken down.[57] In this Catholic environment, complaints against movies, theater plays, female fashion, and even sports press were frequent. In a rapidly changing city where female citizenship had a strong presence, it was as if they considered that the modern world was against traditional Catholic values.

De la Calle's photographs embody and materialize a challenging attitude toward the conservative discourse. Sierra, Celada, and Echavarría not only appear dressed provocatively but also show their legs and arms, wear visible makeup, and deploy a body language that went against all the rules of modesty and chastity imparted by the Church. They embody the New Woman, but not the working proletariat woman marching and fighting for women's rights, such as the famous social activist María Cano.[58] Neither do they deploy a sexualized body. Rather, they embody the bourgeois woman concerned with modern appearances and seduced by emerging mass culture and an international lifestyle. Although this might initially seem contradictory, we should understand the decision to embrace a seemingly superficial attitude as a political act. The active appropriation of a bourgeois style is exploited here to alter the hegemonic discourse by disrupting precisely the social circle the sitters came from and, more importantly, the one that perpetuated the myth of the Antioquian race. One can imagine that a man such as Echavarría, who, judging by his last name, was part of one of Medellín's wealthiest families, challenged that precise context.[59]

The dress worn by Echavarría complicates even further the reading of these images since it looks more like a costume than a proper everyday dress. One might wonder if he selected the attire from a repertoire of props that de la Calle had for his sitters to choose from (as did most photographers during this period) or if Echavarría himself brought the outfit to the studio and used it in other contexts as well. These types of portraits show how gender was understood and performed. In this sense, these photographs cannot be read as pictures of men dressed as women; instead, these images show how the sitters understood the working of concepts such as femininity and manhood. As stated by Jorge Coronado when analyzing a picture of women dressed as men in Peru in the 1930s, "This is not simply a picture of women in costume, but rather an appreciation of knowledge of how gender roles and their expression function and animate society. That knowledge can be assigned to the subjects and/or to the photographers. But it also dwells within the image."[60]

The question of the costume is more pressing in this picture than in other photographs of cross-dressed men also taken by de la Calle, in which the brief descriptions added by the photographer to the negatives help explain the occupation of the sitters. Again, the information on the negative allows us to better understand the photograph's function. These handwritten texts were usually not included in the positive versions of the images but were cropped and kept out of sight of the public. In conjunction with the images, these handwritten aspects show the prevalence of cross-dressing for theatrical and performative activities. That is obvious, for instance, in the photographs of Jesús Quiñones taken in 1906. In one photograph, he appears wearing a velvet gown with large lace ruffles on the sleeves, a bow around his neck, and a wig with a headpiece that emphasizes the artificiality of the costume (fig. 3.12). He was probably performing the role of Cossette for the *Bohemios zarzuela*. Quiñones has been identified as a Mexican actor, and the photograph was possibly used to promote the show during their stay in Medellín or as a

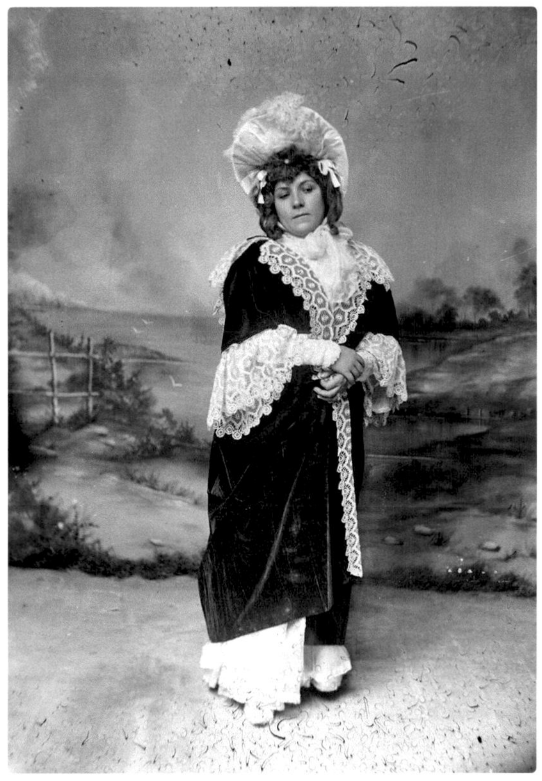

3.12. Benjamín de la Calle, *Jesús S. Quiñones*, 1906. Digital positive from gelatin dry plate, 18 × 13 cm. Biblioteca Pública Piloto de Medellín / Archivo fotográfico.

collectible item of a famous person after his departure. This was a common use for portrait photography during the time. Indeed, in the archives of these photographers in Medellín, there are numerous portraits of foreign actors and actresses in their roles. Although by the time this picture was taken, women in Colombia were allowed to act, men still performed some women's roles. As explained by Rondy Torres, during the nineteenth century, "In Latin American cities, going on the stage was synonymous with dishonor for local women."[61] Men acting as women was still a common practice during the first decades of the twentieth century, as evidenced by these photographs.

Other pictures of cross-dressed men, such as those of Ricardo Correa (figs. 3.13 and 3.14), also reinforce the fact that many men posed for the camera in their theatrical attire and roles to promote their performing identities. In one picture, Correa rests his head in his left hand and smiles directly at the camera (fig. 3.15). Smiling was not a common

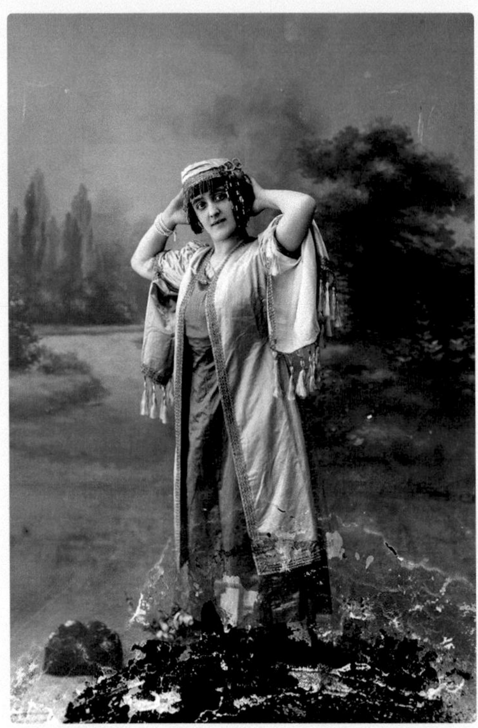

3.13. Benjamín de la Calle, *Ricardo Correa A.*, 1910. Digital positive from gelatin dry plate, 18 × 13 cm. Biblioteca Pública Piloto de Medellín / Archivo fotográfico.

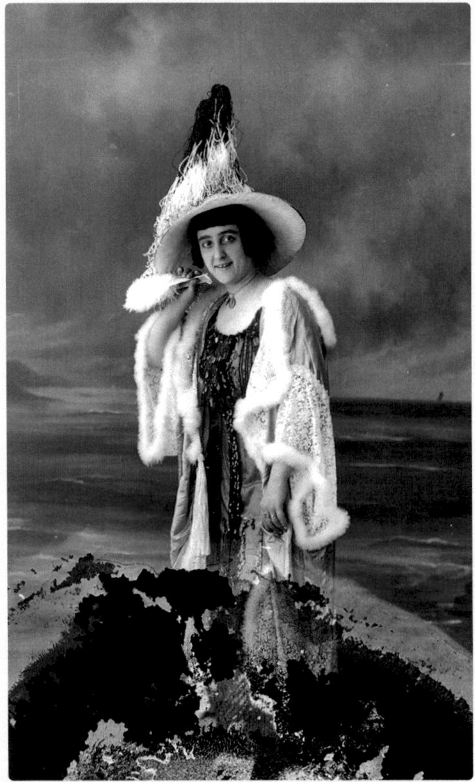

3.14. Benjamín de la Calle, *Ricardo Correa A.*, 1914. Digital positive from gelatin dry plate, 18 × 13 cm. Biblioteca Pública Piloto de Medellín / Archivo fotográfico.

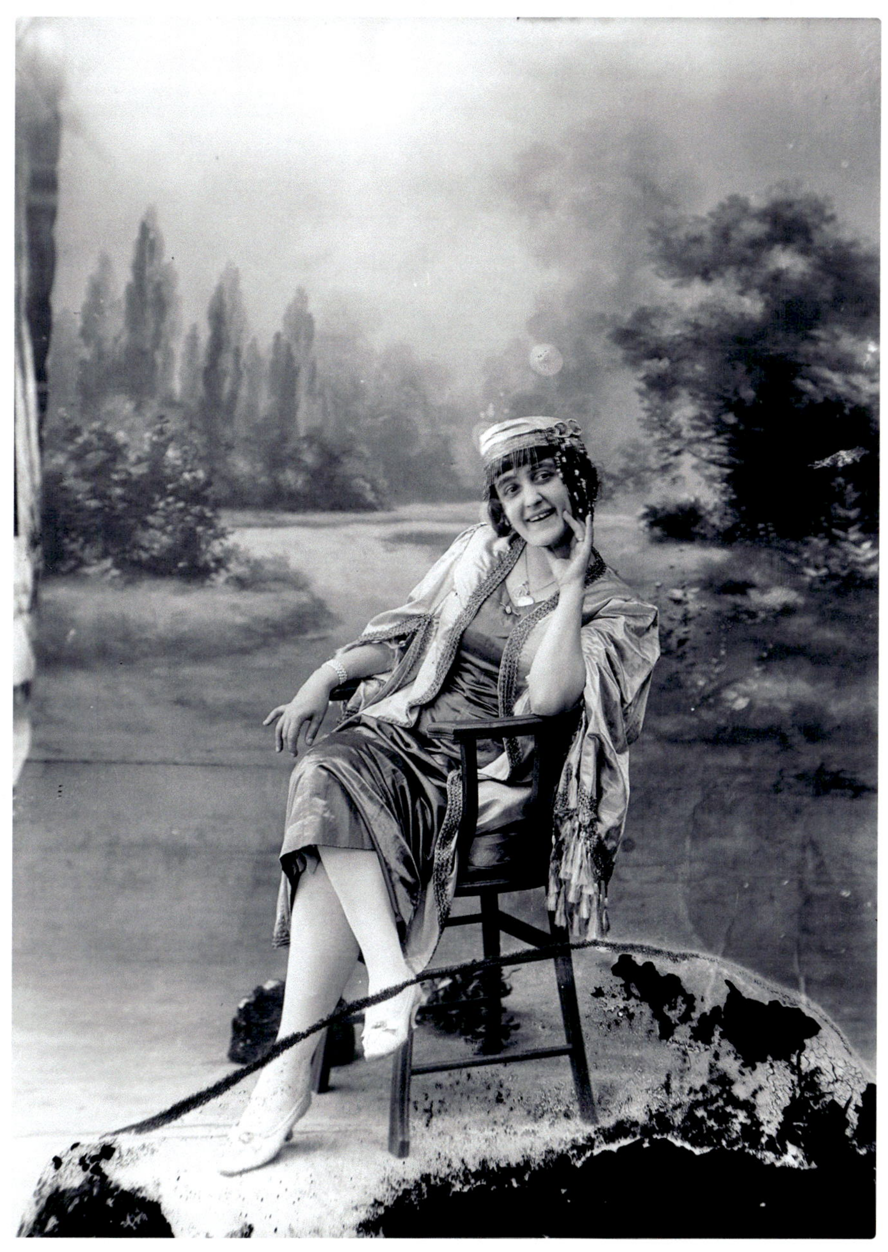

3.15. Benjamín de la Calle, *Ricardo Correa A.*, 1910. Digital positive from gelatin dry plate, 18 × 13 cm. Biblioteca Pública Piloto de Medellín / Archivo fotográfico.

gesture in portrait photography during that time. People posed for the camera with grave looks or pensive expressions, especially for commemorative portraits. As Tanya Sheehan has argued, smiling and excessive laughter—particularly "the toothy smile"—were seen as transgressive gestures most commonly found in persons who inhabited the margins of society.[62] Indeed, smiling became a trope only in the 1940s, when people assimilated the efforts made by Kodak since the 1920s to sell the idea of photography as a pleasurable hobby.[63] This small but revealing gesture in Correa's photograph might explain why the pictures of Echavarría, Sierra, and Celada are so intriguing. Although the men wear costumes for the pictures, their gestures and poses are not as overtly exaggerated as in the photographs of actors in female roles. They pose with a more natural look. Although they are performing an identity, it is not a theatrical performance. There is something more subtle in their gestures, which speaks to the instability of their identities in the photographs.

These images of cross-dressed men play with the instability of identity and the deployment of a continuous masquerade. These "new" bodies became signifiers of the cultural politics in the city. De la Calle's photographs established new parameters in which other subjectivities could explore the ambiguous and complex relationship between the hegemonic racial discourse and another, perhaps more tolerant, world. However, they remained at a purely visual level, ultimately raising the provocative question of visualization's actual power. As Butler wondered, "can the visibility of identity suffice as political strategy, or can it only be the starting point for a strategic intervention, which calls for a transformation of policy?"[64]

Criminal Bodies: The Woman-Man Case

In 1912, the journal *Progreso* published an article announcing "a curious case."[65] The article recounts the story of a man who, dressed as a woman, worked as a maid in Medellín's elite households. Her given birth name was Roberto Durán, but she used the name Rosa Emilia Restrepo.[66] She became a suspicious individual because, after being employed for a while, she would disappear. She was captured by the police and sent to doctors who identified her as a man. According to the article, she claimed that her mother had dressed her as a woman since she was a child, and she

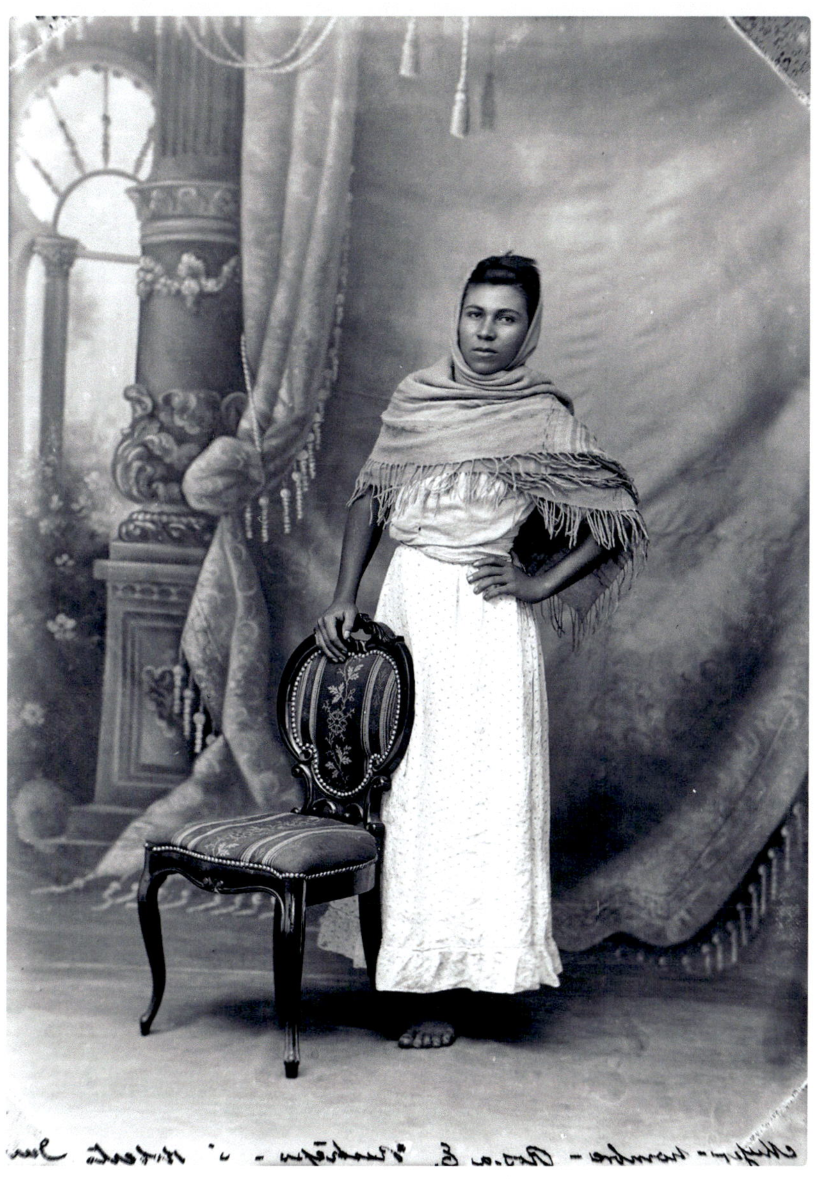

3.16. Benjamín de la Calle, *Mujer-hombre (Rosa Emilia Restrepo o Roberto Durán)*, 1912. Digital positive from gelatin dry plate, 16 × 12 cm. Biblioteca Pública Piloto de Medellín / Archivo fotográfico.

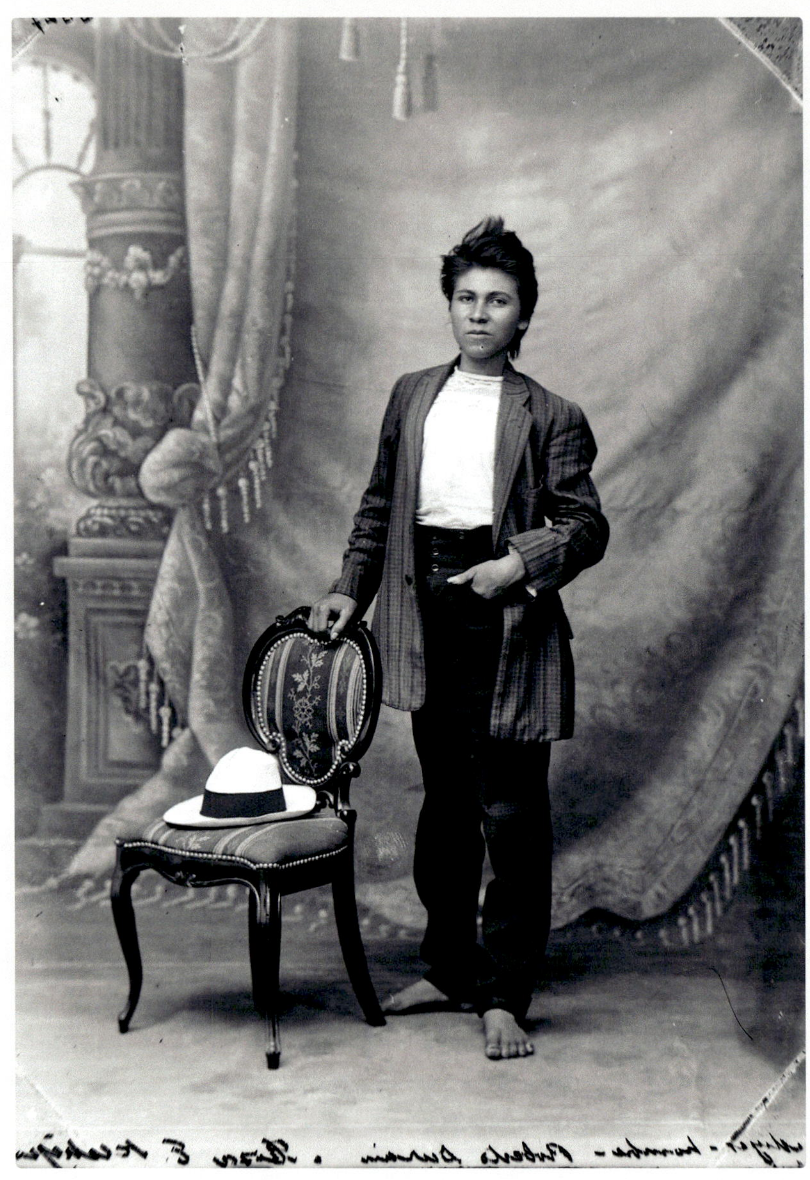

3.17. Benjamín de la Calle, *Mujer-hombre (Rosa Emilia Restrepo o Roberto Durán)*, 1912. Digital positive from gelatin dry plate, 16 × 12 cm. Biblioteca Pública Piloto de Medellín / Archivo fotográfico.

had refused to wear men's clothing ever since. They ultimately sent Rosa Emilia to jail, removed her dress, and forced her to wear men's clothes.

Two studio photographs taken by de la Calle accompanied the article: one of Rosa Emilia Restrepo and one of Roberto Durán (figs. 3.16 and 3.17). To be more specific, de la Calle took two photographs of the same sitter: one performing the role of a woman, the other the role of a man. The sitter poses similarly in both images. Standing behind a chair, resting her right hand on its back and her left hand at the waist, Rosa Emilia or Roberto appears in front of a conventional interior backdrop depicting a big curtain and an ornate column. In the photograph where the sitter appears dressed as a woman, she wears a simple white dress, no shoes, and a shawl. In the other one, she wears black pants, a white shirt, no shoes, and a dark striped blazer. In this last photograph, there is a hat on the chair. Gender identifiers are either concealed or reinforced in both images with the inclusion of props, such as the hat, or even subtle gestures of the sitter. For example, she wears short hair in both photographs, an uncommon characteristic for a woman during this period. The shawl wrapped over her head and shoulders hides this feature in the first image, thus concealing a characteristic that did not align with the normative female appearance. In the second photograph, in which she appears to perform the identity of a man, her right hand is tucked inside a frontal pocket of the pants, thus reinforcing a masculine or male attitude.

The photographs operate hand in hand. As in the negative/positive process, one photo cannot work without the other. These pictures are so powerful precisely because they intervene together. Without one of the images, the other loses its force. In that sense, we can think of this pair of pictures as dependent on one another to convey their meaning. Their binarism reinforces the significance of the pictures in the same way the negative expands the meaning in photography.

Nevertheless, these photographs are curious in and of themselves, considering that they were taken partly for judicial documentation and partly to display what was considered an eccentricity or a "curious case." The images do not align with the internationally standardized photography used to document criminals, as introduced by Alphonse Bertillon in Paris during the 1890s. Bertillon's method, or bertillonage, called for two photographs, one frontal and one in profile, included in a card file containing the criminal history of individuals. Eleven anthropological measurements of the corresponding subject—which Bertillon considered invariable in adults—accompanied the photographs. Among these were height, width of head, length of the middle finger, size of left foot, and so on. Bertillon's anthropometric method spread rapidly in Europe and America, but the mug shot arrived in Medellín only in 1914. Indeed, the type of bertillonage introduced in Antioquia was a variation of the original method since it already included other identification technologies, such as dactyloscopy, that is, fingerprinting.

The acquisition of the anthropometric kit was enthusiastically announced in *Progreso*, the same journal that two years before had published the photographs of the woman-man. Accompanied by a photograph of the first anthropometric file created in Medellín, the article announced that the "instrument for judicial photography and anthropometric measurements" was a tool for "progress" that would help the police department improve the "deficient methods" they used until then.[67] The article, written by Manuel F. Calle, director of the Police Department, was also printed in a specialized journal called *Revista de la Policia Departamental* (Magazine of the Departmental Police). Although this iteration did not include illustrations, a lengthy note on judicial photography followed the article. Written by photographer Rafael Mesa, perhaps the most direct business competitor of de la Calle and the Rodríguez brothers, the article described the advantages and deficiencies of this new type of judicial photography, which he called, using Bertillon's term, "signaletic photography."[68] According to Mesa, these portraits were paradoxical because the result was a correct and direct impression of the subject in scientific terms, but the resulting image lacked likeness to the sitter. In other words, a signaletic portrait was of no value to recognize a subject in real life. It was useful to compare two different signaletic portraits and determine if they corresponded to the same subject, if both images depicted the same graphic characteristics. Nevertheless, it would be hard to determine the exact relationship between such a photograph and the real-life sitter.

In Mesa's opinion, for a portrait to be a likeness of its sitter, it should be taken under correct lighting conditions (for him, probably only achievable in the studio) that no police department could ever have.[69] Moreover, in this type of "straight photography," the correspondence between light and color and its translation into a monochromatic color scheme was not directly proportional. The photographic emulsion was more sensitive to certain colors—blue or violet—and less so to red and yellow. Thus, the portrait of a blond person with blue eyes would result in the image of someone with very light eyes and darker hair.[70] The same would happen with a sitter whose skin had reddish or yellowish gradations, which would appear darker on the photographic plate. According to Mesa, these photographic deficiencies could be corrected with scientific and technical procedures in the studio but not in the police department. Professional photographers had other tools, like lenses, that helped blur extremely defined contours and could use orthochromatic methods such as retouching, consequently balancing the color mistakes of the translation from the colorful real-life referent into a monochrome image.

Mesa's emphasis on the importance of likeness in a traditional portrait and the lack thereof in a signaletic one speaks to the dialectic function of the photographs of Rosa Emilia Restrepo and Roberto Durán. Appropriating Allan Sekula's terms, one could say that these images embody the tensions between the repressive and the honorific portrait.[71] One could also argue that they represent a positive and negative depiction of the sitter, the female version embodying the negative. Considering that the anthropometric system had not yet arrived in Medellín when these images were taken, the intention of the photographs seems twofold: on the one hand, they served as judicial documents of this person's double identity—that is, they played a repressive/negative function as surveillance—but on the other, they also embraced what was already a traditional aspect of portrait practice, that of photographing oneself as a sort of ceremonial presentation, in other words, the creation of an honorific/positive portrait. These two photographs by de la Calle do not formally differ from any of his other portraits and, unlike the later criminal photographs, they present an individual with both likeness and identity. Although initially conceived as bearers of legalistic or indexical truth, they did not withhold that unique function and instead embraced a more complex and unstable photographic identity.

Approximately a month after their original publication, the two images appeared in *Avanti* magazine, accompanied by an ironic article. The unknown author, writing under the pseudonym Juanita Arredondo, questioned the number of people that the suspect might have fooled: from receiving "hot stares, cries of enthusiasm," and even "gallant phrases from shoemakers, carpenters, and tailors" to the "love claims and even kisses she might have received."[72] The author concludes the article by narrating the judicial decision not to let Rosa Emilia go free until she agreed to wear the clothes that her biological sex dictated. In simpler terms, she had to wear trousers to be free. Yet, in the final paragraph, the author reveals a surprisingly progressive opinion stating that, if she were the chief of police, she would force Rosa Emilia to wear skirt-pants, therefore leaving "moral, sexual integrity, and individual guarantees" safe.[73] The ambivalence of skirt-pants again plays with the idea of a nonbinary image, an image that simultaneously inhabits positive and negative values, thus putting the binary opposition in suspense.

By including the photographs in the printed press, the subject became an object of public exposure regardless of the written information accompanying the images. Not coincidentally, the two times the pictures appeared in the news, it was in magazines devoted to promoting civility.[74] Indeed, the photographs became signifiers of what was right (positive) and what was wrong (negative), thus performing a judicial function and a moral one. The wide circulation of these images created a vigilant network of people, introducing a diluted version of the panoptic principle into daily life. This idea of scrutinizing, surveilling, and defining the body, both morally and physically, agreed very well with the eugenic and racial discourses being disseminated in the medical and political spheres during the same period, as discussed in chapter 1. One might even wonder if Rosa Emilia was indeed arrested for committing a crime or if her capture had to do with her position as a vulnerable subject in Medellín's society. The article that appeared in *Progreso* did not state why she was arrested; rather, it suggested that being a suspicious person was enough to pursue a prosecution. The article noted that "the police had information that a woman who looked like a man was placed as a servant in houses in this city and then disappeared, with some *suspicions* falling on her. Yesterday morning she was captured and taken to the police command, where she was examined by the official doctors and recognized as a male."[75]

The definition and visualization of a new criminal body in Colombia had begun a few years earlier with other cases in which photography had played a critical role. Two of those cases are relevant in this context. The first is a similar instance of a cross-dresser caught by the police and photographed by a commercial photographer. The second is the last public execution in Colombia, an event photographed by de la Calle himself.

In 1899, the Medellín-based commercial photographers Botero y Gregory announced the sale of photographs of the "notable character" of a woman-man from Jericó.[76] In this case, a married woman had left her husband and children to pursue a homosexual relationship. According to an article published in the newspaper, the woman, named Eulalia Sánchez, not only dressed as a man but also married the woman she was living with. Since homosexuality could not be legally penalized in Colombia—just morally—conservative citizens in Medellín sought other ways to punish the woman for her actions. Insisting that the "abominations of the female-man were criminal acts," some argued that marrying another person while the first partner was still alive was against the law and had to be penalized.[77]

According to the newspaper ads, photographers Botero y Gregory were the only ones who held the rights to reproduce these images, which sold as a pair for 1.60 pesos. Unfortunately, these photographs have not been identified, and thus, a comparative visual analysis with de la Calle's pictures is not possible. However, the announcements suggest the images seemed to follow the same logic as de la Calle's portraits: one picture deployed the sitter dressed as a man and the other as a woman. Their existence is certainly a significant precedent in this type of photography, which might have been available to de la Calle when he took Rosa Emilia's photographs.

The second relevant criminal case in which photography played a critical role resulted in a series of pictures taken by de la Calle. His role as a police photographer did not start with the pictures of the woman-man case. Indeed, in 1906, he photographed the last public execution by firing squad in Antioquia.[78] Only three images from this series survive, and no further documentation has been identified. The first photograph shows the death scene just after the execution (fig. 3.18). The corpse, with blood on his left cheek still visible, appears in the middle of the image. Two young police officers with ammunition belts and rifles with bayonets stand on each side. In the foreground, to the viewer's right, an open casket awaits the body. The photograph is a direct frontal shot, unlike the other two images in the series, which show close-ups of the convict's face taken at different moments (fig. 3.19). The first depicts the sitter alive and upright just before the execution. He wears what appears to be a *ruana* or poncho over a white shirt. A plaque, presumably with the convict's information, hangs from his neck. The second photograph, taken right after the execution, appears to be a cropped close-up of the execution photograph described above. However, the position of the plaque reveals that it is indeed a different image. The convict's head falls toward his right shoulder, and the bloodstain on his face is even more visible in the close perspective. The plaque is slightly moved forward for better legibility.

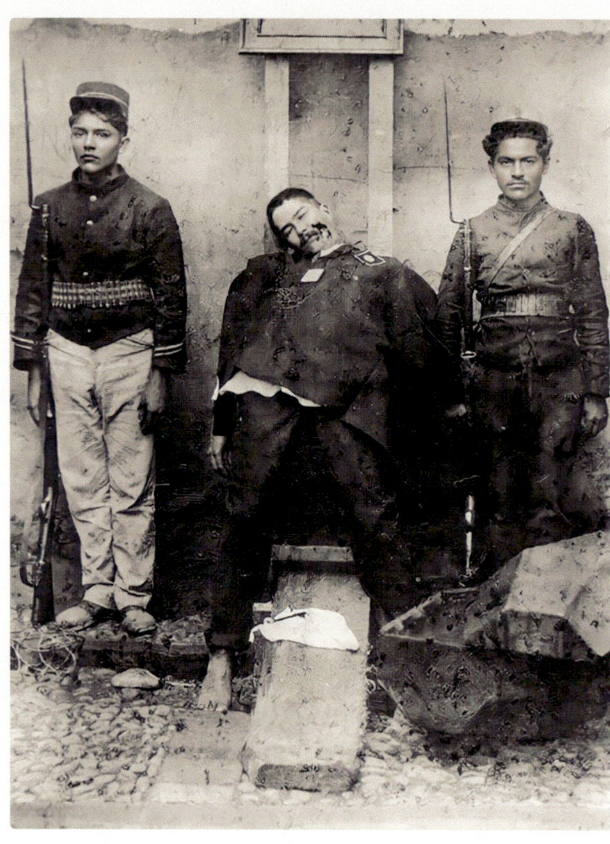

3.18. Benjamín de la Calle, *Untitled (After the Execution)*, ca. 1906.

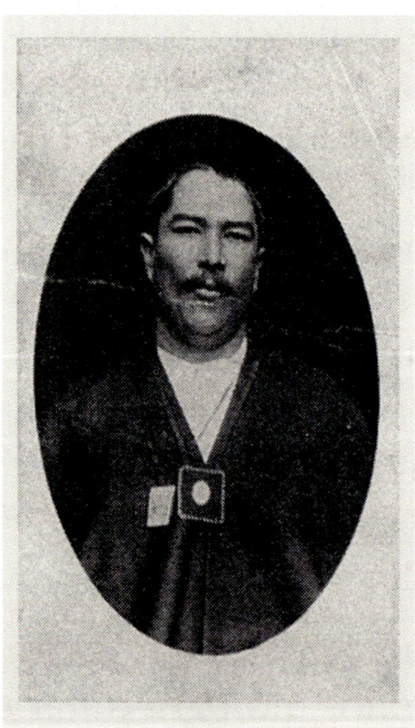

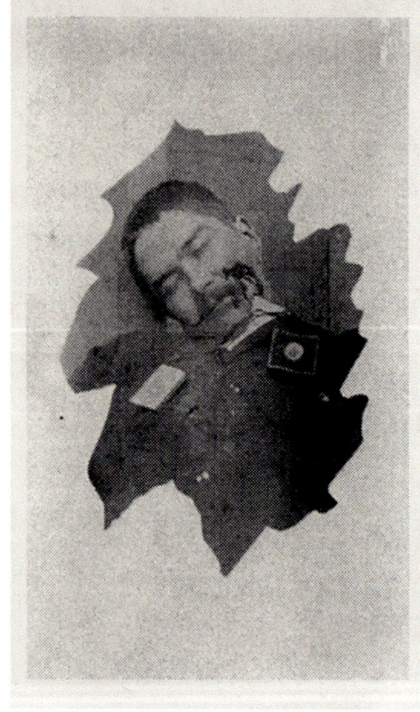

3.19. Benjamín de la Calle, left: *Untitled (Before the Execution)*, ca. 1906; right: *Untitled (After the Execution)*, ca. 1906.

Allegedly, de la Calle took these images without charging the police department, for which he worked for over fifteen years as a judicial photographer.[79] The question of why he might have undertaken this free enterprise could be explained by the commercial success he envisioned from selling the photographs as cartes de visite. Although he did not know that these images were to become the visual documentation of the region's last death sentence, the before and after effects of the dramatic scene made them commercially desirable. Capital punishment was being debated in the county, and it was about to be abolished, which happened in 1910. If photography could document reality, freezing a potentially relevant historical subject became the perfect theme for a photographer who struggled to keep his studio running.

De la Calle was smart enough not to sell the images without intervention. Not only did he create a pair of photographs that visualized the condition of the sitter, both dead and alive, but he also used frames that reflected the status of the convict through visual conventions. Following traditional pictorial representations, the first photograph—in which the sitter appears posing alive in front of a dark background—employs an oval frame referencing traditional portraiture conventions. The second image, which deploys the tragic scene of the sitter's face after being shot, uses a formless vignette that recalls the shape of a liquid spot, visually doubling the bloody mark on the convict's face. This subtle intervention made the images more dynamic and thus more attractive to potential clients. These photographs became valuable historical references, not only due to what they represented as the last execution in the country but also, perhaps more importantly, due to what they evoked: the state's power. They performed a double function. On the one hand, they worked as reminders of the consequences for citizens that went against the law, and on the other, they shaped the visual construction of a criminal body.

These pictures differ from de la Calle's photographs of the woman-man case. Formally, they are two different types of portrait. The before-and-after execution scenes were taken outdoors and are less staged, although still maintaining a degree of performativity. The sitter looks vulnerable and unprepared to be exposed to the photographic lens. On the other hand, we have a pair of photographs carefully arranged at the photographer's studio: chosen props, a practiced pose, and a carefully illuminated setting.

Thematically, the images differ even further. Although at first glance, all these photographs seem to belong to the same genre, that of crime photography, when closely inspected they reveal different intentions. Rosa Emilia Restrepo or Roberto Durán's portraits emphasize gender identity issues rather than the crime itself. Indeed, the criminal act is always secondary in these photographs. When looking at the pictures, it takes a while to remember what the crime was. In contrast, the execution pictures are closer to the type of criminal photography that was finally consolidated in Bertillon's method. His anthropometric system, today considered the first modern police record method, intended to "fix the human personality, give each human being an identity, a certain individuality, durable, invariable, always recognizable and easily demonstrable."[80] Yet the photographs of the woman-man case did exactly the opposite: they presented an unstable, mutable identity, nonidentifiable, and thus, difficult to categorize. Moreover, they destabilized the ideology of the *raza antioqueña* as they visually questioned the status quo regarding gender, an essential feature of the discourse imparted by the elites and the church. They also play with the dichotomy of positive and negative, presenting an honorary and a repressive portrait side by side, thus enhancing the tensions between them. Together, these two photos embody the concept of the nonbinary image as they resist photography's duplicity. Yes, they are two, but work together as a single entity. The subject they represent cannot be categorized as a stable identity. Rosa Emilia or Roberto embodies the possibility of being male and female simultaneously, positive and negative in a single body/image.

• • • • •

The series of photographs analyzed in this chapter highlights the different instances in which cross-dressing played a fundamental role: whether as a tool for self-empowerment and aspiration, as in the case of María Anselma Restrepo; as a way of revealing or suggesting a different identity that did not align with hegemonic discourses, as in the case of Alfonso Echavarría, Emilio Sierra, and José Celada; as a tool to promote a career, as in the pictures of José Quiñones and Ricardo Correa; or as a repressive or honorary portrait, as seen in the pictures of Rosa Emilia Restrepo. These pictures reveal that cross-dressing was a practice rather than a series of subjects in the context of the turn of the century in Medellín and that, as a practice, its meanings and effects could be contradictory and diverse. They also reveal the ambivalences of a photographer whose work is usually associated with an interest in these Othered subjectivities but who, as shown in this chapter, also worked for governmental institutions and their disciplinary apparatuses.

The bodies and subjects in these images are examples of a wider and more complicated identity history of a region that was trying to position itself as civilized, cosmopolitan, and modern. What they reveal is that rhetorical modernity opposed the real modernity that grew in the margins and was thus invisible to hegemonic racial discourses. While sometimes de la Calle's photographs produce and maintain difference, in others, they challenge the negative/positive binary opposition. His pictures, with their representation of multiple identities, complicate the idea of constructing a unified *raza antioqueña*. In some cases, his photographs reveal his rejection of this racial discourse in favor of a more emotional expression of regional identity, visualizing the repressed negative Other in positive terms, while in others, they align with it.

CHAPTER FOUR

Orientalism in the Andes

ITINERANT IMAGES AND DISTANT NEGATIVES

IN 1910, Melitón Rodríguez created a picture titled *Cosecha de rosas* (Rose harvest, fig. 4.1). The photograph depicts an Orientalist scene of female conviviality: two women dressed in traditional Middle Eastern clothes working together, picking up roses and plucking petals to place in an urn. The photographer set the scene with traditional vases of different sizes and flowers lying on the floor as evidence of their work. The painted backdrop refers to a Middle Eastern building with profusely decorated columns and a tapestry in the background. It is a picture set in no specific time or place, following the tropes of common stereotyping of Orientalist photography, trendy in Europe during the second half of the nineteenth century. The scene takes as a point of reference the painting *La cueillette des roses* by Austrian artist Rudolf Ernst (1854–1932), who became a prolific Orientalist painter during the late nineteenth century in France (fig. 4.2). The composition of the two pictures is almost identical: the woman sitting on the floor plucking the roses appears on the left side of both the painting and the photograph; the roses scattered on the floor are precisely in front of the urn in both images; there is another urn standing on a wooden support on the right side of both pictures; the second character in the images appears from the right side, carrying roses in a basket that rests on her right shoulder; and even the smaller, fallen urn in the foreground appears in the same place in both pictures.

How can two closely linked images be produced in entirely different spatial and temporal spaces? How did Melitón learn about Orientalism,

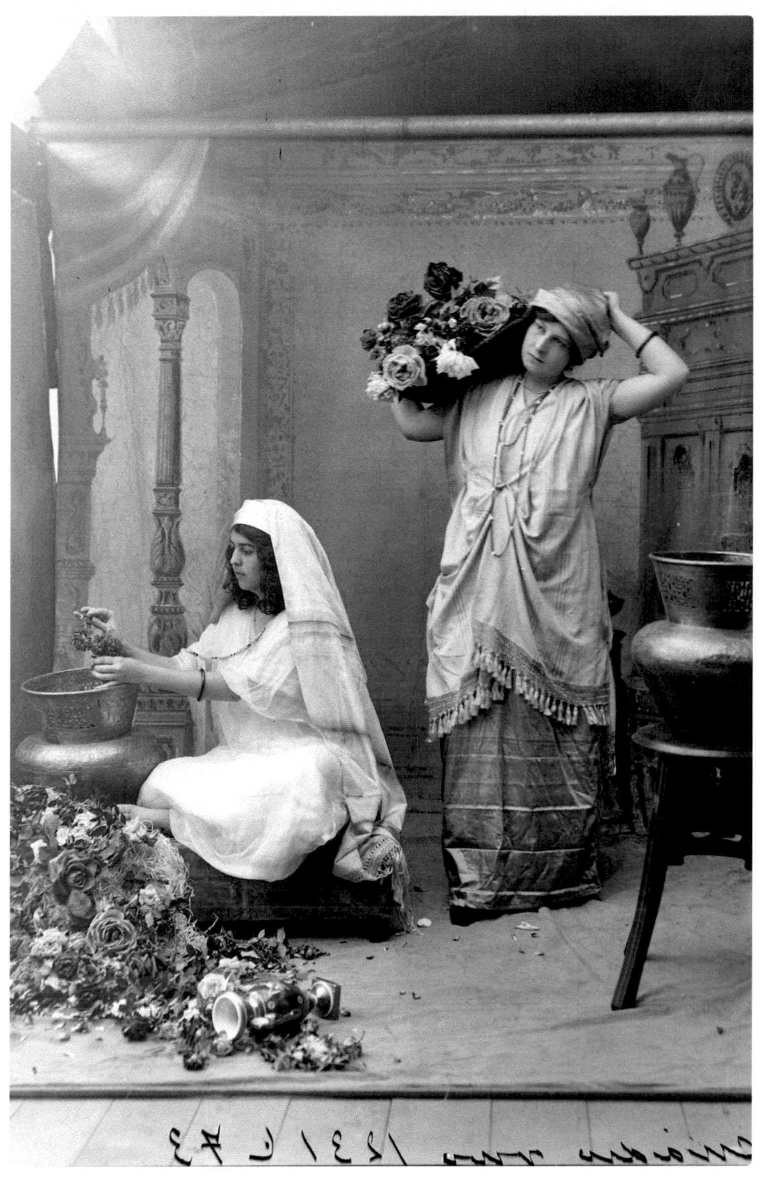

4.1. Fotografía Rodríguez, *Cosecha de rosas*, 1915. Digital positive from dry plate negative, 20 × 15 cm. Biblioteca Pública Piloto de Medellín / Archivo fotográfico.

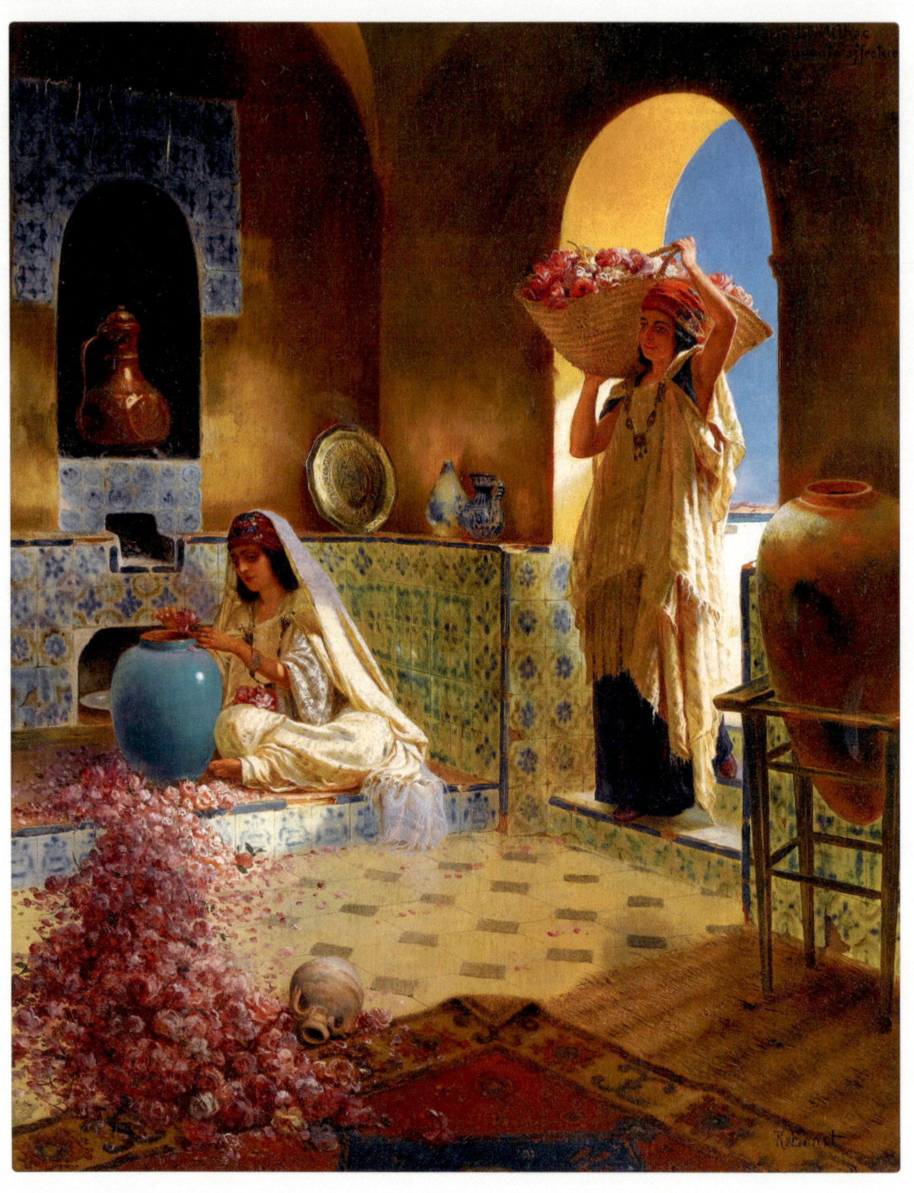

4.2. Rudolf Ernst, *La cueillette des roses*, n.d. Oil on canvas, 55 × 45 cm. Private collection.

considering the isolation and context of Medellín at the time? Did Orientalism transcend the European colonizing gaze to become a global trend? If so, why has it been so poorly explored within Latin American visual production? What is the meaning of Oriental imagery produced outside the European colonizing territories? Does it challenge or support European dominance? These are some questions that emerge when looking at *Cosecha de rosas*. In this chapter, I explore the appropriation of Orientalism by both Rodríguez and de la Calle, which was possible partly due to the wide circulation of photographs, mostly in their postcard form. The negative/positive process of photography permitted such an extensive distribution of images, allowing distant tropes such as Orientalism to arrive in unexpected places, such as Latin America. Orientalism permeated and worked in different ways in the marginal spaces of the colonial world, complicating the notion of Orientalism proposed by Edward Said. In the 1970s, when Said published his Orientalist theory, his ideas were based on a binary opposition led by a clear world division between East and West, and thus between good and evil, right and wrong, positive and negative.[1] As I argue in this chapter, this binary view is not so black and white when one looks at the Orientalist visual production created in marginal places of the world that had no colonial interests or had been colonies themselves, such as Colombia. Here, Orientalist tropes were rather used to promote internal divisions within the same society, and they spoke to racial divides among a highly stratified and racist population. In this sense, the issue of race, namely of the *raza antioqueña*, was intrinsic to these Orientalist ideas that circulated in literary form and visually, as demonstrated by the photographs analyzed here.

The construction of Orientalizing tropes served as a way to acknowledge and visualize difference, namely that between the white antioqueño elite and other subaltern subjects. Thus, Orientalism served as a way to distance the presumed white elite from other racialized and therefore negative subjects, namely the Indigenous and black populations. However, as I will demonstrate, Orientalism also served as a strategy to identify with a racialized Other and thus to create a more horizontal dialogue with a distant trope. In this sense, Orientalism was used for different purposes, and the reading of the photographs in this chapter is evidence of the tensions between these two apparently opposing perspectives.

In previous chapters, I analyzed the negative from a material and metaphorical perspective. In this one, I further explore the idea of alterity and the subaltern in photographic representations as supposedly negative subjects, but I also use the negative as the driving force of photography's itinerancy. Eduardo Cadava and Gabriella Nouzeilles led, in 2013, a research project titled *The Itinerant Languages of Photography*.[2] The project emphasized the migratory character of photographs, that is, their capacity to circulate not only through geographical spaces but also across historical periods and various media.[3] Taking this idea as a point of departure, I argue that this circulation of photographs on a massive scale was only possible thanks to the photographic negative. The negative permitted the creation of multiple photographic copies, leading to questions regarding originality and allowing the wide circulation of the same image around the world. In one of the texts in *The Itinerant Languages of Photography*'s catalog, Cadava follows Walter Benjamin's proposal that photography comes into being only "as a consequence of reproduction, displacement and itinerancy."[4] Indeed, what really defines the medium is photography's capacity to circulate. Photographs are itinerant in and of themselves.

In some cases, they were designed to travel across the globe, bringing with them—for the first time—a sort of fidelity to things themselves that, before the invention of photography, was only available through imagination. This radical change in how we experience the world was only possible through the negative/positive process. The spread of Orientalism was partly due to this phenomenon, and here I analyze one of the many forms in which its appropriation took place. In sum, we will explore how Orientalism was appropriated by a group of elite subjects in Antioquia and how it arrived at and worked in such an unexpected place. I also use the notion of the negative Other and its racial connotations to understand further the visual representation of Orientalist subjects created in Medellín.

Orientalisms

Going back to the first photograph in this chapter, *Cosecha de rosas*, and to the questions that emerged from such an image, it is necessary to clarify first what Orientalism is. Edward Said defined Orientalism as a line of thought that imagined, distorted, and exoticized cultures of Islamic and Asian origin. It was an ideology defined by the Western hegemonic cultural sphere, which embodied distinctions between the Orient—mainly North Africa, the Middle East, and Asia—and the European West to control and authorize a distinctive view of the East as defined by the West. Orientalism saw the East as an inferior culture and became an ideology of political domination that justified colonialism and perpetuated European dominance.[5] The subjects of Orientalist tropes were often depicted in a sexualized, racialized, and feminized manner: in other words, as negative Others that were ready and available for the colonial world.

Moreover, the images were presented as realistic documents representing life in these largely unknown territories; a fact reinforced through photographic representations. The photographs, mostly taken inside a photographer's studio, were carefully composed and embellished to re-create the fantastic world with which the Orient was associated. This way of seeing spread throughout the Western cultural sphere—especially during the nineteenth century—producing pieces of literature, theater, painting, and photography exaggerating clichéd cultural tropes. In photography, the invention of the negative/positive process of reproducing images coincided precisely with the nineteenth-century Orientalist craze.

More recently, Orientalism has been redefined against Said's initial binary analysis. He presumes that the ideas of the West and the East are stable and mutually exclusive political, cultural, and ideological constructs. It has been argued that his approach obscures nuances within bodies of work that can be more diverse and complex and that his perspective has occluded other narratives and counternarratives in which the Orientals themselves were participants.[6] More recently, an inclusive and less binary-based definition has emerged.[7] Homi Bhabha, for example, saw in Said's proposal a problem of ambivalence.[8] For Bhabha, Said fell into the same logic as Western hegemonic strategies. Said's binary proposal—for example, that of power versus powerlessness, knowledge versus ignorance, and even latent versus manifest Orientalism—replicated the same structures of Western thought, thus failing to establish a cohesive epistemic framework for protest or subversion that encompasses various polarities and remains inherently flexible in its dynamics.[9] This new approach to Orientalism understands it as a "network of aesthetic, economic, and political relationships that cross national and historical boundaries."[10] This later characterization complicates the unidirectional forces initially attributed to the ideology, complicating its uses and contexts. This is the definition I use to analyze the Rodríguez brothers' and de la Calle's photographs in this study.

The division between East and West is problematized with the production of Orientalist imagery outside European centers because it challenges its binary understanding based on direct relationships of power where the East was portrayed in negative terms and the West in positive ones. These new nonbinary definitions speak to the circulation, appropriation, and transformation of ideas within Western and non-Western cultures. When Orientalist depictions were produced in places such as Colombia, which, given its marginal position, had no political or colonial engagement with the East, Orientalist imagery played a different role. Nonhegemonic Orientalism, as I shall call it, was a process that intended to position non-European cultures in direct relation to hegemonic cultural traditions. In other words, it was a process that aimed to present their own cultures as modern by identifying with leading international trends. It was also a process that sought to link their culture to the East as exotic other.[11] In addition to the traditional perspective of European Orientalism, which, as art historian Linda Nochlin noted, presented its subjects as "irredeemably different from, more backward than, and culturally inferior to those who construct and consume the [Orientalist] picturesque product," in Latin America the pictures also functioned as a way to align with the European milieu and thus to a superior culture.[12] Moreover, they exoticized and created an Other's Other.

At the beginning of this chapter, I outlined how the composition of *Cosecha de rosas* resembles that of *La cueillette des roses*. But both pictures also refer to a series of characteristics that delineate the construction of Orientalist painting starting in the late eighteenth century: absence of history, lack of Western presence (only the presence of a controlling gaze), and a projection of Western imagination.[13] The photograph appropriates all the characteristics of European Orientalism, which perpetuated political power and justified the dominance of Western culture. However, it was used not as a political tool for colonial domination but as a strategy to align with a racist hegemonic culture, namely that of the Antioquian race. Orientalism was yet another aspect of the discourses of Latin American modernism: racial, hygienic, anthropological, criminal, and sexual.[14] Yet it was an ironic move since it went against Latin America's differentiating intentions. If Latin Americans—or more specifically, antioqueños—wanted to create an image of their own culture to distinguish from the rest of the country, they were not crafting an original one but frustrating their own discourse.

Although the presence of Orientalism in South America might initially seem surprising, the south-to-south relationship between the Americas and the "Orient" has been constant throughout its history since colonial times. It even predates the academic interest in Orientalism of the European-Atlantic powers by centuries.[15] Indeed, it can be traced back to Christopher Columbus's mistake of confusing the new continent with India. Thus, from the conquest period onward, the native inhabitants of these lands were presumed to have a connection with the Orient. Later on, during colonial times, commerce between the East and the Americas was constant and abundant, as demonstrated by the Manila-Acapulco Galleon, which traveled from 1565 until 1815.[16] This shipping line circulated not only all kinds of goods but also persons and ideas that fostered intercontinental exchanges between Asia, the Americas, and Europe. In addition to this, from the 1880s until the 1930s, a wave of Christian immigrants from Syria, Palestine, and Lebanon arrived in the Americas escaping from the Ottoman Empire.[17] In Colombia, in particular, they settled on the Caribbean shore, most of them in Barranquilla, which, at the time, was the country's principal port and its third most developed city.

Colombia was not a particularly attractive destination because the country was immersed in civil wars and consequently suffered economically and socially. However, some immigrants who arrived by mistake decided to stay, and others found the Colombian situation enough of an improvement to develop their lives here. Eastern culture manifested both culturally—through food and music—and in commercial strategies. The impact of Middle Eastern culture on Colombia was significant even though the number of immigrants was not very high.[18] Indeed, Middle Eastern immigrants introduced "personal credits" in Colombia, which allowed clients to pay monthly.[19] This new market tactic revolutionized commerce and stimulated new consumption practices.[20] Although Antioquia was one of the few places in the country where the Middle Easterners did not have a big impact, it is possible to think that the repercussions of this transnational encounter might have hit the imaginary of the Antioquian cultural sphere at an early stage. Not coincidentally, the name of the department itself, Antioquia, recalls a relationship to the so-called Orient. The connections between Colombia, the Middle East, and Asia were thus not a novelty by the end of the nineteenth century, attesting, once again, that the process of exoticization of Oriental subjects as negative Others was in some ways similar to the one pursued in Europe, particularly in France around the same time, and in others very different from its European counterparts.

Orientalism in Antioquia

A well-documented connection between the Antioquian cultural sphere and Orientalist imagery is the art of the department's quintessential nineteenth-century painter and sculptor, Francisco Antonio Cano. Born in Yarumal, Antioquia—the same town as Benjamín de la Calle—Cano moved to Medellín in 1885, intending to travel to Bogotá to study engraving. That same year, however, a civil war exploded in response to the Regeneración project, a new centralized type of government supported by President Rafael Núñez and Miguel Antonio Caro.[21] With the country amid a civil war, Cano had to stay in Medellín, settling in the house of his cousins, the Rodríguez brothers, for five years. During this time, he learned painting and photography, opened the photographic studio with Horacio Marino, collaborated with different literary magazines—including *El Repertorio* and *El Montañés*—and organized some of the first art exhibitions in the city.[22] Cano taught painting to his peers, including Melitón, Horacio Marino's younger brother, who would become the head photographer of the Rodríguez atelier after Horacio Marino's withdrawal from the business in 1898.

After the war, in 1897, Cano finally departed for Bogotá. In the capital, he was in contact with the most prominent academic painters of the time, including Epifanio Garay and Ricardo Acevedo Bernal. He painted important political figures and positioned himself as a recognized artist in Bogotá's growing cultural sphere. He returned to Medellín and continued with his quest to become an artist, not a naive or self-taught one, but an academic painter and sculptor. In 1898, Cano received a grant from the government to travel to Paris and study painting at the Académies Julian and Colarrosi.[23] His sojourn overlapped with the last current of Orientalism in France. Although the Parisian art scene was effervescent, and modern art was on the rise, Cano eschewed the vanguard agenda and remained closer to the academy. He studied with an older generation of artists, including Jean-Baptiste Constant, also called Benjamin Constant (1845–1902), who had turned to Orientalist painting after a trip to Morocco in 1872.[24]

The impact of Orientalism in the work of Cano is evident in some of his paintings, particularly *El Cristo del Perdón* (The Forgiving Christ, 1910), *Rebeca* (Rebecca, 1910), and *El Soko* (The Souk, 1901, fig. 4.3). In the first two paintings, the effect of Orientalism is hidden behind historical religious themes. Cano does not create paintings with explicit exoticization of Middle Eastern culture. However, he subtly engages with sexual

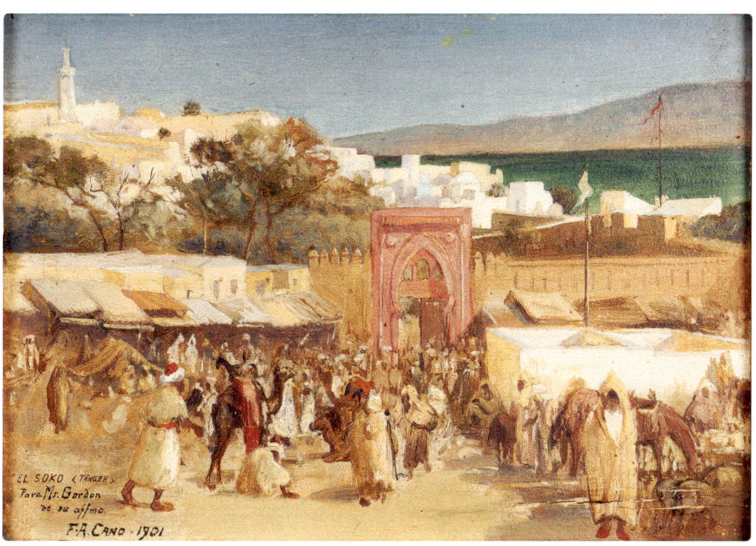

4.3. Francisco Antonio Cano, *El Soko,* 1901. Oil on canvas, 18 × 26 cm. Private collection, Medellín. Photo: Carlos Tobón.

desires embodied in Oriental female characters and idealizes the landscape of the scenes. For example, in *El Cristo del Perdón,* he creates a realist scene of the eighth station of the cross, and in *Rebeca,* Cano represents the moment when she meets Abraham's servant and offers him water. The painter sets the scene in a deserted Oriental landscape and paints Rebecca carrying the water vase on her shoulder, a common way to depict her. She is represented as a sensual woman, leaving her left shoulder uncovered, a gesture emphasized by the position of her hand. In *El Soko,* Cano opts for a view of the gate of El Soko, a relatively common perspective of the city of Tangiers. Here, the city looks untouched by Western influence and is instead depicted in an idealized way.

After returning from Paris, Cano taught painting and sculpture to many artists from Medellín, including Melitón Rodríguez.[25] In a painting titled *Estudio del pintor* (The painter's studio, 1885, fig. 4.4), Cano depicted a scene from his studio. Melitón, still a young boy, appears on the right side of the composition, turning away from his easel, and looking at a drawing by Gabriel Montoya, the man sitting next to him. From Melitón's easel hang two objects: a drawing or painting, still a work in progress, and a small carte de visite he uses as a model for his picture.

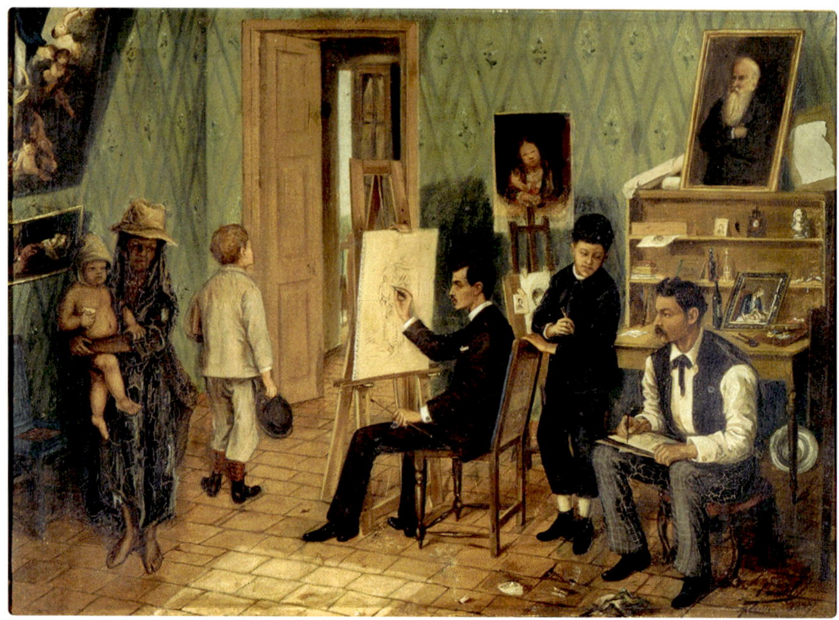

4.4. Francisco Antonio Cano, *Estudio del pintor*, 1885. Oil on canvas, 42 × 59 cm. Private collection. Photo: Carlos Tobón.

Cano differentiates Melitón's practice from that of the other two artists included in the composition. While the others utilize the live models standing on the left side of the painting, Melitón uses a photograph, foreshadowing not only the vital role that photography would play in his life but also the future intrinsic connection between painting and his work as a photographer. Moreover, the carte de visite can be read as a reminder of photography's mechanical reproduction capacity, which, as stated earlier, was only possible due to the negative/positive process.

The idea of multiple copies of a single image also materializes in the carte de visite format, particularly in its complete negative form. Cartes de visite were usually created using collodion glass plates and a multiple-lens camera. This new technology, popularized by Parisian photographer André-Adolphe-Eugène Disdéri, permitted the creation of multiple copies of the same image or variations thereof on a single negative plate. As seen in *Mlle Rousseau dans l'Africaine* (fig. 4.5), a series of Orientalist photographs by Disdéri in 1865, cartes de visite play with the notions of duplication and reproduction on different levels. In this positive version of a cartes de visite negative, it is possible to see how each pose is

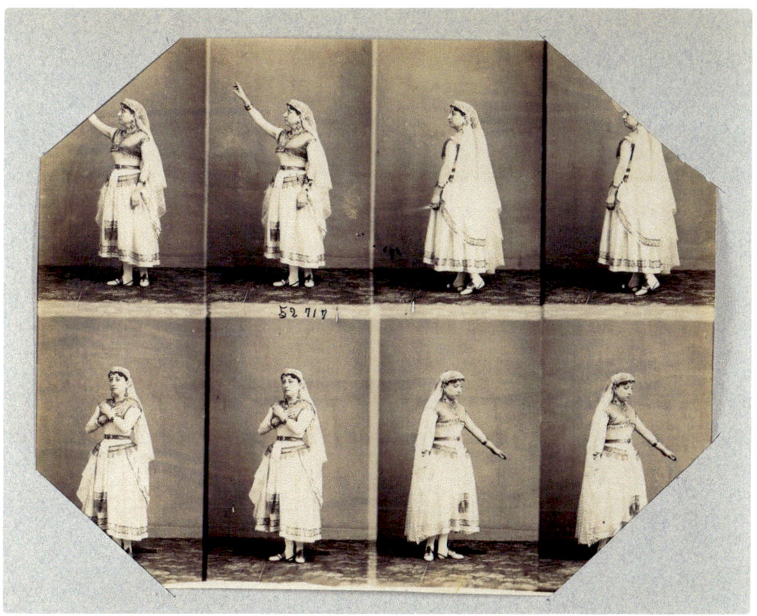

4.5. André-Adolphe-Eugène Disdéri, *Mlle Rousseau dans l'Africaine*, 1865. Albumen silver print from glass negative, 18.8 × 23.5 cm. Gilman Collection, gift of The Howard Gilman Foundation, 2005. Metropolitan Museum of Art.

repeated twice in the photographic sequence. This type of negative signals photography's capacity to create multiple copies of the same image through the repeated documentation of the sitter with a multiple-lens camera and the reproduction of the negative itself.

As opposed to the wide popularization of the daguerreotype and tintype processes in Europe and the United States, the carte de visite revolutionized photography in Colombia. The invention of the carte de visite in 1854 and its consequent popularization during the 1860s coincided with the implementation of a new liberal constitution in Colombia, in force from 1863 until 1886. The liberal government politics of this period benefited foreign exchange and commerce, particularly exports, which included photographic materials.[26] This historical coincidence advanced photography as a mechanical reproduction technique in the country and made the medium available to a broad population. Moreover, the new photographic process based on a negative matrix had an economic impact on photography's dissemination, making the technology affordable to a wide public for the first time. Cano's painting, created in 1885, clearly evidences this phenomenon, showing the popularity of cartes de visite and how the artistic milieu used them.

This dialogue between Cano's and the Rodríguez brothers' work manifested throughout their careers. Cano brought photographs, postcards, engravings, books, and magazines that might have informed the photographer's production. The visual connection between *Cosecha de rosas* and *La cueillette des roses* is so close that it is hard to think that Melitón created this photograph without having access to a direct referent of the painting. I have written elsewhere that Melitón must have learned about the painting through some reproduction of the original.[27] Here, I want to propose that he had access to the original through a postcard. This idea is supported by some of the photographic reproductions of artworks in postcard form that are part of Cano's archive, which we presume he brought back from his trip to Europe. And although none of these pictures represents *La cueillette des roses*, they reinforce that Cano was collecting these types of images and that he brought them back to Colombia and probably shared them with his peers. Postcards were a primordial mode of artistic reproduction and, as stated by Cadava and Nouzeilles, "they evoke the itinerancy of images in general."[28] Indeed, beginning in the 1880s, with the introduction of the halftone printing process, photographic postcards became the primary vehicle through which images circulated worldwide.[29] Jeffrey Meikle explains in detail how in 1878, American inventor Frederick Ives created the halftone process, in which the negative played a fundamental part, thus permitting massive photographic reproduction in postcard form:

> He [Frederick Ives] created the so-called halftone screen by etching two plates of glass with parallel ruled lines and filling the etched lines with dark pigment. He then joined the two sheets of glass in a wooden frame, with the dark lines facing inward and at right angles. The result was a smooth, transparent glass screen covered with small, precise squares similar to those on graph paper. To prepare a printing plate, this screen was mounted in a camera between a reversed *photographic negative* of the image to be printed and a photosensitized zinc or copper plate. Light shining through the *negative* created patterns of varying high and low light intensities, which were then diffused by the ruled squares of the screen, casting dots of light (or shadow) onto the plate. The more intense the light, the larger the dots on the plate, though their center points were all arranged in precisely even rows. In the case of completely dark areas

of the *negative*, no dots of light were cast onto the plate's surface. After an exposed plate was chemically fixed and washed, an acid bath dissolved the surface of the plate around the dots, thereby creating a raised or relief surface with which a halftone image could be printed.[30]

It is clear from this description that the negative was crucial in developing the process to mass-produce realistic-looking cards. But this extensive circulation of images was not limited to the images themselves. It also meant that the ideas these images perpetuated were disseminated as well. Postcards became one of the main channels through which Orientalist tropes circulated.[31]

Considering that both the painting *La cueillette des roses* and the photograph *Cosecha de rosas* were created during the "postcard craze" period, it is very feasible to think that Melitón had access to the painting through a postcard. However, the fact that the images look alike does not mean they operate similarly. Indeed, by appropriating the Ernst painting within a completely different context, the function of the picture changed. By imitating the Orient, the Antioquian elite was defining itself in opposition to it and thus moving closer to the Western understanding of culture—and that was, indeed, the ultimate goal of the discourse promoted by the myth of the *raza antioqueña*.

The myth gained strength by exoticizing the negative Other with which their own culture was originally associated but from which they wanted to distance: the *indio*, the black, the mestizo, the peasant, as a sort of surrogate or even underground self. Ultimately, the *raza antioqueña* discourse worked very similarly to Eurocentrism, to which the construction of Orientalism and the Other was crucial. It was, as Edward Said explained, "a collective notion identifying 'us' Europeans against all 'those' non-Europeans, and indeed it can be argued that the major component in European culture is precisely what made that culture hegemonic both in and outside Europe: the idea of European identity as a superior one in comparison with all the non-European peoples and cultures."[32] Said's statement translates perfectly to the discussion of the Antioquian race. If *Europe* and *European* are substituted for *Antioquia* and *Antioquian*, the same argument for the construction of a superior race would apply.

Latin American intellectuals from the nineteenth century, especially writers, appropriated different forms of Orientalism in their work.[33] In their writings, many created an Orientalized, imagined, and exoticized space that, in many cases, departed from the European view and not their own.[34] In Latin America, Eurocentrism was—and in many cases continues to be—the hegemonic line of thought, a fact that might be partially explained through the particularities of the emancipation processes. Here, independence was not led by the native Indigenous peoples (as in Africa or India) but was orchestrated by the "criollo elites who wanted to govern themselves . . . dominate the Indians and build nations based on ideals of linguistic and racial purity."[35] The necessity to position their own culture at the level of the European one, which they ultimately believed they pertained to, led the elites to appropriate a negative Other in the Oriental tradition. However, as Laura J. Torres-Rodríguez asserts, Orientalism was also useful to the white criollo elites of the nascent Republics to proclaim their own identity based on difference and independence from Europe.[36] In this way, Orientalism played a double, and even contradictory, role. On the one hand, it was a strategy used to identify with the European tradition, and on the other, it was a mechanism used to mark a stark difference with that same referent as it "opposed European notions of morality, time, space, and personal identity."[37] In other words, the Latin Americans claimed their own distinctiveness by identifying with subjectivities considered morally negative from a European standpoint. As is explored later in this chapter, this apparent contradiction is also present in the work of the Colombian photographers analyzed here. However, it is important to first take a look at the Orientalist tradition in photography in more general terms to understand the place where these Colombian photographers inserted themselves.

Photography's Orientalism

Photography, in particular, had a relationship with the mythical Orient right from its invention. Indeed, in François Arago's speech to the French Chamber of Deputies in 1839 announcing the invention of photography, he emphasized the advantages that photography would bring to the documentation and exploration of the Middle East.[38] Only eighty days after Arago's intervention, daguerreotypist Frederic Goupil-Fesquet and a group of French painters and scholars led by Horace Venet traveled to Algeria and Egypt to document ancient monuments.[39] From the 1850s onward, when the negative/positive process was already in use in most European countries, many photographers embarked on cumbersome trips to Egypt and the Holy Land to capture parts of the world that Westerners had barely seen. Among these photographers were Maxime du Camp, Francis Frith, August Salzman, Jacques Antoine Moulin, and Felix Bonfils. Their images fascinated European consumers and became a complete market success.[40] The negative process permitted their reproduction in different formats: albums, postcards, cartes de visite, and so on, and was crucial for their economic success and dissemination.

During the collodion period, when photographers had to travel with their portable darkrooms to develop the pictures in situ, the negative played a fundamental role in Orientalist photography. As Sean Willcock noted, Orientalist portraiture was a technical and theatrical process that involved not only the shooting of the camera and final positive print but also "the preparation, exposure, developing, fixing, rinsing and varnishing of a negative, during which the intended final product, the positive, remained absent."[41] The negative was made immediately public precisely because these traveling photographers were forced to develop the plates while the collodion was still wet. Moreover, the negative captured "chemical reactions, environmental conditions and material flows—that went into its own formation."[42] Working in the field meant new challenges for Orientalist photographers as the negatives were exposed to new and unknown environmental conditions, capturing on the surface of the plates the challenges that the weather imposed. In this way, as noted by Willcock, negatives were not limited to depicting the geometric space of the Cartesian perspective, which is typically associated with positive prints. Instead, they also captured elements of the surrounding environment that translated into cracks, bubbles, and other material impressions on the negative plates.[43] In the late 1870s, with the invention of gelatin-based negative processes, Orientalist photographs became easier to produce and circulate. They satisfied an emerging tourist industry and the desire of collectors for Orientalist imagery.[44] The expeditions to the Middle East were part of a set of political, cultural, and economic relations between the East and the West, and the resulting images should be understood as consequential from these interchanges and networks.[45]

The large number of Orientalist images produced during that period covered a wide range of subjects, from the documentation of historical monuments to studio photography. Photography was presumed to be an objective and transparent medium, which made producing this sort of image even more problematic. The distorted reality portrayed in paintings was interpreted as a genuine document of life; with photographic representations, the images were attributed an even greater documentary value. It was taken for granted that the camera acted as a witness to what came in front of it since this was a medium that relied on the presence of a referent as a condition for producing the image. However, as we well know today, that referent could be widely manipulated, allowing for the creation of scenes that were carefully selected, framed, and even staged in scenarios intended to portray a reality that did not exist but sold very well. The demand was so heavy that both foreign and local photographers produced this sort of images, and their conventions were far from uniform, as they shifted depending on the customer and the function the image should fulfill.

With the Victorian fascination for dressing up, which was partly a way of escaping from the constrictions of daily life, Orientalist studio photography emerged as a widespread trend worldwide. For commercial purposes, photographers created pictures of highly sexualized harem women, or odalisques. This iconography had a longer genealogy starting in the nineteenth century, with painters such as Ingres, Delacroix, and Gérôme. Among the photographic studio mise-en-scènes are, for example, those created by Jacques Antoine Moulin, who was a "specialist in *academies*," as he listed himself in the Paris directories.[46] *Académies* was the term used to describe nude studies, which he specifically created for artists and which, in many cases, verged on the pornographic. This is seen, for example, in images such as *A Moorish Woman with Her Maid* from ca. 1856 (fig. 4.6). The photograph depicts a woman lying on a set of cushions, resting her bare feet on her maid's lap, while the maid protects her mistress by holding her feet with one hand and her knees with the other. The legs and arms of the lying woman are uncovered provocatively and further enhanced by the ankle cuffs and bracelets she is wearing for the picture. Here, the woman's body further enhances sexual desire and thus the subordination of the female.[47] In other words, she appears as a negative subject. This photograph was part of an album created in 1865 to celebrate the visit of Napoleon III to Algeria and was probably seen, in a different setting, by Roger Fenton (1819–69), one of the most famous English photographers to create Orientalist pictures.[48]

Indeed, Fenton created a photograph of a reclining odalisque as part of his *Orientalist Suite* from 1858 (fig. 4.7). In his picture, the woman

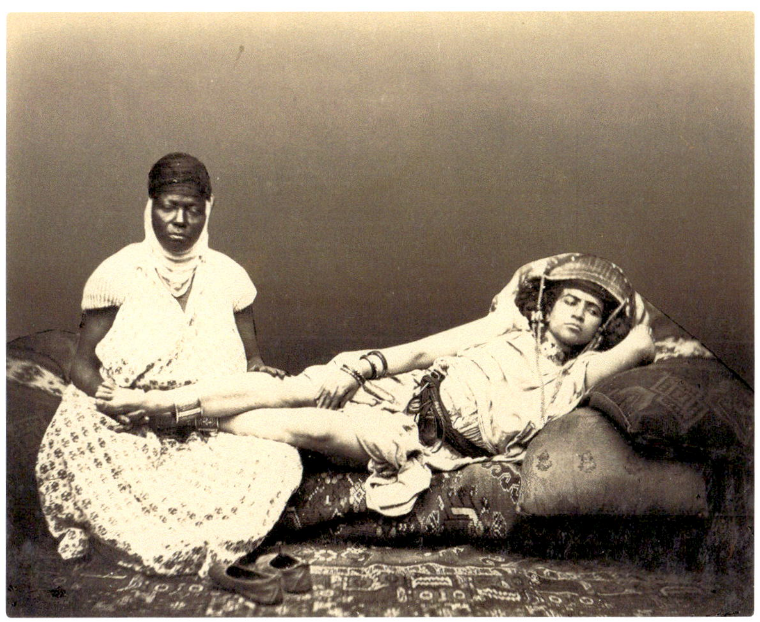

4.6. Félix Jacques Antoin Moulin, *A Moorish Woman with Her Maid*, ca. 1856. Albumen print, 18.1 × 22.8 cm (7⅛ × 9 in.). The J. Paul Getty Museum, Los Angeles.

appears in a pose similar to the one in the Moulin photo; this time, however, she is alone. The woman is also depicted in a setting of cushions, carpets, vases, and other Orientalist props, and while her legs are covered, her blouse is suggestively open, exposing part of her left breast. This pose became the standard way of portraying Eastern women for Western eyes. Sexual overtones were intentional, and the exploitation of women's bodies was at play, especially when they were women of color, perceived as symbols of "sexual regression and promiscuity."[49] This iconography was repeated in paintings, drawings, and engravings, and even more profusely in cartes de visite and postcards.[50] Here, the picture was not only cheap and therefore accessible to a large part of the population; it was also an image that traveled due to the facilities that the negative/positive provided. Thus, the possibility of possessing the eroticized negative Other and the widespread circulation of these images turned the iconography of the odalisque into a "cultural cliché" and simultaneously "naturalized the mythology of Oriental eroticism."[51]

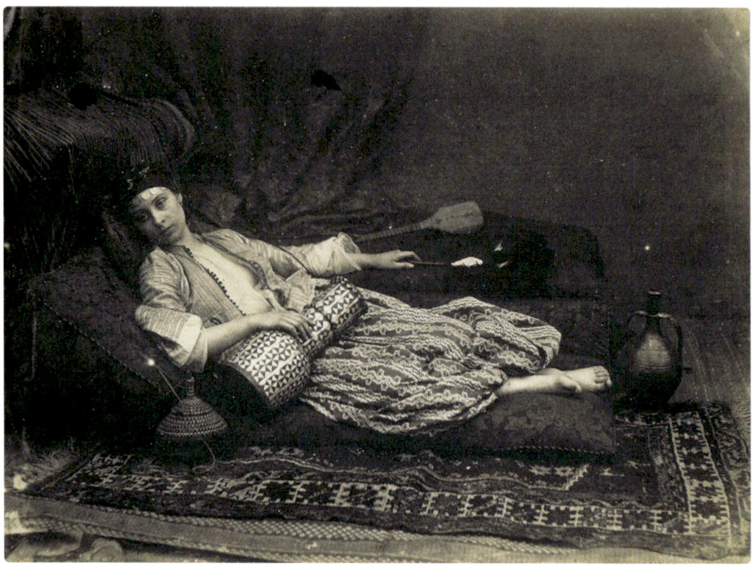

4.7. Roger Fenton, *Reclining Odalisque*, 1858. Salted paper print, 28.5 × 39 cm. The Rubel Collection, purchase, Lila Acheson Wallace, anonymous, Joyce and Robert Menschel, Jennifer and Joseph Duke, and Ann Tenenbaum and Thomas H. Lee, gifts, 1997, Metropolitan Museum of Art, New York.

The Orientalist Costume

Cosecha de rosas is not the only Orientalist photograph of the antioqueño photographers' body of work. Another striking image, commonly known under the title *Odaliscas* (Odalisques), was taken by Benjamín de la Calle in 1915 (fig. 4.8). In this photograph, a group of five women pose in the image. Unlike the more common representation of the topic, which usually depicts one or two persons, this photograph is charged with excess, not only in terms of the number of women in the picture but also by the exuberance of the costumes and props: Cushions, carpets, Oriental headpieces, pearl necklaces, eccentric textiles, and even a jewelry box in the back exacerbate the theatricality of the scene. In the back of the image, a woman places her hand inside a small chest filled with jewels, as if it were a treasure found in a scene from *One Thousand and One Nights*.

The photograph is also very frontal, especially compared to Moulin's or Fenton's images. Here, the women face the spectator directly, with their bodies confronting the camera and suggestively inviting the person

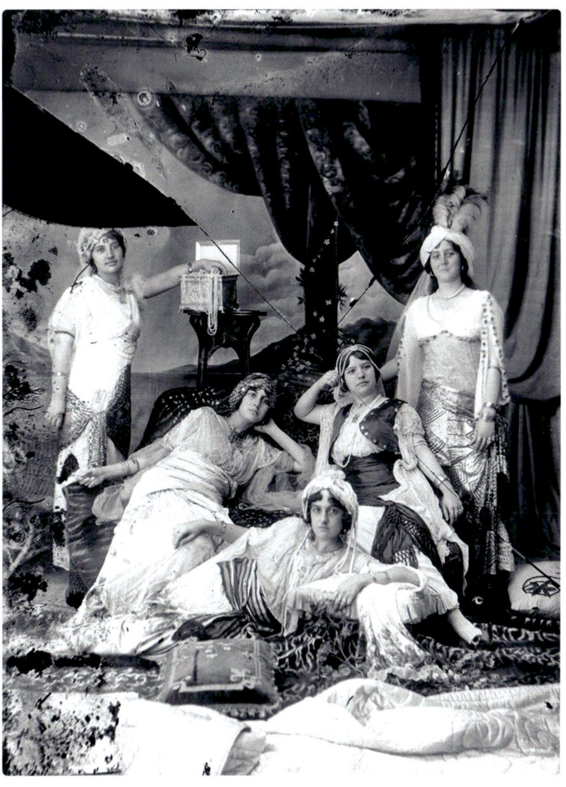

4.8. Benjamín de la Calle, *Untitled (Grupo de Odaliscas)*, 1915. Digital positive from dry plate negative, 25 × 20 cm. Biblioteca Pública Piloto de Medellín / Archivo fotográfico.

on the other side of the lens—or the picture—to look further. They are, however, fully covered and, therefore, less sexualized than their European variants. The multiplicity and the excess of the photograph recall a harem fantasy, a dream of polygamy that, in the context of Medellín, becomes a suggestive provocation that could have produced scandalous reactions from the very conservative spectators. In this sense, the sitters embody the notion of the negative. This idea can be read here on two different levels. First, the odalisques portray a distant sexualized subject that implies negative terms. In other words, they embody the idea of a distant negative Other. But they also embrace Orientalism as a way of redeeming that negative subject through an identification with the remote Other performed through the costume, the poses, and the photograph itself.

During the same photographic session, de la Calle took another two photographs: one of Alicia Botero and one of Alicia Sánchez, the two sitters in the middle of the group photograph (figs. 4.9 and 4.10). Botero preserves

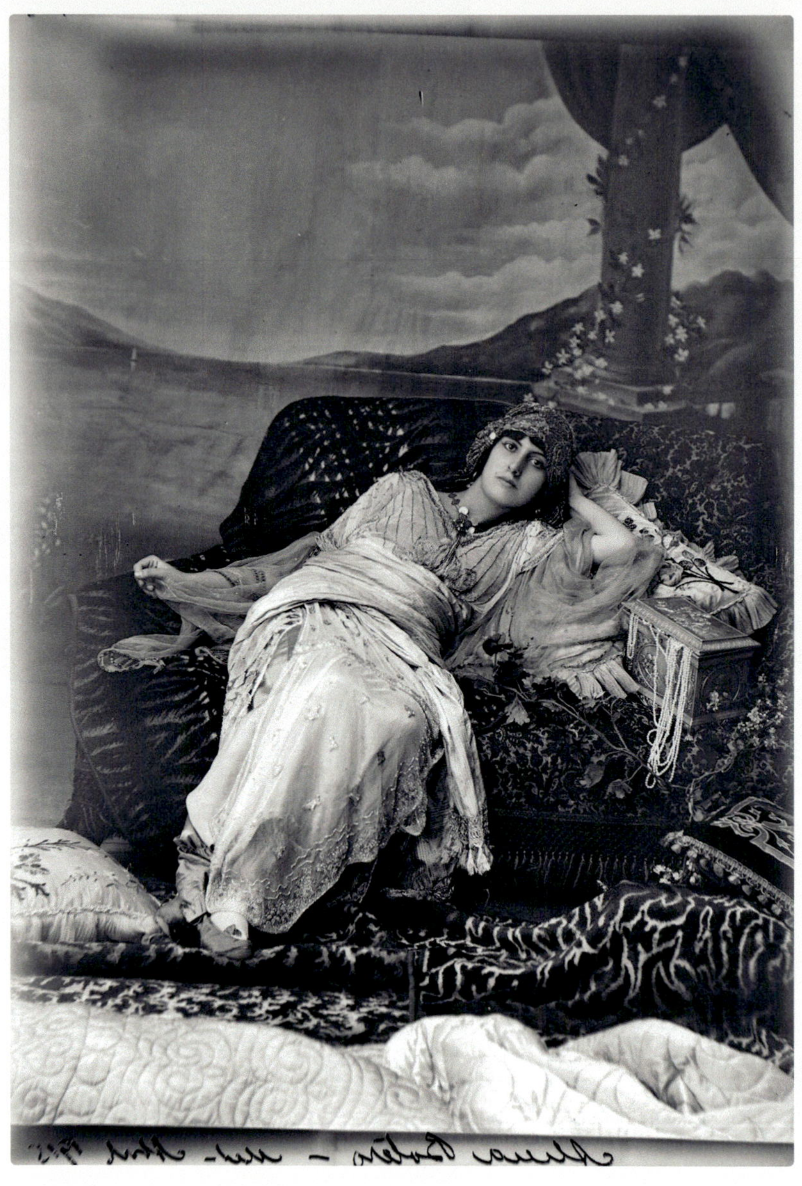

4.9. Benjamín de la Calle, *Alicia Botero*, 1915. Digital positive from dry plate negative, 16 × 12 cm. Biblioteca Pública Piloto de Medellín / Archivo fotográfico.

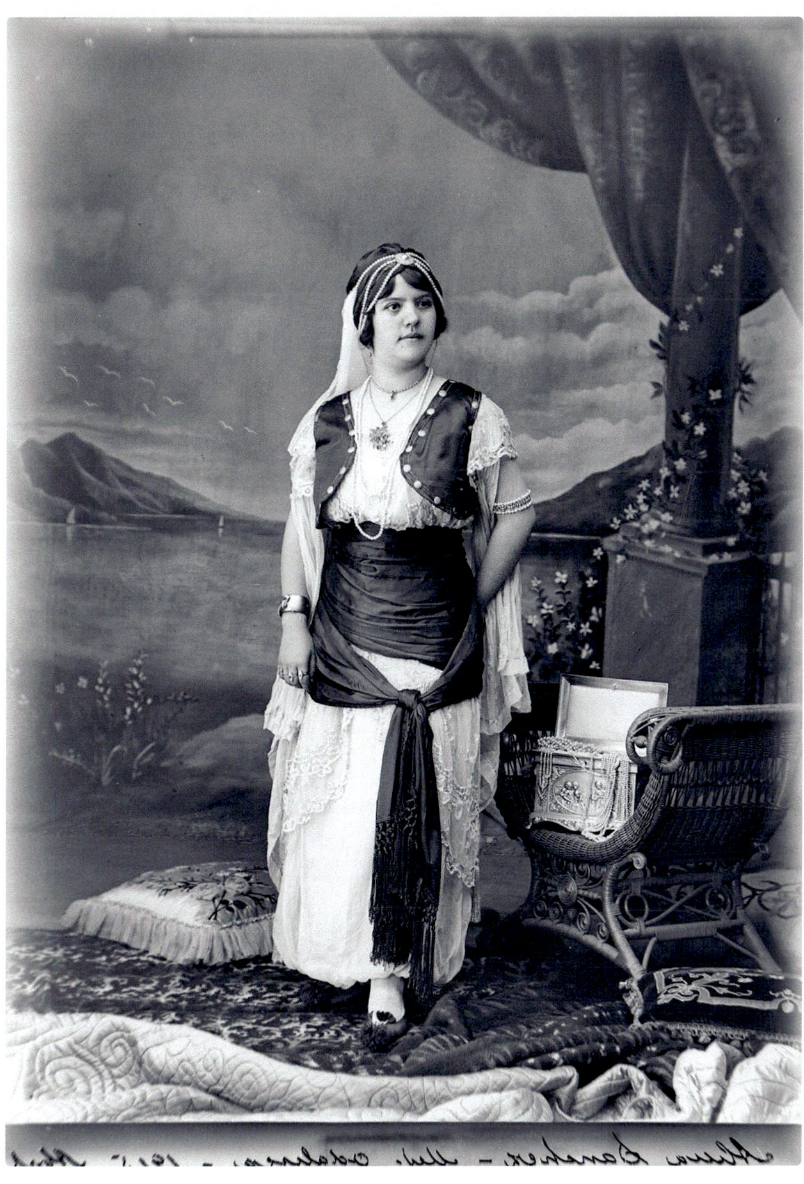

4.10. Benjamín de la Calle, *Alicia Sánchez*, 1915. Digital positive from dry plate negative, 16 × 12 cm. Biblioteca Pública Piloto de Medellín / Archivo fotográfico.

the suggestive reclining pose from the previous picture, while Sánchez stands more hieratically. Yet they both perform the distant negative subject. They both embody the notion of alterity, an alterity that describes the tensions between an identification with an Othered subject and simultaneously the distance between themselves and an unknown culture. This lack of familiarity partially manifests in the props included in the pictures, such as the jewelry box, the cushions, and the carpets, all manifestations of the Orientalist imagination. Moreover, the sexualized poses and Orientalist costumes contrast with the backdrop, the negative space, which depicts an idyllic landscape of a large lake surrounded by mountains. The backdrop painting breaks the coherence of the idealized Oriental scene as it does not represent a stereotypical Middle Eastern landscape, again making the contradictions at work in these photographs evident.

That de la Calle agreed to create an image of the negative Other, a difference embodied in an exotic construction, speaks to the fact that he could not escape being a man of his time. However, the provocative aspect of the image challenges the sanctimonious attitude of Medellín's society by giving space to women to perform their sexuality without the necessity of uncovering their bodies to satisfy the viewer's desire. More importantly, even if the image could recall a fantasy space upon which desires could be projected with impunity, the women are posing for themselves and not another's imposed gaze. It is a commissioned portrait, not an image created by de la Calle to be sent to an exhibition or sold and circulated as a carte de visite or postcard. Indeed, the picture format is bigger than his usual photographs—about twenty-five by twenty centimeters—indicating the higher price he might have charged for it and its potential use. This was most likely a picture meant to be framed and held in private hands. Contrasting with *Cosecha de rosas*, where the two women work in congeniality and suggest a submissive attitude, in *Odaliscas*, the women present themselves as challenging and empowered characters. Thus, Benjamín de la Calle's photograph is an example of subversion against the racist and hostile discourse of the elite, which promoted the self-righteous behavior of women. In pictures such as this one, Orientalism works as a way of recovering an excluded domain.

The picture of the odalisques displays a duality that renders it unique. On the one hand, it is an image of feminine liberation, a liberation that was possible only within the space of performance enabled by the costumes and the photographic setting. In other words, performing another identity by wearing an outfit not worn in daily life allowed them to act freely and disregard the severe restrictions imposed by the codes of behavior and the Marian model of Catholicism. On the other hand, the Orientalist costume inevitably relied on an exoticization of the Other and, to that extent, aligned itself with the same structures of power against which the image appeared to take a stand. By virtue of this duality, the image is ambivalent or even contradictory. However, the sense of subversion against the discourse of the elite, against the discourse of *la raza antioqueña* that promoted a patriarchal attitude toward women, would have carried the most weight within the context in which the image was produced. Thus, *Odaliscas* must be understood as an instance of counterdiscourse, a picture of liberation that, beyond creating a vision of the unknown as an inferior culture, functions as a symbolic space of radical alterity, removed from the conventions of its own culture. By embodying a character alien to the dress codes proper to their own culture, the women may have felt a certain degree of freedom; by portraying a fictitious character, they could play a role on the margins of their sociocultural anchorage. In other words, by Orientalizing themselves, the women gained recognition and freedom.

De la Calle is better known for his work portraying—although not only—the other half of Antioquia's society, the mestizo, peasant, and lower-middle-class populations: the negative Others in a community that proclaimed itself white, Catholic, and heterosexual. He was a controversial figure in Antioquian society, not only for his supposed homosexuality but also because, through his photographic work, he often positioned himself against the discourses promoted by the myth of *la raza antioqueña*. The fact that de la Calle would also create Orientalist images—that is, photographs that materialize an exotic construction of the unknown—shows that even someone like him could hardly escape his historical context.

The group portrait of the odalisques points to similar representations of the harem motif, specifically those taken in the Ottoman Empire by foreign and local photographers who sought to satisfy the European rage for Orientalist eroticism. These photographs typically depicted groups of Turkish women but, unlike those taken by European photographers in North Africa or Europe, were less risky and relatively chaste. In fact, the women are hardly ever depicted nude, although, as Ali Behdad has noted, they always pose without the hijab and partially display their bodies.[52] These photographers also dignified their models by giving the image the title of *Dames turques*, perhaps complying with regulations regarding the use of

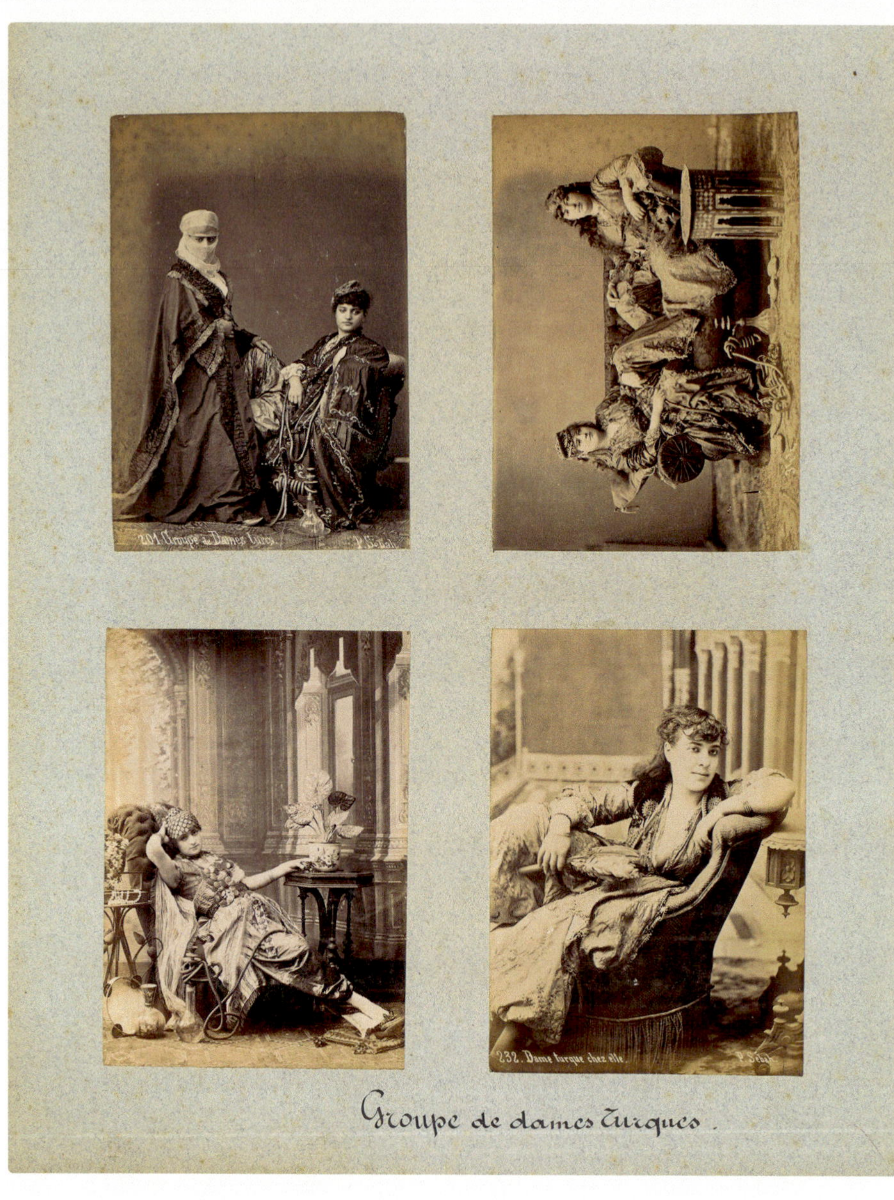

4.11. Various photographers, *Groupe de dames turques*, n.d. Page of the album *Turquie*, 1852–1920, 43 × 32.5 cm. Pierre Gigord Collection of Photographs. Getty Research Institute Special Collections, Los Angeles.

photography within the Ottoman Empire and intended to project a positive image (fig. 4.11).[53] Although these images were more innocuous and did not present their subjects in the nude, they were not less erotic or Orientalist. Many photographers took advantage of this partial unveiling to encourage play with the fantastic idea of the inaccessible harem. Although the veil is part of a woman's social dress code within the Muslim religious context, the interior scenes produced by Orientalist artists opened the way for an erotic interpretation of this item of clothing. Such images traveled around the world, especially to Europe, where other photographers would use them as a reference to re-create similar scenes. In turn, those new images were distributed in different contexts, thus creating a worldwide economy of visual Orientalism, an economy enabled by the photographic negative.

A photograph like *Favorite of the Harem* (1901, fig. 4.12), published by the American company Underwood and Underwood, could well have served as the model for de la Calle's *Odaliscas*. Produced as a stereograph, the image presents five women striking sensual poses on a set filled with pillows and textiles while a man, possibly the Sultan, chooses his favorite. The photograph is staged and relies on the same tropes used by de la Calle; oddly, both photos refrain from using stereotypical props like hookahs, tea sets, or musical instruments like the tambourine. We do not know where this image was taken since the stereograph publishing house Underwood and Underwood was one of the largest in the world, with offices in New York, London, Toronto, and Ottawa (Kansas). The women do not appear naked, so eroticism in this image functions similarly to that of the Ottoman photographs: in both cases, the absence of nudity produced a scene that is not any less sensual and Orientalist. Consumers of stereographs privileged erotic scenes because the image gained more realism as it became three-dimensional when viewed through the stereoscope.

But regardless of the specific referent de la Calle might have used for his *Odaliscas* picture, the association with the Orient that the sitters of this photograph perform is simultaneously close and distant from their own bodies. It is distant insofar as the sitters associate themselves with a fairly unknown culture but close as they relate with other subjects that have also experienced an Othering process. As Sara Ahmed explains, "the East is associated with women, sexuality and the exotic, with what is 'behind' and 'below' the West, as well as what is on the other side," an idea clearly related to the concept of the negative.[54] As explained in chapter 3, the negative is what stands "on the other side" of the photographic positive. It is

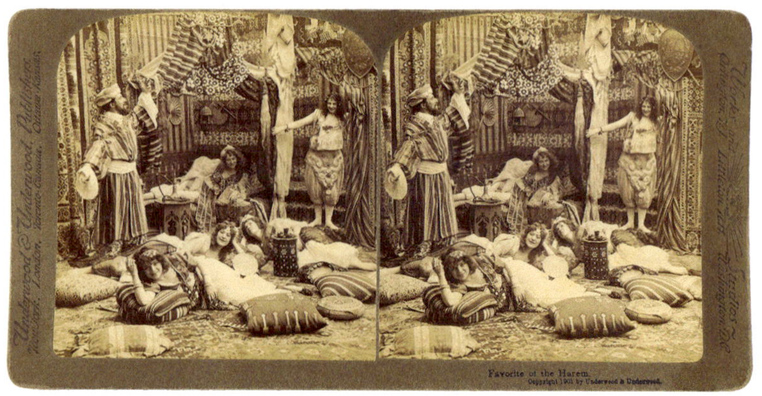

4.12. Underwood and Underwood, *Favorite of the Harem*, 1901. Albumen silver print. The J. Paul Getty Museum, Los Angeles, 84.XC.1158.169.

what is not shown and kept away from sight; it is alterity and thus photography's Othered object. We can then argue that the negative is an "orientated" object, as it has acquired a connotation by taking its subaltern position as a given. But the negative is not only orientated in this way; it is also orientated through the demarcation of a neglected physical space, that is, the negative space in photography. This overlooked space is further explored in the final chapter of this book. Still, it is imperative to remind readers that by referring to the negative, we are also dealing with the marking of a geographical/physical distinction in the same way in which Orientalism delimits differences based on the arbitrary demarcation of a place.

Returning to the photos analyzed in this section, unlike *Cosecha de rosas*, a pictorialist photograph conceived as a work of art for a photography contest, the odalisque photographs are individual or group portraits of members of Antioquian society, whose names and last names occasionally appear on the negative plates. The habit of dressing up was among the traditions of the nineteenth century in Medellín: adults and children alike appear in a profuse collection of images wearing angel, monk, gypsy, and even baker costumes. The odalisques' photographs are likely related to this tradition, which became increasingly popular in Medellín as the century advanced, perhaps because of the diffusion of the theater, opera, and other performing arts. In his 1909 book *Apuntes para la historia del teatro en Medellín y vejeces* (Notes for the history of theater in Medellín and old matters), Eladio Gónima recalls that

> in the year [18]39 a famous costume ball was held in the home of Doctor Gabriel Echeverri, and this ball was the talk of the town for long after, for there was a great display of luxury, good music, and above all the cordiality and courtesy with which Mr. Echeverri, his wife, and children performed the honors of their house.
>
> Among the costumes worn by the ladies and young ladies, one could find Cleopatra, Mary Stuart, Esther, Rachel, etc., and the gentlemen wore the old Spanish suit from the days of Louis XIV, Louis XV, Hungarian costume, old Venetian costume, etc.[55]

Judging by this recollection, in the early nineteenth century, the Medellín elite already exhibited a lively interest in performing exotic characters as part of the costumes they wore for these private celebrations.

De la Calle was not the only photographer to take pictures of elite members of Antioquian society dressed in Orientalist costumes. The Rodríguez brothers' body of work includes another Orientalist photograph from 1899, featuring fourteen men dressed up as Arab types (fig. 4.13). The men pose before the camera in different postures, some sitting in the foreground while others remain standing in the background with their gazes turned in different directions. One is turning his back to the viewer. What is most worthy of attention in the image is the costumes worn by the men, of which the most visible element is a mask that exaggerates the black skin of the "Arab" that it purports to depict and features a mustache, large almond-shaped eyes, and thick eyebrows. The men wear striped pants and white shirts, a short cape in a darker tone, a hat that hints at a turban and has a half-moon on top, and bathing towels that a few of them wear as long capes or over their heads, in the manner of a traditional headscarf (keffiyeh) but without the black string that holds it in place. The costume chosen by this group is a pastiche of elements drawn from an imaginary space and various sources, such as albums of exotic types, paintings, engravings, photographs, and written and spoken narratives.

This photograph is also exemplary of a mise-en-scène, on this occasion deprived of artistic intent, wherein the figure of the negative Other, the Arab, is reduced to simplistic visual stereotypes. Unlike *Cosecha de rosas*, in this image, the photographer's creative intention plays a minor role, and what he captured reflects the deeply ingrained ideology of *la raza antioqueña*. The black mask is a profoundly symbolic element that highlights the alleged whiteness of the skin behind it. Here the costume unmasks

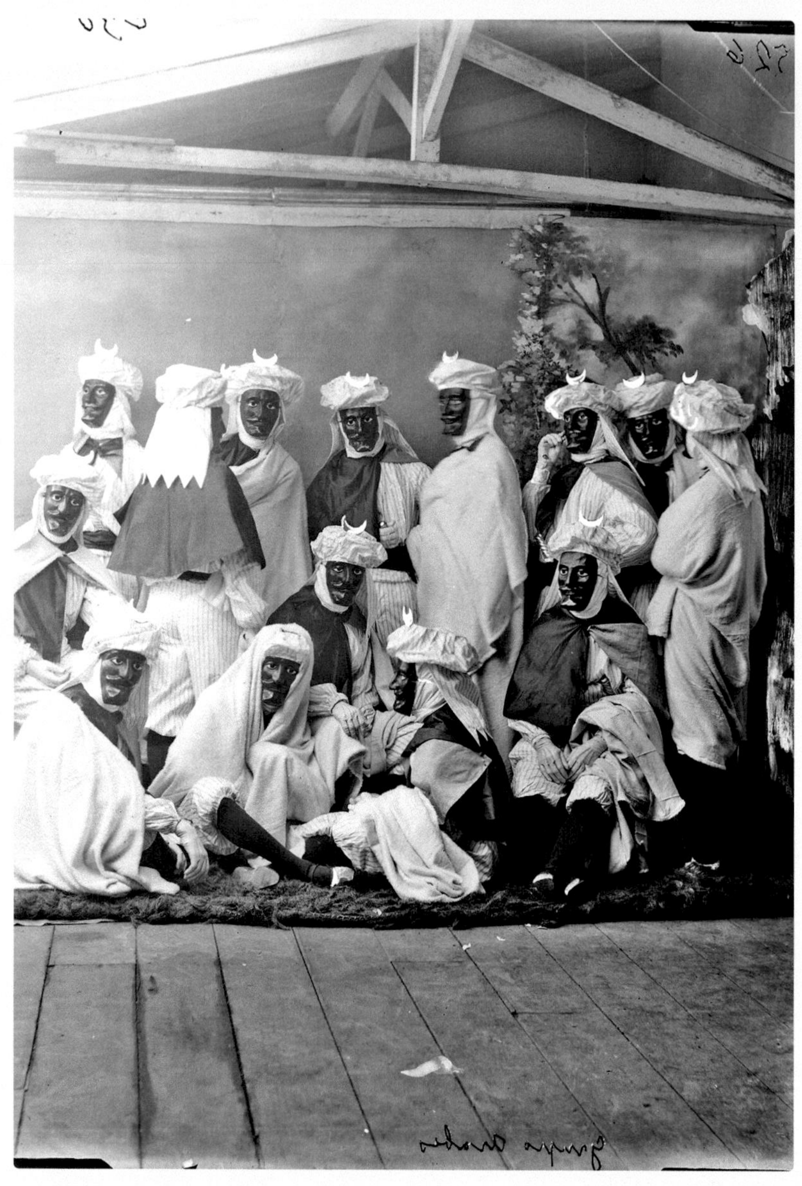

4.13. Fotografía Rodríguez, *Grupo árabe*, 1899. Digital positive from dry plate negative, 25 × 20 cm. Biblioteca Pública Piloto de Medellín / Archivo fotográfico.

a naturalized way of thinking, creating a space for the mise-en-scène of the politics of costume. Moreover, the black mask on top of the white skin plays also with the opposition of the photographic positive and negative. The black color of the face mask is physically and rhetorically associated with blackness in the same way in which the photographic negative, since its invention, was loaded with a racialized discourse. As noted by Batchen, as early as February 1839, John Hershel wrote in his diary that in the photographic negative, "fair women [were] transformed into negresses" thus establishing a pejorative and gendered reading of the darker version of the image.[56] Curiously, however, none of these racially inflicted readings of the negative appear in the Rodríguezes' writing, although they are certainly at work in the images themselves.

Returning to the relationship between the black mask and the negative, it is important to point out how both are based on the objectification of blackness. Both treat it as a commodity that can be manipulated for commercial or personal profit. While the positive versions of photographic images are usually seen and thought of as images, the negatives are treated as objects.[57] They are touched and retouched; they are primary sources for something else, not objects/images in and of themselves. Through the colonizing imperial eyes, Middle Eastern persons were also objects that could produce something (sexual desire, products, money, etc.) for Western civilization. Rather than seeing them as equal subjects, they were pictured as objects capable of meeting Westerners' needs.

As a sociopolitical notion constructed by hegemonic nations, skin color functions as an invisible norm and thus institutes an asymmetrical ontological relation between white and black beings.[58] The civilizing fantasy upon which the discourse of *la raza antioqueña* was built treats the Other as a fiction wherein the black/mestizo/Indian person is not only a nonwhite but also plays a fundamental role, as a negative Other, in the construction of an idea of the white man. In other words, they are interdependent, just as in photography the positive is contingent on the negative. In the *Grupo árabe* photograph, the black/mestizo/Indian is replaced by the Arab, a figure of the Other around which a copious negative symbolic arsenal had already been assembled in Spain. America inherited this arsenal from Europeans. In fact, as Hernán G. Taboada explains, the embodiment of religious alterity attributed to the Moors functioned as a model for the ideological construction of the figure of the Amerindian.[59] This entails that the Arab costume featured in Fotografía Rodríguez's photograph not only corresponds to a construction of difference personified by an exotic, homogeneous, and essentialized being, but it also reflects the values inherited by the criollos and perpetuated among the middle and upper classes of what today is Colombia. Despite this, we must be careful and understand that the Orientalism reflected in these images is not driven by an ill-meaning intent of the models or the photographer; instead, as Said himself explains, such Orientalism functions as a way of cataloging and contextualizing knowledge that is available at a given historical moment.

Such knowledge is also visible in other aspects of the photograph. In the Arab group, we see that while some sitters look at the camera, others look back or show their covered faces in profile. This representation partially follows the prototypical way of depicting anthropological and criminal types that circulated widely during this period, primarily as photographs and prints, both technologies based predominantly on a positive/negative matrix. As noted by Marta Penhos, these typologies based on frontal and profile pictures were related to the necessity of identifying and observing marginal peoples as objects of study rather than as subjects themselves.[60] In Colombia, scientific and artistic approaches to this representation type were promoted mainly by the watercolors of the Chorographic Commission, *costumbrista* painting, and photography. In many of these images, the represented subjects appear in the same three perspectives the Arab group photo uses to present Orientalized subjects. That is, looking to the front, in profile, and back. This is particularly evident when one compares the photograph with a watercolor such as *Notables de la capital* (Distinguished persons from the capital), where a group of men and women from different socioeconomic backgrounds appear floating in a blank space and facing different directions (fig. 4.14). The two subjects on the left and right sides face backward, displaying their various costumes, while the three subjects at the center of the composition look in profile or a three-quarter view. These two images, the Arab group and *Notables de la capital*, are only two examples of the multiple pictures in which the disposition of the bodies presented from different perspectives was used to classify Othered bodies in the visual culture of Colombia's nineteenth century.

The Arab group photograph is not intended as a group portrait in the traditional sense since none of the subjects represented are identifiable as individuals. In fact, this photograph goes against the very promises of portraiture, a genre in which the features and physical characteristics make the sitters recognizable individual subjects. In portraiture, the

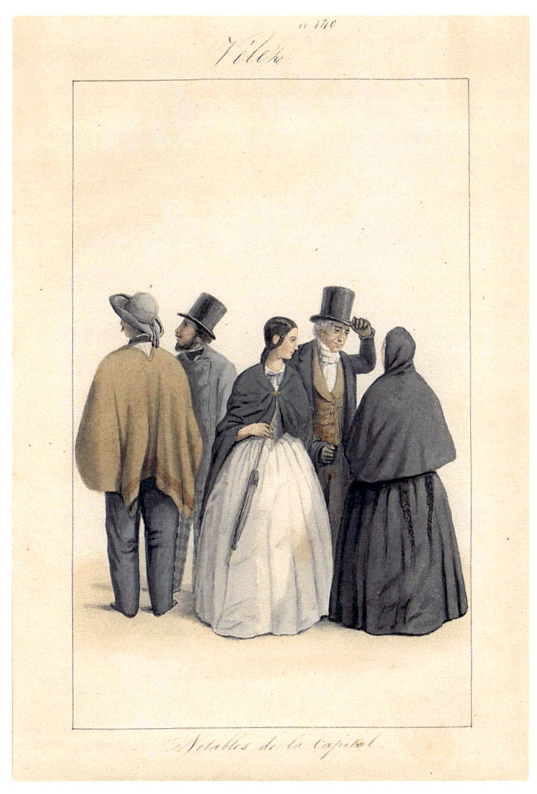

4.14. Carmelo Fernández, *Notables de la capital*, 1850. Watercolor on paper, 30 × 21 cm. Biblioteca Nacional de Colombia.

face becomes one of the most critical aspects of the depicted person because it is through it that the particularities of the sitter and their resemblance become evident. But in the Arab group photo, all individuals look the same. Their particularities are homogenized through the use of more or less the same costume and the same mask. There seems to be a contradiction here: Although there are no apparent differences among the sitters, their homogeneity emphasizes the difference between them as a group of presumed white male subjects and the Orientalized individuals they are performing. The racialized association of the photographic negative with a black/colored subject materializes in this image. The mask references that which is distant, alien, and thus negative.

The photos analyzed in this chapter are not the only Orientalist images from this extensive archive. Other photos, such as the pictures of Libia Restrepo and Virginia Jaramillo (figs. 4.15 and 4.16) taken in 1910, portray women in Asian costumes. These pictures suggest that the Orientalizing tropes explored in this book are only a minor example of

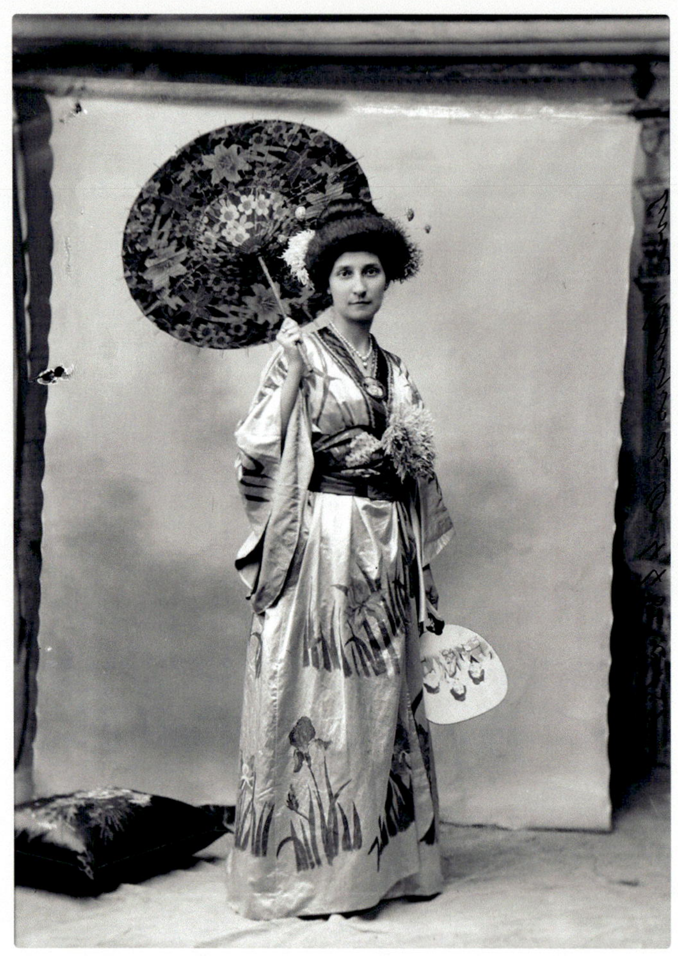

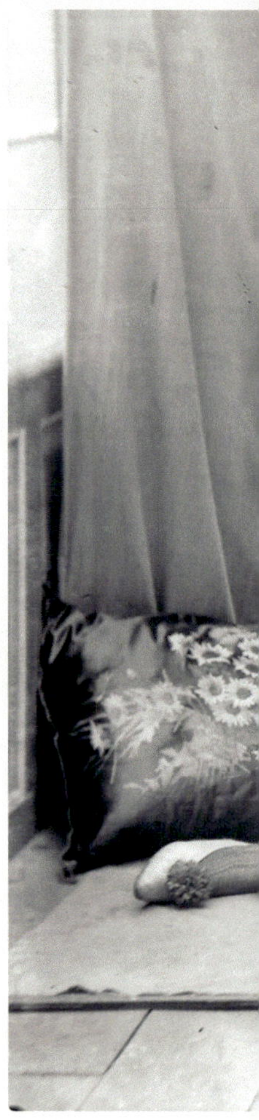

4.15. Fotografía Rodríguez, *Libia Restrepo de O.*, 1910. Digital positive from dry plate negative, 18 × 13 cm. Biblioteca Pública Piloto de Medellín / Archivo fotográfico.

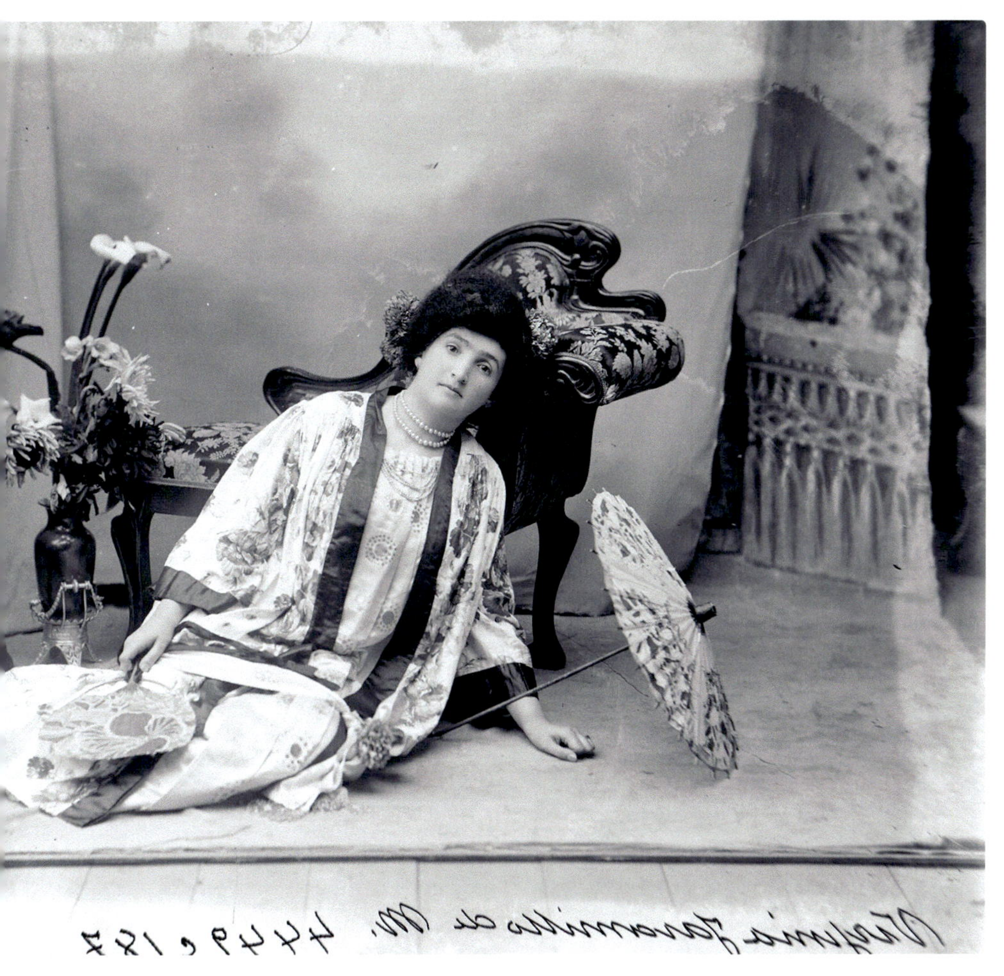

4.16. Fotografía Rodríguez, *Virginia Jaramillo de M.*, 1910. Digital positive from dry plate negative, 13 × 18 cm. Biblioteca Pública Piloto de Medellín / Archivo fotográfico.

the connections and visual exchanges between Colombia and the Eastern world. However, the relations between Colombia and Asia differ from the analysis presented in this chapter focusing on the Middle East. Libia Restrepo's and Virginia Jaramillo's photos seem to take Japanese types as a point of departure for creating the Orientalizing tropes. Their robes and sashes imitate Japanese kimonos; the sitter's hairstyle in a high bun was popular in Japan during the Edo Period; and the fixed fan, known as *uchiwa*, is also Japanese (or an imitation thereof). As stated at the beginning of this chapter, objects coming from Asia circulated in Colombia's territory from colonial times onward due to the Manila-Acapulco Galleon shipping line. Therefore, the visual reference for creating these photos could have come from a variety of objects ranging from prints to photographs, screens, plates, and even fans and umbrellas, like the ones the sitters hold in the pictures.[61] For example, the sitters' hairstyles recall the ones depicted on the fan in figure 4.15.

But further study is required to understand the meanings of these photos and establish a more critical reading. Few investigations address the connections between East Asia and Colombia, particularly during the nineteenth century.[62] We can speculate that these photographs were a response to Europe's Japanism craze, but the reality is that this research still has to be done. It is not an exaggeration to think that prints, photographs, or postcards produced in Japan could have reached Medellín, especially taking into account the fascination for everything Japanese, Chinese, and Turkish, in vogue in Europe since the end of the nineteenth century, and the exchanges between Medellín, France, and England during the same period.[63] Although the Colombian photographs imitate in some ways Japanese studio photography from the nineteenth century, it is hard to determine without further study the functions, connections, and differences between these photographs and those produced in Japan.[64] I close this chapter with these pictures as an invitation to other researchers to delve into the possible meanings of these fascinating photographs and encourage them to think through the negative. Negatives call for an inversion of our usual way of thinking. We look at them to imagine how they would look in their positive version. The images analyzed here are also an invitation to read them in more nuanced terms, thus surpassing simplistic readings.

CHAPTER FIVE

Negative Spaces

THE BACKDROPS IN BENJAMÍN DE LA CALLE'S AND FOTOGRAFÍA RODRÍGUEZ'S PHOTOGRAPHS

LET'S BEGIN BY comparing two images. The first one is a photograph of a man named Leonardo Posada taken by Fotografía Rodríguez in 1892, and the second is a portrait of Rafael Rúa taken in 1897 by Benjamín de la Calle (figs. 5.1 and 5.2). Each picture depicts a local man dressed in dark pants, leather shoes, a collared shirt, and an antioqueño poncho, posing in front of a painted backdrop that deploys a European-like environment. Regardless of whether the painting represented an indoor or outdoor setting, the backdrops do not correspond to the time and place where the pictures were taken. In the first photograph, the backdrop simulates the stylized environment of an upper-middle-class house interior: a wall decorated with a painted mirror, a flower vase, and trompe l'oeil moldings, typical of nineteenth-century Western European interior decorations. The props employed to further set the scene include a posing chair with a tall back, velvet upholstery, and long fringe, and a patterned rug contrasting with the painted wall in the background.[1] The second photograph depicts an outdoor scene with an idyllic painted landscape in the background. The backdrop includes—on the right side of the image—the corner of a house's porch built in a nineteenth-century neoclassical style. The house's single visible column—which reveals the architectural style of the building—stands on the corner of the porch and is decorated with a climbing plant. In this picture, an unidentifiable studio prop replaces the usual chair (somewhat imitating its shape), and a fur shawl and a hat lie on top.

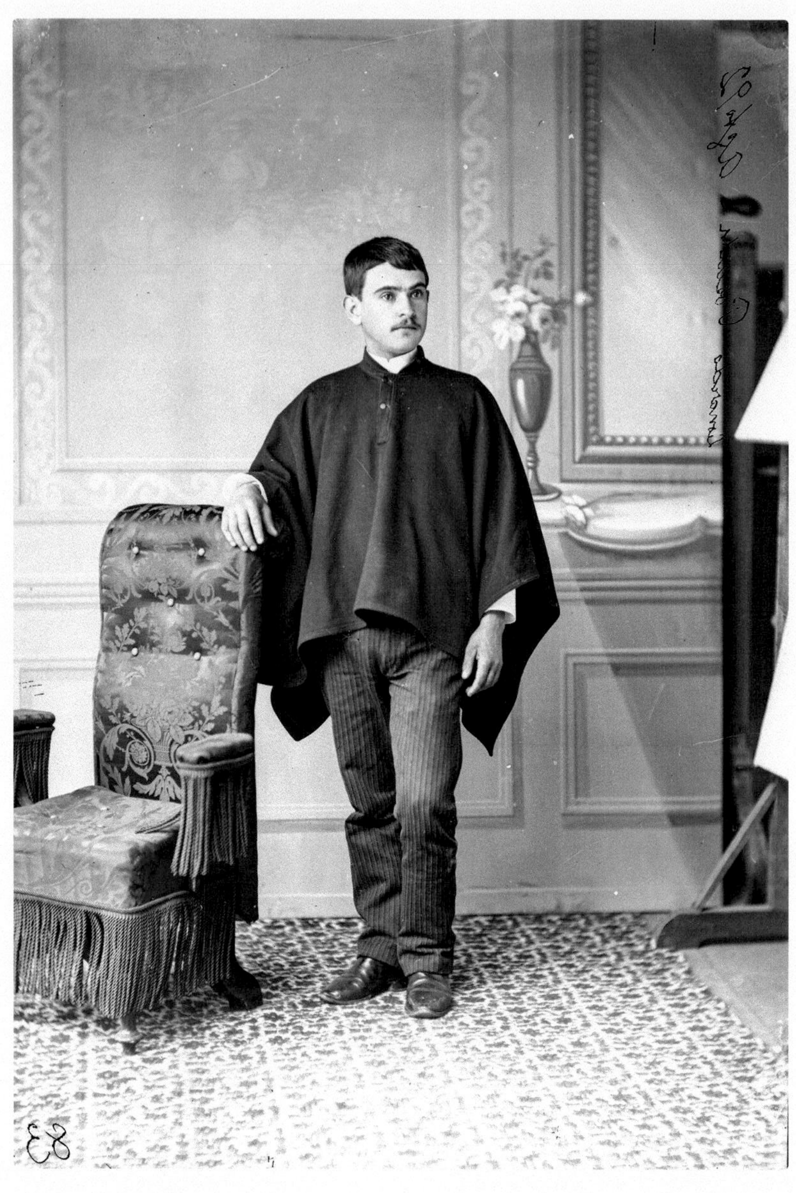

5.1. Fotografía Rodríguez, *Leonardo Posada*, 1892. Digital positive from gelatin dry plate. Biblioteca Pública Piloto de Medellín / Archivo fotográfico.

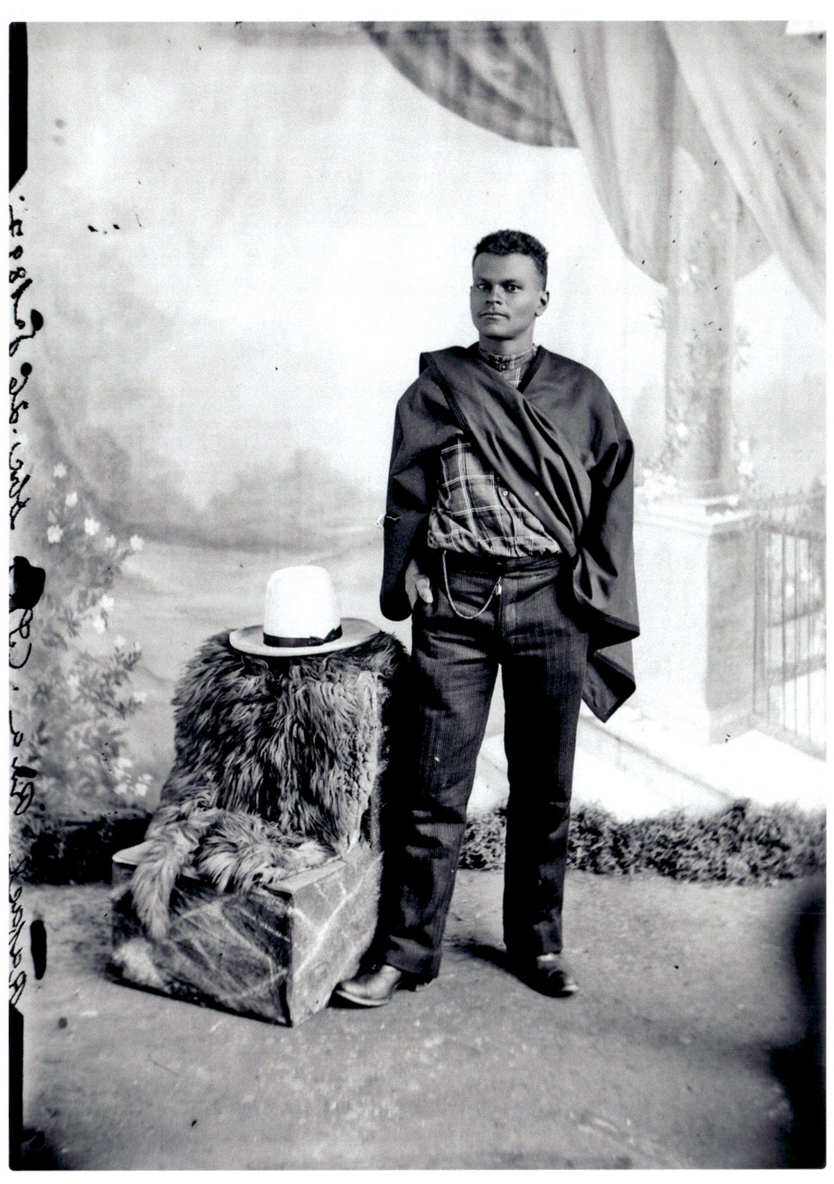

5.2. Benjamín de la Calle, *Rafael Rúa*, 1897. Digital positive from gelatin dry plate, 18 × 13 cm. Biblioteca Pública Piloto de Medellín / Archivo fotográfico.

This lengthy description of the photographs serves to note the ubiquity of standardized compositions in studio photography: the selection of similar poses, props that simulate comparable shapes, the use of similar clothing, and so on. More significantly, it helps evidence the lack of contradictions that both photographers and sitters saw in the juxtaposition of local signifiers—such as the antioqueño hat and, more prominently, the poncho—with backdrops that depicted distant and foreign environments. The production of the two photographic studios studied in this book converges within the context of these contradictory but culturally assimilated representations. By looking at the ordinary portraits (i.e., images that, at the time of their production, could go unnoticed even by a curious eye because they did not stand out for their artifice nor the identity of the sitters), one finds common ground in the representational strategies of both photographic studios. But why did sitters, photographers, and critics not see a contradiction in this form of representation? Why was it normal for an antioqueño to pose wearing traditional local clothes in front of European landscapes and foreign interiors? Why was this contradictory juxtaposition prevalent in the work of both Fotografía Rodríguez and de la Calle? How can we understand this trope in relation to the discourse of the *raza antioqueña*? Are these photographs stabilizing the contradictions inherent in the concept of the *raza antioqueña*—or are they destabilizing them by revealing them so bluntly? Do the backdrops used by the photographers enhance definitions of gender, class, and race? And, if they do, how?

To address some of these questions, the focus of the analysis of the photographs in this chapter shifts from the sitters to the backdrops, in other words, to the negative space of the pictures. These often-overlooked background paintings add to the meaning of the photographs and raise questions regarding antioqueños' understanding of their own identity. In the same way that retouching became a photographic supplement of which both photographers took advantage, the photo's negative space also enhanced the meaning of the images, often in apparently contradictory ways.

This chapter analyzes the different styles of backdrops used by each studio and the contradictions, changes, and challenges that emerged within their production. In the case of Fotografía Rodríguez, it addresses the distinct development in the style of their backdrops, which changed from figurative to abstract, as seen in Teresa Santamaría's portrait (fig. 5.3). By the end of the 1920s, Fotografía Rodríguez's background

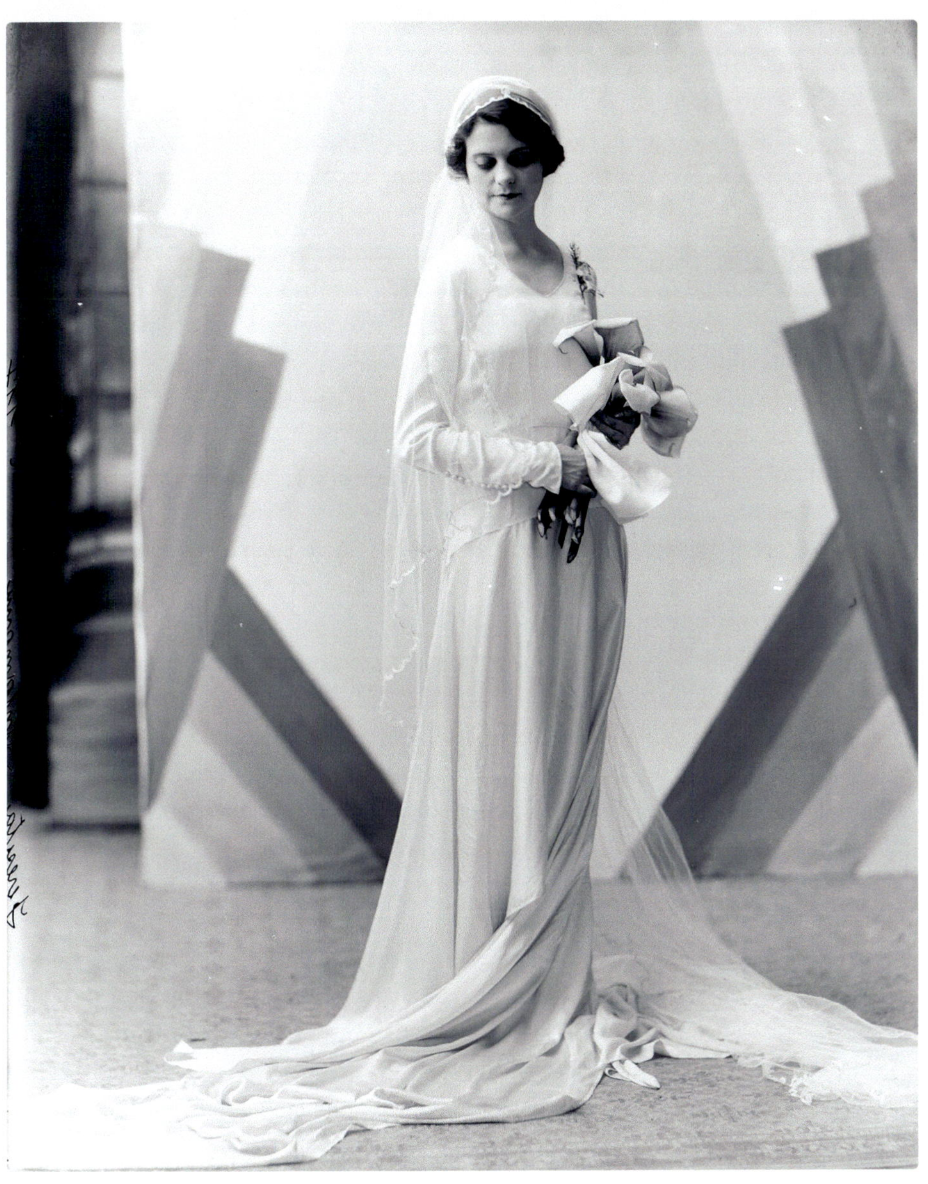

5.3. Fotografía Rodríguez, *Teresa Santamaría*, 1930. Digital positive from gelatin dry plate, 25 × 20 cm. Biblioteca Pública Piloto de Medellín / Archivo fotográfico.

paintings exhibited abstract forms when the most progressive painters in the country had not even considered abstraction as a painterly subject.[2] Indeed, this did not happen anywhere in Latin America until 1934, with the return of Uruguayan painter Joaquín Torres-García to his home country and his ideas about abstraction based on constructive universalist theories.[3] It is true that these backdrops were not thought of as paintings by that era's standards, but let's take them as if they were—as legitimate objects of study—and examine the implications of this abstract turn. It is surprising to find these modern abstract paintings as backdrops in the work of a photo studio in Medellín. Yet the Rodríguez brothers' photographs are neither modern nor abstract and continue to deploy traditional subjects—such as weddings, first communions, and other social events. The themes of their photographs never changed, and their work continued to present their subjects conventionally. Although avant-garde visual language was literally standing in front of their eyes, they did not take a step toward modern and experimental photography. However, the abstract backdrops suggest a new rhetoric was about to emerge in the country. Where were these abstract images coming from, and how were they understood? What does this paradoxical juxtaposition between modernity and tradition suggest?

On the other hand, de la Calle's backdrops did not evolve stylistically. He used idyllic landscapes as backdrops for his photographs, avoiding the depiction of exclusively interior settings. His work, ultimately progressive not so much in terms of style as in his subjects and the strategies developed to represent his sitters, was, until his death in 1934, a continuation of traditional studio portraiture imitating pictorial forms. Whereas in Fotografía Rodríguez's backdrops one can trace a chronology from figuration to abstraction, and thus an estrangement from pictorialist language, in de la Calle's photography there is no stylistic change, and that is precisely what draws the attention to his backdrops. Throughout his career, he mainly utilized backdrops depicting outdoor scenes. Was there something about landscape painting that attracted him? What can we learn from this particular selection of scenery? Without changing the background paintings, he subtly changed the settings by adding hand-painted details on the negatives and introducing collage techniques to create specific environments. These additions worked as supplements that made his images more attractive to potential clients. They played an auxiliary role, enhancing the effects of the photographic illusion. Throughout his forty-three-year career as a photographer, de la Calle used only twelve different backdrops, modifying them by inserting hand-painted details such as clouds, tree branches, and flying herons. Was his fixation on the traditional backdrops a deliberate decision? Was this insistence on utilizing mostly exterior views one of his visual strategies? If so, why?

These apparent paradoxes force us to question canonical readings of photography and how local visual traditions have mediated modernity in ways that are independent of and critical of European modernity.[4] Moreover, to investigate the negative space of photography is also to question the hierarchies assigned to certain aspects of the image. This chapter aims to take a fresh approach and look at the entire picture as an integral part of the composition to question where the photograph's meaning lies. In this section, the negative again takes a different form. Rather than focusing on its material, symbolic, or metaphorical aspects, I study the negative as space to reveal new interpretations through a detailed examination of often overlooked aspects of the photographic image and to understand how these aspects intertwine with the racial discourse of the *raza antioqueña*. As we will see, whiteness was also coded into landmarks, architecture, and even the natural landscape.[5]

The Backdrop as Negative Space

Taking as a point of departure James Elkins's approach to photography as if it were "judged by the square inch," in a photographic portrait we should consider an analysis of aspects apart from the sitter. Considering the premise "photographs of people—that is, most photographs—are not mainly photographs of people," the image's negative space should also be considered when examining a photograph.[6] Indeed, other things occupy most of the area of the photographic image, most times unwanted material that adds nothing to the meaning and was not even intended to be captured. This unwanted material is usually the negative space of the picture. As pointed out by Elkins, what in the traditional painting made up the background—a space put in "mark by mark" by its author and thus intentionally included in the picture—in photography could be contingent and therefore serves a different function.[7] To distinguish this not-necessarily-wanted photographic space from the specifically designed painterly background, he coined the word "surround."[8]

However, studio photography challenges this idea of the surround. Although usually perceived just as a negative space, often ignored or seen solely as a decorative element, this space is hardly neutral. Not only do both the photographer and the sitter select it (although from a limited variety of choices), but it also informs and enhances the individuals' projection of their identity. It is also a space painted "mark by mark" and, although not created by the photographer or the sitter, they ultimately selected it, making its representation intentional and thus significant. In this sense, the nonhuman parts in this genre of photography occupy an intermediate space between Elkins's notions of background and surround.

Using these standardized backdrops was a common feature in the international scene of studio photography. During the daguerrean era, backdrops were usually simple pieces of cloth hung in the background of pictures. It was not until the advent of the carte de visite that the painted full-length backdrop flourished. Indeed, as James Wyman noted, one could trace a genealogy of backdrop paintings to other popular technologies of vision during the nineteenth century, such as the panorama and the diorama.[9] Partly owing to the intense debate regarding the status of photography as art, backdrops introduced painterly references and, thus, traditional artistic elements to the new medium. In this sense, backdrops also elevated photography to the level of painting, incorporating not only its tropes but also parts of its physical traces. Backdrops could reveal and emphasize certain aspects of the sitters' personalities. By the 1870s, backdrops were regarded as an essential part of studio photography, and debates concerning their use became a popular topic in the photographic literature of the period.[10] The use of painted backdrops derived directly from traditional full-length portraiture in painting, specifically from portraits prioritizing the public presentation of the sitters rather than glimpses into their personal values, personalities, or domesticity.[11] From its inception, photographic portraiture was coded within the painterly tradition, with traces of this heritage emerging not only materially (as seen in the work of pictorialist photographers and their use of intricate techniques intended to imitate painterly finishes) but also in the visual content of the images. In this latter case, the painterly traces revealed themselves in the depiction of cloths and curtains in the background, which in most cases broke the coherence of the depicted scene but continued a tradition introduced in painterly portraiture. That is the case, for example, for de la Calle's portrait of Rafael Rúa, where a hanging curtain appears depicted in the upper right section of the backdrop. The suspended textile wraps around a column, ensuring a theatricality that does not correspond to a real-life scene. The contrast between these theatrical elements and the real-life quality of photography ironically emphasized illusion rather than the objective truth that the photographic medium claimed to reveal.

In hegemonic places of photography production, such as France and England, the contraposition of sitters against these invented pictorial environments brought about mismatches between the depicted subjects and the backdrops. But these representations were incongruous, not so much because of the contraposition of the sitters' identity and the simulated places (unless the photographs were of nonwhite people), but rather due to class distinctions. The backdrops used in these cases usually reflected aspirational motivations. The sitters posed against timeless Arcadian landscapes or scenes with pillars, balustrades, and furniture that referred to a recent past. The emergent middle class could hide behind the simulacrum of these hand-painted aristocratic environments. But as the nineteenth century advanced, some of these images began to be read in codes of taste, that is, in terms of class. Ironic descriptions mocking these visual incongruities, such as the following by Henry Peach Robinson, emerged: "the palatial column and curtain, so suitable for the middle-class citizen; the raging sea and profile rocks, with a carpet on the sands to save the feet of the delicate young lady out in the storm in an evening dress; the pasteboard terrace and distant mole-hills, with fountains squirting out of the sitter's head."[12] For many nineteenth-century photographers, good taste (and therefore high class) was synonymous with simplicity and equated with the photographer's ability to produce a portrait that conveyed the sitter's personality with the fewest potential distractions. Too many details and props drew attention away from the face of the portrayed person and made the observer focus on other aspects of the photograph.

The backdrop industry flourished rapidly in the United States, with L. W. Seavy's company becoming one of its most famous producers.[13] The German Engelmann und Schneider from Dresden were the leading manufacturers in Europe. Photographic suppliers in the United States and Europe advertised these background paintings according to their potential uses (romantic scene, couple, heroic portrait) rather than describing what they represented. These scenic backgrounds repeatedly utilized the same artistic tropes. Designed specifically for full-length portraits, they deployed invented landscapes or indoor environments painted with

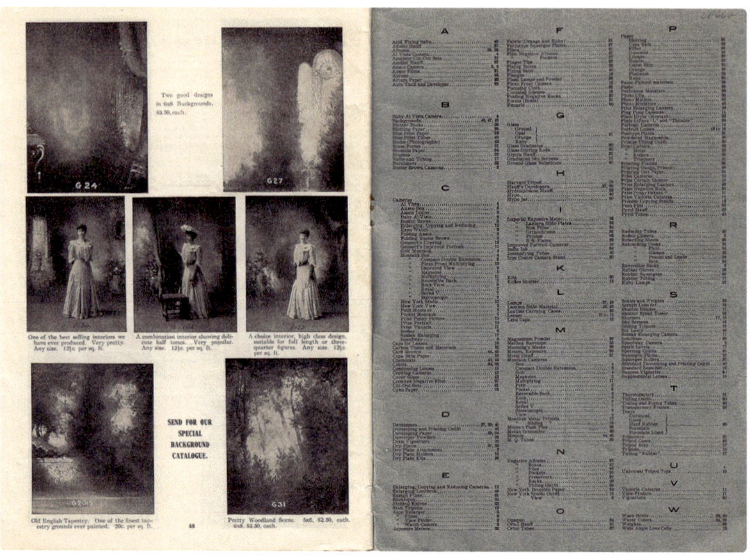

5.4. Spread from *Catalogue of Photographic Apparatus and Supplies*, no. 58, ca. 1908.

loose, spontaneous brushstrokes that played with intense light contrasts. The sides of the paintings featured curtains and columns decorated with abundant plants and flowers, usually immersed in dark-toned settings. Frequently, a bright area crossed the center of the composition, giving the overall picture a chiaroscuro appearance that made the sitters stand out in contrast to the otherwise dark environments (fig. 5.4). These generic scenarios aimed to convey points of reference with presumed familiar landscapes or domestic settings, although rarely grounded in specificity. This is partially reflected in the language used to describe the backdrops, which ranged from vague local descriptions such as "Old English Tapestry" to completely generic ones like "Pretty Woodland Scene."[14] Not assigning geographic specificity to these paintings neutralized them to highlight the photographic subject.[15]

If, by the end of the nineteenth century, European critics and photographers saw the proliferation of detail as a sign of bad taste, by the twentieth century such a reading was further entrenched. The most prominent example was perhaps Walter Benjamin's perception of backdrop paintings and studio sceneries as a "place between an execution and a representation, between a torture chamber and a throne room."[16] But as the years went by, backdrops—the negative space of the photos—became more conventional to avoid accusations of bad taste. The fewer details or references to specific places these paintings had, the easier it was to pose individuals from different economic and social classes in front of them. Furthermore, with Kodak's introduction of the Brownie camera in 1900 and its rapid popularization, outdoor scenes no longer had to be re-created in the studio. It was possible to take photographs in front of natural landscapes. This did not mean that studio photography died, but its aesthetic principles shifted toward less decorative representations, with a return to the stark backdrops used during daguerrean times. More importantly, the return to simplicity also meant a solution to one of the most debated subjects: With the reintroduction of neutral backdrops, the potential for visual mismatches between sitter and background disappeared. However, the history of backdrop evolution was different in nonhegemonic places.

Convergences: *La raza antioqueña* and Western Civilization

While by the end of the nineteenth century, Europeans saw tastelessness and incoherence in the depiction of middle-class citizens against the aristocratic sceneries of the backdrops used by studio photographers, in Medellín, these juxtapositions did not seem as controversial. Indeed, perhaps the mismatch was not even perceived because it was so common that there was never an obvious alternative. The relationship between the backdrops and the sitters is probably more complex in this context, especially when considering the ideological environment in which they lived. One of the most peculiar characteristics of the antioqueños was their pride in identifying simultaneously as both peasants and high-class citizens. They saw fluidity in their roles, thus allowing a more comprehensive incorporation of local and traditional signifiers into the higher social atmosphere. Libardo López described the phenomenon in his book *La raza antioqueña*: "That muleteer who, among rejections and jokes, with his pants rolled up to the top of the calf, goes bordering with his mules the muddy road to the port, is the same appropriately dressed gentleman of aristocratic ways with whom you meet any other day in the Club."[17] This duality became one of the most distinctive characteristics of male antioqueños, visually reflected by incorporating traditional clothes into everyday life, regardless of class background. Wearing a poncho or a ruana became an identity signifier that reflected the antioqueños' commitment to hard labor and closeness to the land. For the higher social classes, dressing down had nothing to do with contradicting their social status; on the contrary, it was a way of stressing their identity roots. However, dressing down integrated key aspects and symbols of a popular rural lifestyle but did not challenge the power structures embedded in antioqueño culture. Whiteness was also coded through behavior and not only through material culture or skin color. Social status was directly related to the relationship one had with the land, not with the cultural symbols of a rural lifestyle. Ultimately, everyone had a direct relationship with the land: whether collective ownership in the case of Indigenous people, private ownership for the high and middle classes, or no ownership in the case of the lower social classes that worked the land itself. Therefore, regardless of class, it was common practice to pose for photographic portraits wearing traditional clothes that usually conflicted with the painted backgrounds of the local photographic studios.

This type of photography in the work of de la Calle and Fotografía Rodríguez can be attributed to the particularity of antioqueño culture to allow an unprecedented fluidity of social classes rarely seen in other parts of Colombia. Scholars and historians have argued that the barriers between social classes were relatively modest during this period. In particular, the success of typically middle-class businesses such as *arriería* (mule-train driving), coffee plantations, and roadside inns for muleteers, and the paternalism of industrialization encouraged this flexibility.[18] Additionally, there were no substantial variations in consumption patterns and beliefs among the different social classes.[19] This phenomenon explains why, in these photographs, there are no radical differences between the work of Fotografía Rodríguez and Benjamín de la Calle, despite serving distinct social classes.

The study of backdrops has been mostly addressed in postcolonial photography. Scholars such as Christopher Pinney and Arjun Appadurai have argued that the use of backdrop paintings, in particular in Indian and African photography, negotiates the tensions between explicit settings—such as bazaars, courts, and palaces—and the categorization of colonial and social-cultural types.[20] Pinney also argues that the backdrop is used as a framework for representation, intended to direct both the subjects and the camera, but also as a strategy for minimizing and controlling the contingency of photography.[21] In this sense, the backdrop's function exists between the control and designation of a particular context for the subject portrayed and the reasons that motivated the photographic event, often related to associative qualities. In this context, the backdrop's function overcomes its iconic status as an allegory of class, romance, and even modernity and becomes indexical of those realities.[22] Backdrops are part of the transformative space of the photographic studio, where, as Pinney notes, sitters can perform new identities "*in advance* of society."[23] That is, in a kind of prophetic way. With this in mind, one of the most critical functions of the backdrop is to place the photographic event, but place it where?

Although the photographs by the Rodríguez brothers and de la Calle seem to place their subjects in a completely different context from the one they belong to—a European past that they did not experience firsthand—in reality, they are placing them not in a specific location, but in a particular discursive setting in which they believed they belonged. As stated by Appadurai,

> The role of the backdrop in "locating" the photograph is more complex. Although it often locates the photographic subject in a certain sort of context, it also locates the photograph in a certain sort of public discourse. In the case of photographic backdrops, this public discourse can and does take many forms, but a frequent referent is the discourse of modernity as a visual fact. That is, in one way or another, many photographic backdrops place the photograph in a potential space of debate about visual modernity as it is expressed in clothes and machines, as well as in bodily comportment and bodily accessories.[24]

The public discourse of these photographs was not only that of the *raza antioqueña* but also, more importantly, of the West. If, by the turn of the century, antioqueños did not see a contradiction between the juxtaposition of the local with the foreign, it was because they did not read the backdrop paintings as something external to their identity roots. Instead, they saw them as an extension of the tradition they claimed to be part of, that is, Western society. Indeed, antioqueños saw themselves as part of the Judeo-Christian tradition of the West. As stated in chapter 1, rather than trying to define their roots from a local Indigenous perspective, the early twentieth-century arguments used to explain both the rapid development of the region and the accumulation of wealth in Medellín—and thus the invention of a new race—always referred to characteristics inherited from their alleged Spanish descent. Among these were the beliefs of descending from Basque and Castilian origins, from a "Spanish clean caste" (*casta limpia española*), and of lesser *mestizaje* thanks to the annihilation of the Indigenous people in the region.[25]

It is pertinent to keep in mind that the myth of the *raza antioqueña*, as epitomized in López's book, was inspired by Gustave le Bon's writings claiming that the "Latin race" had degenerated and that "the causes of this decadence lie entirely in the mental constitution of a race possessing neither energy, strength of will, nor morality."[26] López's reaction to this defamatory description of his people was an attempt to redeem them, by showing not only that they did not lack any of the characteristics which constitute the character of "superior races" but also that there was a direct connection with their white European ancestors. The proliferation of photographs intentionally juxtaposing the local with the foreign speaks precisely to this reaction. The images materialize the idea that, for the antioqueños, there was no actual contradiction between a poncho and a Mediterranean landscape; for them, a *carriel* (the local purse used by male muleteers) was as Latin as a Roman column.

Nineteenth-century Latin Americans were the first generation of Spanish and Portuguese descent to call themselves Latin Americans. Indeed, as stated by José Luis Falconi, the term *Latin America*, like many other nationalist discourses, emerged from both nostalgia and homesickness in the Paris of the 1850s, where many intellectuals from the region gathered and formed for the first time a circle of men who supported the Pan-American dream.[27] However, the concept's origin was connected to the imperialist impulses of the French state during the nineteenth century. As pointed out by historian Thomas Holloway,

> Historically, the first use of the term *Latin America* has been traced only as far back as the 1850s. It did not originate within the region, but again from outside, as part of a movement called "pan-Latinism" that emerged in French intellectual circles, and more particularly in the writings of Michel Chevalier (1806–79). A contemporary of Alexis de Tocqueville who traveled in Mexico and the United States during the late 1830s, Chevalier contrasted the "Latin" peoples of the Americas with the "Anglo-Saxon" peoples (Phelan 1968; Ardao 1980, 1993). From those beginnings, by the time of Napoleon III's rise to power in 1852, pan-Latinism had developed as a cultural project extending to those nations whose culture supposedly derived

from neo-Latin language communities (commonly called Romance languages in English). Starting as a term for historically derived "Latin" culture groups, L'Amerique Latine then became a place on the map.[28]

Besides Chevalier, in Parisian circles, a Colombian named José María Torres Caicedo (1830–89) became one of the first Spanish-speaking intellectuals to describe the region as "Latin." During the second half of the nineteenth century, Torres Caicedo became one of the most widely known and representative intellectual figures from Latin America in Europe.[29] He intended to connect the roots of his people with a Latin European past to legitimize his status as a Colombian in Paris. Interestingly, Torres Caicedo began the conceptualization of the idea of a Latin race, not using this term but rather the concept of Spanish race to refer to South Americans in contrast with what was called the Anglo-Saxon race, that is, those from the United States and Canada.[30] Only after 1856 did he begin to use the term *Latin race* as the introduction to a poem starting with the verse "La raza de América Latina / al frente tiene la raza sajona" (The Latin American race / faces the Saxon race).[31] However, his idea of the Latin race was concerned with the defense and exaltation not of an Indigenous past but of a Spanish one, stating, "Of course, the Spanish Americans are not Latin for their Indigenous past, but for the Spanish one."[32] Not surprisingly, this assertion resonates strongly with the European genealogies sought by the antioqueño elites, many of whom shared the Parisian intellectual circles of the nineteenth century with Torres Caicedo. Thus, if the myth of the *raza antioqueña* placed the antioqueños within the Latin American race, as understood by nineteenth-century intellectuals in Paris, it was only to refer to a direct connection with a Latin European past.

Therefore, images such as the photographs of Marco Antonio Chalarca by Fotografía Rodríguez and Francisco Uribe by de la Calle, in which a foreign environment in the negative space of the photo contrasts strongly with local traditional clothing and accessories, did not seem to pose a contradiction for the sitters and observers of the period (figs. 5.5 and 5.6). On the contrary, it made sense to juxtapose them as they made a statement regarding their claimed European past. Indeed, Marco Antonio Chalarca's photograph recalls Pompeo Batoni's portraits of young men painted during their Grand Tour in the eighteenth century.[33] As in Batoni's paintings, the Rodríguez brothers included a sculptural figure referencing classical sculpture. Batoni used this trope to establish the sitters as men of culture,

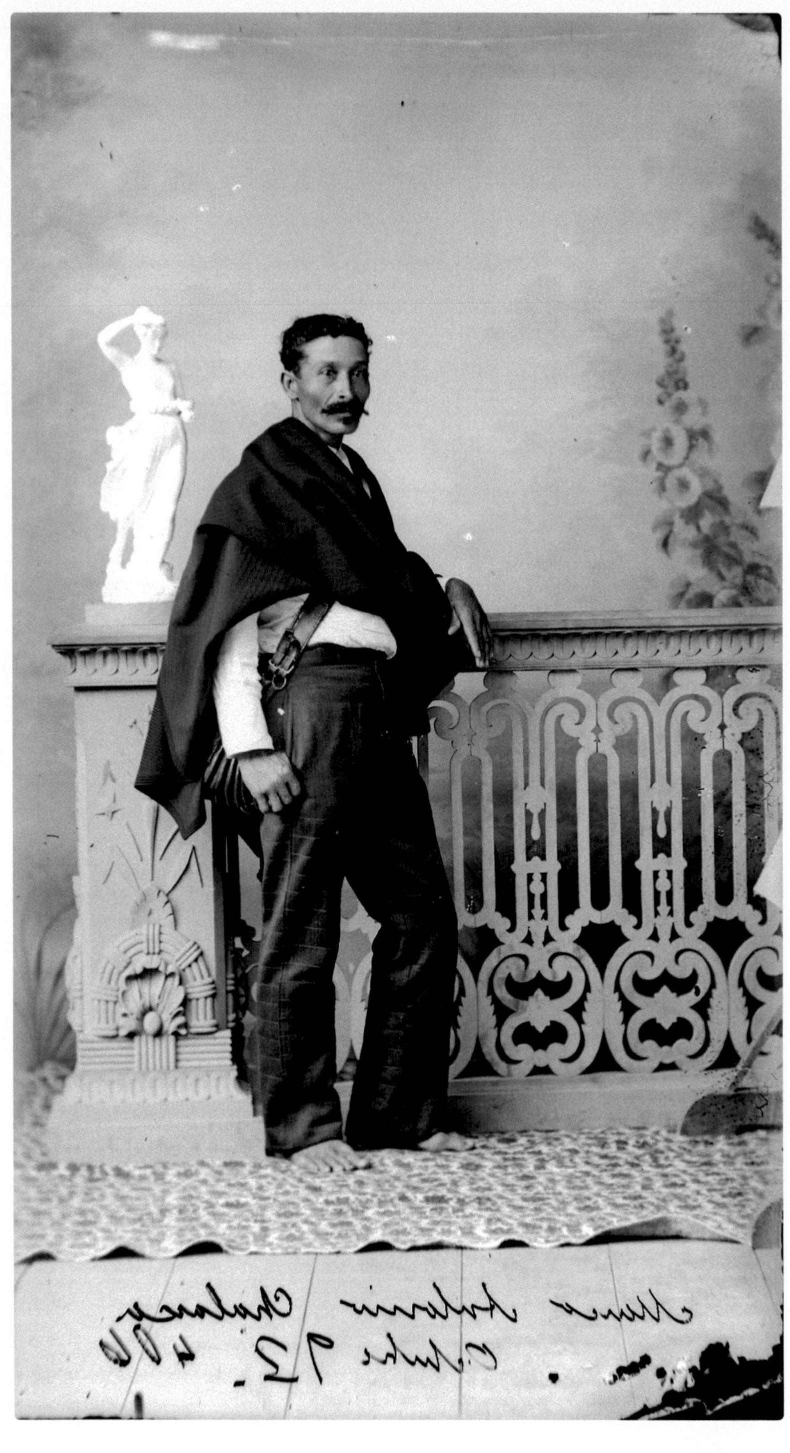

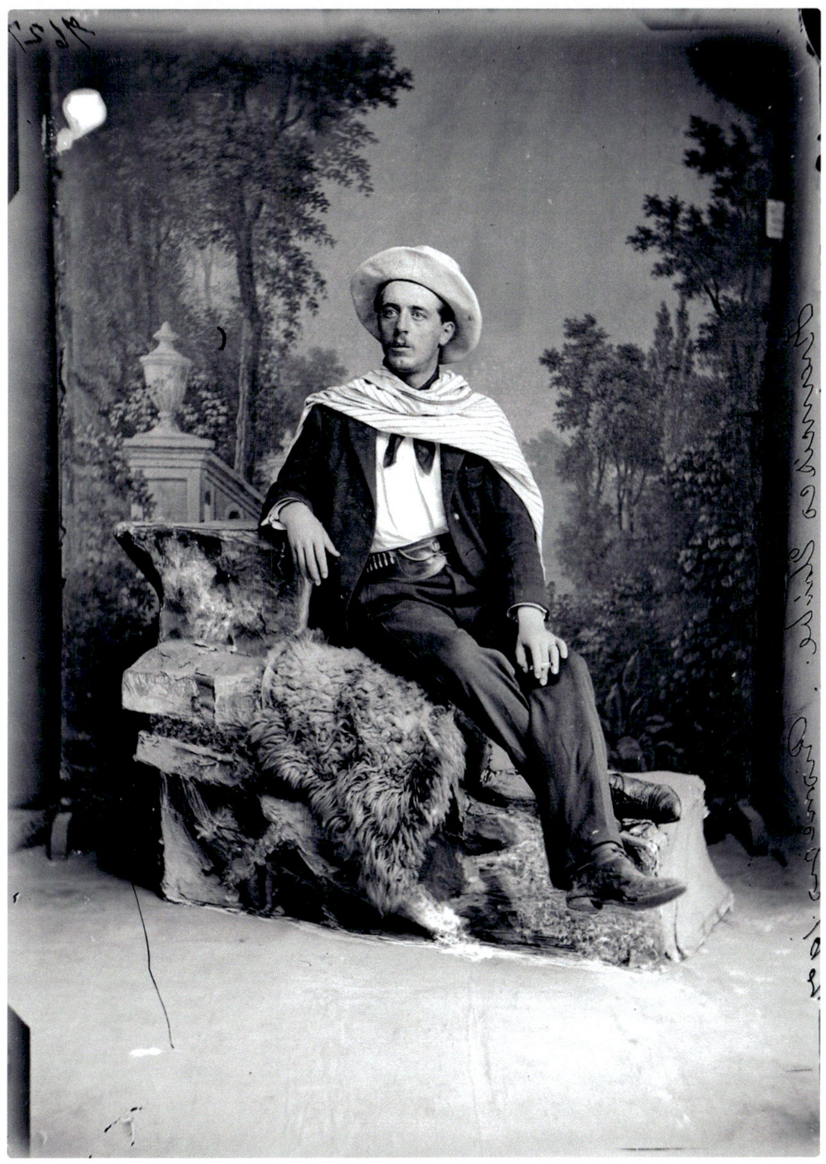

5.5. Fotografía Rodríguez, *Marco Antonio Chalarca*, 1893. Digital positive from gelatin dry plate, 13 × 7 cm. Biblioteca Pública Piloto de Medellín / Archivo fotográfico.

5.6. Benjamín de la Calle, *Francisco Uribe*, 1900. Digital positive from gelatin dry plate, 18 × 13 cm. Biblioteca Pública Piloto de Medellín / Archivo fotográfico.

knowledge, and refinement. The same can be said of Chalarca's photograph in which he appears nonchalantly, wearing local clothing, barefoot, and set against an Arcadian backdrop, with a balustrade and the already mentioned white sculpture. In sum, through detailed attention to the negative space, these photographs visualize the discursive rhetoric of a strongly embedded ideology from which it was almost impossible for the sitters to distance themselves completely. Even for a progressive photographer such as de la Calle, these images did not pose a conflict. In this type of photographs, the work of both studios converges. Their world was ultimately understood from their society's point of view at the turn of the twentieth century in Medellín, Colombia.

Abstraction as Negative Space

Around the end of the 1920s, the negative space of the photographs by Fotografía Rodríguez underwent a radical change. Instead of representing figurative scenes, their photographic backdrops became abstract and completely nonrepresentational. In images such as the bridal portraits of Teresa Santamaría and Aura Mejía (figs. 5.3 and 5.7), the backdrops depict geometric figures. Teresa Santamaría's photograph emulates art deco decorative forms with a rectilinear framework in the corners, forming a rhomboidal figure at the center. Aura Mejía's background painting juxtaposes a series of geometric figures—such as circles, triangles, and rectangles—in different colors and dimensions. The abstract paintings that appear as environmental elements in the background of the photographs by Fotografía Rodríguez are surprising because of the early years in which they were created, especially when compared with the emergence of abstract painting in Colombia and Latin America. If the earlier figurative backdrops were used to refer through photography to a painting tradition—in particular to painterly portraiture, as discussed earlier—the new abstract backdrops distance themselves entirely from that tradition of referring to other artistic forms, specifically the decorative arts and architecture. Indeed, painting could hardly have inspired these abstract images, since painterly abstraction emerged in Colombia only in the late 1930s and early 1940s with the work of Carolina Cárdenas and Marco Ospina, both artists based in Bogotá.[34] Their work and that of their contemporary Colombian abstract painters had little to do with the large-scale geometric pictures in

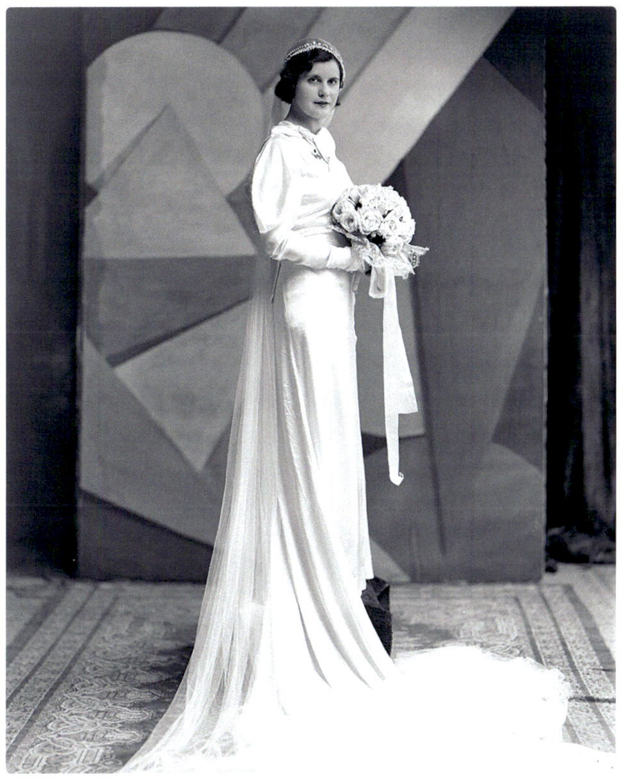

5.7. Fotografía Rodríguez, *Aura Mejía*, 1934. Digital positive from gelatin dry plate, 25 × 20 cm. Biblioteca Pública Piloto de Medellín / Archivo fotográfico.

the backgrounds of these photographs.[35] Painting was no longer a point of reference for photography, but other visual sources became the new triggers to introduce these highly modern settings to a still traditional form of photographic portraiture. In particular, the art deco architectural style seemed to have significantly impacted the selection of backdrops. Although these were not painted by the photographer but most likely imported from Europe and the United States, Melitón selected this set of paintings instead of the traditional backgrounds he had used until then.[36] The decision to change the backgrounds of his pictures to abstract forms might have been stimulated by two particular sources: the architectural work his brother was pursuing in Medellín and international fashion photography.

Melitón's brother, Horacio Marino, with whom he had started the photographic studio back in 1891, retired from photography to immerse himself in a new discipline: architecture. Indeed, in 1902 Horacio Marino opened an architectural firm with Salvador Ángel, which lasted until 1920, when he founded H. M. Rodríguez e Hijos (H. M. Rodríguez and

Sons).[37] Some of the projects constructed in the 1920s included buildings in art deco style, such as the Palacio de Bellas Artes and the Palacio Municipal—today, this building hosts the Museo de Antioquia. Nel Rodríguez, Horacio Marino's son, in consultation with his father and brother Martín, designed the Palacio de Bellas Artes in 1926, right after his return from Europe and the United States, where he had spent some time studying architecture.[38] The building was a commission intended to represent the power derived from art's social practices, and its inspiration was the European academic buildings of that period.[39] The style of the Palacio de Bellas Artes has both neoclassical and art deco influences. The Palacio Municipal was designed in 1931 and constructed between 1931 and 1937. Its design plays with proportions and the use of space to accentuate its verticality. The details, such as the doors and the gratings, were created in art deco style.[40] Starkly abstract facades with geometric elements and streamlined forms characterize both buildings.

The art deco decorations that characterized the buildings the photographer's brother constructed might have served as a point of reference for him. Similarly, the backdrop employed in photographs such as the portrait of Teresa Santamaría uses geometric decorative elements that recall this architectural style. The significance of modern subjectivity derived from the exploitation of these elements merged in a single image many of the precepts of the progressive conservatism of the time. On the one hand, the abstract elements recalled the foreign and the modern, but the photographs depicted traditional and conservative subjects. These images ultimately reflected the dichotomies of the *raza antioqueña*. They represented a society that pursued economic and technological progress but aimed to maintain its conservative social and cultural beliefs.

Abstraction became a synonym of *upper class* and *feminine*. The photographs with abstract backdrops tended to privilege upper-middle-class sitters, mainly women, further reinforcing the contradictions in this type of photograph. If progress—a touchstone from the *raza antioqueña*'s discourse—was made apparent through abstraction, why was it so blatantly represented through feminine sitters? A possible explanation might involve exploiting feminine beauty to reinforce power dynamics. The presentation of women in front of abstract backdrops was a continuation of the representational apparatus of women as fetishized and silenced subjectivities. Pictorial modernism, in its canonical version, is ultimately structured around sexual politics. As stated by Griselda Pollock,

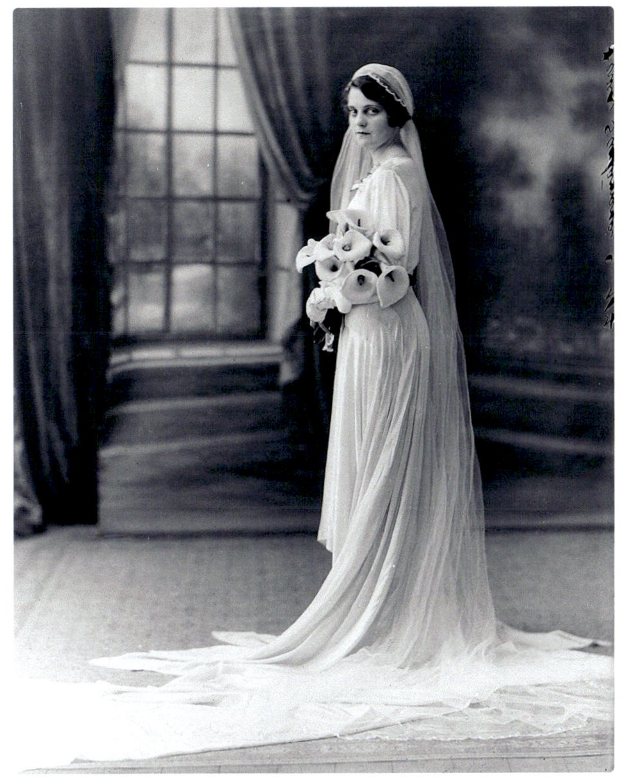

5.8. Fotografía Rodríguez, *Teresa Santamaría*, 1930. Digital positive from gelatin dry plate, 25 × 20 cm. Biblioteca Pública Piloto de Medellín / Archivo fotográfico.

"the figure of the artist always assumed to be masculine in critical and economic practices around art is matched by the sign woman which is its signifier within representational systems."[41] This idea, further translated into nonrepresentational art, was literalized by these photographs by juxtaposing the feminine sitters against the abstract backdrops that constructed the negative space of the pictures.

The idea of progressive conservatism is reinforced when one compares this photograph with another picture of Teresa Santamaría taken, most likely, during the same session as the previous one (fig. 5.8). In this latter image, Santamaría poses wearing her bridal gown in front of a traditional interior background. The backdrop depicts a large window divided into panes, with open curtains, and an empty, darker wall with hints of light coming through the window on the right. The sitter stands slightly to the right, where the two sides of the backdrop meet. Although in both images Santamaría appears in bridal dress (a strong signifier of the

Catholic values reinforced during this time), figure 5.3, with its abstract art deco background, suggests an impulse toward modernism and cultural progress, while figure 5.8, with the traditional interior, recalls outdated nineteenth-century studio photography.

The concept of what some historians have called traditional modernism is epitomized through the unproblematic coexistence of these photographs and the sitter herself.[42] Teresa Santamaría was the director of one of Colombia's most enduring women's magazines of the twentieth century: *Letras y encajes* (Letters and lace), launched in 1926 and published once a month until 1959. Its purpose was to serve as a guide for "modern housewives," boosting education and culture while perpetuating traditional feminine roles such as cooking, cleaning, and raising children.[43] A Christian perspective reinforced these ideas. Just as the photograph with the modern abstract negative space coexists with the traditional subject, the beginning of feminine emancipation coexisted with traditional Christian values. In both the picture and the magazine, modernity appeared as a simulacrum. Modernity was a background literalized by the abstract backdrops utilized by Fotografía Rodríguez in the negative space of their pictures.

As a photographic studio aligned with the region's ideology and for which presenting its sitters as modern subjects was crucial, incorporating these new backgrounds introduced an apparent contemporary rhetoric to the pictures. Architecture was not the only source of inspiration for the novel aesthetic. As seen in other photographic backdrops, such as that in a portrait of Olga Echavarría, also from 1930, international fashion photography might have played a central role (fig. 5.9). In this photograph, the backdrop selected depicts circular shapes of different colors and sizes, sometimes overlapping, and distributed on a homogeneous background that recalled modern paintings such as Kandinsky's *Several Circles* from 1926. Although such a reference was hardly a direct one—most certainly Melitón Rodríguez was not aware of Kandinsky's painting—the knowledge of modern international aesthetics might have been accessible through the study of fashion photography from the period. With the new influence of American culture—a twist from the still present impact of French culture—and the strong interest in fashion, magazines from Europe and America arrived in the Andean city.[44] The influence of Hollywood, through both movies and photography, had a substantial impact on how women embraced fashion and how it was presented to the public in Colombia.[45]

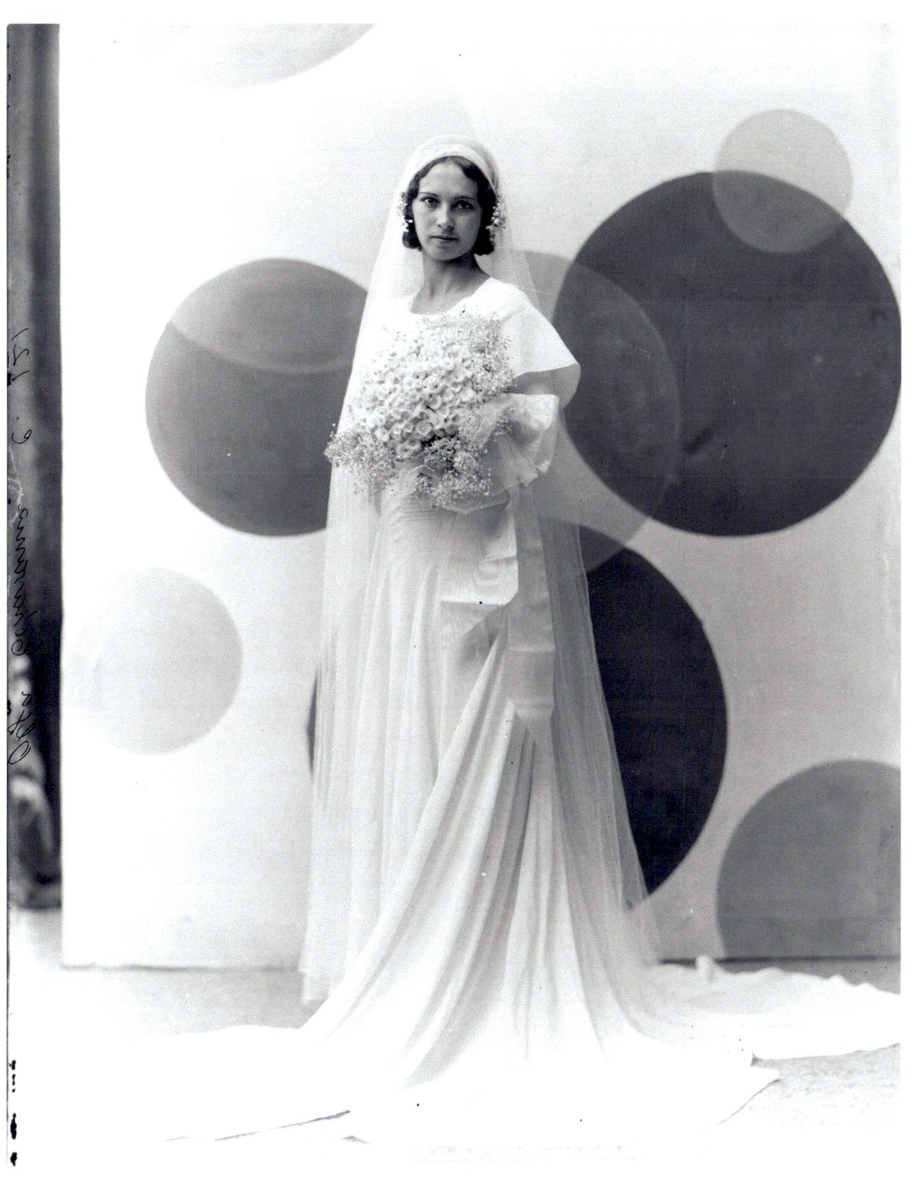

5.9. Fotografía Rodríguez, *Olga Echavarría*, 1930. Digital positive from gelatin dry plate, 25 × 20 cm. Biblioteca Pública Piloto de Medellín / Archivo fotográfico.

The most recognized international fashion photographer of the early twentieth century was Edward Steichen (1879–1973), who, after working with Alfred Stieglitz for his Little Galleries of the Photo-Secession (later known as 291 for its address on New York's Fifth Avenue) and serving in World War I, moved toward straight, sharp-focus photography, and the commercial world. In 1923, Condé Nast hired him to work for *Vanity Fair* and *Vogue*, which he did until 1937.[46] Although he took a step back from pictorialist photography, his time with Stieglitz at the Little Galleries was decisive in his later work. Working with him, Steichen immersed himself in the modern art world, selecting the European paintings and sculptures exhibited in the small gallery space owned by Stieglitz in New York City.[47] His highly complex understanding of art was later influential in his fashion photographs, especially after the 1925 Exposition Internationale des Arts Décoratifs et Industriels Modernes (International Exposition of Modern Industrial and Decorative Arts) held in Paris.[48] This is reflected in photographs such as *Tamaris*, which depicts a model wearing an art deco scarf designed by Sonia Delaunay (fig. 5.10). She poses with her back turned to the camera in front of a set of modernist panels and displaying with her raised arm the scarf that covers her entire body. Steichen accentuated the play of geometric forms with the dramatic reflection of lights and shadows on the set, creating similar patterns that imitated the figures, not only of the scarf but also of the outer backdrop panels painted with abstract geometric forms.

Although it is hard to know if Steichen's photography inspired Melitón, the impact of international studio fashion photography cannot be ignored. We can see the negative space of images, such as Aura Mejía's portrait, as appropriations of the abstract compositions introduced in the high-fashion world. In Melitón's pictures, however, the light effect is less dramatic, and the sitters' poses are stiff and subservient to traditional portraiture conventions. Ultimately, the function of the photos was different, and thus, the results diverged. While American fashion photography was produced with high budgets for the most recognized magazines of the world, Melitón's pictures were done in a small and rather humble studio and intended for personal commemorative events or local publications. Although his photographs never reached a point of complete modern experimentation, and the emphasis on the intrinsic language of the photographic medium (focus, aperture, point of view, or framing of the shots) was evident, the introduction of the abstract backdrops in the negative

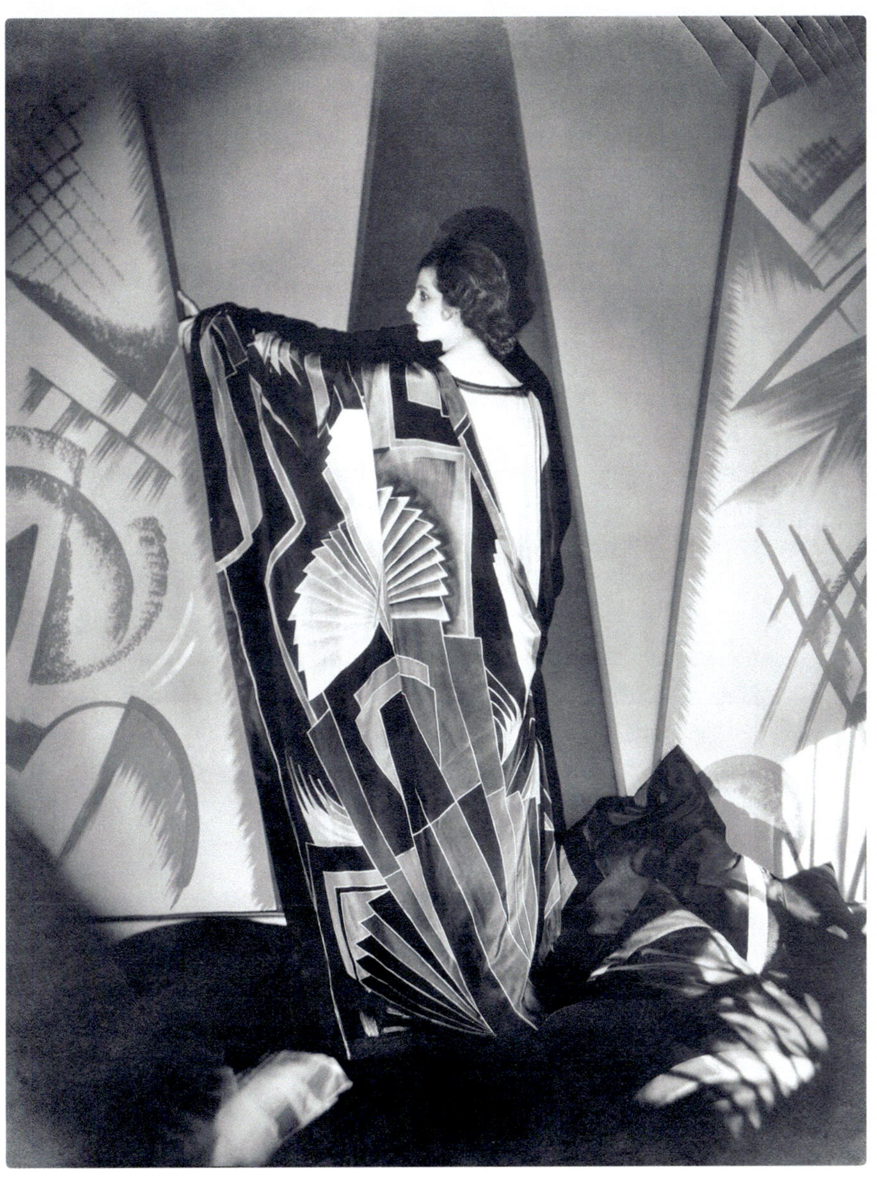

5.10. Edward Steichen, *Tamaris*, June 1, 1925. *Vogue*, © Condé Nast.

space of the photos placed his subjects in the discourse of modernity as a visual fact. The altered self-image created in the photographs with traditional figurative backdrops was radically changed with the introduction of abstract background paintings. While the former seemed to be about metaphorically placing subjects in situations of a desired altered reality, the latter created for the sitters a new modern subjectivity that did not require the depiction of a specific place but simply a visual rhetoric that conveyed a modern attitude.

However, as previously stated, this modern attitude was paradoxical; it presented modernity as a negative space, latently announcing a new chapter in the country's history. Indeed, the 1930s in Colombia began with a new liberal government—led by Enrique Olaya Herrera (1930–34) and later Alfonso López Pumarejo—today remembered as the Revolución en marcha (Revolution underway; 1934–38). Colombia was one of the few Latin American nations to enter the Great Depression without a revolutionary change in the political sphere.[49] Although Olaya Herrera minimized the impact of the global economic recession, and his administration is remembered as a smooth transition from conservative to liberal politics thanks to his moderate position, the actual change came with López Pumarejo's government, one that somewhat paralleled Franklin D. Roosevelt's New Deal in the United States.[50] López Pumarejo's social reforms focused on protecting the working class, providing support for education, expanding and diversifying the communication industries, and constructing highways and transportation media.[51] Thus, modernity was underway, as announced by the backdrop paintings of Melitón's photographs.

Although never conceived as artworks, the Colombian photographer's abstract backdrops ironically served the same purpose as some of the highest examples of modern painting by the mid-twentieth century. In March 1951, *Vogue* magazine published a series of four fashion photographs by Cecil Beaton with Jackson Pollock's paintings as backgrounds (fig. 5.11). The female models posed in front of the mural-size images, in dresses matching their palette and texture. Beaton's photographs signaled the end of an era. Popular culture and capitalism had appropriated and instrumentalized modern art—conceived precisely as autonomous and resistant to bourgeois culture—and Beaton's photographs materialized that idea. Pollock's paintings did not work anymore as sites of resistance and new areas of experience but as framing and decorative devices of the culture they intended to resist.[52] Ironically, while Melitón's backdrops were

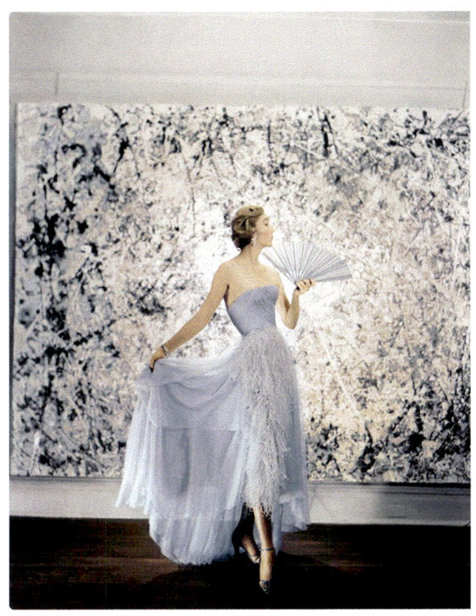
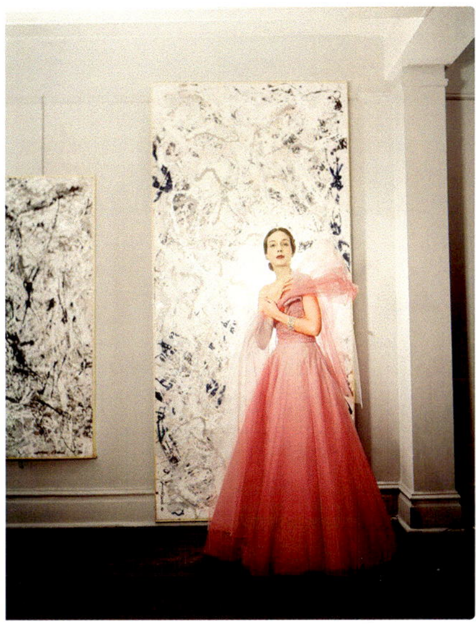

5.11. Cecil Beaton, photographs published in *Vogue*, March 1951. *Vogue*, © Condé Nast.

not conceived as art, they introduced a modern attitude and visual rhetoric predating modern art in Colombia (and Latin America). The negative space of his photos became the latent space of modernism.

Landscape as Negative Space

In Mercedes Rivera's photograph by Benjamín de la Calle, we see one of the earliest backdrops used by the photographer in his studio in Medellín (fig. 5.12). It depicts a lake scene with mountains in the background and a balustrade emerging on the right side of the picture. Another prominent backdrop used during this time appears in the photograph of Nepomuceno Bedoya, representing a serene forest landscape with cypresses on the left side of the picture (fig. 5.13). These trees become a recognizable feature in de la Calle's images because he used this particular backdrop frequently. These are just two examples of de la Calle's fixation on outdoor scenes, ranging from mountain views to seascapes. From the other twelve background paintings identified thus far in his career, only one depicts an interior setting—a fact that stands out when compared with the work of his strongest competitor, Fotografía Rodríguez.

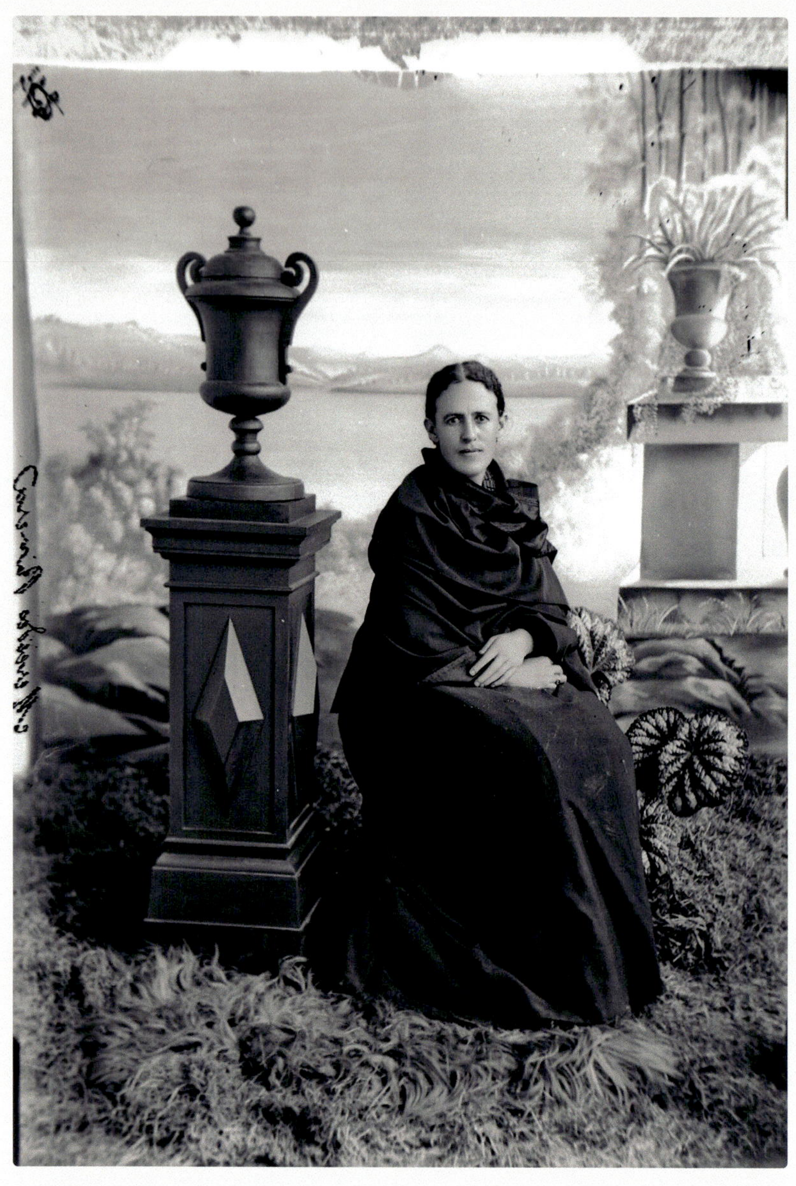

5.12. Benjamín de la Calle, *Mercedes Rivera*, 1898. Digital positive from gelatin dry plate, 18 × 13 cm. Biblioteca Pública Piloto de Medellín / Archivo fotográfico.

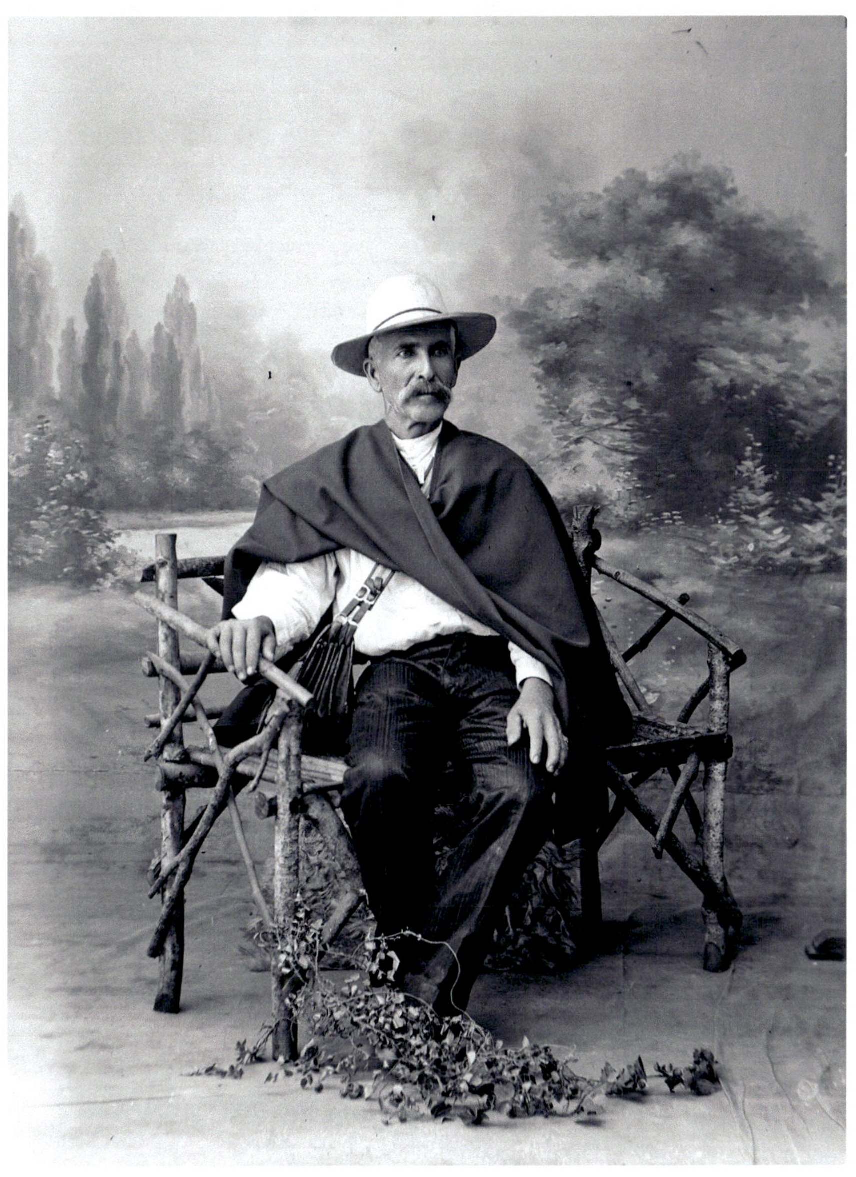

5.13. Benjamín de la Calle, *Nepomuceno Bedoya M.*, 1913. Digital positive from gelatin dry plate, 16 × 12 cm. Biblioteca Pública Piloto de Medellín / Archivo fotográfico.

Why did de la Calle and his clientele have such a strong interest in outdoor scenes? Considering the photographer's fondness for and identification with the disenfranchised, outdoor scenes might have been part of his repertoire of visual strategies to erase class differences or—at least—to elevate the social status of his sitters. Just as adding a painted veil to a wedding portrait heightens the social standing of the sitters, the selection of outdoor scenes seemed to play a similar role. Indoor backdrops usually depicted foreign upper-class architectural environments with opulent ornamentation that highlighted the contrast with the local sitters—especially if they were from the middle and lower social classes. Conversely, landscape backdrops neutralized the differences between the subjects and their chosen settings. Although the outdoor scenes also included balustrades, garden vases, and columns that clearly referred to European culture and thus to whiteness, the scenes seemed to take place in spaces hard to classify as private or public. The strategy to employ landscape scenes as backdrops is not a neutral one. As stated by W. J. T. Mitchell in the opening words of his essay "Imperial Landscape," "like money, landscape is a social hieroglyph that conceals the actual basis of its value. It does so by naturalizing its conventions and conventionalizing its nature."[53] By the time de la Calle was taking his first photographs, landscapes had become synonymous with modernity in Colombia. Challenging the conventions of traditional academic painting, painter Andrés de Santa María introduced landscape as an avant-garde movement.[54] His artworks embraced the unfinished aspect. He used short and heavy brushwork, and his use of color went against the conventions of the Academy. He even worked in plein air, a practice no other artist had embraced in Colombia. Indeed, his pieces were characterized as influenced by the impressionist movement, and they produced controversy among traditional art critics.[55] But, thanks to his European upbringing and high-class background, he managed to insert himself within the conservative Colombian art world and, together with Spanish painter Luis de Llanos, introduced the Cátedra de paisaje (Landscape school) at the Escuela Nacional de Bellas Artes in 1894. Landscape painting had a vigorous moment for a brief period, but it certainly became a symbol of modernity. And yet the backdrop paintings de la Calle used seemed to appeal to a conservative taste. Rather than radically introducing something pictorially new, these paintings point to a long-standing debate in the history of Colombia: the distribution of land.

The notion of territory and its conventionalization has played a crucial part in the history of Antioquia. Beginning in the late eighteenth century and until the early twentieth century, a particular process of massive migration and territorial settlement, today known as the *colonización antioqueña* (antioqueño colonization), took place in the region. Families from the then-called *país* or *comarca de Antioquia* moved to neighboring territories looking for new ground to cultivate and settle.[56] Economic instability and the hope of finding lands untouched since the times of the conquest triggered this massive migration of people. Indeed, this territory was mountainous and hard to cross, making it less attractive to the Spanish conquistadores than the flatlands of other regions. In a roughly hundred-year period, several generations of *colonos* (colonizers)—the word used to describe the new settlers—founded new towns, built roads, established farms, constructed bridges, and developed the coffee industry. New departments, such as Caldas, Risaralda, and Quindío, were founded in Antioquia's southern region, but the colonization process also extended toward the north and the east. It triggered a new market economy protected from the civil wars by the same landscape that was unattractive to the Spanish conquistadores.[57] The *colonización antioqueña* process is considered by contemporary historians one of the most important historical events in the country during the modern period.

From an iconographical perspective, the artwork that best represents this process—although from an idealized viewpoint—is *Horizontes*, a painting by Francisco Antonio Cano created in 1913 (fig. 5.14). The artwork depicts a white peasant family resting on top of a hill with the mountainous landscape of the unconquered territories in the background. The man points toward an unknown horizon, signaling the path the family will travel to settle; both man and woman gaze toward it. The pointing gesture recalls the visual evocation of Manifest Destiny—that is, the idea that the United States was destined to expand across the continent under a divine right or duty. The woman holds a baby wrapped in a white cloth, while the man carries an ax, presumably used to open new roads in the long-untouched wildlands they must cross. The painting simultaneously evokes drama and hope. On the one hand, it depicts a poor, displaced family struggling for a better future. On the other, it represents the prospects of a new, more stable and secure life.

The background landscape of Cano's painting is as vital as the romanticized scene of the family. Without the landscape, the artwork would lack

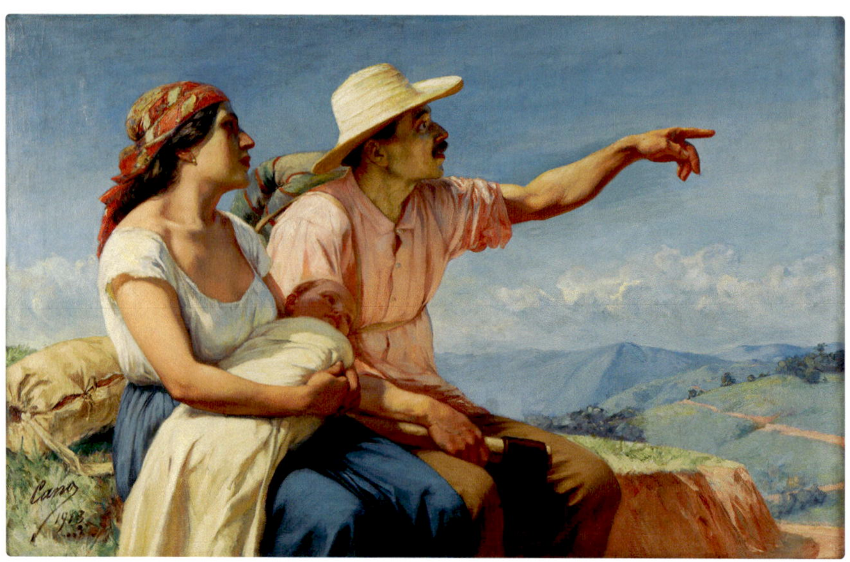

5.14. Francisco Antonio Cano, *Horizontes*, 1913. Oil on canvas, 95 × 150 cm. Museo de Antioquia, Medellín. Photo: Carlos Tobón.

its profound meaning, as it would not be anchored to history. It depicts a land that has gone from untouched and secluded to a new productive territory, reinforcing the narrative of the Antioquian race and its progressive discourse promoting the notion of hardworking white people. This process of territorial colonization should be understood as an enterprise. Indeed, during the twentieth century, many of the new towns founded by the *colonos* became the epicenters of the booming coffee industry in Colombia. In this sense, Cano's painting represents precisely that: a depiction of a land that has gone from savage and untouched to one that is productive and thus civilized. Indeed, we see a touch of this transition to civilization in the human-made road on the right of the painting. As stated by W. J. T Mitchell, "The semiotic features of landscape and the historical narratives they generate, are tailor-made for the discourse of imperialism, which conceives itself (and simultaneously) as an expansion of landscape understood as an inevitable, progressive development in history, an expansion of 'culture' and 'civilization' into a 'natural' space in a progress that is itself narrated as 'natural.'"[58] Historian Juan Camilo Escobar Villegas noted that this painting became the representation of an identity discourse that Antioquia's elite desired to control. Still, we should wonder if the romanticized scene also expressed the drama and conflicts the migrating peasants had to confront to gain actual possession of those untouched lands.[59]

Nevertheless, Cano's painting was not the first visual production rhetorically conveying this complex relationship between land, work, property, and Antioquian identity discourse. The consistent juxtaposition of landscape backgrounds and local people in the photographs of de la Calle not only anticipated Cano's painting but systematically called attention to the gulf between the portrayed sitters and the territorial disputes that were taking place. It has been noted that the backdrop paintings gave subaltern subjects an image—a place in a nation in which they were invisible—through the inscription of their bodies in the rituals of the elite.[60] This is true if we remember that posing for a portrait had been, until then, a privilege of the upper classes. However, that was the role not of the landscape backgrounds but of portrait photography, as it became a new and more democratic system of representation. Instead, I argue that the landscape backgrounds inscribed the sitters in the discourse of the Antioquian race, just like Cano's painting. However, the roles of foreground and background, positive and negative space, were inverted. While the landscape background in the photographs is indeterminate, in the painting it is quite specific: it is the landscape of the Colombian mountain hills of the western part of the country. And if Cano's painting represents the idyllic image of an Antioquian peasant family, the photographs depict specific subjects—with names, last names, and, in most cases, even the towns the sitters came from—as seen handwritten on the negatives of many of de la Calle's photographs. Therefore, the background landscapes, that is, the negative space of the photos, inscribed the subjects in a territory that responded, not to the mimetic depiction of the newly conquered lands, but to the imaginary of territorial expansion and the Antioquian civilizing program that aligned precisely with the European one. Many of the outdoor scenes created by de la Calle included balustrades, garden vases, and columns that referred to European culture. This is clear in pictures such as Francisco Uribe's photograph, where he appears posing in front of a backdrop depicting a natural landscape with a balustrade and a vase on the left of the picture (fig. 5.6). This is not a local site, but an imaginary territory where local culture aligned smoothly with the hegemonic discourse, this time represented by the backdrop scene. Again, the role of the negative space is in the associative qualities it triggers.

In de la Calle's photographs, the scenes repeat themselves often due to the few backdrop choices his clients had. That was problematic in a competitive environment. If other photographers in the city had a greater variety of settings and thus a wider selection of backgrounds to place their sitters, de la Calle had to attract clients by offering a different product. He achieved this by playing with the point of view of the camera. He moved it slightly to capture certain aspects of the backdrops, concealing others by including props and placing the sitters in front of them. The distance from which the photographs were shot and the camera's point of view played an important role in configuring the apparently new environments.

We see this, for example, by comparing photographs of Efraín Acevedo and José María Slait (figs. 5.15 and 5.16). In the first picture, the photographer placed the sitter on a bench at the center of the composition. The backdrop depicts a lake view with a sailboat recognizable in the distance. The second photograph used the same background painting, but the camera was further away from the sitter. Although the overall picture presents a broader view of the scene, the props standing next to the sitter cover a large part of the lake, including the sailboat, thus creating a completely different scene. If one looks at this picture without knowledge of the theme of the background painting, it is almost impossible to tell that there is a lake. Thus, de la Calle used the same backdrop to create a lake scene and a mountainscape view.

De la Calle also altered the repetition of the backdrops by including small details on the surface of the negatives. Hand-painted herons appeared here and there, especially in seascape views whenever the client so demanded, and the skies varied from clear to partly cloudy depending on the mood he wanted to convey (fig. 5.17). The sky section of the negative of Judit Garcés's photograph is heavily retouched, creating a gloomy effect on the overall picture, something not achieved in the other photos that employed the cypress backdrop (figs. 5.18 and 5.19). In other instances, he hand-painted tree branches and added details to complete his compositions, as seen in the photograph of Marta Rosa González (fig. 5.17). In cases like this one, his interventions do not dramatically transform the picture; they just add a personal touch to otherwise standardized images.

Nevertheless, de la Calle's most creative interventions appeared in two photographs depicting romantic and somewhat melancholic views of women under moonlight. The first one is a photograph of a young woman named Sofía Jaramillo, who appears meditative, her head resting on her left hand and looking upward under a full moon (fig. 5.20). De la Calle used a simple black curtain as the backdrop and played with lighting effects to

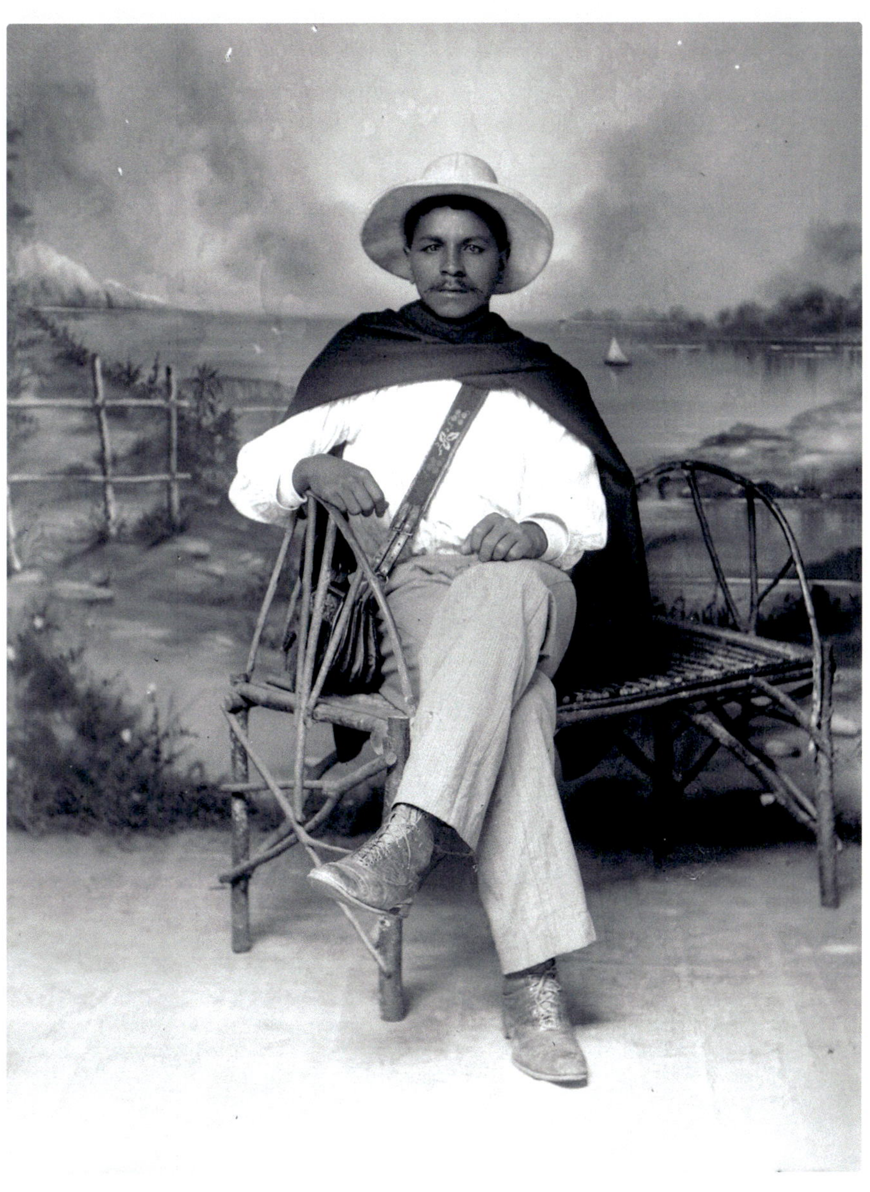

5.15. Benjamín de la Calle, *Efraín Acevedo*, 1905. Digital positive from gelatin dry plate, 12 × 9 cm. Biblioteca Pública Piloto de Medellín / Archivo fotográfico.

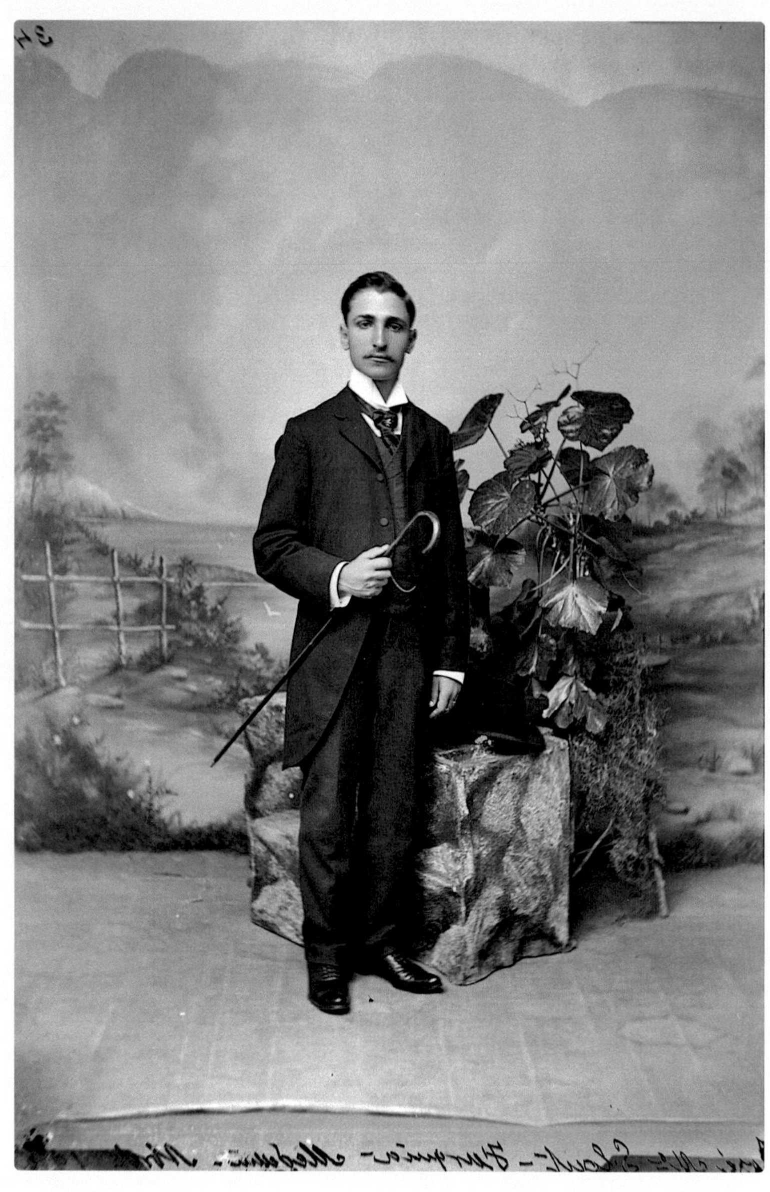

5.16. Benjamín de la Calle, *José María Slait,* 1915. Digital positive from gelatin dry plate, 18 × 13 cm. Biblioteca Pública Piloto de Medellín / Archivo fotográfico.

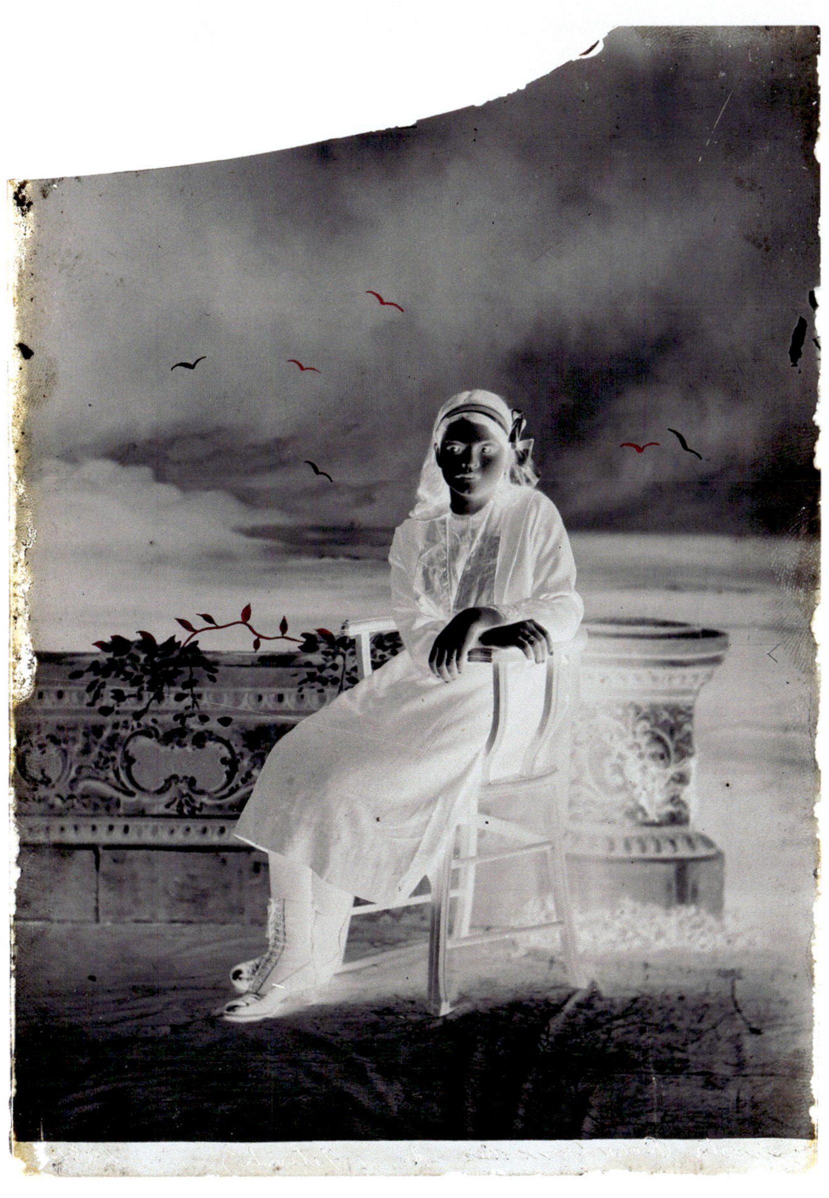

5.17. Benjamín de la Calle, *Marta Rosa González*, 1914. Gelatin dry plate, 16 × 12 cm. Biblioteca Pública Piloto de Medellín / Archivo fotográfico.

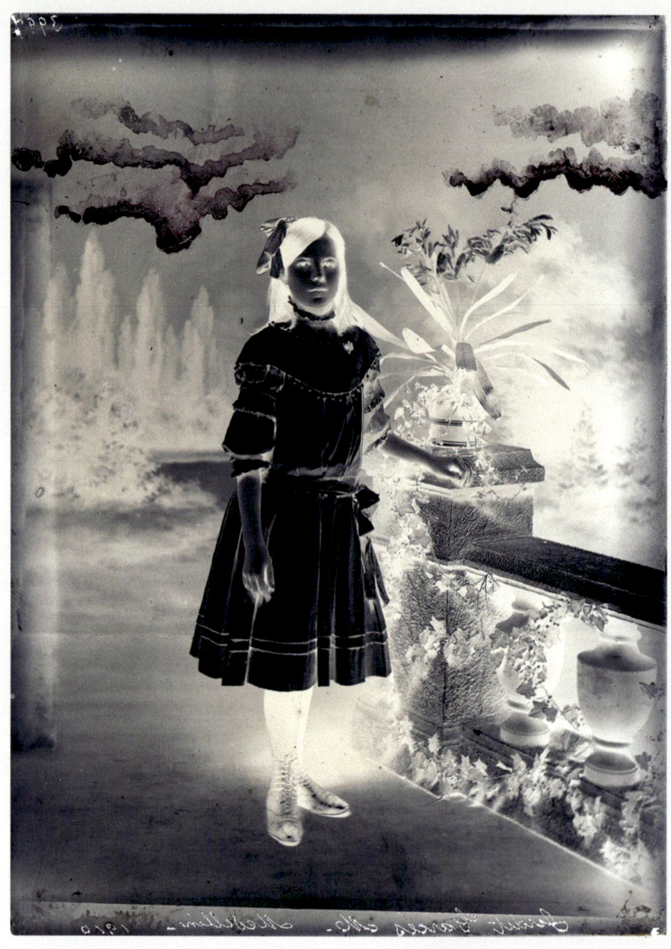

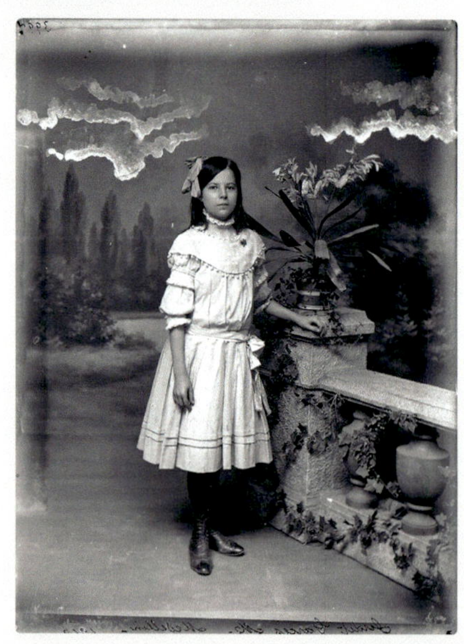

5.18. Benjamín de la Calle, *Judit Garcés M.*, 1910. Glass negative plate with retouching. Gelatin dry plate, 16 × 12 cm. Biblioteca Pública Piloto de Medellín / Archivo fotográfico.

5.19. Benjamín de la Calle, *Judit Garcés M.*, 1910. Digital positive from gelatin dry plate, 16 × 12 cm. Biblioteca Pública Piloto de Medellín / Archivo fotográfico.

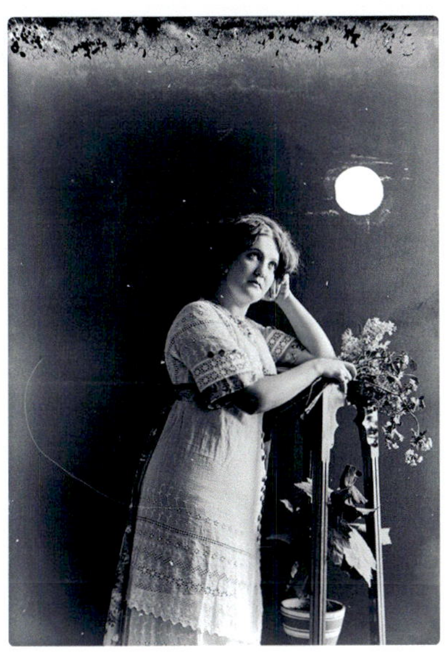

5.20. Benjamín de la Calle, *Sofía Jaramillo V.*, 1913. Digital positive from gelatin dry plate, 18 × 13 cm. Biblioteca Pública Piloto de Medellín / Archivo fotográfico.

5.21. Benjamín de la Calle, *Graciela Gaviria M.*, 1925. Digital positive from gelatin dry plate, 13 × 10 cm. Biblioteca Pública Piloto de Medellín / Archivo fotográfico.

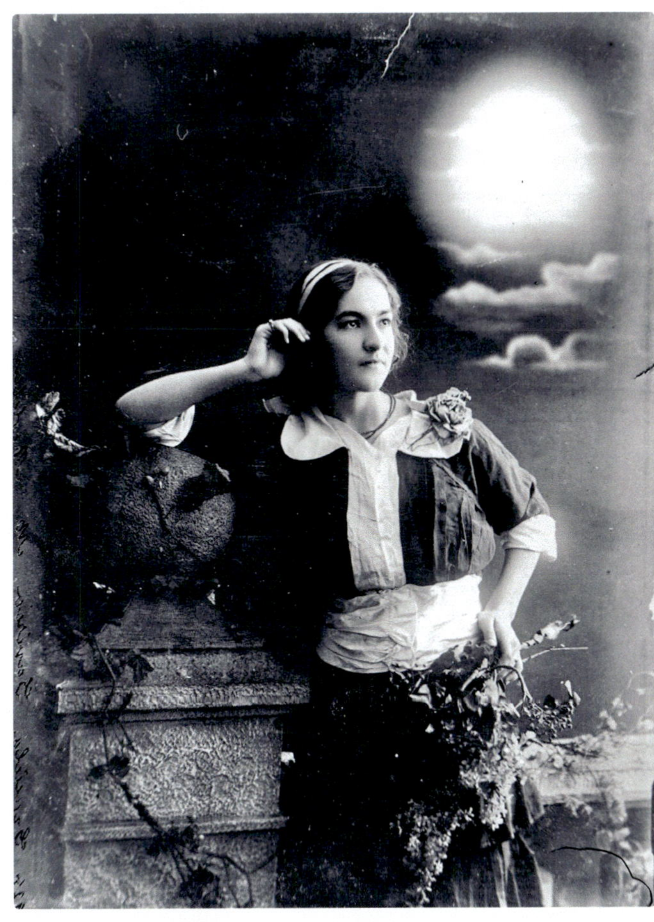

create a strong contrast between the illuminated sections of the image and those remaining in the dark. To simulate the moon, he pasted a black circular piece of cardboard onto the surface of the negative. The second image, created years later, follows a similar technique but, this time, achieves a more elaborate effect. Not only did de la Calle paste on the cardboard to simulate the moon, but he also hand-painted a light halo surrounding it and clouds that became visible with the light projected by the moon (fig. 5.21). The effects de la Calle created, through his collaged and painted interventions, were representations of things that the camera could not record and thus his creativity mediated.

De la Calle's manual interventions worked as supplements to his photographs. By themselves, the images were incomplete; they lacked something. In those cases, retouching played an auxiliary role, enhancing their meaning. The addition of the manual touches distinguished his practice from that of his competitors. Although he continued using the same backdrops throughout his career, he found a way to make his images distinguishable and a strategy to dignify his sitters through a deliberate selection of outdoor scenes. By never changing his style and following the codes of nineteenth-century portraiture until his death in 1934, de la Calle inserted his sitters in the hegemonic discourse of a stratified society. Throughout time his photographs lost their resistance status, and his once-negative subjects began encountering a more open society. Not changing his backdrops meant becoming outdated, and by the 1930s, other types of visual resistance strategies were emerging in the art world.

The negative space in studio portraiture thus remains a place through which the meaning of photography can be enhanced, contested, and challenged. Just as retouching the negatives changed the meaning of a photograph and materialized racial anxieties, the negative space of the pictures registered similar preoccupations. These frequently disregarded elements of nineteenth-century studio portraiture are essential aspects of the phenomenology of photography, a fragmented medium that I invite the reader to look at and think through the negative.

Notes

INTRODUCTION

1 Colombia has a centralized government, but the country is divided into thirty-two regions called departments. These subdivisions have a certain degree of autonomy and are ruled by a governor, who is elected through popular vote.

2 "Que hay un lugar en la América Latina en que existe esa roca ideal de una raza superior, y ese lugar es Antioquia." López, *La raza antioqueña*, 7–8. All the translations are mine unless otherwise noted. It is important to note here that in Colombia this type of regionalist discourse developed parallel to a national identity. See Appelbaum, *Muddied Waters*.

3 The Thousand Days' War was one of the many civil wars between Conservatives and Liberals during the nineteenth century in Colombia. It lasted from 1899 to 1902 and was the first war to be photographically recorded in the country. Indeed, both Melitón Rodríguez and Benjamín de la Calle photographed some of the generals and civilians involved in this war. Some of these pictures are discussed in chapter 3.

4 Melo, "¿Raza antioqueña?"

5 Azoulay, *Civil Imagination*, 18–27.

6 Quoted in Batchen, *Negative/Positive*, 104n1.

7 Lavédrine, "The Negative Image," 141.

8 Grimaldo Grisby, "Negative-Positive Truths," 16–38.

9 Lavédrine, "The Negative Image," 144.

10 Valverde, *Photographic Negatives*, 14.

11 Valverde, *Photographic Negatives*, 15.

12 Lavédrine, "The Negative Image," 146.

13 Batchen, *Negative/Positive*, 4.

14 Cook, *Victorian Negatives*, xviii.

15 Holmes, "Doings of the Sunbeam," 5.

16 "Los trabajos mejor en todo sentido. Mejores negativos y más trabajo." Rodríguez, "Cuaderno de caja," 89.

17 "Se terminó con dos negativos de niños que estarán muy buenos, los que voy a desarrollar en el acto." Rodríguez, "Cuaderno de caja," 89.

18 Grimaldo Grisby, "Negative-Positive Truths," 22.

19 Grimaldo Grisby, "Negative-Positive Truths," 22.

20 Quoted in Batchen, *Negative/Positive*, 7.

21 Morley and Wills, "Photography," quoted in Cook, *Victorian Negatives*, xxix.

22 Cook, *Victorian Negatives*, xxix.

23 Sheehan, *Study in Black and White*, 12.

24 Pinney with the PhotoDemos Collective, *Citizens of Photography*, 5.

25 Benjamin, "Little History of Photography," 276.

26 See Penhall, "The Invention and Reinvention," 106–12.

27 Riegl, "The Modern Cult of Monuments," 78.

28 See Alpers et al., "Visual Culture Questionnaire," 25–70.

29 See Batchen, "Does Size Matter?," 164–74.

30 Edwards and Hart, "Introduction: Photographs as Objects," 1.

31 See Riegl, *Late Roman Art Industry*, 22–24; Yonan, "Toward a Fusion."

32 See Fineman, *Faking It*; Kriebel and Zervigón, *Photography and Doubt*.

33 Barthes, *Camera Lucida*, 6.

34 Barthes, *Camera Lucida*, 59.

35 Azoulay, *The Civil Contract of Photography*, 112.

36 Christopher Pinney discusses this idea of minimizing contingency through overpainting or Photoshopping images in their positive versions. See Pinney with the PhotoDemos Collective, *Citizens of Photography*, 6.

37 Photographers have always been aware that photography does not capture everything. The most famous example is Daguerre's Boulevard du Temple daguerreotype from 1838. Due to the long exposure time of the process, in this photograph only a person getting his shoes shined was captured. The people in motion on a busy Parisian boulevard were missing from the picture. For a more contemporary reflection of this particularity of the negative, see Koester, "Nanking Restaurant."

38 Batchen, *Negative/Positive*, 7.

39 Cerón-Anaya et al., "A Conceptual Roadmap," 177.

40 López Rodríguez, *Blancura y otras ficciones*, 16–17.

41 Rappaport, *The Disappearing Mestizo*, 4–7.

42 Rappaport, *The Disappearing Mestizo*, 5.

43 For more information on this, see Katzew, *Casta Painting*.

44 Rappaport, *The Disappearing Mestizo*, 4.

45 Rappaport, *The Disappearing Mestizo*, 7.

46 Codazzi's project exceeds Alexander von Humboldt and Aimé Bonplant's initial expedition to South America and José Celestino Mutis's Botanic

Expedition in its achievements and scientific results. For more information on this, see Uribe Hanabergh, "Translating Landscape"; González Aranda and Uribe Hanabergh, *Manual de arte del siglo XIX*; and Appelbaum, *Dibujar la nación*.

47 López Rodríguez, *Blancura y otras ficciones*, 23–30.

48 Rappaport, *The Disappearing Mestizo*, 7.

49 There is a lot of literature regarding this topic; see Hering Torres, "La limpieza de sangre," 32–55.

50 For more information about the historical understanding of the concept of race, see Banton, *Racial Theories*; and Wade, "The Meaning of Race and Ethnicity," 4–23.

51 Wade, "The Meaning of Race and Ethnicity," 13.

52 Wade, "The Meaning of Race and Ethnicity," 14.

53 Wade, "The Meaning of Race and Ethnicity."

54 This is true except for the "indigenous race." Indigenous people were commonly placed outside the map entirely and thus outside of the regions that compose the nation. For more on this, see Appelbaum, *Muddied Waters*. Scholars such as Peter Wade and Michael Banton adapted the concept of racialization to refer to the process of creating and naturalizing human differences in groups characterized by certain biological or cultural traits. This concept's scope is to avoid the reification of a single meaning of *race* and to study how it has been understood throughout history.

55 Appelbaum, *Muddied Waters*, 15.

56 Sociedad Geográfica de Colombia, "Antioquia."

57 Londoño-Vega, *Religion, Society, and Culture*, 16.

58 See Appelbaum et al., *Race and Nation*.

59 "Estimado amigo y colega: suplícote que si no tienes para ello inconveniente, y lo consideras acto de justicia, te dignes a decirme a continuación tu que bien conoces mis trabajos fotográficos—si en tu concepto poseo suficientes conocimientos en el arte, y si por tanto estoy en capacidad de abrir un establecimiento en cualquier sociedad adelantada, en la seguridad de que satisfaré los gustos más refinados. Motivan esta exigencia los inconvenientes con que a veces pueda tropezar por no ser suficientemente conocido mi nombre como fotógrafo en las poblaciones que visite. Perdona la molestia que te ocasiona tu amigo afectísimo, que te desea felicidades. Benjamín Calle Muñoz." De la Calle and Rodríguez, "Fotografía."

60 "Estimado colega y amigo, con el mayor gusto doy contestación a tu súplica, en los mismos términos con que, espontáneamente, te lo he manifestado varias veces: tus trabajos, en mi humilde concepto, pueden figurar al lado de los mejores del país, en material de buen gusto y exquisito acabado; algunos de ellos me han causado envidia, te lo confieso sinceramente. Otra persona de tus aptitudes y conocimientos en el arte, estaría

á la hora presente, no digo en Medellín, que es poco: en la misma Bogotá o en cualquier otra de las capitales suramericanas. Si esto te sirve de algo, quedará contento tu amigo. H.M. Rodríguez." De la Calle and Rodríguez, "Fotografía."

61 De la Calle and Rodríguez, "Fotografía."

62 Most of the photographs discussed in this book exist only in their negative version. Since both studios were commercial enterprises, the positive versions remain in family albums and private collections. During this time, photographers only kept the negatives of their work, which in some cases were inherited or passed along to another photographer who might have acquired the studio. The positive images analyzed here are contemporary scans of the negatives or digital inversions from the photograph of a negative.

63 Londoño Vélez, *Testigo ocular*, 104.

64 Londoño Vélez, *Testigo ocular*, 104.

65 Betancur, *Moscas de todos los colores*, 153.

66 As opposed to that of the Rodríguez brothers, which qualified as a first-class atelier. See Londoño Vélez, *Testigo ocular*, 149–50; and Londoño Vélez, *Benjamín de la Calle*, 12.

67 Londoño Vélez, *Testigo ocular*, 150.

68 Domínguez Rendón, *Vestido, ostentación y cuerpos*, 132. The term *urbanidad* in Spanish connotes a sense of belonging to the city and thus of being civilized. Benjamín de la Calle came from a small town where the rules of civility and etiquette did not follow the standards of the capital.

69 Domínguez Rendón, *Vestido, ostentación y cuerpos*, 134.

70 Betancur, *Moscas de todos los colores*, loc. 6535.

71 Betancur, *Moscas de todos los colores*, loc. 6576.

72 Prager, "Four Flowering Plants."

73 Ruiz Gómez, *Benjamín de la Calle*, 15.

74 See Lemaitre, *Rafael Reyes*.

75 The book was not a photo book as the term is now understood. It was a part of the propaganda program of the president, but it can be argued that it constitutes a photo book due to the importance of the images accompanying the text. It was also the first book that compiled images from the entire country, utilizing photogravure as a printing technique in Colombia. See Serrano, *Historia de la fotografía en Colombia*, 183.

76 "El Presidente titular de Colombia, saluda al Sr. D. Benjamín de Calle, le da cumplidas gracias por los trabajos Fotograficos que ha ejecutado durante su corta permanencia en Medellín, y por medio de la presente lo recomienda como fotografo habil y cumplido caballero." Reyes, "El Presidente."

77 Rafael Mesa also took very similar views of the congregation of masses in the plazas of Medellín, but the president did not mention or acknowledge

his work. I attribute these images to de la Calle, but I have not found any further evidence.

78 Ochoa, "La Fotografía," 294.

79 The difference between likeness and resemblance is further discussed in chapter 1. For a thorough discussion of this topic during the nineteenth century, see von Brevern, "Resemblance After Photography."

80 Francisco Antonio Cano became the first independent artist from Antioquia. He organized the first fine arts exhibition in Medellín in 1892 and, together with Horacio Marino Rodríguez and the poet Luis de Greiff, he published the first illustrated magazine in the region, titled *El Repertorio* (1896–97). In 1897 he traveled to Bogotá, where he became part of the capital's artistic circle, and in 1898 he went to Paris on a government fellowship to study painting and sculpture at the Academie Julian and the Academie Colarossi. By 1901, Cano was considered a "symbol of artistic redemption" in Antioquia. See Londoño Vélez, *La mano luminosa*.

81 *El Montañés* (1897–99) was a literary magazine edited by Gabriel Latorre, Francisco Gómez, and Mariano Ospina. It was one of the first magazines that aligned with the progressive discourse driven by the intellectual elite in Medellín. Through its texts and images, it supported modern ideals and promoted the modernizing project of the region. Horacio Marino founded the architecture firm H. M. Rodríguez e Hijos, active from 1903 until 1973. This firm was responsible for changing the provincial look of Medellín and importing a modern architectural style to the city. It was the first firm to design and construct buildings in Medellín.

82 Mejía, *El taller de los Rodríguez*, 7.

83 Tabares, *Melitón Rodríguez en blanco y negro*, 35.

84 These books were in their library as study guides and are held by Melitón's grandson in Medellín. *La pratique en photographie, avec le procédé au gélatino-bromure d'argent* was published by the Librairie illustrée in 1896, and *L'art en photographie* was published by the same company in 1893.

85 See Stanfield, *Of Beasts and Beauty*.

86 Stanfield, *Of Beasts and Beauty*, 2.

87 "El cuerpo y la apariencia física . . . ocupan la imaginación de escritores y artistas, construyendo un círculo argumentativo en el que los blancos son más bellos y, por tanto, moralmente superiores, de manera que quien es bello y moral es considerado como blanco." López Rodríguez, *Blancura y otras ficciones*, 36.

88 *El Bateo*, "No habrá feos."

89 *El Bateo*, "No habrá feos."

90 "Feas que quieren quedar bonitas, tuertos y bizcos con los ojos buenos, blancos que no se acomodan con las sombras y negros a quienes hay que

hacer blancos." P. N. G., "Pequeña historia de la fotografía en Antioquia"; Escobar Villegas, *¡Hágase la luz!*, 77–83.

91 Tagg, *The Burden of Representation*, 36.

92 In 1957, Arturo Uribe, a member of the tourist bureau of Medellín, organized the first official festival, called Feria de las Flores. It was his idea that the state of Antioquia and the city of Medellín should host a tribute to the thriving flower industry of Colombia. However, there has always been a fascination with the production of flowers in the region, perhaps due to its yearlong spring weather. It seems likely that the beauty contest promoted through *Sábado* for the Fiesta de las Flores was a precedent for the official festival. What is remarkable in both cases is the association of flower production (and the idea of eternal spring) as part of the Antioquian identity and the explicit co-relation between flowers and women. All the festivals include a beauty contest. For more information about *Sábado*, see Arango de Tobón, *Publicaciones periódicas en Antioquia*, 334–36; Posada Callejas, *El libro azul de Colombia*.

93 For example, in his notebook Melitón specifies that the photograph of Elisa Botero was taken for a beauty pageant.

94 Ramirez M. et al., *Moda femenina en Medellín*, 61.

95 See Stanfield, *Of Beasts and Beauty*.

96 For more details, see López, *La raza antioqueña*.

97 For a deeper discussion about the topic of witnessing, see Baer, *Spectral Evidence*.

98 *Paisa* is the demonym used to designate the people from the departments of Antioquia, Caldas, Risaralda, and Quindío.

99 "Tiene la humanidad tres pequeños martirios en la vida cotidiana, los causan nuestros mismos benefactores y son: el sastre, el peluquero y el dentista. Antiguamente eran cuatro, porque se añadía el fotógrafo. Cuando alguno tomaba la resolución de retratarse, allá en los tiempos viejos, debía someterse a lo siguiente: pedir turno y manifestar si quería grupo, viñeta o cuerpo entero; operación de alta cirugía. Llegado que era el día, se necesitaba engalanarse, ponerse la ropita dominguera, y sobre todo, si el agraciado pertenecía al bello sexo. Ya éste en la galería, y cuando el fotógrafo estaba listo, se principiaba por colocar al paciente; se lo situaba en pose; generalmente recostado a una mesa, donde había varios libros esparcidos, uno que otro abierto, como si fuera un gran pensador, después . . . aunque él no supiera leer. En tal posición se le sujetaban por detrás unos ganchos de hierro, que para el caso había preparados; éstos le cogían la cabeza, principalmente, y parte del cuerpo. Todo ello para guardar completa quietud. No podía pestañearse durante un minuto que duraba la retratada. En esta situación el fotógrafo tomaba una actitud muy seria, como correspondía a tan delicada acción; con una mano agarraba el obturador y con, la

otra el reloj para medir el tiempo. Semejaba un facultativo que pulsara un enfermo. Y contaba muy pausadamente . . . uno, dos y tres. Mas ésto sólo no era suficiente; había que esperar un buen rato, mientras el operador revelaba la placa, para ver si la impresión resultaba buena; la mayor de las veces quedaba imperfecta y mala, y era preciso repetir el retrato hasta obtener un éxito completo." Echavarría, "La fotografía."

100 Tagg, *The Burden of Representation*, 36.

101 Tagg, *The Burden of Representation*, 37.

102 Rafael Mesa (b. 1875) was another studio photographer active in Medellín. His most significant contribution to the history of photography in Antioquia was perhaps the introduction of the photogravure technique in conjunction with Horacio Marino Rodríguez. Together they published the first photogravures in the magazine *El Repertorio*. See Londoño Vélez, *Testigo ocular*, 172–87.

103 "Cualquier individuo anónimo para el mundo, es para su familia un personaje que quiere inmortalizar. Antes estaba vedado al mayor número de los mortales legar a sus descendientes la imagen de sus antepasados. . . . La fotografía ha puesto al mundo todo en condiciones idénticas, pintando con igual fidelidad y baratera a un emperador con sus escudos y blasones que un arriero con su sombrero de anchas alas y su camiseta tunjana. La luz del cielo es una gran demócrata: pinta desde su cámara oscura cuanto se le pone delante, no importa sea harapo. Hoy el novio más destituido y el padre más infeliz, pueden, sin ir hasta Jamaica regalar retratos a sus novias y tener los de sus hijos. Y la luz que así lleva al santuario del hogar tantos tesoros de veneración y de ternura, nos conduce de pueblo en pueblo y de nación en nación hasta los confines del planeta." Fernández, "Bellas Artes."

104 For more information about this topic, see Escobar and León Maya, "Siglos de conexiones, no de aislamientos."

105 For a more in-depth discussion about nationalism/regionalism and its consolidation through natural ties, such as skin color, gender, and parentage, see Anderson, *Imagined Communities*.

ONE. ENVISIONING A NEW RACE

1 Reyes, *Aspectos de la vida social*, 56.

2 For a thorough discussion of this topic, see Brew, *El desarrollo económico de Antioquia*; and Melo, *Historia de Antioquia*.

3 Throughout its history, the relationship between Panama and Colombia has been a conflicting one. In 1713, during colonial times in the Americas, the Viceroyalty of New Granada was founded. It included the territories of today's Colombia, Ecuador, Venezuela, and Panama. Although Panama and Colombia are neighboring territories, the long mountain range of the

Darien—that separates them—did not allow complete integration. Therefore, Panama maintained closer ties to the Viceroyalty of Peru. When New Granada achieved independence from Spain under Simón Bolívar's leadership, this territory was named the Gran Colombia. Bolívar's ideal did not last long, and the territory fragmented, but Panama remained part of Colombia. By 1855, American engineers had already constructed a railway that crossed the country from the Atlantic to the Pacific Ocean and envisioned the construction of the famous canal. Nevertheless, the French—under Ferdinand Lesseps—began the first construction attempt. However, France's political and economic situation during the Third Republic interrupted the project. In 1903, Colombia denied the United States permission to complete the project, a decision that led them to support Panama's desire for independence, which took place that same year.

4 For an in-depth study of this phenomenon, see Caballero, *Memorias de la guerra de los mil días*; Salazar, *Memorias de la Guerra*; and Olano, *Memorias*.

5 Reyes, *Aspectos de la vida social*, 57.

6 For a thorough discussion of this topic, see Escobar Villegas, *Progresar y civilizar*.

7 As explained in the introduction of this book, *mestizaje* should be understood here as the process of becoming white. Reyes, *Aspectos de la vida social*, 58.

8 "Origen es español, castellano, con un poco de sangre semítica en las venas," and Isidoro Silva stated, "La raza blanca domina exclusivamente. La raza indígena ha dejado en la población muy pocas huellas; la raza negra, por ella misma por decirlo así, ha desaparecido . . . no ha dejado sino algunos mulatos raros." Quoted by Reyes, *Aspectos de la vida social*, 58.

9 Londoño-Vega, *Religion, Society, and Culture in Colombia*, 10–12.

10 Parsons, *Antioqueño Colonization in Western Colombia*, 4. *Mulato* in Spanish is the designation for one of the races that emerged during colonial times. It specifically refers to a person of mixed-raced ancestry, especially a person with one white and one black parent. Among the other races are *zambos* (persons of mixed race between an Amerindian and black person), mestizos (mixed race between white and Amerindians), and criollos (people of Spanish descent born in the Americas).

11 "Cada cual se jacta de descender en línea recta de hidalgos de sangre azul; pero la verdad es que los colores morenos, amarillos y atezados que se ven en casi todas las familias." Saffray, *Viaje a Nueva Granada*, 93.

12 "Razas blancas, vigorosas y saludables." Codazzi, quoted by Appelbaum, *Dibujar la nación*, 60.

13 Appelbaum, *Dibujar la nación*, 60.

14 For a thorough discussion of this topic, see Barthes, *Mythologies*.

15 According to Rodríguez in his text *Habitantes de Medellín* from 1925, by 1912, only 52 percent of Medellín's population was literate; by 1918, the

number had increased to 61 percent. For a thorough discussion of this topic, see Betancur, *La ciudad*.

16 Gaspard-Felix Tournachon (1820–1910), commonly known as Nadar, became Paris's most recognized photographer during the second half of the nineteenth century. Although he started his career as a caricaturist and was immersed in different enterprises, from journalism to aeronautics, it was photography that made him famous. Nadar photographed the most famous characters of the Parisian bourgeoisie, including Charles Baudelaire, Alexandre Dumas, George Sand, Eugene Delacroix, and Sarah Bernhardt, among many others. For more information about Nadar, see Hambourg et al., *Nadar*; and Begley, *The Great Nadar*.

17 Both the archives of the Rodríguez brothers and those of Benjamín de la Calle are held at the Biblioteca Pública Piloto (BPP) in Medellín. The photographic archives of this library are considered the largest negative archives in Latin America, and UNESCO recently declared them a "regional documentation of world memory." The BPP holds 1,000,700 photographs in different formats dated from 1848 to 2005. The Rodríguez brothers' archive includes approximately 20,000 negatives and Benjamín de la Calle's some 7,000.

18 "El objeto del retoque es corregir dichas imperfecciones únicamente: Tales son la eliminación de las manchas, pecas, cicatrices y demás defectos accidentales de la piel humana; corregir la dureza de algunas sombras y disminuir el efecto que un fuerte alumbrado puedas producir en las arrugas muy profundas." Rodríguez and Rodríguez, *Diez y ocho lecciones*, 36.

19 "Operaciones todas que tienen a destruir el carácter individual y cuyo efecto final es más bien la reproducción de una estatua de porcelana que la de un ser de carne y hueso." Rodríguez and Rodríguez, *Diez y ocho lecciones*, 36.

20 Burrows and Colton, *Concise Instructions in the Art of Retouching*, 21.

21 "El retoque es uno de los primeros y más importantes progresos alcanzados por el arte de Daguerri [*sic*]." P. N. G., "Del Retoque," 622–23.

22 P. N. G., "Del Retoque," 622–23.

23 "Hay algunos teoristas que, demasiado apasionados por el realismo, sostienen que el retoque no tiene razón de existir, disque porque un retrato debe ser todo lo más natural posible." P. N. G., "Del Retoque," 622–23.

24 "Los lentes fotográficos tienen la misma condición de los que no lo son, que es la de aumentar de una manera prodigiosa las cosas pequeñas; de donde resulta que en un retrato 30, 40 o más veces menor que el original, vemos las arrugas, pecas, poros, manchas y muchas otras cosas de la piel, relativamente más grandes de lo natural." P. N. G., "Del Retoque," 622–23.

25 Combination printing was a common practice, especially for inserting clouds in landscape views, which had to be added through montage

techniques. At that time, photographic film was only sensitive to blue light, so skies usually appeared blank. The best-known practitioner of this technique was the French photographer Gustave Le Grey (1820–84).

26 Rice, "Parallel Universes," 61.

27 For a thorough discussion of this topic, see von Brevern, "Resemblance After Photography."

28 Von Brevern, "Resemblance After Photography," 8, 10.

29 "Sin parecerse por $5.00, con aire de familia por $8.00 e igualito, igualito, por $10," in Echavarría, "La fotografía." Escobar Calle, *La ciudad y sus cronistas*, 112.

30 For a thorough discussion of this topic, see Stepan, *"The Hour of Eugenics."*

31 *La raza cósmica* (The cosmic race) was a book published by Minister of Education José Vasconcelos in 1925, where he proposed the idea of a fifth race in the Americas. This new race would be a synthesis of the other four races found in Latin America. Aesthetic functions played an essential role in his theories. For a thorough discussion of this topic, see Vasconcelos, *The Cosmic Race*. *Indigenismo*, broadly defined, was an artistic current and intellectual movement that denounced the political and economic exploitation of the Native American population. It served to negotiate a distinct, yet modern, national identity. For a thorough discussion of this topic, see Greet, *Beyond National Identity*.

32 In the 1920s, a group of artists today remembered as Los Bachués embraced indigenism as a way to rescue national identity and promote the Americanist feeling that characterized the continent in those decades. Historically, the first generation of artists in the 1930s in Colombia has been recognized under the name of Bachués, even though they did not consider themselves a group or a movement. Among the Bachué artists are Rómulo Rozo, Luis Alberto Acuña, José Domingo Rodríguez, Ramón Barba, Josefina Albarracín, and Hena Rodríguez. For a thorough discussion, see Padilla, *La Bachué de Rómulo Rozo*.

33 In the 1940s, Colombian elites started to promote a new identity discourse. The idea of a mestizo country replaced previous eugenic and hygienist beliefs. This new discourse saw mestizos and *mulatos* as good races that could help the country progress. Politically, however, these ideas increased a whitening policy. Only in the 1960s and '70s, with the Indigenous movements and the peasants' struggles, did some changes begin to be implemented. These new political and social orientations were part of President Virgilio Barco's (1986–90) Plan Nacional de la Rehabilitación in the late 1980s. His government opened the space to convene a Constitutional Assembly, which took place in 1991 during Cesar Gaviria's presidency (1990–94). For a thorough discussion, see Pineda Camacho, "La constitución de 1991," 107–29.

34 This continued throughout the first half of the twentieth century, reaching such an incredible level of acceptance that Colombia's president, Laureano Gómez (1950–53), declared in 1922 that the Colombian race came from a combination of Spanish, Indian, and black antecedents and that the latter two were stigmas of complete inferiority. Gómez was a radical Conservative Party leader who wrote actively against the artistic vanguard. He wrote texts such as "El Expresionismo como síntoma de pereza e inhabilidad en el arte" in 1937. This is to suggest that these degenerist ideas continued throughout the twentieth century in Colombia and had important historical repercussions.

35 Cited in Carrizosa, "Reflexiones sobre la tesis doctoral," 488.

36 "La degeneración significaba una regresión de la capacidad vital y de producción de la raza." Miguel Jiménez López, cited in Villegas Vélez, "Raza y nación," 212.

37 "Reforzar nuestra economía futura y nuestra sangre." López de Mesa, *Disertación sociológica*, 409.

38 Villegas Vélez, "Raza y nación," 228.

39 "Parece raro que así lo diga, pero siendo ese Departamento el centro de la República geográficamente, y también como vigor de raza, todo lo que sea robustecerla y depurar su sangre nos es útil." López de Mesa, "Los problemas de la raza," 33.

40 For a thorough discussion, see Maxwell, *Picture Imperfect*.

41 Maxwell, *Picture Imperfect*, 15.

42 Maxwell, *Picture Imperfect*, 3.

43 Poole, *Vision, Race, and Modernity*, 134.

44 Poole, *Vision, Race, and Modernity*, 139.

45 Poole, *Vision, Race, and Modernity*, 140.

46 López, *La raza antioqueña*, n.p.

47 López, *La raza antioqueña*, n.p.

48 For a thorough discussion, see Escobar Villegas, "Andrés Posada Arango," 78–98.

49 Escobar Villegas, *Progresar y civilizar*, 55.

50 "Para probar a muchos que sí es la raza antioqueña de casta limpia española." Quoted in Escobar Villegas, *Progresar y civilizar*, 66.

51 Contemporary artists such as Milagros de la Torre have revealed in their work similar aspects of popular photography from other parts of Latin America. De la Torre deals specifically with issues related to skin whitening in street portrait photography from Peru in her series *Under the Black Sun*, 1991–93. For a thorough discussion, see Rangel, *Observed = Indicios*.

52 "A função era dar maior resistência à passagem da luz e assim conseguir zonas mais claras no positivo, resultando a pele mais clara segundo gostos estéticos da época." Pereira, "O retoque do negativo fotográfico," 45.

53 Coronado, *Portraits in the Andes*, 71.

54 Indeed, in the extensive research done in the archives, I was able to identify just one female photographer from this period in Antioquia. Her name was Ana Zapata.

55 Riches, "Picture Taking and Picture Making," 129.

56 Herrera, "Técnicas de retoque de negativos," 113.

57 Riches, "Picture Taking and Picture Making," 137.

58 Riches, "Picture Taking and Picture Making," 137.

59 Tabares, *Los hermanos Rodríguez Márquez*, 26, 45.

60 Pinney, "Notes from the Surface of the Image," 213–14.

61 Londoño-Vega, *Religion, Society, and Culture in Colombia*, 147.

62 Sekula, "The Traffic in Photographs," 16.

63 For a thorough discussion, see Poole, *Vision, Race, and Modernity.*

64 Ochoa, "La Fotografía," 245.

65 Edwards, "Objects of Affect," 226.

66 González-Stephan, "Cuerpos in/a-propiados," 14–32.

67 "Sacar a la servidumbre de color del campo visible . . . podía crear el efecto de un grupo social moderno, homogéneo y hasta desrracializado e inclusive hasta jugar a la democracia racial." González-Stephan, "Cuerpos in/a-propiados," 25.

68 Campt, *Listening to Images*, 4.

69 Von Brevern, "Resemblance After Photography," 18.

70 For a thorough discussion, see Cole, "A True Picture of Black Skin."

71 Appelbaum, *Dibujar la nación*, 91.

72 For a thorough discussion on the Wills i Restrepo studio, see Escobar Villegas, *¡Hágase la luz!*

73 Levine, "Faces of Brazilian Slavery," 133.

74 Poole, "An Image of 'Our Indian,'" 46.

75 Poole, *Vision, Race, and Modernity*, 133.

76 Poole, *Vision, Race, and Modernity*, 139.

77 Bakongo was an African territory composed of today's Democratic Republic of the Congo, the Republic of the Congo, and the northern part of Angola.

78 Quibdó, the capital of Chocó—the department of Colombia with the largest black population—is only 110 kilometers away from Medellín. Chocó is also one of the poorest departments in the country, a problem that drives the migration of many persons to the closest industrial centers.

TWO. THE PICTORIAL NEGATIVE

1 There are several photographs depicting different allegories. It was a tradition adopted early in the history of photography in Colombia. For a thorough discussion of this topic, see Serrano, *Historia de la fotografía*, 113; and Edwards, "Allegorical Photography," 27–29.

2 See Bunnell, *A Photographic Vision*.

3 See Nordstrom, *Truth Beauty*; Kusnerz, "Pictorialism in Japan"; Toh, *Imagining Singapore*; Fundación la Caixa, *La fotografía pictorialista*; and Penhall, "El Pictorialismo en los Andes," 156–61.

4 Freund, *La fotografía como documento social*, 15–18.

5 For a thorough analysis of the representation of this classical account, see Stoichita, *Short History of the Shadow*.

6 Rosen, *Julia Margaret Cameron's "Fancy Subjects,"* 1.

7 Rosen, *Julia Margaret Cameron's "Fancy Subjects,"* 2.

8 Ripa, *Iconología*, 108–9.

9 Poole, *Vision, Race, and Modernity*, 170.

10 Poole, *Vision, Race, and Modernity*, 172.

11 Photo-paintings by these artists can be found in the collection of the Museo Nacional de Colombia.

12 *La República*, February 19, 1868, 392, quoted in Museo Nacional de Colombia, "Luis García Hevia, 200 años."

13 For more information on women hunting in Victorian England, see Munkwitz, "Vixens of Venery," 74–87.

14 Cerón-Anaya et al., "A Conceptual Roadmap," 182.

15 This photograph has been historically attributed to Horacio Marino's younger brother, Melitón. However, recent scholarship suggests that Horacio Marino was in charge of the photographic studio until 1898, when he turned to architecture. The attribution of the image to Melitón or Horacio Marino is in question; therefore I assign it to the studio.

16 Ramón Torres Méndez went to the Department of Antioquia in 1841. According to his biographer, José Belver, the artist became famous in the regions he visited. However, no documentation supports Torres Méndez's reputation in Antioquia. See Londoño Vélez, *Historia de la pintura y el grabado*, 88. Although most of these images were done during the early and mid-nineteenth century, they were later reproduced for different purposes. We know, for example, that Torres Méndez created a series of "types" and views with artistic intentions and that they were shown in the Exposición Artística de la Sociedad de Dibujo y Pintura in 1848. The following year, the pictures were printed in *El Museo*, and between 1851 and 1852, he published a collection of national custom prints. The latter were reprinted in 1878 and 1910 as an independence commemorative edition. See Gaona Rico et al., *Noticias iluminadas*, 52–53.

17 See Majluf, "Pattern-Book of Nations," 15–56; González Aranda and Uribe Hanabergh, *Manual de arte*; Huertas Sánchez, *Del costumbrismo a la academia*.

18 "La invasión de las minucias fotográficas." Miguel de Unamuno, quoted in Briggs, "An Expansive and Renewed *Costumbrismo*," 331.

19 Gaona Rico et al., *Noticias iluminadas*, 41.

20 For further reference, see the work of Pancho Fierro (1810–79) in Peru or the Ecuadorian watercolors from the album found at the Biblioteca Nacional de Madrid. Kennedy-Troya, "Formas de construir la nación ecuatoriana," 36.

21 See Ochoa, *Cosas viejas de la Villa de la Candelaria*, 78.

22 This is a strategy that de la Calle often used to dignify and elevate the status of his mostly low- and middle-class clientele.

23 "Una especie de San Pedro, preocupado por su trabajo." Ochoa, *Cosas viejas de la Villa de la Candelaria*, 113.

24 Echavarría, "La fotografía," 113.

25 According to French Academy standards, history painting and portraiture were more important genres.

26 Jean Baptiste Louis Gros was a French diplomat who traveled throughout Latin America precisely at the time of the invention of photography. He first visited Mexico in 1831 as secretary of the French Legation. He then traveled to Brazil, Venezuela, and finally to Colombia in 1839. Gros was an admirer of Alexander von Humboldt's work, dedicating time to the study of his legacy in Colombia. He is recognized as one of the many traveling artists who visited the Americas during the nineteenth century. In Colombia, his legacy was extremely significant because he took the first photographic views of the country and passed along the invention of the medium to the Colombian government as dictated by France. Some scholars suggest that he must have taken many more daguerreotypes during his time in Colombia. However, only two survive: *Calle del Observatorio* and *Catedral de Bogotá, costado oriental*, both from 1842. Although there is no record of his earlier work, it is hard to think it took him three years to take the first pictures. Apparently, Gros also instructed the Colombian painter Luis García Hevia on how to take daguerreotypes. Some of García Hevia's daguerreotypes date from 1841. See Serrano, *Historia de la fotografía en Colombia*, 16–32; Moreno de Ángel, *El daguerrotipo en Colombia*, 86–87; González Aranda and Uribe Hanabergh, *Manual de arte*.

27 In 1888, Carlos Endara Andrade (1865–1954) and Epifanio Garay (1849–1903) founded the studio Endara-Garay in Panama City, at the time still part of Colombian territory. Both artists were well versed in painting and produced work together. Endara later became one of Panama's most influential photographers, documenting not only the construction of the canal but also the life of Panamanians for over fifty years. Garay returned to Bogotá in 1892 after living in Panama, New York, Paris, and Cartagena. He became one of Colombia's most important academic painters and was director of the Escuela Nacional de Bellas Artes (National School of Fine Arts) until the beginning of the Guerra de los Mil Días in 1900. His work

focused mainly on portraiture, a rare interest for a successful academic painter. His contemporaries' work in other parts of Latin America was usually devoted to historical paintings, classic and literary stories, *academies* (erotic nude studies), or even genre paintings. His close relationship with photography might have influenced Garay's choice of portraiture. For more information about Endara and Garay, see Medina, "Historiografía y ubicación de Epifanio Garay," 96–116; Susto, "Carlos Endara Andrade y la fotografía"; and Lewis Morgan, "Historia de la fotografía."

28 See Sommer, *Foundational Fictions*.

29 Sanín Cano, "Medellín hace sesenta años," 42.

30 *Frutos de mi tierra* was Carrasquilla's first novel and is considered the first novel based on the culture of the Department of Antioquia. His literary peers believed the costumes of the region were not material for a realist piece of literature; Carrasquilla's result proved them wrong. Carrasquilla followed Flaubert's belief that there were no bad themes but rather bad writers. For more information on Carrasquilla, see Levy, *Tomás Carrasquilla*; and Rodríguez-Arenas, *Tomás Carrasquilla*.

31 Some examples of these magazines are *La Miscelanea* (1894–1901), *La Bohemia Alegre* (1895), *El Montañés* (1897–99), *Lectura y Arte* (1903–6), *Alpha* (1906–12), and *Panida* (1915). For more information, see Arango de Tobón, *Publicaciones periódicas en Antioquia*.

32 Luis de Greiff (1869–1944) was a liberal writer, politician, and intellectual from Medellín. Besides publishing *El Repertorio* and collaborating with other cultural magazines such as *Lectura y Arte* and *Alpha*, de Greiff was president of the Junta Liberal de Antioquia in 1910, deputy of the Asamblea de Antioquia in 1918, member of the House of Representatives between 1911 and 1914 and, in the following two periods, senator for the Department of Antioquia. During the rest of his life, he continued to be involved in politics and was one of the most respected writers of the newspaper *El Correo Liberal*.

33 Photogravure was a revolutionary reproduction technique developed by Henry Fox Talbot (1800–1877) and later improved by Karel Klíč (1841–1926). It combines photographic and intaglio printing technologies. Photogravure images are rendered in ink and therefore are considered nonphotographic. The technique permitted the reproduction of high-quality photographic images in books, magazines, and other publications, making it an attractive medium for artists and photographers, particularly pictorialists such as Alfred Stieglitz. For detailed information about the process, see Stulik and Kaplan, *The Atlas of Analytical Signatures*.

34 For a detailed discussion of ekphrasis, see Mitchell, "Ekphrasis and the Other." For a connection between ekphrasis and *costumbrismo* in Latin America, see Giannandrea, *Literatura y pintura en el costumbrismo argentino*.

35 Escobar Calle, *El Repertorio*, 8.

36 There is a version of this photograph dated 1912 in the postcard collection at the Biblioteca Luis Ángel Arango in Bogotá.

37 Rojas Cocoma, "Unidad, paisaje y lugar."

38 Benerman and Wilson, *The Photographic Journal of America*, 287. According to a short note about *Los zapateros* published in *El Repertorio*, the contest took place on July 28, 1895. See Escobar Calle, *El Repertorio*, 270. I have conducted extensive research to locate the publication, but it is missing from most periodical collections related to photography or Latin American culture in the United States. It is feasible that, as a small publication, it was classified as a trade catalog rather than a periodical and placed in archives and special collections rather than libraries. The Maurice G. Gennert archives at UC Santa Barbara do not have the publication either. The journal is part of the archives of the Universidad de Antioquia in Medellín, but the issue of the photograph's publication is missing.

39 Rodríguez, "Fotozincografía"; Rodríguez, "Fotomicrografía."

40 Aristides Ariza (1894–1948) was one of Bogotá's most recognized photographers during the first decades of the twentieth century. He specialized in photography for advertising campaigns and in Colombia's early stages of photojournalism. Ariza also worked on portraiture. One of his most notable works in this genre was a collection of 180 salient Colombian characters titled *Galería de notabilidades colombianas*. Quintilio Gavassa (1861–1922) was an Italian photographer who settled in Bucaramanga, Colombia. He is recognized for documenting the Thousand Days' War in Colombia. See Serrano, *Historia de la fotografía en Colombia*.

41 *Luz y Sombra* 2, no. 12 (December 1895): 292.

42 See *Luz y Sombra* 2, no. 12 (December 1895). The image that won the prize is unknown. For more on the Valleto brothers, see Negrete, *Valleto Hermanos*.

43 The award received for this photograph is a recurrent topic in the literature on the history of photography in Colombia. See Serrano, *Historia de la fotografía en Colombia*, 142; Roda et al., *Crónica de la fotografía en Colombia*, 21; Londoño Vélez, *Testigo ocular*, 119; Osorio Gómez, *Fotografía en Antioquia*, 59.

44 This is a part of the history of photography in Colombia that has been very poorly studied. Without further in-depth research, it is hard to know if other photographers in the country were pursuing similar goals. What is definitely known is the practice of other types of pictorial photography, such as the one deployed by Martin Chambi in Peru. See Penhall, "El Pictorialismo en los Andes," 156–61.

45 Poole, *Vision, Race, and Modernity*, 190.

46 The main point of reference was the French photographic tradition. Most Latin American photographers were trained following French photo-

graphic publications, such as the Rodríguez brothers, or through peer-to-peer apprenticeship, which started with photographers trained in Paris, such as Emiliano Mejía, who instructed Benjamín de la Calle. Although Antioquia and Britain had a direct commercial connection, there is no evidence that these particular images traveled back to Colombia.

47 Poole, *Vision, Race, and Modernity*, 189.

48 Ortiz-Echagüe and Montero Díaz, "Documentary Uses of Artistic Photography."

49 See Schwarz, *Misplaced Ideas*.

50 Poole, *Vision, Race, and Modernity*, 185.

51 Taylor, "Transculturating Transculturation," 91.

52 Mejía, *El taller de los Rodríguez*, 7.

53 Tabares, *Melitón Rodríguez en blanco y negro*, 66.

54 Leja, "Mumler's Fraudulent Photographs," 21–58.

55 Chéroux et al., *The Perfect Medium*, 15.

56 The iconology related to the guardian angel is usually the angel leading a child by the hand. The Rodríguezes might have altered the usual imagery to create their version of a different, less popular angel. See Castellanos de Losada, *Iconología cristina y gentilica*.

57 "A falta de un nombre más apropiado, le hemos dado el de El Angel del Trabajo, que es a nuestro entender el que más se aproxima al bellísimo ideal que representa." *Avanti*, no. 8 (1912): 136.

58 "El ferrocarril de Amagá es, pese a sus tachas y la mala voluntad que muchos le tienen, una obra de alta civilización, demostrativa de que el alcohol y otros males no han logrado todavía destruir por completo las energías de la Raza Antioqueña." *Avanti*, no. 1 (1912): n.p.

59 Not only were photographers trying to capture spirits from beyond but recognized scientists in the twentieth century, such as Thomas Alva Edison to cite an example, were carrying out experiments to prove the existence of spirits and ghosts.

60 Tovar Bernal, "Introducción a la religión y la ciencia," 38.

61 For more information on radical liberals, see Delpar, *Rojos contra azules*.

62 Londoño-Vega, *Religion, Society, and Culture in Colombia*, 40.

63 Londoño-Vega, *Religion, Society, and Culture in Colombia*, 42.

64 Londoño-Vega, *Religion, Society, and Culture in Colombia*, 26–27.

65 Ramírez M. et al., *Moda femenina en Medellín*, 73.

66 Reyes, "Cambios en la vida femenina."

67 Reyes, *Aspectos de la vida social y cotidiana*, 172.

68 For a longer discussion, see Orvell, "Photography and the Artifice of Realism," 73–102.

69 Londoño-Vega, *Religion, Society, and Culture in Colombia*, 127.

70 Reyes, *Aspectos vida social y cotidiana*, 50.

71 See Medina, "Oswald Spengler y la revista Mundial," 292–304; Medina, "La exposición francesa de 1922," 317–29.

72 One of the first photo books in the history of photography was a publication created by Henry Fox Talbot titled *The Pencil of Nature*. The book, published in installments between 1844 and 1848, promoted the idea that photography was a creation of nature itself. Talbot wrote that the images were "executed by the new art of Photogenic Drawing, without any aid whatever from the artist's pencil" and were "impressed by Nature's hand." See Talbot, *The Pencil of Nature*.

73 Hincapié, "Amor, matrimonio y educación," n.p.

74 "La joven soltera debe evitar en todo hacerse notable, tanto en la calle, como en los diversos lugares donde se vea pasar . . . debe proscribir por completo toda manifestación de exuberancia intempestiva." Condesa de Tramar, "La señorita en la calle," in *Avanti*, no. 9 (1912): 155.

75 "Un hombre serio no aceptará nunca por esposa a una jovencita que, sin haberse comprometido por completo, haya permitido a la crítica cebarse en ella," in *Avanti*, no. 9 (1912): 155.

76 Ramírez M. et al., *Moda femenina en Medellín*, 74.

77 Barthes, *Camera Lucida*, 10.

78 Molloy, "La política de la pose," 3.

79 Molloy, "La política de la pose," 4.

80 Pinney, "Seven Theses on Photography," 143–48.

81 Barthes, *Camera Lucida*, 4.

82 Ertem, "The Pose in Early Portrait Photography," n.p.

83 Franco Diéz, *Mirando solo a la tierra*, 57.

84 Herrera, "Entre máscaras y tablas," 138.

85 For more information, see Herrera, "Actores, actrices y otras gentes," 49–65.

86 Herrera, "Actores, actrices y otras gentes," 64.

87 This did not necessarily mean that through photography women were liberated from the ideological discourse in which they were immersed. The other, new identity could still follow patriarchal and hegemonic values. For a further discussion on the role of photography in relationship to women's portraiture, fetishism, and identity performativity, see Solomon-Godeau, "The Legs of the Countess."

88 Solomon-Godeau, "The Legs of the Countess," 76.

89 In 1888, the Kodak camera was introduced with the slogan "You press the button—we do the rest." This new system revolutionized photography since, for the first time, unskilled amateurs could take a photograph. This moment is also considered the birth of snapshot photography. For more information, see Sarvas and Frohlich, *From Snapshots to Social Media*.

90 See Fineman, *Faking It*.

91 Mejía, *Diccionario biográfico y genealógico*, 89–90.

92 Barthes, *Camera Lucida*, 14.

93 Belting, *An Anthropology of Images*, 3–4.

94 Cuarterolo, *De la foto al fotograma*, 75–76.

95 "Con gran atención nos dedicamos al estudio de los trabajos expuestos, y nos complacemos en manifestar que en medio de tanta belleza artística descollaron las fotografías que á la Exposición enviaron nuestros amigos Rodríguez y Jaramillo, propietarios del mejor establecimiento fotográfico del país." *El Espectador*, "Exposición de pintura."

96 "Los hermanos Rodríguez que lo dirigen, no sólo son entendidos en el arte fotográfico, sino artistas consumados, por el exquisito gusto que muestran en el desempeño de los trabajos que les confían." Villegas, "Informes," 486.

97 Sheon, "William-Adolphe Bouguereau in Paris," 109.

98 Ventura, "Intention, Interpretation and Reception," 219.

THREE. THE NEGATIVE IN SUSPENSE

1 Chervonik quoted in Batchen, *Negative/Positive*, 104.

2 The history of the *carriel* is unknown. Some argue it is an adaptation of the purses used by the Spaniards during the colonization process. Others say it derives from the English who came to work in the gold mines in Antioquia and that its name is an adaptation of the English *carry all*. In any case, the purse became very popular due to its usefulness for the *arrieros* (muleteers) who used it to carry all sorts of objects, including candles, playing cards and dice, pocketknives, tongs and hammers, handkerchiefs, combs, and amulets.

3 See Hall, "The Work of Representation," 13–75.

4 The online archive of the Biblioteca Pública Piloto, where de la Calle's archive is, has particularly encouraged this reading. The photograph itself has no description besides the name of the sitter and the place where she comes from, but the description written posthumously on the archive's database describes her as "*guerrillera*."

5 There is extensive literature about the *soldaderas*, including Arce, *Mexico's Nobodies*; Mraz, *Photographing the Mexican Revolution*; and Poniatowska, *Las Soldaderas*.

6 For more information on this topic, see Segura, *Las guerras civiles*; Cardona, *Los caudillos del desastre*; and Camacho et al., *Paz en la República*.

7 For more information, see Randall, "Nations in Crisis," 72–106. The separation of Panama from Colombia took place the following year, in 1903, but the war itself, which ultimately was the motor for independence, ended in 1902.

8 Jaramillo, "Mujeres en guerra," 60.

9 The Guerra de los Supremos took place between 1840 and 1842. It was a revolution led by leaders from across the country against the centralist constitution instituted after Santander's death. Santander was one of the Independence leaders, a federalist, and Simón Bolívar's opponent. The centralist government ultimately won the war due to the lack of organization among the many regional uprisings. For more information about the role of women in war, see Martínez Carreño, "Las capitanas de los Mil Días"; and Martínez de Nisser, *Diario de los sucesos*.

10 Martínez de Nisser, *Diario de los sucesos*, 49.

11 Contrary to what has been stated elsewhere, in the diary, Martínez de Nisser described how she joined the troops driven by her political commitment in defense of the constitution and not solely because of love for her husband, who had been previously recruited. See Alzate, "María Martínez de Nisser," 30.

12 Educated men such as Dr. Lorenzo María Lleras responded that his "modesty was offended" when the congress offered Martínez de Nisser a medal for participating in the war. See Rodríguez-Arenas, "María Martínez de Nisser (1843)," 107.

13 Alzate, "María Martínez de Nisser," 27.

14 See Jaramillo, "Las Juanas," 60–74.

15 In Andean countries such as Bolivia and Peru, the word *chola* describes a mixed-race woman with strong Indigenous features. In Colombia, the use of this word is less common.

16 See Espinosa, *Memorias de un abanderado*; and González Aranda, *José María Espinosa*.

17 Chicangana-Bayona, "La Campaña del Sur," 75.

18 For more on the role of women in these paintings, see Chicangana-Bayona, "La Campaña del Sur."

19 On the *soldaderas*, see Arce, *Mexico's Nobodies*; Mraz, *Photographing the Mexican Revolution*; Poniatowska, *Las Soldaderas*. In the Mexican Revolution, women occupied high ranks such as colonel and captain; see Jáuregui et al., *Emiliano Zapata*. For more information about Brazilian *cangaceiras* women, see Doeswijk, "Una entrevista a Lampião"; and Haag, "Sin una idea."

20 Mraz, "Sara Castrejón," 134.

21 Mraz, "Sara Castrejón," 134.

22 It is usually worn hanging from the left shoulder. In María Anselma's photo, she wears it hanging from the right. This could indicate that the picture is flipped, but this is how it has been published in the digital archive.

23 The idea of a nonbinary image is from photo historian Olena Chervonik.

24 See Villegas, "Mazamorreo y población negra libre."

25 Gutiérrez de Pineda, "Tensiones del odio en la pequeña comunidad," 294.

26 Serrano, *Historia de la fotografía*, 116.

27 See Fernández, "Las obras del Museo de Antioquia."

28 For more information, see Appelbaum, *Dibujar la nación*.

29 Giraldo, *Retratos en blanco y afro*, 59.

30 Quoted in Giraldo, *Retratos en blanco y afro*, 59.

31 Sheehan, *Study in Black and White*, 26.

32 I use the male pronoun to refer to Benjamín de la Calle's male cross-dressed sitters for two reasons. First, there is no other information regarding the identity of the sitters. Their gender identities are unknown today, and there is no way to decipher them by looking at the photographs. Second, the titles of the photographs, which usually correspond to the name of the sitters and presumably were given to the photographer by the sitters themselves, are male names.

33 Sheehan, *Study in Black and White*, 25.

34 Based on the Napoleonic code, in Colombia, as in most of Latin America, homosexuality was decriminalized with Independence, until 1887. It was again penalized from 1937 until 1980. See Bustamante Tejada, *Invisibles en Antioquia*.

35 Strassler, *Refracted Visions*, 79.

36 Strassler, *Refracted Visions*, 79.

37 Favero, "Backdrops," 32.

38 Darío Ruiz is one of the first to point out that de la Calle was a gay man. However, maybe due to the still conservative environment dominating the 1980s in Colombia, he never states this directly. However, he suggests it by saying that de la Calle "assumed his sexual singularity"; see Ruiz Gómez, "Benjamín de la Calle," 15. Perhaps the first person to address de la Calle's sexuality directly in writing was Constantine Alexander Payne in his honors thesis for Stanford University in 1984, titled "Growth and Social Change in Medellín, Colombia, 1900–1930."

39 White, "Haciendo carambolas," 357.

40 These comments are taken from a series of interviews by Jorge Mario Betancur between 1993 and 1996 during his research for the book *Moscas de todos los colores*. Betancur shared these interviews with me in 2016. Unfortunately, the interviewees had already passed away by the time I started this research. Jorge Mario Betancur, interview with the author, 1993.

41 Betancur, interview, 1993.

42 Betancur, interview, 1993.

43 Sedgwick and Koestenbaum, *Between Men*, 3–4.

44 Bustamante Tejada, *Invisibles en Antioquia*, 141.

45 The word *cacorro* was specifically used to refer to a man penetrating another man, and *marica* to identify the penetrated counterpart. As pointed out by

José Fernando Serrano, the difference lies in that the first does not lose his condition as a male while the second does. Being penetrated means to be effeminized and thus homosexual. According to Serrano, a *marica* is expected to act like a woman, or at least to imitate her, playing a passive role. A *cacorro*, on the contrary, maintains male behavior but is proud of sleeping with *maricas*. See Serrano, "Entre negación y reconocimiento."

46 See Serrano, "Entre negación y reconocimiento."

47 Butler, "Imitation and Gender Insubordination," 314.

48 Sifuentes-Jáuregui, *Transvestism*, 3.

49 Butler, *Gender Trouble*, viii.

50 Butler, "Imitation and Gender Insubordination," 312–13.

51 Butler, "Imitation and Gender Insubordination," 312–13.

52 For more information on the relationship between the New Woman and photography, see Nelson, *New Woman Behind the Camera*.

53 Archila, "Colombia 1900–1930," 333.

54 Reyes, *Aspectos de la vida social*, 179.

55 Reyes, *Aspectos de la vida social*, 172.

56 Ramírez et al., *Moda femenina en Medellín*, 109.

57 Stanfield, *Of Beasts and Beauty*, 20.

58 María Cano (1887–1967) is considered the first female socialist leader in Colombia. She was born in Medellín in a middle-class family directly related to the city's intellectual elite. In the 1920s, proletariat workers named her *la flor del trabajo* (the flower of labor), a title that referred to her struggle for better working conditions and socialist reforms. Her name today is related to socialist militancy, gender struggle, and a transgression of class subjectivities. See Robledo, *María Cano*.

59 The Echavarría family was one of the wealthiest in the department of Antioquia. They are recognized for their entrepreneurial efforts in founding the two biggest textile companies in the country: Coltejer and Fabricato. They also founded important institutions such as the Hospital San Vicente de Paul, the first electric energy company in Antioquia, and the Banco Alemán Antioqueño.

60 Coronado, *Portraits in the Andes*, 100.

61 "En las ciudades latinoamericanas, subir al proscenio era sinónimo de deshonra para las mujeres locales." Torres, "Las miradas cruzadas en la ópera," 259.

62 Sheehan, *Study in Black and White*, 77.

63 For more information on the history of smiling for photography, see Kotchemidov, "Why We Say 'Cheese.'"

64 Butler, "Imitation and Gender Insubordination," 311.

65 "Caso Curioso. El suceso de ayer," *Progreso*, no. 57 (1912), cited in Londoño, *Benjamín de la Calle, fotográfo*, 23.

66 In this section, I refer to the sitter for these two photographs consistently using the female pronoun. This decision is based on the declarations given to the police, where it is implied that the sitter identified as a female.

67 Calle, "Servicio antropométrico," 2.

68 Mesa, "Fotografía judicial," 384.

69 Mesa, "Fotografía judicial," 386.

70 This is an interesting concern considering that most of the population had dark eyes and darker hair. That a traditionally high-class photographer considered this an issue worth highlighting speaks again to the embedded idea of the *raza antioqueña*.

71 See Sekula, "The Body and the Archive," 6.

72 Arredondo, "Rosa Emilia," 90.

73 Arredondo, "Rosa Emilia," 90.

74 Patricia Londoño discusses how a correct civic attitude was a way of living that could be taught through the example it set and that those who did not follow it should be penalized. Indeed, she mentions that some exemplary citizens to be admired included Ricardo Olano, the editor of *Progreso*, the magazine in which the woman-man case photographs were first published. See Londoño-Vega, *Religion, Society, and Culture*, 264.

75 "Tenía aviso la policía de que una mujer que parecía hombre se colocaba como sirvienta en casas de esta ciudad y después desaparecía, recayendo sobre ella algunas sospechas. Ayer por la mañana se la capturó y fue conducida a la comandancia, donde examinada por los médicos oficiales fue reconocida como varón." *Progreso*, no. 57, emphasis added.

76 *El Cascabel*, no. 121 (July 13, 1899): n.p.

77 X.X.X., "El hombre-mujer de Jericó," n.p.

78 Londoño Vélez, *Benjamín de la Calle*, 26.

79 Londoño Vélez, *Benjamín de la Calle*, 13.

80 Bertillon, cited in Ellenbogen, *Reasoned and Unreasoned Images*, 30.

FOUR. ORIENTALISM IN THE ANDES

1 Said, *Orientalism*.

2 This project materialized in an exhibition at Princeton University Art Museum and a book with the same name.

3 Cadava and Nouzeilles, *The Itinerant Languages of Photography*, 17.

4 Cadava and Nouzeilles, *The Itinerant Languages of Photography*, 25.

5 See Said, *Orientalism*.

6 Behdad, "The Orientalist Photograph," 12.

7 See Ganguly, "Roundtable."

8 See Young, "The Ambivalence of Bhabha," 141–56.

9 Chakrabarti, "Moving Beyond Edward Said," 9.

10 Chakrabarti, "Moving Beyond Edward Said," 9.

11 Beaulieu and Roberts, "Orientalism's Interlocutors," 4.

12 Nochlin, "The Imaginary Orient," 51.

13 For a further description of these characteristics, see Nochlin, "The Imaginary Orient," 33–59.

14 Morán, "Volutas del deseo," 385.

15 Kushigian, *Orientalism in the Hispanic Literary Tradition*, 11.

16 See Carr et al., *Made in the Americas*; and Cortés, *Viaje y Tornaviaje*.

17 Christian immigrants escaping the Ottoman Empire sought a safer place to live. The main destinations were the United States of America, followed by Argentina, Mexico, and Brazil. These countries had laws that protected immigrants from ethnic and religious persecutions.

18 See Fawcett and Posada Carbó, "Árabes y judíos."

19 Igiro Gamero, "El legado de los inmigrantes," 309.

20 Igiro Gamero, "El legado de los inmigrantes," 309.

21 The political movement today known as La Regeneración was an alliance between the conservative party and moderate liberals against the radical liberals. It intended to change the Constitution of 1863, which had created the United States of Colombia, a federal government that lasted only until 1886. That year, a new constitution was introduced and became Colombia's political charter until 1991. See Bushnell, "La regeneración y su secuela," 195–214.

22 See Londoño Vélez, *Francisco Antonio Cano*.

23 See Londoño Vélez, *Francisco Antonio Cano*, 19.

24 Londoño Vélez, *La mano luminosa*, 66. Londoño also mentions René-Francois Prinet (1861–1946) as a possible Orientalist influence in the work of Cano, but his painting style was closer to impressionism than Orientalist imagery.

25 See Barrera, *F.A. Cano*.

26 Serrano, *Historia de la fotografía*, 92–93.

27 Solano Roa, "Orientalism in the Andes," 207.

28 Cadava and Nouzeilles, *The Itinerant Languages of Photography*, 17.

29 Meikle, *Postcard America*, 21–22.

30 Meikle, *Postcard America*, 23, emphasis added.

31 See Teulié, "Orientalism and the British Picture Postcard Industry"; Alloula, *The Colonial Harem*; Mégnin, *La photo-carte en Algérie*; Sebbar et al., *Femmes d'Afrique*; Stétié and Belorgey, *Égyptiennes*.

32 Said, *Orientalism*, 15.

33 Some of these authors include José Juan Tablada, Arturo Ambrogi, Efrén Rebolledo, Enrique Gómez Carrillo, Rubén Darío, and Julián del Casal.

34 It is important to note that this does not apply to all writers. Laura J. Torres-Rodríguez claims, for example, that writers such as José Juan Tablada had a direct interest in Asian cultures such as Japan. His interest

in Japan was thus a modern referent as important as European culture. See Torres-Rodríguez, *Orientaciones transpacíficas*, 52.

35 The term *criollo* designates Spanish people born in the Americas. Nagy-Zekmi, *Moros en la costa*, 18.

36 Torres-Rodríguez, *Orientaciones transpacíficas*, 27.

37 Kushigian, *Orientalism in the Hispanic Literary Tradition*, 8.

38 Arago, "Report," 15–27.

39 Behdad, "The Orientalist Photograph,"14.

40 See Nickel, *Francis Firth*.

41 Willcock, "Developing Orientalism," 127.

42 Willcock, "Developing Orientalism," 140.

43 Willcock, "Developing Orientalism," 140.

44 Behdad, "The Orientalist Photograph," 2.

45 Behdad, "The Orientalist Photograph," 12.

46 J. Paul Getty Museum, "Félix Jacques Moulin," n.p.

47 It is an image that recalls Manet's *Olympia* (1863), but it predates the painting's creation. Once again, in both *Olympia* and the photograph, issues of race and class are raised explicitly with the inclusion of the black woman as a servant in the background. For a broader discussion of *Olympia*, see Clark, "Olympia's Choice," 79–146.

48 Baldwin, *Roger Fenton*, 24.

49 Low, *White Skin/Black Masks*, 21.

50 Alloula, *The Colonial Harem*, 5.

51 Behdad, "The Orientalist Photograph," 27.

52 Behdad, *Camera Orientalis*, 63.

53 Behdad, *Camera Orientalis*, 63.

54 Ahmed, *Queer Phenomenology*, 14.

55 Gónima, *Apuntes para la historia*, 108.

56 Batchen, *Negative/Positive*, 7.

57 Batchen, *Negative/Positive*, 5.

58 Low, *White Skin/Black Masks*, 222.

59 Taboada, "La sombra del Oriente," 22.

60 Penhos, "Frente y perfil," 20.

61 See, for example, Acosta Luna and Forero Montoya, "El mundo en un plato," 284–99.

62 Japanese immigration to Latin America began in the twentieth century, and Colombia received just a handful of Japanese people during the first decades of the century. As pointed out by my colleague Betsy Forero—an expert on Japanese visual culture—few studies explore the connections between Japan and Colombia. See Sanmiguel, "Japoneses en Colombia."

63 Escobar and León Maya, "Siglos de conexiones."

64 For information about nineteenth-century Japanese studio photography, see Gartlan and Wue, *Portraiture and Early Studio Photography*.

FIVE. NEGATIVE SPACES

1 This type of chair was commonly used by photographic studios and sold by the same photographic suppliers that equipped the photographers with cameras, negatives, and chemicals. For more examples of posing chairs sold by photographic suppliers, see Gennert, *Descriptive Catalogue of Photographic Apparatus and Supplies*, 103–8.

2 Based on today's historical perspective, abstract painting in Colombia emerged in 1943 with the work of Marco Ospina. See Castles and Jaramillo, *Marco Ospina*.

3 Pérez-Oramas, "The Anonymous Rule," 28.

4 Pinney and Peterson, *Photography's Other Histories*, 202.

5 Cerón-Anaya et al., "A Conceptual Roadmap," 189.

6 Elkins, *What Photography Is*, 116.

7 Elkins, *What Photography Is*, 116–17.

8 Elkins, *What Photography Is*, 116–17.

9 Wyman, "Introduction."

10 See, for example, a relatively long illustrated article published in two installments: Seavey, "How to Use Photographic Backgrounds."

11 Wilton, cited by Pinney, *Camera Indica*, 74.

12 Robinson, *The Studio*, 28.

13 Robinson, *The Studio*, 22.

14 Gennert, *Photographic Apparatus and Supplies*, 48.

15 Appadurai, "The Colonial Backdrops," 4–7.

16 Benjamin, "Little History of Photography," 282.

17 "Aquel arriero que entre reniegos y chistes, remangado hasta arriba de la pantorrilla, va orillando con su recua los fangales camino del puerto, es el mismo caballero de maneras aristocráticas con quien topa usted cualquier día en el Club, correctamente vestido." López, *La raza antioqueña*, n.p.

18 Londoño-Vega, *Religion, Society, and Culture*, 20.

19 Londoño-Vega, *Religion, Society, and Culture*, 20.

20 See Appadurai, "The Colonial Backdrops"; and Pinney, *Camera Indica*.

21 Favero, "Backdrops," 30.

22 Appadurai, "The Colonial Backdrops," 4–7.

23 Favero, "Backdrops," 32.

24 Appadurai, "The Colonial Backdrops," 4–7.

25 Escobar Villegas, *Progresar y civilizar*, 67.

26 Le Bon, *Psychology of Peoples*, 150.

27 Falconi, "No Me Token," n.p.

28 Holloway, "Introduction," 7.

29 Ardao, *Génesis de la idea*, 76.

30 Ardao, *Génesis de la idea*, 78–79.

31 Torres Caicedo cited in Ardao, *Génesis de la idea*, 83.

32 "Claro es que los Americanos Españoles no hemos de ser latinos por lo Indio, sino por lo Español." Torres Caicedo, quoted by Ardao, *Génesis de la idea*, 74.

33 I want to thank Verónica Uribe for noticing this relationship and pointing it out.

34 In contrast to the work of his contemporaries in Argentina and Brazil, who conceptualized painting as a concrete form that rejected any references to the real world, Ospina's paintings emerged from an analysis of the natural forms surrounding him. His earlier abstract painting *Capricho Vegetal* (Vegetable caprice) from 1943 depicts a series of organic shapes that together recall a sort of landscape. For more information about Ospina's work, see Castles and Jaramillo, *Marco Ospina*.

35 Although Carolina Cárdenas's drawings echo some of the geometric forms of Fotografía Rodríguez's backdrop paintings, they are small-scale exercises and it is not known whether she showed them or intended to create large paintings based on them. For more information about her abstract drawings, see Badawi, "La artista Carolina Cárdenas," 133–36.

36 They continued using just one of the traditional backdrops depicting an upper-class interior.

37 González Escobar, "Horacio Marino Rodríguez," 190.

38 Vélez White, *Arquitectura contemporánea en Medellín*, 58.

39 Vélez White, *Arquitectura contemporánea en Medellín*, 57.

40 Vélez White, *Arquitectura contemporánea en Medellín*, 67.

41 Pollock, *Vision and Difference*, 159.

42 Reyes, *Aspectos de la vida social*, 50.

43 Londoño Vega, "Las publicaciones periódicas," 17.

44 The interest in fashion in Medellín can be traced back to the early development of the textile industry in Antioquia. This interest is still present today, as reflected by the international fashion fairs taking place in Medellín every year. Among them is the largest textile and confection fair in the Americas, called Colombiatex.

45 Cruz Bermeo, *Grandeza*,14.

46 See Ewing and Brandow, *Edward Steichen*.

47 Daniel, *Stieglitz, Steichen, Strand*, 16.

48 Squiers, "Edward Steichen at Condé Nast," 112.

49 Bushnell, *Colombia, una nación*, 261.

50 Bushnell, *Colombia, una nación*, 267.

51 Paralleling the example dictated by Lázaro Cárdenas's administration in Mexico—the other point of reference of López Pumarejo's

administration—the Revolución en marcha also supported the emergence of public art in Colombia. In particular, in Medellín, a series of public art murals were commissioned to decorate the internal walls of a public building. Pedro Nel Gómez was the artist selected to paint the frescoes of the Palacio Municipal, the building recently constructed by Horacio Marino Rodríguez's architectural firm. The murals denounced social discomfort in themes related to migration, lack of food, and mining, among other issues.

52 For more information about Cecil Beaton's photographs, see Clark, *Farewell to an Idea*; and Crow, *Modern Art in the Common Culture*.

53 Mitchell, "Imperial Landscape," 5.

54 Badawi, "La vida secreta del paisaje," 123; González Aranda, "Fin del sueño académico," 323–47.

55 For more information, see González Aranda, "Fin del sueño académico," 323–47.

56 In the late eighteenth century, part of the territory today known as Colombia was divided into *paises* or *comarcas*. These were the names given to specific regions as opposed to the modern notion of departments or states.

57 For more information, see Parsons, *La colonización antioqueña en el occidente*; and Melo, *Historia de Antioquia*.

58 Mitchell, "Imperial Landscape," 17.

59 Escobar Villegas, *Progresar y civilizar*, 381.

60 Flórez, "La fotografía de telón de fondo," 26.

Bibliography

Abelove, Henry, Michele Aina Barale, and David M. Halperin. *The Lesbian and Gay Studies Reader*. New York: Routledge, 1993.

Acosta Luna, Olga Isabel, and Betsy Forero Montoya. "El mundo en un plato: De Jingdezhen al camarín del Rosario en Tunja." In *Historias del Arte en Colombia*, edited by Olga Acosta, Natalia Lozada, and Juanita Solano. Bogotá: Ediciones Uniandes, 2022.

Ahmed, Sara. *Queer Phenomenology: Orientations, Objects, Others*. Durham, NC: Duke University Press, 2006.

Alloula, Malek. *The Colonial Harem*. Minneapolis: University of Minnesota Press, 1986.

Alpers, Svetlana, Emily Apter, Carol Armstrong, et al. "Visual Culture Questionnaire." *October* 77 (1996): 25–70.

Alzate, Carolina. "María Martínez de Nisser: Una opinión y un cuerpo que se exponen." *Cuadernos de literatura* 13, no. 25 (2008): 24–36.

Anderson, Benedict. *Imagined Communities: Reflections on the Origin and Spread of Nationalism*. London: Verso, 1991.

Appadurai, Arjun. "The Colonial Backdrops." *Afterimage* 24, no. 5 (1997): 4–7.

Appelbaum, Nancy. *Dibujar la nación: La comisión corográfica en la Colombia del siglo XIX*. Bogotá: Ediciones Uniandes and Fondo de Cultura Económica, 2017.

Appelbaum, Nancy. *Muddied Waters: Race, Region, and Local History in Colombia, 1846–1948*. Durham, NC: Duke University Press, 2003.

Appelbaum, Nancy, Anne Macpherson, and Karin Alejandra Rosemblatt. *Race and Nation in Modern Latin America*. Chapel Hill: University of North Carolina Press, 2003.

Arago, Dominique François. "Report." In *Classic Essays on Photography*, edited by Alan Tratchenberg. Sedgwick, ME: Leete's Island Books, 1980.

Arango de Tobón, María Cristina. *Publicaciones periódicas en Antioquia 1814–1960: Del chibalete a la rotativa*. Medellín: Fondo Editorial Universidad EAFIT, 2006.

Arango Mejía, Gabriel. *Genealogías de Antioquia y Caldas*. 2nd ed. 2 vols. Medellín: Imprenta Departamental, 1942.

Arango Mejía, Gabriel. "Origen de la raza antioqueña." *Boletín de Historia y Antigüedades* 5, no. 59 (1909).

Arce, Christine B. *Mexico's Nobodies: The Cultural Legacy of the Soldadera and Afro-Mexican Women*. Albany: State University of New York Press, 2017.

Archila, Mauricio. "Colombia 1900–1930: La búsqueda de la modernización." In *Las mujeres en la historia de Colombia*, edited by Magdala Velásquez Toro. Bogotá: Grupo Editorial Norma, 1995.

Ardao, Arturo. *Génesis de la idea y el nombre de América Latina*. Caracas: Centro de Estudios Latinoamericanos Rómulo Gallegos, 1980.

Arredondo, Juanita. "Rosa Emilia." *Avanti* 1, no. 5 (May 1912).

Azoulay, Ariella Aïsha. *The Civil Contract of Photography*. Brooklyn: Zone Books, 2008.

Azoulay, Ariella Aïsha. *Civil Imagination: A Political Ontology of Photography*. Translated by Louise Bethlehem. New York: Verso, 2015.

Badawi, Halim. "La artista Carolina Cárdenas y los orígenes de la abstracción en Colombia." In *Historia urgente del arte en Colombia*. Bogotá: Editorial Planeta, 2019.

Badawi, Halim. "La vida secreta del paisaje: Andrés de Santa María, la Hacienda el Vínculo, la propiedad de la tierra y los inicios de la pintura de paisaje en Colombia." In *Decir el lugar: Testimonios del paisaje colombiano*, edited by Nicolás Gómez Echeverri. Bogotá: Banco de la República, 2017.

Baer, Ulrich. *Spectral Evidence: The Photography of Trauma*. Cambridge, MA: MIT Press, 2002.

Baldwin, Gordon. *Roger Fenton: Pasha and Bayadere*. Malibu, CA: J. Paul Getty Museum, 1996.

Banton, Michael. *Racial Theories*. Cambridge: Cambridge University Press, 1998.

Barrera, Humberto. *F.A. Cano: De Yarumal a París*. Yarumal, Colombia: Alcaldía de Yarumal, 2010.

Barthes, Roland. *Camera Lucida: Reflections on Photography*. New York: Hill and Wang, 2010.

Barthes, Roland. *Mythologies*. New York: Hill and Wang, 2012.

Batchen, Geoffrey. "Does Size Matter?" In *Negative/Positive: A History of Photography*. Abingdon, UK: Routledge, 2021.

Batchen, Geoffrey. *Negative/Positive: A History of Photography*. Abingdon, UK: Routledge, 2021.

Beaulieu, Jill, and Mary Roberts. "Orientalism's Interlocutors." In *Orientalism's Interlocutors: Painting, Architecture, Photography*. Durham, NC: Duke University Press, 2002.

Begley, Adam. *The Great Nadar: The Man Behind the Camera*. New York: Tim Duggan, 2017.

Behdad, Ali. *Camera Orientalis: Reflections on Photography from the Middle East*. Chicago: University of Chicago Press, 2016.

Behdad, Ali. "The Orientalist Photograph." In *Photography's Orientalism: New Essays on Colonial Representation*, edited by Ali Behdad and Luke Gartlan. Los Angeles: Getty Research Institute, 2013.

Belting, Hans. *An Anthropology of Images: Picture, Medium, Body*. Princeton, NJ: Princeton University Press, 2014.

Benerman and Wilson. *The Photographic Journal of America* 34 (1894).

Benjamin, Walter. "Little History of Photography." In *The Work of Art in the Age of Its Technological Reproducibility and Other Writings on Media*, edited by Michael W. Jennings, Brigid Doherty, and Thomas Y. Levin. Cambridge, MA: Harvard University Press, 2008.

Benjamin, Walter. "The Work of Art in the Age of Its Technological Reproducibility." In *The Work of Art in the Age of Its Technological Reproducibility, and Other Writings on Media*, edited by Michael William Jennings, Brigid Doherty, and Thomas Y. Levin. Cambridge, MA: Belknap, 2008.

Bernal Nichols, Alberto. *Miscelanea sobre la historia, los usos y las costumbres de Medellín*. Medellín: Universidad de Antioquia, 1980.

Betancur, Agapito. *La ciudad. Medellín en el 5° cincuentenario de su fundación: Pasado, presente, futuro*. Medellín: ITM, 2003.

Betancur, Jorge Mario. *Moscas de todos los colores: Historia del barrio de Guayaquil en Medellín, 1894–1934*. Bogotá: Ministerio de Cultura, 2000. Kindle ed.

Biblioteca Pública Piloto. *Melitón Rodríguez, fotógrafo: Momentos, espacios y personajes*. Medellín: Biblioteca Pública Piloto, 1996.

Billeter, Erika. *Canto a la realidad: Fotografía latinoamericana 1860–1993*. Madrid: Lunwerg, 1993.

Botero Gómez, Fabio. *Cien años de la vida en Medellín 1890–1990*. Medellín: Consejo de Medellín, 1994.

Brew, Roger. *El desarrollo económico de Antioquia desde la independencia hasta 1920*. Medellín: Editorial Universidad de Antioquia, 2000.

Briggs, Ronald. "An Expansive and Renewed *Costumbrismo*." *A Contracorriente* 13, no. 3 (2016): 331–35.

Bunnell, Peter C. *A Photographic Vision: Pictorial Photography, 1889–1923*. Salt Lake City, UT: Peregrine Smith, 1980.

Burrows and Colton. *Concise Instructions in the Art of Retouching*. London: Marion and Company, 1876.

Bushnell, David. *Colombia, una nación a pesar de sí misma: De los tiempos precolombinos a nuestros días*. Bogotá: Editorial Planeta, 1996.

Bushnell, David. "La regeneración y su secuela: Una reacción positivista y conservadora (1885–1904)." In *Colombia, una nación a pesar de sí misma: De los tiempos precolombinos a nuestros días*. Bogotá: Editorial Planeta, 1994.

Bustamante Tejada, Walter Alonso. *Invisibles en Antioquia 1886–1936: Una arqueología de los discursos sobre la homosexualidad*. Medellín: La Carreta Editores, 2004.

Butler, Judith. *Gender Trouble: Feminism and the Subversion of Identity*. New York: Routledge, 1990.

Butler, Judith. "Imitation and Gender Insubordination." In *The Lesbian and Gay Studies Reader*, edited by Henry Abelove, Michele Aina Barale, and David M. Halperin. New York: Routledge, 1993.

Caballero, Lucas. *Memorias de la guerra de los mil días*. Bogotá: El Áncora Editores, 1980.

Cadava, Eduardo, and Gabriela Nouzeilles, eds. *The Itinerant Languages of Photography*. Princeton, NJ: Princeton University Art Museum, 2013.

Calle, Manuel F. "Servicio antropométrico." *Progreso*, November 24, 1914.

Camacho, Carlos, Margarita Garrido, and Daniel Gutiérrez. *Paz en la República: Colombia, siglo XIX*. Bogotá: Universidad Externado de Colombia, 2018.

Campt, Tina. *Listening to Images*. Durham, NC: Duke University Press, 2017.

Cardona Tobón, Alfredo. *Los caudillos del desastre: Guerras civiles en el siglo XIX*. Manizales: Universidad Autónoma, 2006.

Carr, Dennis, Gauvin Bailey, Timothy Brook, Mitchell Codding, Karina Corrigan, and Donna Pierce. *Made in the Americas: The New World Discovers Asia*. Boston: MFA Publications, 2015.

Carrizosa Moog, Jaime. "Reflexiones sobre la tesis doctoral 'La raza antioqueña es única y no está degenerada.'" *IATREIA* 26, no. 4 (2013): 487–93.

Castellanos de Losada, Basilio Sebastián. *Iconología cristina y gentilica: Compendio del sistema alegórico, y diccionario manual de la iconología universal*. Madrid: Imprenta de D.B. González, 1850.

Castles, John, and Jorge Jaramillo. *Marco Ospina: Pintura y realidad*. Bogotá: Fundación Gilberto Alzate Avendaño and Alcaldía Mayor de Bogotá, 2011.

Cerón-Anaya, Hugo, Patricia de Santana Pinho, and Ana Ramos-Zayas. "A Conceptual Roadmap for the Study of Whiteness in Latin America." *Latin American and Caribbean Ethnic Studies* 18, no. 2 (2022): 177–99.

Chakrabarti, Sumit. "Moving Beyond Edward Said: Homi Bhabha and the Problem of Postcolonial Representation." *International Studies Interdisciplinary Political and Cultural Journal* 14, no. 1 (2012): 5–21.

Chéroux, Clément, Jean-Loup Champion, and Trista Selous. *The Perfect Medium: Photography and the Occult*. New Haven, CT: Yale University Press, 2005.

Chicangana-Bayona, Yobenj Aucardo. "La Campaña del Sur (1813–1816) en las telas de José María Espinosa Prieto." *Historia y Sociedad*, no. 17 (2009): 69–95.

Clark, T. J. *Farewell to an Idea: Episodes from a History of Modernism*. New Haven, CT: Yale University Press, 1999.

Clark, T. J. "Olympia's Choice." In *The Painting of Modern Life: Paris in the Art of Manet and His Followers*. New York: Alfred A. Knopf, 1985.

Cole, Teju. "A True Picture of Black Skin." *New York Magazine*, February 18, 2015.

Cook, Susan E. *Victorian Negatives: Literary Culture and the Dark Side of Photography in the Nineteenth Century*. Albany: State University of New York Press, 2019.

Coronado, Jorge. *Portraits in the Andes: Photography and Agency 1900–1950*. Pittsburgh: University of Pittsburgh Press, 2018.

Correa Montoya, Guillermo. *Raros: Historia cultural de la homosexualidad en Medellín, 1890–1980*. Medellín: Universidad de Antioquia, 2017.

Cortés, Ana María. *Viaje y Tornaviaje: Bienes y rutas del Galeón de Manila. Colección Museo Franz Mayer*. Bogotá: Museo Nacional de Colombia, 2021.

Crow, Thomas E. *Modern Art in the Common Culture*. New Haven, CT: Yale University Press, 1998.

Cruz Bermeo, William. *Grandeza: Rastros de la moda internacional en Medellín 1890–1950*. Medellín: Editorial Universidad Pontificia Bolivariana, 2016.

Cuarterolo, Andrea. *De la foto al fotograma: Relaciones entre cine y fotografía en la Argentina (1840–1933)*. Montevideo: Ediciones CdF, 2013.

Daniel, Malcolm R. *Stieglitz, Steichen, Strand: Masterworks from the Metropolitan Museum of Art*. New York: Metropolitan Museum of Art, 2010.

de la Calle, Benjamín, and Horacio Marino Rodríguez. "Fotografía." *El Espectador*, July 30, 1898.

Delpar, Helen. *Rojos contra azules: El partido liberal en la política colombiana, 1863–1899*. Bogotá: Procultura, 1994.

Doeswijk, Andreas. "Una entrevista a Lampião: El Rey de los Cangaceiros." *Revista de Historia Oral* 3, no. 12 (2001): 8–18.

Domínguez Rendón, Raúl. *Vestido, ostentación y cuerpos en Medellín: 1900–1930*. Medellín: Instituto Tecnológico Metropolitano, 2004.

Echavarría, Enrique. "La fotografía." *Letras y Encajes* 9, no. 113 (1935).

Edwards, Elizabeth. "Objects of Affect: Photography Beyond the Image." *Annual Review of Anthropology* 41 (2012): 221–34.

Edwards, Elizabeth, and Janice Hart. "Introduction: Photographs as Objects." In *Photographs, Objects, Histories: On the Materiality of Images*, edited by Elizabeth Edwards and Janice Hart. London: Routledge, 2004.

Edwards, Steve. "Allegorical Photography." In *Encyclopedia of Nineteenth-Century Photography*. New York: Routledge, 2008.

El Bateo. "No habrá feos en el taller de belleza." October 10, 1907.

El Espectador. "Exposición de pintura." July 30, 1892, 373.

Elkins, James. *What Photography Is*. New York: Routledge, 2011.

Ellenbogen, Josh. *Reasoned and Unreasoned Images: The Photography of Bertillon, Galton, and Marey*. University Park: Pennsylvania State University Press, 2012.

Ertem, Fulya. "The Pose in Early Portrait Photography: Questioning Attempts to Appropriate the Past." *Image and Narrative*, no. 14 (2006). https://www.imageandnarrative.be/inarchive/painting/fulya.htm.

Escobar, Felipe. *Melitón Rodríguez: Fotografías*. Bogotá: El Áncora Editores, 1985.

Escobar, Juan Camilo, and Adolfo León Maya. "Siglos de conexiones, no de aislamientos." *El Eafitense*, no. 104 (2017): 8–15.

Escobar Calle, Miguel. *La ciudad y sus cronistas*. Medellín: ITM, 2003.

Escobar Calle, Miguel. *El Repertorio: Revista mensual ilustrada bellas artes, literatura y variedades*. Medellín: Secretaría de Educación para la Cultura de Antioquia, 2004.

Escobar Villegas, Juan Camilo. "Andrés Posada Arango: El conocimiento de la naturaleza, el 'Progreso,' la 'Civilización' y las 'Razas superiores.'" *IATREIA* 18, no. 1 (2005): 78–98.

Escobar Villegas, Juan Camilo, ed. *¡Hágase la luz! Pastor Restrepo Maya, fotógrafo (1839–1921)*. Medellín: Fondo Editorial Universidad EAFIT, 2014.

Escobar Villegas, Juan Camilo. *Progresar y civilizar: Imaginarios de identidad y élites intelectuales de Antioquia en Euroamérica, 1830–1920*. Medellín: Fondo Editorial Universidad EAFIT, 2009.

Espinosa, José María. *Memorias de un abanderado*. Bogotá: Imprenta el Tradicionalista, 1876.

Ewing, William A., and Todd Brandow. *Edward Steichen: In High Fashion, the Condé Nast Years, 1923–1937*. Minneapolis: Foundation for the Exhibition of Photography and Musée de l'Elysée, 2008.

Falconi, José Luis. "No Me Token; or, How to Make Sure We Never Lose the * Completely." Guggenheim Museum, October 30, 2013. https://www.guggenheim.org/blogs/map/no-me-token-or-how-to-make-sure-we-never-lose-the-completely.

Favero, Paolo S. H. "Backdrops: Conversation with Chris Pinney." *Membrana—Journal of Photography, Theory and Visual Culture* 5, no. 1 (2018): 30–36. https://doi.org/10.47659/m5.030.int.

Fawcett, Louise, and Eduardo Posada Carbó. "Árabes y judíos en el desarrollo del Caribe colombiano, 1850–1950." *Boletín Cultural y Bibliográfico* 35, no. 49 (1998): 3–29.

Fenalco. *El comercio en Medellín, 1900–1930: Fotografías*. Medellín: Fenalco Antioquia, 1982.

Fernández, Carlos Arturo. "Las obras del museo de antioquia . . . una visita guiada: Antioquia militante." *Vivir en el Poblado*, no. 279 (2011).

Fernández, Pedro. "Bellas Artes." *Voz de Antioquia*, no. 117–18 (July 26, 1889).

Fineman, Mia. *Faking It: Manipulated Photography Before Photoshop*. New York: Metropolitan Museum of Art, 2012.

Flórez, C. V. "La fotografía de telón de fondo." Premio Nacional de crítica y ensayo: Arte en Colombia. Accessed February 3, 2021. https://premionalcritica.uniandes.edu.co/wp-content/uploads/C.V.-Fl%C3%B3rez.pdf.

Franco Diéz, Germán. *Mirando solo a la tierra: Cine y sociedad espectadora en Medellín (1900–1930)*. Bogotá: Pontificia Universidad Javeriana, 2013.

Freund, Giselle. *La fotografía como documento social*. Barcelona: Gustavo Gili, 2017.

Fundación la Caixa. *La fotografía pictorialista en España: 1900–1936*. Barcelona: Fundación la Caixa d'Estalvis i Pensions, 1998.

Ganguly, Keya. "Roundtable: Revisiting Edward Said's Orientalism." *History of the Present* 5, no. 1 (2015): 65–82.

Gaona Rico, Óscar Franklim, Paula J. Matiz, Juan R. Rey, and Carolina Vanegas. *Noticias iluminadas: Arte e identidad en el siglo XIX*. Bogotá: Fundación Gilberto Álzate Avendaño, 2011.

García Barrientos, Federico. *Lujo, confort y consumo: Medellín 1900–1930*. Medellín: Universidad Pontificia Bolivariana, 2014.

Gartlan, Luke, and Roberta Wue. *Portraiture and Early Studio Photography in China and Japan*. London: Routledge, 2017.

Gennert, G. *Catalogue of Photographic Apparatus and Supplies*. No. 58, ca. 1908.

Gennert, G. *Descriptive Catalogue of Photographic Apparatus and Supplies*. ca. 1893.

Giannandrea, Beatrice. *Literatura y pintura en el costumbrismo argentino, siglo XIX: Écfrasis*. Saarbrücken: VDM Verlag, 2009.

Giraldo, Sol Astrid. "La fotografía en Antioquia: Carne y hueso para un mito." In *Antioquia Imaginada*, edited by Efrén Giraldo. Medellín: EAFIT, 2013.

Giraldo, Sol Astrid. *Retratos en blanco y afro*. Bogotá: Ministerio de Cultura, 2014.

Gónima, Eladio. *Apuntes para la historia del teatro de Medellín y vejeces*. Medellín: Tipografía de San Antonio, 1909.

González Aranda, Beatriz. "Artistas en tiempos de guerra: Los fotógrafos." *Boletín Cultural y Bibliográfico* 37, no. 54 (2000): 11–22.

González Aranda, Beatriz. "Fin del sueño académico." In *Manual de arte del siglo XIX en Colombia*. Bogotá: Universidad de Los Andes, 2013.

González Aranda, Beatriz. *José María Espinosa: El abanderado del arte en el siglo XIX*. Bogotá: Museo Nacional de Colombia, Banco de la República and El Áncora Editores, 1998.

González Aranda, Beatriz, and Verónica Uribe Hanabergh. *Manual de arte del siglo XIX en Colombia*. Bogotá: Universidad de los Andes, 2013.

González Escobar, Luis Fernando. "Horacio Marino Rodríguez (1866–1931): El modernismo arquitectónico de Medellín y la transformación de una ciudad." In *Piedra, papel y tijera: Horacio Marino Rodríguez Márquez (1866–1931)*. Medellín: Editorial EAFIT, 2018.

González-Stephan, Beatriz. "Cuerpos in/a-propiados: Carte-de-visite y las nuevas ciudadanías en la pardocracia venezolana postindependentista." *Memoria y Sociedad* 17, no. 34 (2013): 14–32.

Green, Jonathan. *Camera Work: A Critical Anthology*. New York: Aperture, 1973.

Greet, Michele. *Beyond National Identity: Pictorial Indigenism as a Modernist Strategy in Andean Art, 1920–1960*. University Park: Pennsylvania State University Press, 2009.

Grimaldo Grisby, Darcy. "Negative-Positive Truths." *Representations* 113, no. 1 (2011): 16–38.

Gutiérrez de Pineda, Virginia. "Tensiones del odio en la pequeña comunidad: Antagonismos en los estratos sociales." *Revista Colombiana de Antropología* 9 (1960): 277–99.

Haag, Carlos. "Sin una idea en la cabeza y un arma en la mano: Lampião supo usar su imagen para crear un mito inmortal." *Revista Pesquisa*, no. 137 (2007). https://revistapesquisa.fapesp.br/es/sin-una-idea-en-la-cabeza-y-un-arma-en-la-mano.

Hall, Stuart. "The Work of Representation." In *Representation: Cultural Representations and Signifying Practices (Culture, Media, and Identities)*. London: Sage in association with Open University, 1997.

Hambourg, Maria Morris, Françoise Heilbrun, and Philippe Néagu. *Nadar*. New York: Metropolitan Museum of Art, 1995.

Handy, Ellen, Brian Lukacher, and Shelley Rice. *Pictorial Effect, Naturalistic Vision: The Photographs and Theories of Henry Peach Robinson and Peter Henry Emerson*. Norfolk, VA: Chrysler Museum, 1994.

Hering Torres, Max S. "La limpieza de sangre. Problemas de interpretación: Acercamientos históricos y metodológicos." *Historia Crítica*, no. 45 (2011): 32–55.

Herrera, Cenedith. "Actores, actrices y otras gentes de teatro en Medellín, 1830–1950." In *Memorias, II Foro de estudiantes de Historia 2003*. Medellín: Universidad Nacional de Colombia, 2004.

Herrera, Cenedith. "Entre máscaras y tablas apuntes para una historia del teatro en Medellín, 1830–1950." *Kabai*, no. 10 (2002): 135–45.

Herrera, Rosina. "Técnicas de retoque de negativos fotográficos: Historia y conservación." *Pátina*, no. 16 (2011): 111–22.

Hincapié, Luz M. "Amor, matrimonio y educación: Lecturas para mujeres colombianas del siglo XIX." *Revista Credencial Historia*, no. 277 (2013). https://www.banrepcultural.org/biblioteca-virtual/credencial-historia/numero-277/amor-matrimonio-y-educacion-lecturas-para-mujeres-colombianas-siglo-xix.

Holloway, Thomas H. "Introduction." In *A Companion to Latin American History*. Malden, MA: Wiley-Blackwell, 2008.

Holmes, Oliver Wendell. "Doings of the Sunbeam." *Atlantic Monthly*, July 1863, 1–15.

Huertas Sánchez, Miguel. *Del costumbrismo a la academia: Hacia la creación de la Escuela Nacional de Bellas Artes*. Bogotá: Museo Nacional de Colombia, 2014.

Igiro Gamero, Katya Inés. "El legado de los inmigrantes árabes y judíos al desarrollo económico de la costa Caribe colombiana y a la conformación de su empresariado entre 1850–2000." *Clio América* 2, no. 4 (2008): 300–328.

Jaramillo, Carlos Eduardo. "Las Juanas y los niños de la revolución." In *Los guerrilleros del novecientos*. Bogotá: Fondo Editorial CEREC, 1991.

Jaramillo, Carlos Eduardo. "Mujeres en guerra: Participación de las mujeres en conflictos civiles." In *Las mujeres en la historia de Colombia*, vol. 2. Bogotá: Grupo Editorial Norma, 1995.

Jáuregui, Carlos, David Solodkow, and Karina Herazo. *Emiliano Zapata: 100 años, 100 fotos*. Bogotá: Ediciones Uniandes, 2022.

J. Paul Getty Museum. "Félix Jacques Moulin." Accessed June 12, 2023. https://www.getty.edu/art/collection/person/103KJX.

Katzew, Ilona. *Casta Painting: Images of Race in Eighteenth-Century Mexico*. New Haven, CT: Yale University Press, 2005.

Kennedy-Troya, Alexandra. "Formas de construir la nación ecuatoriana: Acuarelas de tipos, costumbres y paisajes." In *Imágenes de identidad, Acuarelas quiteñas del siglo XIX*. Quito: FONSAL, 2005.

Koester, Joachim. "Nanking Restaurant—Tracing Opium in Calcutta." *Camera Austria* 125 (2014): n.p.

Kotchemidov, Christina. "Why We Say 'Cheese': Producing the Smile in Snapshot Photography." *Critical Studies in Media Communication* 22, no. 1 (2005): 2–25.

Kriebel, Sabine T., and Andrés Mario Zervigón. *Photography and Doubt*. New York: Routledge, 2017.

Kushigian, Julia A. *Orientalism in the Hispanic Literary Tradition: In Dialogue with Borges, Paz, and Sarduy*. Albuquerque: University of New Mexico Press, 1991.

Kusnerz, Peggy Ann. "Pictorialism in Japan." *History of Photography* 28, no. 4 (2004): 387.

Lavédrine, Bertrand. "The Negative Image Before the Photographic Negative." *Journal of the American Institute for Conservation* 59, no. 3–4 (2020): 141–47.

Le Bon, Gustave. *The Psychology of Peoples*. London: T. Fischer Unwin, 1898.

Leja, Michael. "Mumler's Fraudulent Photographs." In *Looking Askance: Skepticism and American Art from Eakins to Duchamp*. Berkeley: University of California Press, 2004.

Lemaitre, Eduardo. *Rafael Reyes: Biografía de un gran colombiano*. Bogotá: Editorial Norma, 1994.

Levine, Robert M. "Faces of Brazilian Slavery: The *Cartes-de-Visite* of Christiano Júnior." *Americas* 47, no. 2 (1990): 127–59.

Levy, Kurt L. *Tomás Carrasquilla*. Boston: Tawyne, 1980.

Lewis Morgan, Mario. "Historia de la fotografía en Panamá." *Canto Rodado: Revista especializada en patrimonio*, no. 9 (2014): 129–40.

Londoño Blair, Alicia. *El cuerpo Limpio*. Medellín: Universidad de Antioquia, 2008.

Londoño Vega, Patricia. "Cartillas y manuales de urbanidad y del buen tono: Catecismos cívicos y prácticos para un amable vivir." *Revista Credencial Historia*, no. 85 (1997): 10–24.

Londoño Vega, Patricia. "Las publicaciones periódicas dirigidas a la mujer, 1858–1930." *Boletín Cultural y Bibliográfico* 27, no. 23 (1990): 3–23.

Londoño-Vega, Patricia. *Religion, Society, and Culture in Colombia: Medellín and Antioquia, 1850–1930*. Oxford: Clarendon Press, 2002.

Londoño Vélez, Santiago. *Benjamín de la Calle, fotógrafo*. Bogotá: Banco de la República, Fundación Antioqueña para los Estudios Sociales (FAES) and Biblioteca Pública Piloto, 1993.

Londoño Vélez, Santiago. *Francisco Antonio Cano: Dibujos, grabados, pinturas y esculturas*. Bogotá: Ediciones Gamma, 2014.

Londoño Vélez, Santiago. *Historia de la pintura y el grabado en Antioquia*. Medellín: Editorial Universidad de Antioquia, 1995.

Londoño Vélez, Santiago. *La mano luminosa: Vida y obra de Francisco Antonio Cano*. Medellín: Editorial EAFIT, 2002.

Londoño Vélez, Santiago. *Testigo ocular: La fotografía en Antioquia, 1848–1950*. Medellín: Editorial Universidad de Antioquia and Biblioteca Pública Piloto, 2009.

López, Libardo. *La raza antioqueña: Breves consideraciones sobre su psicología*. Medellín: Imprenta de la Organización, 1910.

López de Mesa, Luis. *Disertación sociológica*. Medellín: Bedout, 1970.

López de Mesa, Luis. "Los problemas de la raza en Colombia." *El Espectador*, 1920.

López Rodríguez, Mercedes. *Blancura y otras ficciones raciales en los Andes colombianos del siglo XIX*. Madrid: Iberoamericana Editorial Vervuert, 2019.

Low, Gail Ching-Liang. *White Skin/Black Masks: Representation and Colonialism*. London: Routledge, 1996.

Majluf, Natalia. "Pattern-Book of Nations: Images of Types and Costumes in Asia and Latin America, 1800–1860." In *Reproducing Nations: Types and Costumes in Asia and Latin America, ca. 1800–1860*. New York: Americas Society, 2006.

Majluf, Natalia, Luis Eduardo Wuffarden, Herman Schwarz, and Adelma Benavente. *La recuperación de la memoria. El primer siglo de la fotografía: Perú, 1842–1942*. Lima: Museo de Arte de Lima and Fundación Telefónica, 2001.

Martínez Carreño, Aida. "Las capitanas de los Mil Días: Participación de las mujeres en la guerra y apasionado testimonio de una de ellas." *Revista Credencial Historia* 121 (2000). https://www.banrepcultural.org/biblioteca-virtual/credencial-historia/numero-121/las-capitanas-de-los-mil-dias.

Martínez de Nisser, María. *Diario de los sucesos de la revolución en la Provincial de Antioquia en los años 1840–41*. Medellín: Fondo Editorial Universidad EAFIT, 2012.

Maxwell, Anne. *Picture Imperfect: Photography and Eugenics, 1870–1940*. Brighton, UK: Sussex Academic Press, 2008.

Medina, Álvaro. "Historiografía y ubicación de Epifanio Garay." *Ensayos* 3 (1996): 93–114.

Medina, Álvaro. "La exposición francesa de 1922." In *Procesos del arte en Colombia: Tomo I (1810–1930)*. Bogotá: Laguna Libros and Universidad de Los Andes, 2014.

Medina, Álvaro. "Oswald Spengler y la revista Mundial contra las vanguardias." In *Procesos del arte en Colombia: Tomo I (1810–1930)*. Bogotá: Laguna Libros and Universidad de Los Andes, 2014.

Mégnin, Michel. *La photo-carte en Algérie au XIXe siècle*. Paris: Non Lieu Éditions, 2007.

Meikle, Jeffrey L. *Postcard America: Curt Teich and the Imaging of a Nation, 1931–1950*. Austin: University of Texas Press, 2015.

Mejía, Juan Luis. *El taller de los Rodríguez*. Medellín: Suramericana de seguros and Centro Colombo Americano, 1992.

Mejía Cubillos, Javier. *Dicccionario biográfico y genealógico de la élite antioqueña y viejocaldense: Segunda mitad del siglo XIX y primera del XX*. Pereira: Sello Red Alma Mater, 2012.

Melo, Jorge Orlando. *Historia de Antioquia*. Medellín: Suramericana de Seguros, 1996.

Melo, Jorge Orlando. *Historia de Medellín*. Medellín: Suramericana de Seguros, 1987.

Melo, Jorge Orlando. "La historiografía sobre la Antioquia del siglo XIX." 1998. https://jorgeorlandomelo.org/2025/03/09/la-historiografi%c2%bda-sobre-la-antioquia-del-siglo-xix-2/.

Melo, Jorge Orlando. "¿Raza antioqueña?" *El Tiempo*, August 15, 2013. https://www.eltiempo.com/archivo/documento/CMS-12992040.

Mesa, Rafael. "Fotografía judicial." *Revista de la Policía Departamental* 1, no. 11 (1914).

Mitchell, W. J. T. "Ekphrasis and the Other." In *Picture Theory: Essays on Verbal and Visual Representation*. Chicago: University of Chicago Press, 1994.

Mitchell, W. J. T. "Imperial Landscape." In *Landscape and Power*. Chicago: University of Chicago Press, 2002.

Molloy, Sylvia. "La política de la pose." *Cuadernos LIRICO* 16 (2017). https://doi.org/10.4000/lirico.3576.

Morán, Francisco. "Volutas del deseo: Hacia una lectura del orientalismo en el modernismo hispanoamericano." *MLN* 120, no. 2 (2005): 383–407.

Moreno de Angel, Pilar. *El daguerrotipo en Colombia*. Bogotá: Bancafé, Fondo Cultural Cafetero, 2000.

Mraz, John. *Photographing the Mexican Revolution: Commitments, Testimonies, Icons*. Austin: University of Texas Press, 2012.

Mraz, John. "Sara Castrejón: Fotografiar la revolución, representar a la mujer." *Fotocinema*, no. 22 (2021): 119–47.

Munkwitz, Erika. "Vixens of Venery: Women, Sport, and Fox-Hunting in Britain, 1860–1914." *Critical Survey* 24, no. 1 (2012): 74–87.

Museo Nacional de Colombia. "Luis García Hevia, 200 años: La realidad versátil." September 20, 2017. https://museonacional.gov.co/colecciones/piezas-en-dialogo/Piezas-en-dialogo-2016/Paginas/Agosto%20-%20septiembre%20-%20octubre.aspx.

Nagy-Zekmi, Silvia. *Moros en la costa: Orientalismo en Latinoamérica*. Madrid: Iberoamericana Editorial Vervuert, 2008.

Negrete Álvarez, Claudia. *Valleto Hermanos: Fotógrafos mexicanos de entresiglos*. Mexico City: Universidad Nacional Autónoma de México, Instituto de Investigaciones Estéticas, 2006.

Nelson, Andrea. *The New Woman Behind the Camera*. Washington, DC: National Gallery of Art, 2020.

Newhall, Nancy Lynne. *P.H. Emerson: The Fight for Photography as a Fine Art*. New York: Aperture, 1975.

Nickel, Douglas R. *Francis Frith in Egypt and Palestine: A Victorian Photographer Abroad*. Princeton, NJ: Princeton University Press, 2004.

Nochlin, Linda. "The Imaginary Orient." In *The Politics of Vision: Essays on Nineteenth Century Art and Society*. New York: Harper and Row, 1989.

Nordstrom, Alison. *Truth Beauty: Pictorialism and the Photograph as Art, 1845–1945*. Vancouver: Vancouver Art Gallery, 2008.

Ochoa, Lisandro. *Cosas viejas de la Villa Candelaria*. Medellin: Instituto Tecnologico Metropolitano, 2004.

Ochoa, Lisandro. "La Fotografía." In *Cosas viejas de la Villa Candelaria*. Medellín: Instituto Tecnológico Metropolitano, 2004.

Olano, Ricardo. *Memorias*. Medellín: Fondo Editorial Universidad EAFIT, 2004.

Ortiz-Echagüe, Javier, and Julio Montero Díaz. "Documentary Uses of Artistic Photography. Spain. Types and Costumes by José Ortiz Echagüe." *History of Photography* 35, no. 4 (2011): 394–415.

Orvell, Miles. "Photography and the Artifice of Realism." In *The Real Thing: Imitation and Authenticity in American Culture, 1880–1940*. Chapel Hill: University of North Carolina Press, 2014.

Osorio Gómez, Jaime. *Fotografía en Antioquia*. Bogotá: Villegas Editores, 2013.

Ourdan, J. P., and Burrows and Colton. *The Art of Retouching*. London: Marion, 1876.

Padilla, Christian. *La Bachué de Rómulo Rozo: Un ícono en el arte moderno colombiano*. Bogotá: Fundación Proyecto Bachué, 2013.

Parsons, James Jerome. *Antioqueño Colonization in Western Colombia*. Berkeley: University of California Press, 1968.

Parsons, James Jerome. *La colonización antioqueña en el occidente de Colombia*. Medellín: Imprenta departamental de Antioquia, 1950.

Payne, Constantine Alexander. "Growth and Social Change in Medellín, Colombia, 1900–1930." *Estudios Sociales* 1, no. 1 (1986): 111–94.

Penhall, Michele M. "El Pictorialismo en los Andes." In *La recuperación de la memoria, el primer siglo de la fotografía en Perú, 1842–1942*, edited by Natalia Majluf. Lima: Museo de Arte and Fundación Telefónica, 2001.

Penhall, Michele M. "The Invention and Reinvention of Martin Chambi." *History of Photography* 24, no. 2 (2000): 106–12.

Penhos, Marta Noemí. "Frente y perfil: Una indagación acerca de la fotografía en las prácticas antropológicas y criminológicas en Argentina a fines del siglo XIX y principios del XX." In *Arte y antropología en la Argentina*, edited by Marina Baron Supervielle. Buenos Aires: Fundación Telefónica, Fundación Espigas, and Fondo para la investigación del Arte Argentino, 2005.

Pereira, Catarina. "O retoque do negativo fotográfico: Estudo de uma colecção do Arquivo Fotográfico da Câmara Municipal de Lisboa." *Estudos de Conservação e Restauro*, no. 2 (2010): 38–57.

Pérez-Oramas, Luis. "The Anonymous Rule: Joaquín Torres-García, the Schematic Impulse, and Arcadian Modernity." In *Joaquín Torres-García: The Arcadian Modern*, edited by Luis Pérez-Oramas. New York: Museum of Modern Art, 2015.

Pineda Camacho, Roberto. "La constitución de 1991 y la perspectiva del multiculturalismo en Colombia." *Alteridades* 7, no. 14 (1997): 107–29.

Pinney, Christopher. *Camera Indica: The Social Life of Indian Photographs*. Chicago: Reaktion, 1997.

Pinney, Christopher. "Notes from the Surface of the Image: Photography, Postcolonialism, and Vernacular Modernism." In *Photography's Other Histories*, edited by Christopher Pinney and Nicolas Peterson. Durham, NC: Duke University Press, 2003.

Pinney, Christopher. "Seven Theses on Photography." *Thesis Eleven* 113, no. 1 (2012): 141–56.

Pinney, Christopher, and Nicolas Peterson, eds. *Photography's Other Histories*. Durham, NC: Duke University Press, 2003.

Pinney, Christopher, with the PhotoDemos Collective, eds. *Citizens of Photography: The Camera and the Political Imagination*. Durham, NC: Duke University Press, 2023.

P. N. G. "Del Retoque." *Las Novedades*, September 19, 1896.

P. N. G. "Pequeña historia de la fotografía en Antioquia." *El Esfuerzo*, 1895.

Pollock, Griselda. *Vision and Difference: Femininity, Feminism and Histories of Art*. London: Routledge, 1988.

Poniatowska, Elena. *Las Soldaderas: Women of the Mexican Revolution*. El Paso, TX: Cinco Puntos, 2006.

Poole, Deborah. "An Image of 'Our Indian': Type Photographs and Racial Sentiments in Oaxaca, 1920–1940." *Hispanic American Historical Review* 84, no. 1 (2004): 37–82.

Poole, Deborah. *Vision, Race and Modernity: A Visual Economy of the Andean Image World*. Princeton, NJ: Princeton University Press, 1997.

Posada Callejas, Jorge. *El libro azul de Colombia: Historia condensada de la República*. New York: J. J. Little and Ives, 1918.

Prager, Sarah. "Four Flowering Plants That Have Been Decidedly Queered." *JSTOR Daily*, January 29, 2020. https://daily.jstor.org/four-flowering-plants-decidedly-queered/.

Ramirez M., Gladys Lucía, Patricia Bonnet, and Oscar Mario Arango. *Moda femenina en Medellín: Aportes de la moda al ideario femenino en Medellín, de 1900 a 1950*. Medellín: Tragaluz Editores, 2012.

Randall, Stephen. "Nations in Crisis: The Loss of Panama, 1890–1921." In *Colombia and the United States: Hegemony and Interdependence*. Athens: University of Georgia Press, 1992.

Rangel, Gabriela, ed. *Observed = Indicios: Milagros de la Torre*. New York: Americas Society, 2012.

Rappaport, Joanne. *The Disappearing Mestizo: Configuring Difference in the Colonial New Kingdom of Granada*. Durham, NC: Duke University Press, 2014.

Reyes, Catalina. *Aspectos de la vida social y cotidiana de Medellín, 1890–1930*. Bogotá: Colcultura, 1996.

Reyes, Catalina. "Cambios en la vida femenina durante la primera mitad del siglo XX: El hogar y el trabajo, escenario de las mayores transformaciones." *Revista Credencial Historia*, no. 68 (1995): 10–13. https://www.banrepcultural.org/biblioteca-virtual/credencial-historia/numero-68/cambios-en-la-vida-femenina-durante-la-primera-mitad-del-siglo-xx.

Reyes, Rafael. "El Presidente." *El Bateo*, May 19, 1908.

Rice, Shelley. "Parallel Universes." In *Pictorial Effect, Naturalistic Vision: The Photographs and Theories of Henry Peach Robinson and Peter Henry Emerson*, edited by Ellen Handy. Norfolk, VA: Chrysler Museum Library, 1994.

Riches, Harriet. "Picture Taking and Picture Making: Gender Difference and the Historiography of Photography." In *Photography, History, Difference*, edited by Tanya Sheehan. Hanover, NH: Dartmouth College Press, 2015.

Riegl, Alois. *Late Roman Art Industry*. Rome: Giorgio Bretschneider Editore, 1985.

Riegl, Alois. "The Modern Cult of Monuments: Its Essence and Its Development." In *Historical and Philosophical Issues in the Conservation of Cultural Heritage*, edited by Nicholas Stanley Price, M. Kirby Taller Jr., and Alessandra Melucco Vaccaro. Los Angeles: Getty Conservation Institute, 1996.

Ripa, Cesare. *Iconología*. Madrid: Akal, 2002.

Robinson, Henry Peach. *The Studio: And What to Do in It*. 1891. Reprint, New York: Arno Press, 1973.

Robledo, Beatriz Helena. *María Cano, la virgen roja*. Bogotá: Penguin Random House Grupo Editorial, 2017.

Roda, Marcos, Roberto Rubiano Vargas, and Juan Carlos Rubiano Vargas. *Crónica de la fotografía en Colombia, 1841–1948*. Bogotá: Carlos Valencia Editores, 1983.

Rodríguez, Horacio Marino. "Fotomicrografía." *Luz y Sombra* 4 (October 1897): 231.

Rodríguez, Horacio Marino. "Fotozincografía." *Luz y Sombra* 4 (March 1897): 62–63.

Rodríguez, Horacio Marino, and Melitón Rodríguez. *Diez y ocho lecciones sobre fotografía y cuaderno de caja*. Medellín: Fondo Editorial EAFIT, 2011.

Rodríguez, Jorge. "Habitantes de Medellín." In *La Ciudad 1675–1925*, by Agapito Betancur. Medellín: ITM, 2003.

Rodríguez, Melitón. "Cuaderno de caja de la fotografía de Rodríguez, 1906." In *Diez y ocho lecciones sobre fotografía y cuaderno de caja*. Medellín: Fondo Editorial EAFIT, 2011.

Rodríguez-Arenas, Flor María. "María Martínez de Nisser (1843)." In *¿Y las mujeres? Ensayos sobre literatura colombiana*. Medellín: Universidad de Antioquia, 1991.

Rodríguez-Arenas, Flor María. *Tomás Carrasquilla: Nuevas aproximaciones críticas*. Medellín: Editorial Universidad de Antioquia, 2000.

Rojas Cocoma, Carlos. "Unidad, paisaje y lugar en la fotografía colombiana alrededor de 1900." *Aisthesis*, no. 68 (2020): 179–207.

Rosen, Jeffrey. *Julia Margaret Cameron's "Fancy Subjects": Photographic Allegories of Victorian Identity and Empire*. Manchester: Manchester University Press, 2016.

Ruiz Gómez, Darío. "Benjamín de la Calle: El rostro singular." In *Benjamín de la Calle: Fotógrafo, 1869–1934*. Medellín: Museo de Arte Moderno de Medellín and Biblioteca Pública Piloto, 1982.

Ruiz Gómez, Darío. *Benjamín de la Calle M.: Fotógrafo, 1869–1934*. Medellín: Museo de Arte Moderno de Medellín and Biblioteca Pública Piloto, 1982.

Ruiz Gómez, Darío. *Proceso de la cultura en Antioquia*. Medellín: Ediciones Autores Antioqueños, 1987.

Saffray, Charles. *Viaje a Nueva Granada*. Bogotá: Ministerio de Educación Nacional, 1948.

Said, Edward. *Orientalism*. New York: Vintage, 1994.

Salazar, Víctor Manuel. *Memorias de la Guerra*. Manizales: Imprenta Departamental, 1992.

Samuel, Ewing. "The Courbet of England: Peter Henry Emerson's East Anglian Photographs and the Imperial Ordering of Labour." *History of Photography* 39, no. 1 (2015): 18–32.

Sanín Cano, Baldomero. "Medellín hace sesenta años (1949)." In *La Ciudad y sus cronistas*, edited by Miguel Escobar Calle. Medellín: Instituto Tecnológico Metropolitano, 2003.

Sanmiguel, Inés. "Japoneses en Colombia: Historia de inmigración, sus descendientes en Japón." *Revista de Estudios Sociales*, no. 23 (2006): 81–96.

Sarvas, Risto, and David M. Frohlich. *From Snapshots to Social Media: The Changing Picture of Domestic Photography*. London: Springer, 2011.

Schwarz, Roberto. *Misplaced Ideas: Essays on Brazilian Culture*. London: Verso, 1992.

Seavey, L. W. "How to Use Photographic Backgrounds." *Scientific American* 2, no. 48 (1876): 765–66.

Seavey, L. W. "How to Use Photographic Backgrounds." *Scientific American* 2, no. 49 (1876): 782.

Sebbar, Leila, Christelle Taraud, and Jean-Michel Belorgey. *Femmes d'Afrique du nord: Cartes postales 1885–1930*. París: Bleu Autour, 2002.

Sedgwick, Eve Kosofsky, and Wayne Koestenbaum. *Between Men: English Literature and Male Homosocial Desire*. New York: Columbia University Press, 2015.

Segura, Martha. *Las guerras civiles desde 1830 y su proyección en el siglo XX: Memorias de la II cátedra anual de historia "Ernesto Restrepo Tirado."* Bogotá: Museo Nacional de Colombia/Ministerio de Cultura, 2001.

Sekula, Allan. "The Body and the Archive: The Use and Classification of Portrait Photography by the Police and Social Scientists in the Late 19th and Early 20th Centuries." *October* 39 (1986): 3–64.

Sekula, Allan. "The Traffic in Photographs." *Art Journal* 41, no. 1 (1981): 15–25. https://doi.org/10.2307/776511.

Serrano, Eduardo. *Historia de la fotografía en Colombia*. Bogotá: Museo de Arte Moderno, 1983.

Serrano, José Fernando. "Entre negación y reconocimiento: Estudios sobre homosexualidad en Colombia." *Nómadas*, no. 6 (1997): 67–81.

Sheehan, Tanya. *Study in Black and White: Photography, Race, Humor*. University Park: Pennsylvania State University Press, 2018.

Sheon, Aaron. "William-Adolphe Bouguereau in Paris." *Burlington Magazine* 108, no. 755 (1966): 107–9.

Sifuentes-Jauregui, Ben. *Transvestism, Masculinity, and Latin American Literature: Genders Share Flesh*. New York: Palgrave, 2002.

Sociedad Geográfica de Colombia. "Antioquia." Accessed May 10, 2018. https://sogeocol.edu.co/Home_B/esgeo/departamentos/antioquia-2/.

Solano Roa, Juanita. "Orientalism in the Andes: Photographs by Melitón Rodriguez and Benjamín de la Calle in the Long 19th Century." *H-ART: Revista de Historia, Teoría y Crítica de Arte*, no. 7 (2020): 201–24.

Solomon-Godeau, Abigail. "The Legs of the Countess." *October* 39 (1986): 65–108.

Sommer, Doris. *Foundational Fictions: The National Romances of Latin America*. Berkeley: University of California Press, 1991.

Squiers, Carol. "Edward Steichen at Condé Nast Publications." In *Edward Steichen: In High Fashion, the Condé Nast Years, 1923–1937*, edited by William A. Ewing and Todd Bradow. Minneapolis and Lausanne: Foundation for the Exhibition of Photography and Musée de l'Elysée, 2008.

Stanfield, Michael Edward. *Of Beasts and Beauty: Gender, Race, and Identity in Colombia*. Austin: University of Texas Press, 2013.

Stepan, Nancy Leys. *"The Hour of Eugenics": Race, Gender, and Nation in Latin America*. Ithaca, NY: Cornell University Press, 1991.

Stétié, Salah, and Jean-Michel Belorgey. *Égyptiennes: Cartes postales (1885–1930)*. Paris: Bleu Autour, 2004.

Stoichita, Victor. *Short History of the Shadow*. London: Reaktion, 1997.

Strassler, Karen. *Refracted Visions: Popular Photography and National Modernity in Java*. Durham, NC: Duke University Press, 2010.

Stulik, Dusan, and Art Kaplan. *The Atlas of Analytical Signatures of Photographic Processes*. Los Angeles: Getty Conservation Institute, 2013.

Susto, Juan Antonio. "Carlos Endara Andrade y la fotografía en Panamá." *Lotería*, no. 137 (1967): 47–54.

Tabares, Maribel. *Los hermanos Rodríguez Márquez: Grabados, pinceles, luces y sombras para crear una estética en el retrato fotográfico femenino de estudio, Medellín, 1890–1930*. Medellín: Universidad EAFIT, 2020.

Tabares, Maribel. *Melitón Rodríguez en blanco y negro*. Medellín: Universidad de Antioquia, 2011.

Taboada, Hernán G. H. "La sombra del Oriente en la independencia americana." In *Moros en la costa: Orientalismo en América Latina*, edited by Silvia Nagy-Zekmi. Madrid and Frankfurt: Iberoamericana and Vervuert, 2008.

Tagg, John. *The Burden of Representation: Essays on Photographs and Histories*. Minneapolis: University of Minnesota Press, 1993.

Talbot, William Henry Fox. *The Pencil of Nature*. London: Longman, Brown, Green and Longmans, 1844.

Taylor, Diana. "Transculturating Transculturation." *Performing Arts Journal* 13, no. 2 (1991): 90–104.

Teulié, Gilles. "Orientalism and the British Picture Postcard Industry: Popularizing the Empire in Victorian and Edwardian Homes." *Cahiers Victoriens et Édouardiens* 89 (2019). https://doi.org/10.4000/cve.5178.

Toh, Charmaine. *Imagining Singapore: Pictorial Photography from the 1950s to the 1970s*. Leiden: Brill Academic, 2023.

Torres, Rondy. "Las miradas cruzadas en la ópera: Reflexiones sobre el cuerpo e identidad en Bogotá en el siglo XIX." *Cuadernos de música iberoamericana* 32 (2019): 245–68.

Torres-Rodríguez, Laura J. *Orientaciones transpacíficas: La modernidad mexicana y el espectro de Asia*. Chapel Hill: University of North Carolina Press, 2019.

Tovar Bernal, Leonardo. "Introducción a la religión y la ciencia en la escuela colombiana (1863–1930)." *Nodos y Nudos* 4, no. 35 (2013): 35–46.

Upegui Benitez, Alberto. *Guayaquil: Una ciudad dentro de otra*. Medellín: ITM, 2004.

Uribe Hanabergh, Verónica. "Translating Landscape: The Colombian Chorographic Commission." *Journal of Arts and Humanities* 3, no. 1 (2014): 126–36.

Valverde, María Fernanda. *Photographic Negatives: Nature and Evolution of Processes*. Rochester, NY: Advanced Residency Program in Photograph Conservation, Image Permanence Institute and Foundation George Eastman House, 2005.

Vasconcelos, José. *The Cosmic Race: A Bilingual Edition*. Baltimore, MD: Johns Hopkins University Press, 1997.

Vélez White, Mercedes Lucía. *Arquitectura contemporánea en Medellín*. Medellín: Instituto Tecnológico Metropolitano, 2003.

Ventura, Gal. "Intention, Interpretation and Reception: The Aestheticization of Poverty in William Bouguereau's Indigent Family." *Visual Resources* 33, no. 3–4 (2017): 204–33.

Villegas, Lucely. "Mazamorreo y población negra libre en Antioquia 1770–1820." *Boletín de Antropología* 7, no. 23 (1990): 29–51.

Villegas, Luis Eduardo. "Informes." *El Espectador*, November 5, 1892.

Villegas Vélez, Álvaro Andrés. "Raza y nación en el pensamiento de Luis López de Mesa: Colombia, 1920–1940." *Revista de Estudios Políticos*, no. 26 (2005): 209–32.

von Brevern, Jan. "Resemblance After Photography." *Representations* 123, no. 1 (2013): 1–22.

Wade, Peter. "The Meaning of Race and Ethnicity." In *Race and Ethnicity in Latin America*. London: Pluto Press, 2010.

White, Byron. "Haciendo carambolas entre cárceles, cuarteles y batallones: La metamorfosis de Carabobo." In *Raros: Historia cultural de la homosexualidad en Medellín*, by Guillermo Antonio Correa Montoya. Medellín: Universidad de Antioquia, 2017.

Willcock, Sean. "Developing Orientalism: Negative/Positive Ecologies 'in the Field' of the British Empire, c. 1850–1888." *World Art* 13, no. 1 (2023): 125–45.

Wyman, James. "Introduction: From the Background to the Foreground. The Photo Backdrop and Cultural Expression." *Afterimage* 24, no. 5 (1997): 1–2.

X.X.X. "El hombre-mujer de Jericó." *El Cascabel*, April 26, 1899.

Yonan, Michael. "Toward a Fusion of Art History and Material Culture Studies." *West 86th: A Journal of Decorative Arts, Design History, and Material Culture* 18, no. 2 (2011): 232–48. https://doi.org/10.1086/662520.

Young, Robert. "The Ambivalence of Bhabha." In *White Mythologies: Writing History and the West*. London: Routledge, 1996.

Index

Note: Page numbers followed by f refer to figures.